A CULTURAL HISTORY OF TRAGEDY

VOLUME 1

A Cultural History of Tragedy
General Editor: Rebecca Bushnell

Volume 1
A Cultural History of Tragedy in Antiquity
Edited by Emily Wilson

Volume 2
A Cultural History of Tragedy in the Middle Ages
Edited by Jody Enders, Theresa Coletti, John T. Sebastian, and Carol Symes

Volume 3
A Cultural History of Tragedy in the Early Modern Age
Edited by Naomi Liebler

Volume 4
A Cultural History of Tragedy in the Age of Enlightenment
Edited by Mitchell Greenberg

Volume 5
A Cultural History of Tragedy in the Age of Empire
Edited by Michael Gamer and Diego Saglia

Volume 6
A Cultural History of Tragedy in the Modern Age
Edited by Jennifer Wallace

A CULTURAL HISTORY OF TRAGEDY
IN ANTIQUITY

VOLUME 1

Edited by Emily Wilson

BLOOMSBURY ACADEMIC
LONDON • NEW YORK • OXFORD • NEW DELHI • SYDNEY

BLOOMSBURY ACADEMIC
Bloomsbury Publishing Plc
50 Bedford Square, London, WC1B 3DP, UK
1385 Broadway, New York, NY 10018, USA
29 Earlsfort Terrace, Dublin 2, Ireland

BLOOMSBURY, BLOOMSBURY ACADEMIC and the Diana logo are trademarks of
Bloomsbury Publishing Plc

First published in hardback in Great Britain 2020
This paperback edition 2023

Copyright © Emily Wilson and contributors, 2020

Emily Wilson and contributors have asserted their right under the Copyright, Designs and
Patents Act, 1988, to be identified as the Authors of this work.

Series design by Raven Design

Cover image: Fragment of a Yellow Fresco Panel with Muse
© Elie Borowski/The J. Paul Getty Museum

All rights reserved. No part of this publication may be reproduced or transmitted
in any form or by any means, electronic or mechanical, including photocopying,
recording, or any information storage or retrieval system, without prior permission
in writing from the publishers.

Bloomsbury Publishing Plc does not have any control over, or responsibility for, any
third-party websites referred to or in this book. All internet addresses given in this
book were correct at the time of going to press. The author and publisher regret
any inconvenience caused if addresses have changed or sites have ceased to
exist, but can accept no responsibility for any such changes.

A catalogue record for this book is available from the British Library.

Library of Congress Control Number: 2019949117.

ISBN:	HB:	978-1-4742-8789-0
	Set:	978-1-4742-8814-9
	PB:	978-1-3504-1652-9
	PB Set:	978-1-3504-1692-5

Series: The Cultural Histories Series

Typeset by RefineCatch Limited, Bungay, Suffolk
Printed and bound in Great Britain

To find out more about our authors and books visit www.bloomsbury.com
and sign up for our newsletters.

CONTENTS

List of Illustrations		vi
Notes on Contributors		viii
Series Preface		x
	Introduction *Emily Wilson*	1
1	Forms and Media *Naomi Weiss*	17
2	Sites of Performance and Circulation *Rosa Andújar*	35
3	Communities of Production and Consumption *Eirene Visvardi*	49
4	Philosophy and Social Theory *Austin Busch*	65
5	Religion, Ritual and Myth *Isabelle Torrance*	83
6	Politics of City and Nation *Robert Cowan*	101
7	Society and Family *Marcel Widzisz*	117
8	Gender and Sexuality *Kirk Ormand*	131
Notes		149
Bibliography		191
Index		213

LIST OF ILLUSTRATIONS

INTRODUCTION

0.1   Apulian mixing vessel with members of a chorus dressed as satyrs, *c.* 410–380 BCE, attributed to the Tarporley Painter.   5
0.2   Apulian mixing vessel showing the madness of Lycurgus, *c.* 350–340 BCE.   15

CHAPTER 1

1.1   Attic mixing vessel, featuring chorus members performing before an altar, *c.* 500–490 BCE.   21
1.2   The Pronomos Vase, an Attic mixing vessel showing a troupe of actors, chorus members, and musicians, *c.* late fifth century BCE.   22
1.3   Attic mixing vessel, depicting the poet Phrynichos, *c.* 425 BCE, attributed to the Kleophon Painter.   25
1.4   Roman sardonyx cameo with four theater masks, *c.* first century CE.   31
1.5   Roman marble relief showing a scene from a comedy, *c.* first century CE.   32

CHAPTER 2

2.1   Silver coin showing the head of Herakles, *c.* 336–323 BCE.   38
2.2   Marble relief showing the Apotheosis of Homer, made by Archelaos of Priene. *c.* 225–205 BCE.   41
2.3   Greek (Sicilian) terracotta mask of a satyr, *c.* 200–100 BCE.   42
2.4   Roman terracotta figurine of a boy in Greek attire holding a tragic mask, *c.* 100–200 CE.   45
2.5   Roman carnelian cameo engraved with the god Pan, *c.* first century CE.   45

CHAPTER 3

3.1   Paestan mixing vessel depicting Orestes seeking sanctuary from the Furies, *c.* 360–320 BCE, attributed to the Python painter.   50
3.2   Gold ring engraved with an actor holding a theater mask, *c.* 325–300 BCE.   56
3.3   Detail of a mosaic from the House of the Tragic Poet in Pompeii, depicting actors and an *aulos* player, *c.* first century CE.   61

CHAPTER 4

4.1   Roman fresco from Pompeii, depicting Medea planning the murder of her children, *c.* first century CE.   71

LIST OF ILLUSTRATIONS vii

4.2 Hellenistic, Megarian pottery relief in the form of a bearded blind man, possibly Oedipus, *c.* 300–100 BCE. 79

CHAPTER 5

5.1 Attic wine vessel depicting Pompe between Eros and Dionysos, *c.* mid-fourth century BCE. 84
5.2 Apulian mixing vessel, showing the sacrifice of Iphigeneia, *c.* 370–350 BCE. 86
5.3 Paestan mixing vessel depicting Alcmene seated on an altar, entreating Zeus for aid. Attributed to the Python painter, *c.* 360–320 BCE. 88
5.4 Marble bust of the Roman emperor Commodus dressed as the demigod Heracles, *c.* 192 CE. 97

CHAPTER 6

6.1 Attic amphora showing Ajax and Achilles playing a board game in the presence of the goddess Athena, *c.* 510 BCE. Attributed to Leagros Group. 105
6.2 Detail of a Lucanian nestoris possibly depicting the scene from Sophocles' *Antigone* in which Antigone is brought before Creon, *c.* 390–380 BCE. 107
6.3 Attic amphora showing a Greek warrior fighting a Persian warrior, *c.* 480–470 BCE. 108

CHAPTER 7

7.1 Attic pyxis showing preparations for a marriage, *c.* 440–415 BCE. 119
7.2 Attic drinking cup showing Tecmessa covering the body of her husband, Ajax. Attributed to the Brygos Painter, *c.* 490–470 BCE. 122
7.3 Lucanian mixing vessel, showing Medea riding off in a chariot. Attributed to "near the Policoro Painter," *c.* 400 BCE. 125
7.4 Amphora depicting Orestes murdering his mother, Clytemnestra, *c.* 340 BCE. 127

CHAPTER 8

8.1 Attic wedding bowl showing preparations for a wedding, *c.* 420 BCE. 133
8.2 Attic *pelike* showing Heracles about to receive a poisoned garment, *c.* 430 BCE. 137
8.3 Attic *loutrophoros* depicting a deceased young man surrounded by female mourners, *c.* late sixth century BCE. 139
8.4 Attic *hydria* showing Medea brewing a potion to renew Jason's youth, attributed to the Copenhagen Painter, *c.* 480–470 BCE. 142
8.5 Fragmentary Roman wall-painting from Pompeii showing Phaedra with her nurse, *c.* 20–60 CE. 147

NOTES ON CONTRIBUTORS

Rosa Andújar is Deputy Director of Liberal Arts and Lecturer in Liberal Arts at King's College London. She is the co-editor of two volumes which address her two main areas of research: *Paths of Song: the Lyric Dimension of Greek Tragedy* (2018) and *Greeks and Romans on the Latin American Stage* (forthcoming, Bloomsbury). She is currently completing a monograph on the tragic chorus entitled *Playing the Chorus: Greek Tragedy Beyond the Choral Ode*.

Austin Busch is Associate Professor of Early World Literature and Associate Director of the Honors College at the College at Brockport. He has published articles on Latin poetry and drama, as well as on the New Testament and other early Christian literature. He co-edited the New Testament and Apocrypha volume of the Norton critical edition of the King James Bible.

Robert Cowan is Senior Lecturer in Classics at the University of Sydney, having previously held posts in Exeter, Bristol, and Oxford. His research interests range over much of Greek and Latin poetry, and he has published on Sophocles, Aristophanes, Plautus, Lucretius, Catullus, Cicero, Cinna, Ticida, Virgil, Horace, Ovid, Seneca, Columella, Martial, Suetonius, and Juvenal, as well as ancient graffiti and the operatic reception of Greek tragedy. However, his main specialisms are Imperial epic and Republican tragedy.

Kirk Ormand is the Nathan A. Greenberg Professor of Classics at Oberlin College. He is the author of *Exchange and the Maiden: Marriage in Sophoclean Tragedy* (1999), *Controlling Desires: Sexuality in Ancient Greece and Rome* (2009), and *The Hesiodic Catalogue of Women and Archaic Greece* (2014), editor of *A Companion to Sophocles* (2012) and co-editor (with Ruby Blondell) of *Ancient Sex: New Essays* (2015). He has published articles on Homer, Hesiod, Hipponax, Sophocles, Euripides, Ovid, Lucan, the Greek novel, Clint Eastwood's *Unforgiven*, and Michel Foucault.

Isabelle Torrance is Associate Professor of Classics and Research Fellow at the Aarhus Institute of Advanced Studies, Aarhus University, Denmark. She is author of *Aeschylus: Seven Against Thebes* (2007), *Metapoetry in Euripides* (2013), *Euripides* (2019), *Euripides: Iphigenia among the Taurians* (2019), and co-author of *Oaths and Swearing in Ancient Greece* (2014).

Eirene Visvardi is an Associate Professor of Classical Studies at Wesleyan University. She works on Greek drama and its role in ancient intellectual and political life. She is the author of *Emotion in Action: Thucydides and the Tragic Chorus* (2015). She is currently working on a book on utopian and dystopian thinking. She is also interested in the rhetoric of confession and the different fictional and institutional contexts for its performance both in antiquity and today.

Naomi Weiss is Assistant Professor in the Department of the Classics at Harvard University. She is the author of *The Music of Tragedy: Performance and Imagination in Euripidean Theater* (2018) and is currently working on a book about the aesthetics of theatrical spectatorship in classical Athens.

Marcel Widzisz has taught Classics at the University of Exeter (UK), the University of Houston, Boston University, Rice University, St. John's College at Annapolis, and, most recently, Southern Virginia University where he has started both a minor and major in Classical Studies. His research interests include Greek tragedy, Homer, Greek religion, and Roman Comedy.

Emily Wilson is a Professor of Classical Studies and Chair of the Program in Comparative Literature at the University of Pennsylvania. She is the author of *Mocked with Death: Tragic Overliving from Sophocles to Milton* (2005) as well as books on Socrates and Seneca and verse translations of *Six Plays of Seneca*, four tragedies of Euripides (in *The Greek Plays*, 2016), *Oedipus Tyrannos* (forthcoming), and the *Odyssey* (2017).

SERIES PREFACE

A cultural history of tragedy faces a daunting task: how to address tragedy's influence on Western culture while describing how complex and changing historical conditions have shaped it over two and a half millennia. This is the first study with such an extensive scope, investigating tragedy's long-lived cultural impact and accounting for its material, social, political, and philosophical dimensions.

Since antiquity, tragedy has appeared in a myriad of forms, reinvented in every age. It has been performed as opera, dance, film, and television as well as live theater. From the beginning, concepts of tragedy have also surfaced in other literary genres such as narrative poetry and novels, as well as in non-literary forms, including journalism, visual art, and photography. Tragedy never appears in a vacuum: the conditions of performance and production and its communal functions always affect its form and meaning. Tragedy has never belonged solely to elite culture, and who creates and consumes these forms of tragedy also makes a difference. Not only has the status of tragedy's producers—the writers, actors, artists, and performers—evolved over time, but so has the nature of the audiences, viewers, and readers as well, all significantly affecting tragedy's aesthetic and social impact.

Tragedy also does more than simply represent or perform human catastrophe or suffering; it is a mode of thought, a way of figuring the human condition as a whole. Philosophers and social and cultural theorists from Plato to Lacan have long pondered the idea of the tragic, while in turn literary models have influenced philosophy, social thought, and psychoanalysis. Tragedy has always had a complex relationship with religion and ritual practices, both complementing and conflicting with religious orthodoxies concerning fate, the power of the gods, and the meaning of suffering. At the same time, since its earliest staging in fifth-century Athens as a civic as well as religious event, tragedy has both echoed and challenged relationships of power and political events in societies experiencing conflict or change.

While tragedy in all its versions has thus profoundly tapped into broad social, intellectual, and political movements, it has often represented those themes through individual experiences, ranging from the titanic sufferings of princes to the sorrows of ordinary men and women. While tragedy's themes of ambition, authority, transgression, and rebellion are grounded in religion and politics, its plots often play out through family relationships that both mirror and conflict with social and political norms. When tragedy thus engages familial and personal themes, it often involves tensions of gender and sexuality. Sexuality is a powerful driver of tragic catastrophe, when desire is granted its own kind of fatal power.

As with other *Cultural History* series, here the story of tragedy writ large is divided into volumes covering six historical periods from antiquity to modernity. Although the boundaries between those time are necessarily fluid, the volumes are divided as follows: 1. Antiquity (500 BCE–1000 CE); 2. Middle Ages (1000–1400); 3. Early Modern Age (1400–1650); 4. Age of Enlightenment (1650–1800); 5. Age of Empire (1800–1920), and 6. Modern Age (1920–present). While such a history naturally focuses on Western culture and history, at the end it also touches on tragedy's later post-colonial adaptations, which put its fundamentally Western concerns in a global context. Each volume has its own introduction by an editor or co-editors presenting an original and provocative vision of tragedy's manifestations in one historical era. Each volume also covers the same eight topics as the others in the *Cultural History*: forms and media; sites of performance and circulation; communities of production and consumption; philosophy and social theory; religion, ritual, and myth; politics of city and nation; society and family; and gender and sexuality. Readers may thus follow one topic over a wide historical span, or they may focus on all dimensions of tragedy in one period. Either way they read, they will be able to appreciate the power of tragedy to shape our understanding of human experience, and in turn, how tragedy has changed over time, both reflecting and challenging historical conditions.

Rebecca Bushnell, University of Pennsylvania, General Editor

Introduction

EMILY WILSON

Tragedy begins with the ancient Greeks, from whom we get the word: *tragoidia*.[1] Ancient Athenian tragedy had a formative impact on all later concepts and treatments of "tragedy." But the influence was often circuitous or much-mediated. The tradition is not continuous, and glances back to Athenian tragedy, both within antiquity itself and in later periods, often rely on the adaptation or invention of a tradition that might be surprising or unrecognizable to the ancient Athenians themselves.

The English word "tragedy" refers to several quite different things. It can be used for real-life events involving large-scale disaster or premature death or both (*OED* "tragedy" s.v. 4). Or it can refer to particular types of drama or literature, again of several different kinds. It is generally written, the *Oxford English Dictionary* tells us, in an "elevated style," but it can be a medieval narrative of the downfall of an important person (*OED* 1.a); or a "classical or Renaissance verse drama," or later prose drama, again dealing with a protagonist's downfall (*OED* 1.b); or it can be the "genre of literature which consists of tragedies" (*OED* 2.a). We should notice the circularity of this definition, which marks the lexicographers' despair at coming up with an account that covers the whole sweep included in the present six volumes. The signs of what makes a literary artifact count as "tragedy" shift around in different cultural periods, and there is no single feature that is common to every era, except perhaps an association of tragedy with seriousness, with "elevated style," and an implicit contrast between tragedy and comedy. What counts as serious or elevated, and where the boundaries between tragedy and comedy are drawn, vary from one culture to another.

The content of ancient tragedy is quite different from that of later periods. Almost all Athenian tragedies of the classical period are, as Aristotle notes in the *Poetics*, based on a small group of pre-classical myths: the stories of the royal house of Thebes, or Argos, or the warriors who fought at Troy (*Poetics* 1453a).[2] By contrast, post-classical tragedies are based on a wide range of different stories; there is no assumption that tragedies will deal with a limited body of myth, stories already known to the audience or reader.

Moreover, there is a sharp difference in the narrative structures deemed appropriate for tragedy. For the medieval, early modern and modern periods, there was a strong association between tragedy and the final downfall of a protagonist. This is not true of ancient tragedy. A great many extant and lost Athenian tragedies had positive endings: they are dramas of escape from a threatened disaster, or of family members who are happily reunited.[3] Aristotle's discussion of plot types in the *Poetics* implies that some of his contemporaries blame Euripides for having too many plays with unhappy endings: "The critics are wrong, the ones who blame Euripides because he does this in his tragedies, and most of his plays end in misfortune" (*Poetics* 1453a). Aristotle himself argues that the unhappy ending is the type most appropriate to the genre, because it is most liable to arouse the correct emotional response from the audience, of pity and fear; for this reason, "Euripides, even if he mismanages other elements, is perceived as the most tragic of poets" (*Poetics* 1453a). Aristotle's preference for unhappy endings in tragedy was clearly controversial in the fourth century BCE; but his views had an enormous influence on the later perception and development of the genre.

Moreover, Aristotle had access to a far wider body of ancient Athenian tragedy than has survived to our time. We have complete plays from only three ancient Athenian tragedians, Aeschylus, Sophocles, and Euripides, and of these, the majority are those that became part of the standard editions, probably to be used in Byzantine schoolrooms. Our vision of Athenian tragedy is shaped by the tastes of those who selected this canon, at a distant point of time and space from the original audiences and original judges. Our view of the genre might be quite different if more of each of these three survived, and still more different if we had more than fragmentary quotations and titles from the work of other Athenian tragedians: Phrynichus, Agathon, Neophron, and many others.[4] For Euripides, we also have a group of nine more plays in alphabetical order, apparently a surviving section from an edition of the complete works.[5] A much higher proportion of these so-called alphabetical plays have happy or, by later standards, "untragic" endings, than the canonical, non-alphabetical plays; these include the *Helen*, the *Iphigeneia in Tauris*, the *Ion*, and the *Electra*. Our vision of Athenian tragic plot structures would be quite different if more survived.

Moving from plot to formal literary features, we also see little or no continuity between the tragedy of the fifth century and the later works categorized under the same generic title. Tragedies in classical Athens were always composed in groups of four: three tragedies, with a satyr play as the final element in the tetralogy. In later periods, including ancient Rome and pre-modern and modern Europe, tragedies were composed as stand-alone pieces of drama or narrative, not quarters of a larger whole. Moreover, in both Athenian and Roman antiquity, tragedy was always verse drama, not prose, and not verse narrative. The dialogue is always composed in iambic trimeter, imagined to be the meter closest to speech, while the choral passages are composed to be sung to complex melodies and accompanied by an elaborate dance routine, using intricate mixtures of lyric meters. No ancient tragedy has any prose elements, in contrast to the tragedies of Shakespeare, which always include some prose, or the all-prose tragedies of Ibsen or Arthur Miller. A further essential difference is that ancient tragedies always include a chorus, of twelve or fifteen male singer-dancers. There are many other crucial dramaturgical differences, such as the fact that Athenian tragedy was always performed entirely by masked male actors.

More broadly, tragedy in antiquity was assumed to be a theatrical genre. Ancient readers would be puzzled at the idea that a non-dramatic narrative could be labeled "tragedy." We can certainly identify tragic elements, tragic echoes, or tragic allusions, in ancient epic, ancient historiography, ancient oratory, ancient philosophy, and the ancient novel. Tragedy was a dominant, highly respected and influential genre in antiquity, and it had a vast impact on other serious and less serious cultural productions. But it is modern scholars, not ancient critics or readers, who discuss the "tragedy of Hector" in the *Iliad*, or the tragic vision of history in Thucydides.[6]

The sharpest difference between fifth-century Athenian tragedy and all later tragedy, in later ancient periods and beyond, is the performance context. All the tragedies of Aeschylus, Sophocles, Euripides and their contemporaries were created for a dramatic competition at a specific religious and civic festival, the Great Dionysia, as discussed in detail in the first three chapters of this volume.[7] Tragedy in Rome was experienced in more varied settings.

As editor of the present volume, I found it difficult to persuade my contributors that they might be able to discuss both Athenian and Roman tragedy. These two entirely different cultural entities are usually studied in total isolation from one another. All of the contributors to this volume are specialists in only one of these areas; all are fully aware that the social and literary and cultural contexts of these two genres are entirely different.

Both of these ancient genres are also usually discussed in total isolation from the later tragic tradition. Some institutional structures, such as the Cambridge Tragedy Paper for undergraduates in English Literature at Cambridge, UK, encourage a more synoptic view. But the notion of studying the whole genre of tragedy or "the tragic" has come to seem to many scholars problematic, because it can involve a lack of cultural and political specificity, and a neglect of the historical facts about a very discontinuous tradition.[8] There are vast gaps between the cultural, thematic, and literary force and effects of Athenian, Senecan, French neo-classical, and Shakespearean tragedy—to take just four of the several distinct dramatic traditions that can be labeled tragic. Philosophizing generalizations about the nature of the tragic or "the tragic sense of life"[9] are often removed many miles from the actual texts, let alone the original performances, of Athenian and Senecan tragedies, which are more varied, more polyvocal, and often lighter and funnier than the philosophers would have us believe.

How, then, could it make sense to study tragedy across time, as the structure of the Bloomsbury six-volume set would have us do? Does it even make sense to conjoin Athenian with Senecan tragedy, as the present volume does? I would argue that it does, but only if we acknowledge that the tradition is fractured and discontinuous, and is, like so many traditions, invented and reinvented retrospectively, by a series of imitations, creations, distortions, misreadings, and new creations. It is precisely because of the diversity and discontinuity of the tragic tradition that this structure is potentially useful. I hope readers will be able to see radical disparities both across and within the volumes, and unexpected connections.

ANCIENT TRAGEDY AND OTHER GENRES

Athenian tragedy drew on several separate earlier traditions, including hexameter poetry, (several kinds of) lyric, and dithyramb. The meter of dialogue in tragedy, iambic trimeter, was drawn from archaic poetic traditions including satirical blame poetry (*iambos*). Tragedy is, from its beginnings, a poly-generic genre, mixing the dense meanings and complex rhythms of lyric with the narrative drive and psychological subtlety of Homer.[10]

The performance of the Homeric epics had formed part of the civic festivals of Athens since the time of Pisistratos, the tyrant who instituted the Panathenaic Festival in 566 BCE. Tragedy borrows some of its most characteristic elements from the *Iliad* and the *Odyssey*. Athenian tragedy, like some Roman tragedies (the *fabulae crepidatae*), almost always draws on the same body of myth as the Homeric poems and the Cyclic poems: the stories of Troy, Thebes, and the House of Pelops. Both archaic Greek epic and Athenian tragedy are set in a non-contemporary world. But the kinship of these genres goes beyond a shared body of mythic material. Tragedy and epic are the two central genres through which ancient Greece and Rome created serious imaginative constructions of the place of individuals within society. Both grapple with the relationship of a single individual to her or his community, especially when, as is the case for Odysseus or Achilles and numerous tragic protagonists, the individual is separated from the group. Both genres are interested in the costs of social reintegration, for the individual and for the community as a whole. Both explore how the past can haunt the present, and how one narrative pattern can be superimposed on another. Both are interested in whether one person or one body or one story can be traded for another. Both deal with the human impulses towards aggression and destruction, and the effects of war on male warriors and on women and children. Both represent the terrible vulnerability of the mortal human body, and the relationship between mortals and the immortal gods.

Certain key plot elements are common in both genres, as Aristotle recognizes in the *Poetics*. These include the recognition scene, the revenge plot, the culminating act of slaughter, the disastrous falling-out of friends or family members, a focus on physical and mental suffering, and catastrophic misunderstandings.

The social worlds of the two genres are also similar. Both Homeric epic and Athenian and Roman tragedy focus primarily on elite characters, especially elite men, from the Greek-speaking world. Both also include characters from other social categories, including elite women (who take on an even more prominent role in tragedy than in Homer), and slaves, and non-Greeks.[11] Both genres also insist on the presence of gods, who interfere in human lives and whose intentions can be difficult or impossible to unravel.

Despite all this common ground, Athenian tragedy is significantly different from either archaic choral lyric or Homeric epic. Formally, the first key difference is the existence of a raised wooden stage and of actors who are separate from the chorus. Homeric epic and other dactylic poetry was also experienced in antiquity in performance, at festivals and parties, with musical accompaniment; but the elaborate, costumed, multi-actor performances of tragedy were a very different theatrical experience.[12]

Every genre is defined by what it is not—and hence, by the other genres that exist within the same culture. In Athens, a tragedy was defined by not being a satyr play, the kind of drama that appeared after every tragic trilogy in Athens.[13] Satyrs were the wild creatures who accompanied the drunken, lustful nature god, Silenus; the lower half of their bodies was like a goat, with hairy legs and hooves, and they featured constant enormous erections (Figure 0.1).

The pairing of tragedy with satyr play must have invited a keen awareness of the elements in tragedy that were not shared by its sister genre, or are less prominent in it. Whereas satyrs belong in the wild countryside, the world of animals and nature and caves, tragedy is a genre that is deeply preoccupied with defining human communities, especially the city-state or *polis* in its relationship with the household or *oikos*—as well as the relationship of cities to one another and of households to one another.[14]

Moreover, satyrs are figures of excessive masculinity, with their hairy bodies, huge phalloi, and uncurbed appetites for nymphs, wine, violence, and self-assertion; their female counterparts, the maenads (wild female worshippers of Dionysos), seem to have been somewhat less prominent in the genre. By contrast, female characters play a prominent role in many Athenian tragedies, and tragic male characters worry that they may be turning into women, or dress up as women, while female tragic characters are sometimes defined as masculine or inhabiting a male role.[15]

The presence of satyr play must also have reminded ancient Athenian audiences of the specific and limited representation of the physical body in tragedy. Characters in tragedy almost never eat or drink anything, unless it is poison or a family member, like Seneca's Thyestes devouring his own children. Sex appears in tragedy only when it is abnormal or freighted with the potential for disaster, like Phaedra's lust for her stepson Hippolytus. By contrast, eating and having sex just for fun were prominent in satyr plays.

Satyr plays were much shorter than tragedies, a mark of their relative frivolity and of the audience's short attention spans after having been in the theater since dawn. Both genres could engage with important ethical and social questions of the day; in Euripides'

FIGURE 0.1: Apulian mixing vessel with members of a chorus dressed as satyrs, c. 410–380 BCE, attributed to the Tarporley Painter. NM47.5 Nicholson Museum, The University of Sydney.

Cyclops, Odysseus has an extensive discussion with Polyphemus about the nature of justice and moral relativism. But the seriousness with which tragedy takes relationships, in families, cities, and communities contrasts with the free-for-all association of Silenus and his hapless band of hangers-on. Of the three satyr plays for which we have most evidence, Euripides' *Cyclops*, Aeschylus' *Dictyulci*, and Sophocles' *Ichneutae*, all feature an encounter between the satyrs and a pre-civilized being: the Cyclops, in the Euripides play, and a baby, in the other two. By contrast, tragedy deals with relationships between fully adult, fully human, and fully civilized people. The intimate, easy bond between the divine Silenus and his followers contrasts with the fraught complexity of divine–human relationships in tragedy. Satyr plays explore the relationship of humans to animals, whereas animals are usually absent from tragedy, except as metaphors. Finally, the intense focus of tragedy on what human beings can and cannot understand contrasts with the way that satyr plays focused on characters whose bumbling ignorance and incompetence is funny, not terrible, and who succeed in their various quests and discoveries, with little or no effort or skill.

Satyr plays did not exist in Rome, so Roman tragedy is defined rather differently within its own cultural context, as the dramatic genre that contrasts with comedy and mime. Moreover, in Rome tragedy was, from its beginnings, defined as a genre borrowed from the Greeks; Livius Andronicus, the first to write tragedy in Latin, was a Greek freedman, and his tragedies, of which nothing but titles survive, were on subjects borrowed from Greek myth; his contemporary Gnaeus Naevius also wrote tragedies based on Greek mythology, as well as comedies (a combination unknown in ancient Athens, where tragedy was seen as a specialty art). Later Roman tragedy came in two distinct types: it included plays based on Greek subjects (*fabulae crepidatae*), and those based on Roman subjects (*fabulae praetextae*, of which the only surviving example is the pseudo-Senecan *Octavia*). The division of serious drama into these two separate categories invites us to see Roman tragedy in terms of its relationship with two different kinds of past: the partly imaginary world of Greek myth, and the more historical world of Rome.

In fifth-century Athens, tragedy was also structurally contrasted and compared with comedy. Tragedy and comedy sometimes appeared in the same festivals, although not pitted against one another. Both were elaborate forms of metrical verse drama, featuring masks, male actors even for female roles, and singing, dancing choruses. Both were serious art forms, expensively produced and involving a great deal of literary and dramatic labor by citizen-actors and economic input from citizen donors. Athenian men devoted this time, energy, and money to the theater, in all three dramatic genres, to promote their own social status, and as an act of piety, and to provide some kind of civic as well as cultural teaching for their fellow citizens. Both tragedy and comedy could include moments of humor, pathos, surprise, or horror, although of course the proportion of laughter to tears was different for the two genres. As far as we can tell from Aristophanes, the only surviving author of Old Comedy (the comic genre of the fifth century), comedy constantly defined itself against contemporary tragedy, and in some cases, vice versa; Euripides in particular seems to allude to and sometimes lift comic motifs and plot elements.[16] Where tragedy used mythical characters and plots (albeit with plenty of scope to adapt or alter the tradition), comedy often featured characters and plots that were entirely made up. Comedy allowed for much more explicit metatheatricality and breaking of the fourth wall, by which the playwright could use one of his characters to speak as if in his own persona to the audience. Characters in Athenian tragedy never do this, although tragic metatheatricality exists in less direct forms. Moreover, comedy often included references to real people and even brought dramatized versions of real people on stage. Tragedy arguably contains veiled references to contemporary political events and real-life people;[17] but it avoids direct representation of the real contemporary world.

The characters of Old Comedy choruses were often animals (like birds or frogs), or fantastical entities (like the Clouds in the play of that name); by contrast, tragedy was a far more naturalistic genre. Onstage violence is probably more common in comedy than in tragedy, and increases exponentially by the time we reach Roman comedy, in which slave-beating jokes form an essential element in the humor. But offstage violence is generally far more bloody and gruesome in tragedy. In comedy, the body is often subjected to non-life-threatening injuries, whereas in tragedy, bodies are hanged, dismembered, hacked apart with axes or by wild horses, or poisoned, or blinded, or left to rot unburied. People in comedy eat, drink, poop, fart, fall over, flirt, and have fun, non-disastrous sex. People in tragedy, in general, do not. But these two genres also share a great many central preoccupations. Both are, unlike satyr plays, interested in the relationships between husbands and wives, parents and children, the human and the divine, and individuals and communities.

Ancient Athenian tragedians also defined their own work against the new genres that were appearing in the fifth century. Sophocles was friends with Herodotus, and drew on an anecdote from his *Histories* in the *Antigone*. Athenian tragedy was constantly responding to other forms of discourse, including historiography and oratory. Tragedy co-opts these alternative genres into itself, competing with comedy and historiography for the status of most-capacious, most important, and most-truthful kind of literary art. Later, Senecan tragedy is deeply engaged not only with Athenian tragedy and earlier Roman tragedy, but also with other literary genres: Virgilian epic, the poetry of Ovid and Horace, the Roman declamation and other oratorical genres, and Seneca's own philosophical writings.[18]

TRAGEDY AND IDEAS

In the early sixth century BCE, Anaximander of Miletus (in modern Turkey) theorized that there is a fundamental infinite substance from which all components of the physical world are composed, and that from this original substance, things come into being and pass away: "For [he said that they] pay each other justice/balance and reparation for injustice/ imbalance, according to the arrangement of time" (DK12B1).[19] This mysterious quotation presumably came in a discussion about the nature of the tangible material world. But the line also hints at further applications, since the word translated here as "justice/ balance," and the cognate word for "injustice/ imbalance," *dike* and *adikia* respectively, become the standard terms in later Greek for moral and legal instances of justice and injustice. Anaximander's philosophical fragment hints at what will become one of the major preoccupations of ancient tragedy: how exactly balance, order, or justice can be regained, when an imbalance has occurred. Is payback, or revenge, the right or only way to regain balance—or does it create further imbalance? This set of questions haunts one of our earliest ancient Greek tragic texts, Aeschylus' *Oresteia* (458 BCE), which looks back, in the first Choral Ode of the first play (the Parodos of the *Agamemnon*) to the original moment of imbalance: the moment when Agamemnon was faced with an impossible choice at Aulis, to betray his men or kill his daughter, and chose the second, valuing his (public, male) community over his (private, female) family.[20] Later Athenian tragedies revert again and again to this same story of cyclical family murder (Sophocles and Euripides both wrote *Electra* plays), and to other plots about revenge and reparation. Tragedy is preoccupied with questions of balance within a family or community, and of the relationship of social or human kinds of justice to cosmic or divine models. During the latter half of the fifth century BCE, Athenian tragedy was perceived as one of the major means of civic education for the adult population, which raised serious questions about what tragedy taught, and whether its lessons were good or corrupting.[21]

After the fifth century was over, Athens had fallen from its position of pre-eminence in the Greek-speaking world, and the great tragedians, Aeschylus, Sophocles, and Euripides (as well as other lost greats such as Agathon) were dead, philosophers began to theorize the value of the genre in new ways. Plato, who came from a wealthy and well-connected family, supposedly wrote tragedies as a young man (Diogenes Laertius, *Life of Plato* 4); he devoted serious philosophical attention to engaging with, imitating, reinventing, and resisting, the ethical, literary, and metaphysical perspectives of tragedy. The dramatic form of his dialogues owes much to the stage, and Plato's preoccupations with questions of true knowledge, wisdom and the nature of the good life overlap with those of Athenian tragedy.

Plato's most famous discussions of tragedy come in two moments in his *Republic* (composed around 380 BCE).[22] These passages both argue that tragedy is dangerous, although for distinct and somewhat incompatible reasons: because it conveys false ideas about the gods; because it causes elite men to pretend to inhabit lesser social roles; because it encourages dangerous emotions; and because it is far distant from reality. Plato says little about tragic plots. He focuses on the kind of characters evoked by tragedy, on the mode of dramatic imitation, and the kind of emotions stirred up by drama.[23]

Plato's student, Aristotle, responds to his critique of poetry in general, and tragedy in particular, in his *Poetics*, a short pamphlet whose brevity indicates how little the subject interested the author. Characteristically, Aristotle adopts a commonsensical approach, combating his teacher's radical views. Aristotle breaks poetry down into categories and subsets, as he does with other subjects of study. Tragedy is, he claims, the most perfect kind of poetry, superior even to epic because it contains the same material in a more condensed form. He classifies poetry according to three different schemes: the media (rhythm, verse, music, etc.); the objects imitated (such as people, acting well or badly); and the manner, i.e., whether the story is told diagetically or dramatically. Whereas Plato implies that dramatic narrative is inherently problematic, Aristotle lays out the possibilities without judgment, and thereby implies a more positive view of the possible ethical and psychological value of literary art.

Aristotle writes back against Plato's claims that poetry is ethically damaging. He begins the treatise by arguing that imitation or pretending is natural to human beings from childhood onwards; imaginative engagement with lives other than our own is thus not a distortion or falsification of our true selves or of reality, but a fulfillment of an essential human capacity. He suggests that tragedy, far from being emotionally corrupting, is in fact useful emotional training. It arouses pity and fear in the audience, and by so doing, "achieves the *catharsis* of such emotions" (*Poetics* 1449b). *Catharsis* is a medical term suggesting purgation, cleansing or forced vomiting or diarrhea. Within the *Poetics*, Aristotle never defines the term or explains exactly what it means. The phrase has been endlessly studied, and it is open to a number of competing interpretations about how exactly Aristotle imagines the psychological process happening. Does tragedy arouse excessive emotions which are then purged? Or emotions that are not excessive but correctly calibrated as correct responses to excessive disasters? When exactly does the purgation take place? The text does not give explicit answers. What is clear is that Aristotle is combating Plato's claim that tragedy waters emotions that should be repressed, by a counter-claim, that tragedy enables emotional cleansing.

In responding to Plato's attacks on the truth claims of poetry in general and tragedy in particular, Aristotle claims that poetry contrasts with history not because one is false and the other true, but because they deal with different ontologies: history tells what did happen, and poetry, what "would happen" (*Poetics* 1451b); it describes probabilities. This is a fairly implausible claim, given the plots of most extant tragedies; its presence shows how eager Aristotle is to provide poetry with a good claim to some definite kind of truth.

More broadly, Aristotle suggests that tragedy does in fact, *pace* Plato, provide a vision of the human world that is both truthful and ethically valuable, because at its best, it shows us actions performed by people who are just a little better than ourselves, involving a journey towards greater understanding shaped into a complex but ultimately unified and readily comprehensible narrative. He tells us that there are three elements that add complexity to tragedy: suffering (*pathos*), recognition (*anagnorisis*), and reversal of fortune (*peripeteia*). The first of these, suffering, is set more or less aside, because it fits less well into the scheme; the other two are essential for Aristotle's vision of the genre, in that they point to a tragic interest in cognitive questions, whereby characters and audiences both achieve greater understanding in the course of the play. For Aristotle, it is essential to claim that tragedy represents a world that is fundamentally coherent and comprehensible, since the idea that everything ultimately makes sense and has an ultimate purpose (a *telos* or final cause) is an essential element of his ethical and metaphysical thought. It is also essential, in his eyes, that tragedies must be unified, since unity is a way of ensuring that something makes some kind of sense and can be understood by the human mind.

Aristotle claims that the six components of tragedy are spectacle, song, diction, plot, character, and reasoning. Plot turns out to be by far the most important of these, because it is in plot that we see how human behavior plays out and has consequences. He goes through four possible plot types. Either good people suffer; or bad people are successful; or good people are successful; or bad people suffer. None of these turn out to be ideal; rather, the correct plot features a fairly good (not ideal) person changing from fortune to misfortune, through some kind of mistake (the word for "mistake" is *hamartia*, a term which was later wildly misinterpreted to mean "tragic flaw"). This type of plot is ideal because it provides the most opportunity for the correct emotional responses, of pity and fear. Tragedy thus provides a particular kind of mirror on human life, one which Aristotle implies is broadly correct. It shows us a world where fairly good people can discover terrible as well as beneficial things, and can switch from good fortune to disaster in the course of an hour's drama. Aristotle insists in the *Nichomachean Ethics* that a good life, *eudaimonia*, consists of virtuous activity; but he also acknowledges that virtuous activity may not be possible for some, perhaps many people, because we may, through no fault of our own, or through "some kind of mistake," not possess or be deprived of "external goods" that are essential for full human functioning and happiness, such as health, freedom, high class, living children, wealth, good looks, and so on (*EN* 1099a30–1099b10). But Aristotle also insists, even more vehemently, on the idea that the world is ultimately comprehensible, even if it is not always conducive to happiness for every individual. The unified, coherent, comprehensible structure of complex tragic plots is essential to its Aristotelian truthfulness.

Aristotle's representation of tragedy has been hugely influential in discussions of the genre since the *Poetics* was first rediscovered in the seventeenth century, so it is worth pausing to consider how peculiar and debatable many of Aristotle's claims and assumptions are, and how much they omit as an account of Athenian tragedy. We must certainly not assume that, as an ancient Macedonian person who lived a generation or two after the great tragedians and probably experienced tragedy primarily through reading, rather than performance, Aristotle would have got everything right about the genre. Despite his rhetoric trumpeting his own common sense, many of Aristotle's descriptions and prescriptions would have seemed downright peculiar or obviously wrong-headed to his contemporaries, such as his valuing of tragedy over Homeric epic, and his omission of most of the classical and archaic Greek poetic canon. He has no extensive discussion of comedy, although he promises to cover it in a further book; perhaps there was a later pamphlet on comedy, or perhaps not. He has almost nothing to say about other poetic genres, such as satyr play, lyric, dithyramb, hymns, encomia, or mime. These would have fit less well into his structure, because it is difficult to describe a lyric poem in terms of its plot.

Moreover, Aristotle's focus on form leaves out all consideration of the social, cultural, performative, and political contexts of ancient tragedy. Spectacle and music are presented as insignificant elements in the genre, and there is nothing about tragedy's place in a religious festival, or about the ways that tragedy participated in Athenian civic and cultural self-fashioning. Aristotle presents Athenian tragedy as a universal genre that describes human beings, rather than as a specifically ancient Athenian genre that evokes the lives, fears, and fantasies of a very particular group of elite male human beings in the latter half of the fifth century BCE.

ANCIENT TRAGEDY IN CONTEXT

Ancient tragedy is linguistically unlike any other genre in the ancient world. Like comedy, it uses a great variety of meters: iambic trimeter for the majority of the dialogue, but also anapaests for particular passages of high excitement and a vast range of lyric meters for the choral passages. Tragedy also uses dense patterns of metaphor and linguistic riddling that is unparalleled in other dramatic genres. The language is at times, often in the dialogue sections, especially in Euripides, fairly simple and conversational; but it can also, especially in the choral passages, be extraordinarily difficult and dense. It is hard to imagine that everybody in the audience would have been able to understand the choruses of Aeschylus readily, even if they were able to hear every word (which is unlikely, given the acoustics of the theater). The linguistic diversity and density is an essential element in the ways that ancient tragedy dramatizes and performs a human failure to understand language or understand through language. The rich uses of metaphor in tragedy, including threads of repeated metaphor, also play an essential part in how tragedy constructs meaning through the physical resources of the theater: through dance, movement, props and gesture as well as through words. In the *Oresteia*, for instance, we have tropes that seem at first to be abstract, invisible ideas—dogs, snakes, nets, cloth, fire, blood, scales, hunting—each of which becomes literalized on stage, in the cloth Agamemnon steps on when he goes into the house to his death, in the net that entangles him in the bath, and in the bloody, snake-haired, dog-like pack of Furies who hunt Orestes in the final play. In *Oedipus Tyrannos*, Oedipus repeatedly puns on his own name and its suggestion of his ability to see or know the truth about feet, through the Riddle of the Sphinx: the Greek verb *oida* means "to know" or "to have seen," while *pous* means "foot." The play ends with this same "See-Foot" man stumbling blind—a terrible, literal reversion of the words which Oedipus imagined could be merely metaphorical. The booted feet of the actors, the dancing feet of the chorus members, and the masked eyes of all the players, make visible a system of imagery that exists both in words and in dramaturgy.

The resources of the theater itself, as well as its religious context, can partly help us understand why tragic language is so much denser than the poetry of Homer, and so much more heavily invested in double or triple layers of meaning. Athenian and Senecan tragedy represent and respond to contemporary religious practices and beliefs.[24] The genre constantly communicates on multiple different levels at once: with gestures and with words, with song and with speech, with costumes and with dance. Presumably the theatrical experience of tragedy was quite different depending on whether one sat at the very front or right at the back of the huge theater. Tragedy is always speaking to several very different audiences at the same time, including the judges of the competition, the ordinary citizens of Athens, the permanent residents, the visitors passing through, and the gods, under whose watchful eye the performances always took place.

Over the past few decades, scholars of ancient tragedy have become increasingly aware of the precise ways in which the genre emerged from its own specific cultural contexts, in Athens, in the wider Greek-speaking world, and then in Rome.[25] These contexts include the actual theatrical and dramaturgical performance conditions for ancient tragedies, as well as the social, political, and cultural world in which they were produced. The essays in the present volume provide eight careful analyses of how ancient tragedy is embedded in its own social world, and are informed by current critical and theoretical developments.

Tragedy emerged under tyranny, but developed during the great period of Athenian democracy.[26] It spoke to pressing cultural questions about the relationship of three competing political and social structures within Athens: between the model of one-man rule ("tyranny," which was not necessarily a negative term in the Greek-speaking world), and newly emergent democracy, in which all free male citizens above a certain wealth bracket had a vote and a voice in the assembly, and the oligarchic model (like that of Athens' military rival, Sparta) in which a few elite aristocratic families hold all the power—a model which was briefly adopted in the late fifth century after a Spartan-sponsored coup. Tragedy frequently seems to stage a conflict between modes of government, not just between the *demos* and the tyrant (e.g., in *agon* between Creon and Haemon), but also between the old oligarchic aristocracy and the new world of demagoguery (as in Sophocles' *Ajax*). Tragedy has sometimes been described as an essentially democratic genre, because so many different kinds of people get a powerful, compelling public voice, including those who had no vote and little or no legal power in democratic Athens, such as slaves and women and foreign immigrants; it has also been seen as an essentially elitist genre, because it focuses predominantly on the lives of a few well-born and wealthy households. Tragedy flourished in the tyranny of Sicily as well as the democracy of Athens.[27] The political valences of tragedy were ambiguous and fluid enough that the genre became popular in many different later cultural contexts, including under tyrants as well as in Republican and imperial Rome. In Rome, tragedy sometimes had an anti-tyrannical resonance. But there was always plausible deniability; the mythic Agamemnon is not necessarily identical with any particular self-indulgent, soon-to-be-assassinated Roman emperor.

Ormand and Widzisz in this volume provide two distinct perspectives on how Athenian tragedy engages with conflicts facing contemporary elite Athenian families. Both focus on the problematic place of wives within their husband's family, and the ensuing tension between different aristocratic or elite households. The special difficulty for elite men in male-dominated societies of exerting and retaining control over the women in their households is not, of course, a concern that is unique to tragedy; it is already a central subject in both the Homeric poems, composed some three centuries before our earliest extant tragedy. But in the more densely-populated, more politicized, more elaborately structured society of fifth-century Athens, there were new kinds and levels of anxiety about the place of elite wives within their households, and about the relationship of elite households to the new social structure, the democratic city-state. Athenian tragedy was entirely created and performed by men, wearing masks and costumes, for an audience that was entirely or at the very least primarily male. Roman tragedy, too, was created by elite men, primarily for the entertainment and edification of an elite male audience. Neither genre can give us any direct access to the real lived experience of any ancient woman. But both can give us rich insights into the particular concerns, fantasies, and anxieties of free male citizens living in a patriarchal society, about gender relationships and the terrible things that might happen, if their wives ever stepped outside the house or opened their mouths. Athenian tragedy has often been seen as especially preoccupied by the conflict between the household or family (the *oikos*), a space where women have some level of authority and some capacity to speak, and the city-state (the *polis*), to which women have no access. Ormand and Widzisz nuance this model by pointing to essential implications for tragedy of the fact that women, in Athenian practices and law, belonged to two different households: that of their fathers, and that of their husbands. Ormand points to the economic and legal liminality of wives and its repercussions in tragedy, while Widzisz shows how often tragedy stages conflicts not between city-state and household, but between two different elite households.

One can find in Athenian tragedy an awareness of other kinds of social conflict: not between men and women, or one house and another, or between the family and the larger community, but between different classes and different cultures. Slave characters play an important and sometimes crucial role in Athenian tragedy; sometimes the elite household is overturned through the agency of a slave—as in the *Oedipus Tyrannos*, where the slave herdsman is the witness to the original murder of Laius. Other tragedies show how elite characters can be transformed into slaves, either literally, and more realistically, through capture in warfare—as in *Trojan Women* or *Hecuba* or Cassandra in *Agamemnon*—or in a more figurative sense, in the many tragedies that deal with experiences of bondage, disempowerment, and diminishment of social status, including *Prometheus Bound*, the *Electra* plays (where, in Euripides' version, Electra is as it were the slave of her own mother), or, in reverse, the *Ion*, in which a temple slave turns out to be, by birth, a lord. We do not know anything about what access the thousands of slaves living in ancient Athens would have had to the tragic theater, if any. Perhaps their experience of tragedy was confined to images on the vases and pots they scrubbed and filled for their owners. But we can glimpse in this art form created by and for slave-owners some glimmerings of interest in the perspectives of their human tools, and some awareness that there, but for the grace of gods, they went.

Ancient tragedy is particularly interested in defining what lies beyond the normal boundaries of elite male experience, and also what lies beyond the city, the community, the known world. Senecan tragedy shows a preoccupation with exceeding the limits of the Roman Empire, moving beyond past achievements or earlier myths. In Athens, tragedies were performed at a moment of the year at which physical boundaries were opened up. The festival of Dionysos happened in the spring, when sea travel to Athens became possible again after the winter storms, so the audiences for tragedy, unlike comedy (whose festival was earlier in the year) would have included visitors from other Greek cities as well as Athenian natives.[28]

Dionysos, the god of the theater, was associated with mysteries and with the overturning of normal, conventional limits between one world and another. One of the central themes of ancient tragedy is the impossibility of maintaining clear boundaries, either between one household and another, or between a household and the larger community. Tragedy also focuses on the permeable boundaries of the individual human body. Dionysian ritual included the performative tearing apart of an animal, an act known as *sparagmos*. In Athenian tragedy, not animals but human beings are ripped apart—including Pentheus in the *Bacchae*, and Hippolytus in the play of that name, as well as Seneca's *Phaedra*.

Even when the physical body remains more or less intact, characters in ancient tragedy often evoke an experience of mental or psychological *sparagmos*, a sense of being ripped into several different pieces. The chorus in the Parodos (first ode) of the *Agamemnon* evoke the experience of the chief at Aulis, pulled between two incompatible and (in his eyes) equally impossible choices: to betray his men, or to kill his own daughter. As he says, "Which of these things is without evil?" Medea, too, is pulled apart in two incompatible directions, by her desire for revenge and her love for her children. Phaedra in the *Hippolytus* describes a comparable sense of disintegration under the pull of contradictory and illicit desires. Sophocles' *Oedipus Tyrannos* most explicitly thematizes a central question of Athenian tragedy: whether an individual person is one or many. The play creates a muddle over how many people killed Laius: one man, or many? Oedipus, who imagines that he is only one person, turns out to be multiple different people: the child of two sets of parents, the husband and son of Jocasta, the brother and father of his children, the savior of the city and the source of its plague. Scholars of Sophocles have long recognized his interest in contrasting stubborn, unyielding characters—like Antigone, Oedipus, Philoctetes, or Ajax—with those who urge them to compromise and yield. We see different versions of this tragic interest in stubbornness, single-mindedness or *autarkeia* ("self-will" or "self-rule") in the other extant tragedians; for instance, Euripides' *Hippolytus* stages an encounter between an almost-man who refuses to compromise in his sense of his own purity and his loyalty to Artemis, and a woman who is both diseased and invigorated by her passion for him. Aeschylus' Xerxes is a self-willed ruler whose refusal to yield to persuasion or compromise in his yearning to extend his empire brings him to disaster: a body clothed in rags, an empire ripped at the seams. Busch's essay on Senecan tragedy, in this volume, focuses on what he argues is a central preoccupation of those much-later plays: the boundaries of the physical and ontological self, and the possibility that external forces might be able to penetrate a person, against his or her will. Seneca's specific concerns with demarcating and policing the boundaries of the self emerge, as Busch shows, from his own philosophical and political preoccupations, and are not entirely paralleled by the ways that selves and bodies are pierced, multiplied, or ripped apart in Athenian tragedy. But common to both Athenian and Senecan tragedy is an anxiety about the ways that people can be something less or more than whole, and about the costs of an insistence on wholeness and invulnerability.

Aristotle lists *pathos*, suffering, as one of the three central components of tragic plots, along with recognition and reversal, although he shows much less interest in it than in the other two more obviously cognitive elements. Recent critics have had much more interest in the ways that ancient tragedy represents the vulnerability of the physical body, and the ways that bodies, in life and in the theater, can be subject to transformation, manipulation, alienation, and disguise. Pentheus, played of course by a male actor, is urged to dress in women's clothes, in order to spy on the women on the mountain—and eventually be torn to pieces by them.

Dead bodies play a particularly important part in ancient tragedy. Several plays focus on the burial of the dead, including *Antigone*, *Oedipus at Colonus*, and *Ajax*. In others, dead bodies are brought on stage at climactic moments of the action, as in the end of *Agamemnon*, *Choephoroi*, or the *Trojan Women*, which features the tiny brain-mangled corpse of baby Astyanax. Sometimes the most important dead bodies are theatrical fictions, as when Helen, in the play of that name, pretends she needs to bury her former husband, Menelaus; or in Sophocles' *Electra*, which features an empty jar that supposedly contains the ashes of the dead Orestes. As a theatrical genre that creates meaning through the appearance of bodies, tragedy is particularly suited to demonstrate the importance of the dead in the lives of the living, and the problems posed by the continued existence of dead bodies. Tragedy also shows how the dead haunt the living in less material ways. In the *Choephoroi* and in Aeschylus' *Persians*, the dead exert a tangible influence on the living. In Senecan tragedy, the dead become even more powerful; we encounter, for example, the ghost of the dead Tantalus at the start of the *Thyestes*, who warns of further horror for the house of Atreus.

Many ancient tragedies end with violent death averted (such as *Ion, Helen, Iphigeneia in Tauris*), or with a focus that shifts from the dead to the survivors (such as *Heracles*). Everybody dies, so perhaps it is not surprising that serious drama would take an interest in death. But the specific preoccupations with violent death in ancient tragedy, whether achieved or merely threatened, and its effects on family and community, can also be seen in the context of contemporary military conflicts. All our extant Athenian tragedies were composed either in the wake of the Persian Wars (in which Aeschylus himself fought), or during the decades of the Peloponnesian War, in which Sophocles was a general. The festival of Dionysos, at which these plays were performed and judged, also included military processions, the display of booty won in war, the parading of boys newly come of age and ready for recruitment for the army, and the display of children orphaned in war.[29]

It is relevant to this military context that so many ancient Athenian tragedies focus on characters who die young, often killed by, or as a result of actions by, members of the older generation. These include Iphigenia (killed by her father), Polyxena (sacrificed on the grave of Achilles), Antigone (who kills herself, but in the wake of a king's poor decisions), Ajax (suicide), Heracles' wife and children (killed by himself), Pentheus (killed by his mother), Hippolytus (killed by his father's curse), and Medea's children (killed by herself). The violent deaths of young people, and the pollution incurred by the older generation as a result, is a preoccupation of tragedy that is surely connected, however indirectly, to the cultural context in which the Athenian assembly repeatedly voted to send more and more boys to war to be killed. In the world of tragedy, many of those who die are female, not male, and tragedy also gives us glimpses into the experiences of non-combatants in war, from the rage and grief of women whose babies are slaughtered and who are themselves raped and enslaved in the sacking of a city (*Hecuba, Trojan Women*), to the continuing, fragile life of enslaved women in the households of their new owners (like Cassandra in *Agamemnon*, or Tecmessa in *Ajax*).

Athenian tragedy also presents us with several characters who return home from war or other spheres of conflict and triumph, usually with disastrous results (*Hippolytus, Heracles, Ajax*). Several extant plays (*Iphigeneia in Aulis, Philoctetes*) focus on the ethical and psychological dilemmas posed by war, and raise difficult questions about whether any means are justified to achieve one's military ends. Ancient Athenian tragedy has been seen in terms of contemporary understandings of post-traumatic stress disorder, and contemporary veterans' groups have also worked to use Athenian tragedy for community-building and healing.[30]

The contributors in this volume have had to balance the broad, perhaps universal interest and appeal of ancient tragedy against its precise historical cultural, political, and social contexts. Cowan's essay in this volume argues that tragedy was always political in the broadest sense, but its political meanings could become wildly different in different contexts (under tyranny, in Athenian democracy, in Hellenistic city-states, in the Roman Republic, and under the Roman Empire). His analysis, along with those of Weiss, Andújar, and Visvardi, trace how the genre took on different political as well as different aesthetic meanings when performed in different social worlds. The title of the chapter, "Politics of City and Nation," is designed to cover politics in all the six volumes, from ancient Athens to the modern era. There was a particular problem in creating a title for these chapters, since political formations, and the appropriate terminology to refer to them, changed radically over the course of the centuries covered by this series. The *polis* or "city-state" of the Greek-speaking world is the term from which we get the English "political"; but it was not either a modern "city" or a modern "nation"—a term that implies a much larger

FIGURE 0.2: Apulian mixing vessel showing a scene probably inspired by Aeschylus' *Edonoi*: Lycurgus, who has been driven mad by Dionysos, has killed his son Dryas and is about to attack his wife. An old retainer watches and will later report the scene, *c.* 350–340 BCE. The British Museum, London, 1849,0623.48 © The Trustees of the British Museum. All rights reserved.

group than the relatively small territories of Greek-speaking city-states. Ancient Rome, too, was not the same as a modern "nation," either in the period of the Republic or the Empire.

Similarly, there is arguably no such thing as "the family" in antiquity. The Latin term *familia*, like the Greek *oikos*, suggests the whole household, including slaves, rather than simply the nuclear biological family. Ancient tragedy was always engaged with broad questions about family structures, relationships between families, relationships between men and women and parents and children, and tensions between families and larger communities or social units. In some ways, these are universal human themes, and their prominence in ancient tragedy is one of the central reasons for the genre's long-lasting appeal. But the particular legal, economic, and social structures of ancient Athenian and

Roman households and their relationship to each other and to the larger community, and culturally-specific attitudes to gender and families in distinct periods of antiquity, have demonstrable relevance to the particular ways that ancient tragedy grapples with these ostensibly universal questions. The problem of how to maintain the integrity of aristocratic households was a central preoccupation of ancient Athenian society and Athenian law in ways that it is not exactly paralleled in other societies, including ancient Rome. The distinct range of ancient attitudes towards sex and gender are echoed but not exactly replicated by those of other cultures. Widzisz and Ormand both emphasize the importance of Athenian citizenship laws for Athenian tragedy's representation of the household, and both show how distinctive ancient Athenian and Roman perceptions of sex, gender, and the family play out in ancient tragedy. Both also emphasize that tragedy is always a mythical, artificial, and in some ways fantastical genre, never a precise mirror of contemporary lived experience.[31] Ancient tragedy was always religious, in the sense that the genre emerged from ritual performance and was always concerned with the relationships of mortals and the gods; but as Torrance shows in this volume, the particular religious contexts and meanings of Athenian tragedy were very different from those of the later Roman genre.

Ancient tragedy has had, and continues to have, an immense cultural impact on later literature, drama, and the history of ideas. The essays in the present volume cannot hope to cover every possible aspect of this fascinating ancient genre, or set of related genres. But each author lays out some essential groundwork for a better historical understanding of what tragedy in antiquity was. Each shows how ancient tragedy at different periods was embedded in its own cultural, social, political, philosophical, legal, and dramaturgical contexts. The essays analyze the specific conditions that produced ancient Athenian tragedy, which were unparalleled by any later culture even in antiquity. We also learn how this hybrid, complex, multi-generic form of dramatic, literary, musical, spectacular, mythical, civic, and religious art was changed and adapted to suit entirely different cultural contexts, as tragedy spread beyond Athens and all over the Greek-speaking world, and later, was adapted in multiple different ways by Rome. Ancient tragedy itself constantly meditates on questions about time. It shows shifts between one era and another, or from mythic to historical time, or the playing out of an ancestral curse; it evokes how time is experienced as too fast or too slow, complete or incomplete; it maps how time feels in the course of the hours spent in the theater.[32] The essays in this volume show how ancient Athenian tragedy was formed by and spoke to its own times, and how it began to mutate in new times and new places of performance.

NOTE

I would like to acknowledge the extremely helpful work done on this volume by two wonderful young scholars: Amy Lewis, who did many hours of sterling work formatting bibliography and footnotes, and Scheherazade Khan, who found and acquired the permissions for many of the illustrations. Both were excellent, and I wish we could add their names to the cover.

CHAPTER ONE

Forms and Media

NAOMI WEISS

What was Greek tragedy? Despite modern productions and adaptations of plays by Aeschylus, Sophocles, and Euripides, we tend to see tragedy as text, presented to us in a book to be read and studied. In antiquity it was read and studied too—indeed, in Aristophanes' *Clouds*, reciting Euripides is presented as a marker of the "new" type of education in late fifth-century Athens, and from the Hellenistic period onwards school texts frequently included selections from this tragedian's work.[1] But for the audience in the Theater of Dionysus in Athens, tragedy was a multimedia, multisensory experience, combining music, dance, speech, costumes, props, and special effects. It also interacted with multiple other art forms, both those within the theater and those beyond it, from wedding songs to speeches in the assembly. And it was an experience that was closely connected to the civic fabric and identity of the city itself. Since we are unable to immerse ourselves in the life of fifth-century Athens and its performance culture, our understanding of what tragedy is—and what it does—is inevitably limited.

To make matters worse, even the texts that survive represent only a tiny fraction of the thousands of plays that were produced in classical Athens. We have about ten percent of the roughly 300 dramas apparently composed by Aeschylus, Sophocles, and Euripides.[2] There were many other playwrights competing in tragic competitions before, alongside, and long after these giants of fifth-century theater, but their works are lost except for a smattering of fragments. Such different degrees of survival are no accident, but a result of a canonizing process, whereby Athenian tragedy came to be represented by the three "greats."[3] This began even before the fifth century came to a close, as we can see from the competition between Euripides and Aeschylus in Aristophanes' *Frogs* (produced in 405 BCE), at the end of which Aeschylus, the winner, demands that Sophocles take his chair in the underworld.[4] In 330 BCE a law was passed ruling that their statues be erected in the Theater of Dionysus and official copies of their scripts be deposited in the state archives, and it may have been from these texts that Hellenistic scholars eventually made their own editions.[5] At some point between the third and fifth centuries CE, collections of the plays were produced with a selection of ten for Euripides and seven for Aeschylus and Sophocles respectively. Nine more of Euripides' tragedies survive thanks to a section of a complete collection of his works, ordered alphabetically, which was copied in the medieval period. It is primarily upon these thirty-three texts that we base our idea of Greek tragedy today.

The combination of the limited number of surviving plays and our unfamiliarity with their performance context means that we often think about tragedy as a self-contained, discrete genre. Another significant reason for this impression is the influence of Aristotle, whose *Poetics* systematically lays out tragedy's formal aspects, as if there were a model to which all tragic plays should adhere. But tragedy was a much more capacious and malleable genre than his discussion might lead us to assume. To see this, we must move away from the bare texts that survive and look at other literary and visual sources that refer to aspects of tragic performance and its place within Athens. We must also closely examine the texts themselves with an eye (and ear) open to their multimedia, hybrid character—for, as we shall see, they contain numerous references to their own live production within the theater, as well as to a wide range of other performance genres. And we should appreciate the long lifetime of tragedy beyond fifth-century Athens, and how it was transformed both through the Hellenistic period and in Republican and imperial Rome.

ARISTOTLE AND THE FORMAL ASPECTS OF TRAGEDY

While the Greek tragedies that survive today demonstrate a great range of styles, narratives, and plot patterns, they also share a basic structure. Their production involved two or three actors (Aeschylus was said to have added the second; either he or Sophocles introduced the third), a chorus (Sophocles apparently increased its size from twelve to fifteen members), and a player of a set of double pipes called the *aulos*. Each play contains a mix of speech and song. Dialogue and extended speeches are generally performed by actors in iambic trimeters (a "spoken" meter; the trochaic tetrameter was also used), though sometimes the leader of the chorus speaks as well. Most plays include a long messenger speech, describing an offstage event that is critical to the plot. Songs are typically performed by the chorus in a variety of lyric meters, but occasionally actors sing in a lyric exchange or even perform arias of their own. Choral songs are generally strophic—that is, they are composed in pairs of metrically matching stanzas (strophes and antistrophes). Between song and speech are "marching" anapaests, which both actors and choruses regularly perform, often as a prelude to singing in a fully lyric meter. The choral songs would regularly punctuate each part of a drama, dividing it into acts or "episodes"; the length of both songs and episodes can vary enormously. A play usually begins with a spoken prologue, often opening with a monologue. This is followed by the chorus' entrance song (*parodos*); subsequent choral odes are termed stasima. The remaining drama following the final choral song is called the *exodos*.

Aristotle provides us with a different way of approaching tragedy's form, beyond these basic structural units. Indeed, many of our assumptions today about what makes a play a tragedy derive from his theoretical discussion of the genre (and of poetry more generally) in the *Poetics*. Yet this treatise, which became so influential after it was rediscovered in the Renaissance, does not appear to have been well known in antiquity.[6] It should not, then, be interpreted as the theoretical lens through which readers and theatergoers in the ancient world typically tended to view tragedy. It is still invaluable, however, in recording ideas about this type of theater by someone who experienced tragic performances in Athens within fifty years of the deaths of Sophocles and Euripides, and who was drawing on debates and assumptions about the genre stretching back well into the fifth century.

In chapter six of the *Poetics* Aristotle defines tragedy as "a mimesis of an action which is elevated, complete, and of magnitude; in language embellished by distinct forms in its sections; employing the mode of enactment, not narrative; and through pity and fear accomplishing the catharsis of such emotions."[7] He then lists its constituent parts in the order of their importance: plot structure, character, diction, thought, lyric poetry, and spectacle. As his ranking demonstrates, he is above all concerned with plot structure, which for him is not just tragedy's most defining feature but also the one which, more than any other, is able to have a powerful emotional impact on the audience, producing pity, fear, and *catharsis* (he is famously ambiguous regarding the precise meaning of this term). He devotes much of the *Poetics* to the principles of a "complex" structure—one which involves recognition and/or reversal (*peripateia*). The most successful form of the latter, Aristotle claims, is when a character falls from prosperity to adversity as a result of a mistake or fallibility (*hamartia*), though he acknowledges other patterns as well, and indeed one of the tragedies he cites most often is Euripides' *Iphigenia in Tauris*, which is often called an "escape tragedy" on account of its happier ending.

While Aristotle clearly states the preferred type of each of these plot devices, his discussion reveals a keen awareness of the broad range of ways in which they could be effected. This awareness must have been shared by the audiences of fifth- and fourth-century theater, as we can see from the surviving plays themselves. The recognition scene in Euripides' *Electra*, for example, parodies the equivalent one in Aeschylus' *Libation Bearers*, with Electra ridiculing the validity of the tokens that in the earlier play convince her of her brother's presence.[8] The humor here relies on the audience's knowledge not just of Aeschylus' tragedy but of this type of recognition scene in general—one which Aristotle deems inferior, preferring instead a recognition that comes about through the events themselves. And indeed the parodies of Aeschylean and Euripidean drama in the comedies of Aristophanes demonstrate that fifth-century audiences were well-versed not only in the stylistic and structural features of tragedy as a whole but in the distinctive characteristics of each tragedian.[9]

The remaining five constituent elements of tragedy receive far less attention in the *Poetics*. By "character" Aristotle means not psychological depth but primarily the ethical qualities of a protagonist (tragedy is a mimesis of not only ethically serious subjects but "those superior to us")[10] and the appropriateness and consistency with which these are portrayed. He mostly passes over "thought," referring instead to his discussions elsewhere of rhetoric, with which this category is primarily concerned. He devotes several chapters to a discussion of diction (or "the composition of metrical speech"),[11] beginning with linguistic terminology and then moving on to the ways in which poetry can achieve "clarity and avoidance of banality,"[12] but says little that seems exclusive to the tragic genre. He calls lyric poetry (*melopoiia*) the greatest of tragedy's *hēdusmata* ("seasonings"), a word which both works as a culinary metaphor to suggest the crucial spice added to a tragic production by music (and presumably also by dance) and conveys the pleasure (*hēdonē*) it could produce. Later he again suggests the importance of tragedy's musical element when he states that the chorus "should be understood as one of the actors, and should be part of the whole and participate in the action," and complains about the trend for including songs that are merely "thrown in" without any relevance to the plot.[13] But otherwise he is silent about this aspect of tragedy, focusing instead on these plays' ability to affect their audience regardless of their performance. He also says little else about the chorus, even though tragedy was regarded as a choral genre well into the fourth century BCE, as the discussion of it in Plato's *Laws* makes clear.[14] Such a focus also accounts for his disregard for spectacle (*opsis*), which refers to the various visual effects (costumes, masks, scenery, props, stage machinery) employed in a production.

TRAGEDY AS MUSICAL THEATER

As Aristotle's neglect of the musical and visual aspects of a tragic performance suggests, we should not expect the *Poetics* to be a holistic account of the genre, with each of its defining parts analyzed equally. While his interest here lies in the more cerebral aspects of tragedy (especially the plot structure), this does not mean that he is unaware of the impact of music, dance, and *opsis*: on the contrary, he calls the latter "soul-affecting,"[15] and he devotes much of the last book of the *Politics* to an examination of the potent effects of musical performance within education and leisure in general.[16] Presumably for the Athenian audience, these aspects of the live production would be some of the most memorable. A detail in Plutarch's account of the Athenians' devastating defeat in Sicily in 413 BCE is telling in this respect. He tells us that, as a result of singing some of Euripides' choral music, some Athenians were set free and given food and drink. Apparently a group of Caunians, from the south-west coast of Ionia, were also once granted haven from pirates in the harbor at Syracuse after affirming that they knew some songs of Euripides.[17] Whatever their veracity, these stories suggest that, as is the case for any Broadway show today, the songs could be the most renowned parts of a production, and the ones which could travel most rapidly across the Greek world.

We should not, then, take Aristotle's theoretical account as necessarily representative of the average theatergoer's experience of tragedy. For a sense of this experience, we can instead turn to visual representations of theatrical performances. There are unfortunately very few surviving vases with images of tragedy as a performance—with what we might understand as the audience's "view" of a tragic production. The majority of vases with scenes from tragedy come from Apulia in Southern Italy (demonstrating the success of this Athenian cultural export), but, unlike depictions of comedy and satyr play, these do not include evidence of costumes, props, or musical accompaniment, and instead represent the characters as real figures of myth. A few Attic pots survive, however, that give an impression of the musical and visual aspects of a tragic production. The most famous is a red-figure column-krater dated to the early fifth century BCE, on which three pairs of chorus members, dressed as soldiers in elaborate costumes and wearing masks and diadems, face a structure that seems to be either an altar or tomb (Figure 1.1). A bearded figure emerges from this structure—possibly an actor in a ghost-raising scene, or perhaps Dionysus himself, witnessing a dramatic performance in his honor. The chorus members are both singing and dancing before him: beneath the arms of the first pair extends a line of vowels (*aooi(o)*), visual symbols of their song; their raised arms and bent legs suggest choreographed movements. This image used to be linked to the scene in Aeschylus' *Persians* in which the chorus summons the ghost of the Persian king Darius, but actually predates that play by at least a decade. Nonetheless, it displays the range of visual and auditory effects for which Aeschylus came to be especially known, at least according to later tradition: the use of props and impressive costumes; memorable dancing, which Aeschylus was said to have choreographed himself; impressive choral songs.[18] We do not know for sure if this vase depicts a performance of tragedy, but it still provides us with something of an audience's view of a theatrical production. Those aspects that may not appear entirely "tragic," such as the short tunics and bare arms instead of the long robes and sleeves in which tragic performers are elsewhere depicted, might indicate a different genre like the dithyramb, which I discuss below.[19] But we should also be wary of assuming that this is an accurate snapshot of a particular scene, and allow instead for a blend of theatrical artifice and dramatic character that suggests some of the dramatic illusion enjoyed by an audience.[20]

Other vases with theatrical scenes demonstrate the centrality of the piper, to whose tune on the *aulos* the chorus would sing and dance. The most famous is the Pronomos Vase, a late fifth-century Attic red-figure volute krater that shows the entire troupe of actors and chorus members just after a victory in a tragic competition (Figure. 1.2).

FIGURE 1.1: Attic mixing vessel featuring a chorus performing before an altar or tomb and a figure, either an actor or Dionysus, *c.* 500–490 BCE. Antikenmuseum Basel und Sammlung Ludwig, Basel, BS 415. Photograph by Andreas F. Voegetin, courtesy of museum.

Named after the piper Pronomos, who is depicted in the bottom center of the main side, dressed in an elaborate robe and still playing his *aulos*, the vase foregrounds instrumental music as one of the defining features of a dramatic production. This may have especially been the case from the late fifth century onwards, when professional pipe players like Pronomos enjoyed fame across the Greek world and, together with star actors, would have been one of the main attractions of tragic theater.[21]

Such images point to the centrality of music and dance within a tragic production, and so also to the centrality of the chorus. They further demonstrate the importance of viewing tragedy via different media to gain an understanding of its defining features. Indeed, we could even consider tragedy against a couple of papyri fragments from the Hellenistic period, each with musical notations above lyrics from a tragedy of Euripides (*Iphigenia in Aulis* and *Orestes*).[22] Though these scores may not represent Euripides' original compositions a couple of centuries earlier, they do include certain melodic traits for which he came to be well known, including *melisma*, the practice of stretching out a syllable over several different notes.[23] The *Orestes* papyrus also provides evidence of how melody could be divorced from the words' pitch accent in Euripidean strophic lyric.[24] Above all, however, these papyri remind us that tragedy was much more than script—it was musical theater.

The surviving plays also reveal the vital role choral music and dance played within their production. For some this is clear from the sheer proportion of choral song making up a play, as is especially the case for Aeschylus' *Suppliants*, over half of which consists in choral song and dance. In this play the chorus, consisting of the Egyptian daughters of Danaus, is twice joined by an entirely different choral group, resulting in twenty-four

FIGURE 1.2: The Pronomos Vase, an Attic mixing vessel showing actors, chorus members, musicians, and the poet after a tragic competition, *c.* 400 BCE. Museo Archeologico Nazionale, Naples, 81673. Scala/Art Resource, NY.

singing and moving bodies in the dancing space known as the *orchēstra*. The first time this happens, music and action become inseparable as a group of Egyptian men rush in to seize the girls: this scene, which we would normally expect to hear about in a messenger speech, is enacted musically, first with the men's chaotic, astrophic song and then, as a strophic pattern resumes, with the girls' lyrical expressions of distress as they try to escape.[25] Presumably both choruses would perform similarly frantic dance movements, as the one chases the other around the *orchēstra*.

Tragedians could also exploit the centrality of music and dance within a play's production by making them a theme of an entire tragedy. To a large degree this is the case for Euripides' *Bacchae*, which begins with Dionysus summoning his chorus of Bacchants onstage to perform his cultic music and dance so that he can set Thebes dancing as he has Asia; the chorus then appear, singing about the god and summoning him to Thebes, where soon "the whole land will dance."[26] Several plays by Sophocles appear to have had explicitly musical themes.[27] The title of *Tympanistae* ("The Drummers"), for example, suggests that the chorus played tambourine-like instruments called *tympana*, probably in honor of Dionysus or Cybele. In the tragedy *Thamyras*, of which just a few fragments survive, the titular character was the Thracian *kithara* player who fatally boasted that he could beat the Muses with his singing (Sophocles himself was said to have played the kithara in the production of this play).[28] The chorus may have been made up of Muses, in which case we can imagine that the play included a musical showdown between them and Thamyras, with a mix of choral and solo song.[29] The fragments also suggest that much of the tragedy's language was musically self-reflexive, drawing the audience's attention to its performance: in one the chorus sings "these tunes in which we celebrate you get the feet forward, / running, moving, with hands, with feet."[30]

Many surviving tragedies contain explicit references to their own music and choreography. In Sophocles' *Ajax*, for example, the chorus exclaim "now I'm eager to dance!" within an exuberant song that they perform just before the hero's downfall, calling on Apollo and Pan to join their musical celebration in a moment of heightened ritual self-awareness and painful dramatic irony.[31] The choral odes in Euripides' later plays frequently include descriptions of traditional musical figures such as Muses, Nereids, or dancing dolphins, to which the chorus assimilates its own performance.[32] Some of the most powerfully self-referential lyrics in all tragedy occur in the "Binding Song" in Aeschylus' *Eumenides*, which the chorus of Erinyes (Furies) performs around Orestes, singing "leaping high / from above, I bring down the heavy-falling / strike of my foot."[33] The chorus here would enact the threatening movements they describe, driving Orestes crazy through their song and dance. It is no wonder that this particular chorus was said to have been so terrifying that, according to one anecdote, some women miscarried in the theater.[34] Even if we just read the plays themselves, then, we can see that tragedy was a multimedia genre, and that music and dance must have been some of the most powerful parts of its performance.

TRAGEDY IN SIXTH- AND FIFTH-CENTURY ATHENS

Aristotle shows little interest in the performance of the plays he discusses in the *Poetics*; he also makes no mention of their performance context, presenting tragedy as a universal phenomenon rather than a specifically Athenian product.[35] But tragedy was closely bound up with Athens' identity. To try to understand what tragedy was in terms of its broader civic role, we must now consider both the possible origins of the genre in the late sixth century and the context of its performance in the classical period.

The origins of tragedy remain impossibly murky and our sources tend to tell us more about later conceptualizations than about the actual history of the genre. The name itself (*tragoidia*) means "goat song," suggesting it began in the context of a competition at which a goat was the prize and perhaps also a sacrificial offering.[36] This was how it was understood in antiquity, at least as early as the third century BCE: on the Parian Marble, a slab of rock inscribed around 264/3 recording significant political and literary events, an entry for between 540 and 520 is "the time when Thespis the poet first [act]ed, who produced a [dr]a[ma in the c]it[y], and the goat was established as the [prize]."[37] We find the same tradition, also crediting the poet Thespis with the invention of tragedy, recorded in an epigram by the Hellenistic poet Dioscorides that begins "I am Thespis, who first modeled tragic song ... at the season when Bacchus led in the triennial chorus whose prize was still a goat and a basket of Attic figs";[38] some three hundred years later, the Roman poet Horace mentions "the poet who in tragic song competed for a mere goat."[39]

The context for this competition was a ritual one. Peisistratus, who was tyrant of Athens from 546–527 BCE after almost twenty years of gaining and losing power, is said to have established the City Dionysia, a five-day-long annual festival for Dionysus that was grafted upon an older local one.[40] This became the primary site for tragic competitions, though theatrical performances in more rural settings must have preceded their inclusion in this one. By the time Aeschylus won his first victory in 484 BCE, contests for comedies had also become part of the festival, as had those for choral songs called dithyrambs, all performed in the Theater of Dionysus on the southern slope of the Acropolis. For the tragic contest, three playwrights each presented a tetralogy consisting of three tragedies and a satyr play—a type of drama with a lighter tone, named for its chorus of horse-human hybrids called satyrs and their father/leader Silenus.

The date traditionally given for the first tragic competition is 534 BCE, based on an entry in the *Suda*, the tenth-century Byzantine encyclopedia, as well as the inscription on the Parian Marble. The evidence for this date is far from reliable, since it seems unlikely that the city archives recording dramatic productions went back any earlier than 502/1.[41] But even if tragic competitions actually began after the fall of the Peisistratids and the reforms of the lawgiver Cleisthenes that ushered in democracy, it is significant that tragedy was later closely associated with this particular period of Athenian history. Plutarch, writing in the early second century CE, mentions the beginnings of tragic competitions in the context of Peisistratus' own ability "to imitate those virtues which nature had denied him" and his return to power with the theatrical ruse of wounding himself and pretending his rivals had tried to kill him.[42] He presents the notorious late fifth-century aristocrat Alcibiades in a theatrical light as well, recording the tradition of how he returned to Athens in 408 BCE in a trireme alongside the champion *aulos* player Chrysogonus and the actor Callipides, both dressed in elaborate costumes as if performing in the theater.[43] Whatever its actual origins, then, tragedy became a medium for thinking about powerful political figures in Athens, especially those associated with tyranny.[44]

Despite such associations between theater and tyranny, in the fifth and fourth centuries tragedy was a fundamental part and product of the democratic city and its empire. The relationship between tragedy and Athenian democracy has been much debated. Though the plots of the plays themselves are almost always set in the mythical past and focus on royal families and other elite, heroic figures, tragedy can be seen as a parallel for the assembly, an alternative space for testing the city's ideologies and grappling with difficult social issues such as gender relations and aristocratic power.[45] The sheer numbers of citizens watching and participating in tragedy indicate the prominent role it played within the workings of Athenian democracy: by the late fifth century the seating capacity within the Theater of Dionysus was at least 6,000 to 8,000 (not including the slope beyond the precinct itself), providing space for large numbers of locals in addition to visiting foreigners. A significant proportion of the adult male population in Athens would also at some point have performed in a tragedy, whether at the City Dionysia or at other festivals like the Rural Dionysia, during which dramas were restaged in smaller deme theaters. Funding for tragedies in the classical period was secured through *chorēgia* ("leadership of choruses"), a system whereby individual wealthy Athenians paid for these hugely expensive productions as a public service to the city—and could enjoy considerable prestige as a result.[46]

Tragedy also displayed Athens' status as the cultural center of the classical Greek world. When this status came under threat, as it did with the rise of Macedon in the second half of the fourth century BCE, the city's close connection with tragedy was especially emphasized, through measures such as Lycurgus' law about erecting the tragedians' statues in the theater and depositing official copies of their plays in the archives.[47] The extent to which tragedy could be bound up with the city's self-construction and identity is perhaps clearest in Plato's *Laws*. After a long discussion about which forms of choral songs and dances should be allowed within the new, imaginary colony of Magnesia and who should perform them, the Athenian stranger calls himself and his interlocutors, as lawmakers, "composers of a tragedy"; he goes on to call their state "a mimesis of the most beautiful and fine life, which we say is really the truest tragedy."[48]

So while we often think of tragedy primarily in terms of its formal characteristics as an art form, for its fifth-century audiences it was also an institution embedded within the cultural—even physical—fabric of Athens. It was a display of power—of Athenian imperial power, but also of the political and financial clout of the *chorēgos* who made each production possible. And it was part of a festival for Dionysus, performed within his theater, which was itself located within the precinct of his temple. Even though many tragedies do not refer to him (or at least not overtly), presumably, like other types of

FIGURE 1.3: Attic mixing vessel showing four chorus members, probably performers of a dithyramb, with the *aulos* player and *chorēgos* (producer-financer), who faces outwards, 430–420 BCE, attributed to the Kleophon Painter. The *chorēgos* is labeled as Phrynichus and may perhaps be identified with the comic poet of the same name. The National Museum of Denmark in Copenhagen, 13817. Photo by John Lee, courtesy of museum.

choral performance, they acted essentially as offerings to the god, akin to expensive sacrifices or dedications.[49]

THE GENRE(S) OF TRAGEDY

We now return to Aristotle for another account of tragedy's origins that affects how we might classify it as a genre. In the *Poetics* he states that tragedy developed in an improvisatory way from "those leading the dithyramb."[50] As noted above, the dithyramb was also performed at the City Dionysia, as well as at other festivals for Dionysus; it was a large-scale show, involving a chorus of fifty men or boys singing and dancing to the accompaniment of the *aulos*. Aristotle seems to assume that at some point dramatic dialogue began between an individual actor/leader and the dithyrambic chorus, though he may have had little more evidence for this early period of tragedy's formation than we do.[51] Whether or not tragedy derived from dithyramb, it should come as no surprise that Aristotle recognizes an affinity between them. Not only are they both performances for Dionysus within his theater, but some surviving tragedies contain markedly dithyrambic elements. The second stasimon of Aeschylus' *Suppliants*, for example, which includes a description of the wanderings of Io through Asia and her arrival in Egypt, where she bore Zeus' son, evokes a narrative style reminiscent of the dithyramb—indeed, Bacchylides makes this same story the subject of one of his.[52] The story of Io also resembles that of Semele, who, likewise impregnated by Zeus, gives birth to Dionysus; this seems to have been a popular subject of dithyrambic song. Many of the choral odes in the later tragedies of Euripides contain imagery commonly associated with the dithyramb, such as dolphins and Nereids—; the latter tend to be fifty in number, just like the members of a dithyrambic chorus.[53]

Just a few lines after his reference to the dithyramb, Aristotle connects the development of tragedy with another choral genre, stating that its tone became more serious after it changed from being "satyric."[54] Though we should be wary of trusting such an evolutionary model, this comment demonstrates the close association between tragedy and satyr play, which was, after all, the final performance within a tragic tetralogy and a central part of each tragedian's repertoire. So little of satyr play has survived (we have just one full drama, Euripides' *Cyclops*) that it is hard for us to appreciate the role it played alongside tragedy, with which it shared many stylistic traits and elite heroic characters—even if the addition of Silenus and his chorus of satyrs also meant that the tone of the drama, as well as the nature of the audience's response to it, was very different.[55] There was clearly some generic overlap between the two forms of theater, so much so that Euripides seems to have deliberately combined them in his *Alcestis*: performed in the fourth place in its tetralogy, this tragedy contains many satyric elements, most notably the entrance of a drunken Heracles following Alcestis' death.[56] It is also important to remember that the same actors, chorus, and aulete would perform all four plays in a tetralogy—that is, they would perform both the three tragedies and the concluding satyr play. We have already seen an entire tragic-satyric troupe on the Pronomos Vase,[57] which shows them at the end of a performance, with most of the chorus still dressed as satyrs and the three actors in the type of long-sleeved costumes they would wear for the entire tetralogy; all of them are holding their masks except for one satyr-choreut who continues to dance to the tune of the *aulos*.

Aristotle's brief comments about tragedy's connections to satyr play and dithyramb point to the hybridity of the tragic genre, even within a treatise that discusses its defining features. They demonstrate an awareness of the crossover between tragedy and the other types of theatrical performance produced within the same festival for Dionysus. The plays themselves also reveal some cross-fertilization with comedy. Aristophanes' parodies of Aeschylus and Euripides in *Frogs*, as well as his portrayal of Euripides and his younger rival Agathon in *Thesmophoriazusae*, rely on his audience's familiarity with tragedy to achieve their full comic effect. But the direction of influence could work both ways, as we can see in Euripides' *Helen*, in which the chorus sings an ode about the nightingale that combines two songs in Aristophanes' *Birds*, produced at the City Dionysia just two years earlier in 414 BCE.[58] *Helen*, which older critics found hard to accept as a tragedy, includes various other comic elements, such as the confrontation between a bedraggled, shipwrecked Menelaus and a female doorkeeper who bars him from the house and almost reduces him to tears. This scene appears to look toward New Comedy of the late third and second centuries BCE, though it may draw from trends already popular within contemporary fifth-century comedy, of which only eleven plays of Aristophanes and some fragments survive.[59] Pollux, writing in the second century CE, claims that Euripides was unusual in the extent to which he emulated the techniques of comedy,[60] but some sort of dialogue between the different genres performed within the one festival must have regularly occurred.

Tragedy drew from genres of performance beyond the theater too, especially in its choral songs, which combine a wide variety of nondramatic lyric.[61] Particular musical traditions can become closely intertwined with the dramatic narrative. Lament especially dominates several tragedies, even though—or perhaps because—its performance was restricted within classical Athens itself. In fifth-century Athenian culture, lament was conceptualized as an especially female type of performance, associated with excessive displays of emotion by women and foreigners.[62] The theater gave Athenians access to such performances and often reinforced these cultural stereotypes.[63] The antiphonal mourning of Xerxes and the chorus in the closing scene of Aeschylus' *Persians*, for example, underscores his utter defeat by the Athenians, contrasting starkly with the Greek paeans earlier described by the messenger.[64] In Sophocles' *Electra* lament is bound up with the self-identity of the protagonist, who repeatedly refuses to cease her mourning. In Euripides' *Trojan Women* lament appears to govern the play from start to finish, marking the helpless position of the Trojan women as they wait to be divided up among their Greek captors.

Even within *Trojan Women*, however, other types of musical performance are at play, especially those associated with female rites of transition that can no longer be enjoyed by the women in the dramatic present. The initial scenes of mourning are abruptly interrupted by the entrance of Cassandra, singing a painfully distorted version of a wedding song (*hymenaios*).[65] This would typically be a choral performance; Cassandra's solo version here indicates quite how far a wedding is from the reality of her position as Agamemnon's doomed concubine. In the first stasimon the chorus of Trojan women remember the maiden songs (*partheneia*) they performed for Artemis as they brought the horse within the city.[66] Such verbal allusions bring this different—and in the dramatic context impossible—genre of female performance within the ambit of their song and of the tragedy as a whole; we can only speculate as to how far their melody and dance movements could have incorporated elements of *partheneia* as well.

This same ode evokes other song types too, from the opening address to the Muse and dactylic rhythms that are reminiscent of epic and the Homeric hymns, to the painful distortion of an epinician (a song for a victorious athlete) at the end, when the chorus state that the slaughter at Troy has produced "a victory crown of young women, / to bear sons for Greece, / but a source of grief for the Phrygians' fatherland."[67] The epinician theme recurs at the start of the second stasimon, which the chorus begins by looking back to the earlier sack of Troy by Telamon, celebrating him as a victorious hero.[68] At the same time, of course, the current backdrop of the city's destruction undercuts this allusion, and the incongruous scene of captive women performing a victory song becomes a very uncomfortable one.

As *Trojan Women* demonstrates, the different types of performance evoked within a single tragedy can be closely interwoven with the dramatic plot. Certain characters are associated with particular musical genres: Electra, Iphigenia, and Andromache, for example, all tend to lament; Orestes is frequently presented as an athletic figure with epinician language.[69] Choruses can also be defined by their type of performance: choruses of maenads (as in Euripides' *Bacchae*) perform cultic music and dance for Dionysus; in Aeschylus' *Libation Bearers* the chorus, after whom the play is named, sing laments as they bring offerings to Agamemnon's tomb; the Erinyes' Binding Song in *Eumenides* recalls the language and rituals of binding magic (including curse tablets, of which the earliest surviving examples from Athens date back to the fifth century).[70]

Choral songs were not the only parts of tragedy that evoked performances beyond the theater, nor were such performances all musical ones. In particular, many tragedies display the language of contemporary oratory, often in the context of the tragic *agōn*, a scene in which two characters each deliver opposing speeches.[71] Aeschylus' *Eumenides* even brings a proto-law court on stage, with the Erinyes set against Orestes and Apollo, and Athena and the Athenian citizens acting as judges. In Euripides' *Trojan Women* Helen delivers her own defense, arguing against her culpability for the war, while the Trojan queen Hecuba, briefly pausing her lament, gives an extraordinarily skilled speech denouncing her in return.[72] This particular *agōn* derives not just from styles of speaking in the law courts and assembly but from the sort of sophistic exercises exemplified by Gorgias' *Encomium of Helen*. Its performance by female characters demonstrates the ability of tragedy to restage and distort different nondramatic types of performance, presenting an impossible scenario that can only exist within the theater. The speeches and songs that evoke these other genres, however, should not then seem somehow foreign to or separate from tragedy itself: on the contrary, tragedy was a hybrid art form, appropriating multiple styles within the one dramatic performance. All these different forms become "tragic" through being combined in a play produced at and for the tragic competition in Athens.

A CHANGING GENRE

Tragedy was therefore a capacious and flexible genre, able to encompass multiple types of performance.[73] For all its formal characteristics, it was also a rapidly changing one. The showdown between Aeschylus and Euripides in Aristophanes' *Frogs* demonstrates that by the late fifth century theatergoers were aware of some of the differences between the older tragedian's work and the more fashionable plays of Euripides. Aeschylus' lyrics, for example, are characterized here as full of bombastic language and have a monotonously dactylic rhythm. In contrast, Euripides mixes up many different kinds of songs and rhythms, especially, his rival claims, those from low-class sources: he "gets [his honey] from everywhere—porn songs, / Meletus' drinking songs, Carian pipe tunes, / laments and choral dances."[74] The parody of his monodies also highlights the increasing number of solo arias in Euripides' late work, pointing to the prominence of star actors in this period as well.[75] The mention of "porn songs" likewise suggests the hiring of professionals rather than citizen amateurs.[76]

With only fifth-century examples of Greek tragedy surviving intact, it is hard to trace the formal developments in the genre beyond this period. Tragedies by Euripides and Sophocles were regularly reperformed, though Aeschylus appears to have gone out of fashion by the mid- to late fourth century.[77] But references in Aristotle's *Poetics* to contemporary poets (Astydamas, Carcinus, Theodectes, Chaeremon), combined with other literary and documentary evidence, reveal a vibrant culture of new tragic production in Athens in the fourth century. At the same time, most of the plays Aristotle mentions still date to the previous century: for him tragedy is defined by Euripides and, above all, Sophocles, whose name stands virtually as a metonym for the entire genre, as Homer does for epic and Aristophanes for comedy.[78] Lycurgus' law likewise suggests that, even as the genre developed in the hands of new playwrights, the idea of what tragedy was (or should be) remained closely tied to these fifth-century models.

Throughout this chapter I have focused on tragedy as an Athenian art form, closely tied to the city's identity and political make-up. As Rosa Andújar's chapter in this volume makes clear, however, we should not be too Athenocentric in our conception of the genre, especially as we look beyond the fifth century. Already in the 400s it was a successful export, enjoying great popularity elsewhere in the Greek world, particularly in Southern Italy and Sicily.[79] Aeschylus himself visited the court of Hieron of Syracuse at least twice and composed *The Aetnaeans* to celebrate the founding of the city of Aetna.[80] The kings of Macedon became increasingly interested in theater as they began to lay claim to Greek culture, and Euripides is said to have spent some time at the very end of his life at the court of Archelaus, for whom he produced a play of the same name.[81] Some eighty years later, Alexander brought this exemplar of Greek culture with him as he ventured eastwards, sponsoring dramatic competitions at his itinerant court in places such as Karmania in modern-day Iran and perhaps even as far as the banks of the river Hydaspes, now in Pakistan.[82] The building of monumental theaters throughout the Greek world in the fourth century onwards further attests to the popularity of both tragic and comic performances far beyond their Attic origins.[83]

Over the next two centuries there continued to be significant developments not just in the cultural identity of tragedy, but in its subject-matter and certain patterns of its style and structure. Theater continued to function as a significant display of Hellenization, entertaining audiences in which native Greeks were a minority. But many of the tragedians whom we hear about from the Hellenistic period—most notably the members of the third-century group known as the "Pleiad"—were based not in Athens but in Ptolemaic Alexandria, the new center of Greek literary production and scholarship. We also hear of non-Greeks composing tragedy, such as King Artavasdes II of Armenia and the Jewish poet Ezekiel. The international guild of theater professionals, called the "*Technitai* of Dionysus," first attested in the late fourth century,[84] testifies to the continued association of drama with Dionysus, but theaters were now built within the temple complexes of other gods too, such as that of Apollo at Delphi.

So few fragments of tragedy survive from the Hellenistic period that it is hard to make generalizations about its form. Its basic structural elements—prologue, choral songs, episodes—remained the same, though, as in Athenian Middle and New Comedy, they may have become more regular, with five "acts" becoming the norm (Horace's preference for this number in his *Ars Poetica* may echo Hellenistic discussions of tragedy as much as it draws on Roman theater).[85] The fragments suggest that, even while the meters of tragedy remained essentially the same, the Hellenistic playwrights were rather more conservative in this respect than their fifth-century predecessors (especially Euripides in his later plays), avoiding resolutions and strictly adhering to Porson's Law. The chorus still seems to have played an important part in many plays; the plural titles of tragedies like Lycophron's *Marathonians* or Moschion's *Men of Pherae* suggest that it could be the focus of a whole drama. Epigraphic evidence suggests that some tragedies could also be performed in an abridged form without a chorus, pointing perhaps to a development parallel to that in Middle and New Comedy, in which its role was greatly reduced.[86] Yet such an assumption of choral decline usually results from taking at face value Aristotle's complaint in the *Poetics* about the contemporary trend for *embolima*—choral songs that are "thrown in" without any relevance to the plot.

One of the clearest differences between classical and Hellenistic tragedy was the range of subject-matter on which their plots were based. Though mythological themes continued (presumably often harking back to fifth-century plays), both historical and contemporary events also began to be included—a trend that continued in Roman tragedy as well. This was the case for satyr play too: indeed, *Agen*, a satyr drama apparently composed by Python of Catana (or Byzantium) and performed during Alexander's Dionysia celebrations on the banks of the Hydaspes, ridiculed his companion Harpalus, who had just deserted. Yet even while the tragic genre was changing, it appears to have remained sufficiently cohesive to be the subject of theoretical discussion by Hellenistic scholars, who produced numerous treatises (now all lost) on its style, content, and modes of performance, as well as biographies of fifth-century tragedians.[87] The popularity of such biographies suggests that tragedy continued to be closely tied to Aeschylus, Sophocles, and Euripides, whose texts Ptolemy II apparently tricked the Athenians into bringing to Alexandria.[88]

In Rome, too, playwrights looked back to fifth-century Athenian theater as they began to form their own tragic tradition, though they simultaneously transformed it into a uniquely Roman literary product. Greek plays, both old and new, continued to be performed into the imperial period. In Rome, however, a new form of tragedy began, starting—so Roman writers tell us—with a production by the half-Greek freedman Livius Andronicus in 240 BCE, amid celebrations following the end of the First Punic War, during which the Romans had extended contact with the Greek cities of Southern Italy and Sicily. Livius appears to have been the first to adapt Greek plays into Roman *fabulae*, not only taking over traditional subject-matter and plot-structures but rendering in Latin the metrical patterns of Greek tragedy. But for all their reliance on classical models (especially Euripides and Sophocles), we should not assume a direct line of contact between fifth-century tragedy and its new Roman incarnation.[89] Hellenistic tragedy must have had a big impact on these plays too, as must earlier forms of theatrical and musical entertainment in archaic Rome. Indeed, Livy emphasizes the Etruscan origins of Roman drama, describing a development from dancing accompanied by a piper to a form of comic drama involving "medleys full of tunes with song now composed for the piper [*tibicen*] and with matching movement"; finally Livius created *fabulae* with plots.[90] Later playwrights in the Republican period also became known for how they combined multiple Greek models within the one piece, while incorporating elements of Roman works too: the remaining fragments of Pacuvius' *Teucer*, for example, suggest that he drew not only from Aeschylus' *Salaminians* and Sophocles' *Teucer*, but from *Telamo*, a tragedy written by his uncle Ennius, another successful playwright (and epic poet); it also works as a sequel to Pacuvius' own *Judgment of Arms*.[91]

Such a variety of generic influences, all combined and reworked within the one Latin play, therefore made this genre distinct from its fifth-century Athenian ancestor. As several chapters in this volume demonstrate, it also differed in its form and contexts of production.

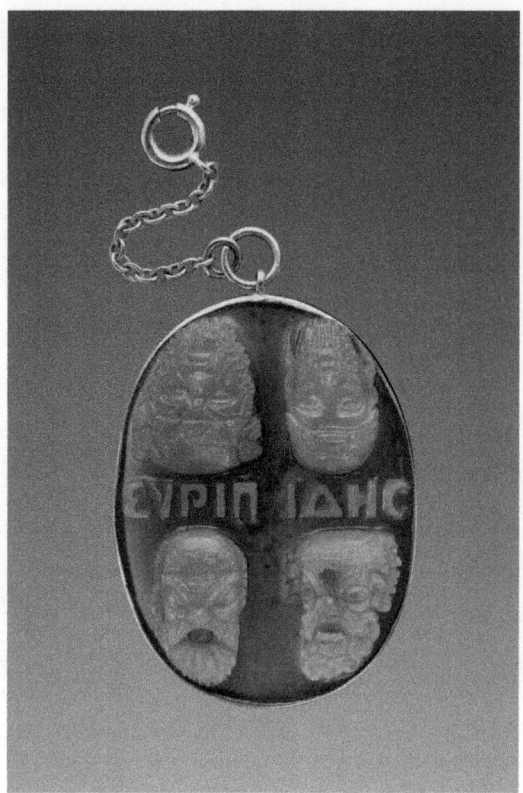

FIGURE 1.4: Roman sardonyx cameo with four theater masks and the name "Euripides" carved on it, demonstrating the tragedian's continued popularity and influence in imperial Rome, c. first century CE. J. Paul Getty Museum 2001.28.7. Digital image courtesy of the Getty's Open Content Program.

The tragedies of Livius and his successors were performed both at religious festivals (*ludi*) for various gods (including Jupiter and Apollo, but not Dionysus) and on special occasions such as the dedication of new temples or the funerals of powerful men. Tragedies were produced individually, without the satyr play with which Greek tetralogies ended; instead they were often accompanied by a type of farce called *fabula Atellana*. The chorus was smaller and less prominent, but the musical element became even greater with more solos performed by actors to the accompaniment of the *tibia*, the Roman equivalent of the *aulos* (Figure 1.5).[92]

In terms of subject-matter, Roman tragedy continued the Greek tradition of dramatizing mythological events. But from the mid-second century BCE tragedians began composing a new type of drama called *fabula praetexta* (named after the *toga praetexta* worn by magistrates), which took its plots from Rome's legendary past or recent history: Naevius' *Clastidium*, for example, was about the consul Marcellus' defeat of the Gauls in 222; the one surviving play, *Octavia* (erroneously attributed to Seneca), concerns Nero's marriage to his mistress Poppaea and ousting of his first wife, Octavia. The *fabula praetexta* was closely related to tragedy itself, resembling it in all but plot, and was regarded by later grammarians as a tragic subgenre.[93]

FIGURE 1.5: Roman marble relief showing a scene from a comedy with a *tibia* player and masked actors against an elaborate stage façade, *c.* first century CE. Museo Archeologico Nazionale di Napoli, Naples, 6687. Azoor Photo/Alamy Stock Photo.

Our only surviving examples of Roman tragedy, a series of plays by Seneca, come from the imperial period. Though we have far less evidence of tragic production between the late Republic and Seneca's work from the first century CE, the genre seems to have continued to be popular. New, permanent theaters were built, beginning with Pompey's, where, at its dedication in 55 BCE, there was apparently a spectacular production of Accius' *Clytemnestra* involving 600 mules; 3,000 mixing bowls were used in Naevius' *Trojan Horse*, the opulence of which was clearly meant to mirror Pompey's own triumphal procession.[94] At the same time, tragic drama was increasingly being performed in more private settings, sometimes only in the form of a read extract rather than an entire play. In the theater it was gradually overtaken in popularity by mime, Atellan farce, and pantomime; the latter seems to have had a dynamic relationship of influence with tragedy.[95]

Seneca's plays are our last surviving examples of ancient tragedy and some of the most influential, becoming a hugely important model for tragic theater in the Renaissance and beyond. In nineteenth-century scholarship, however, they were deemed "rhetorical tragedies," full of emotional declamations and apparently unfit for the stage.[96] More recently, scholars have instead emphasized their theatricality,[97] and it seems likely that they were composed with a range of performance contexts in mind: not just the primary one of the theater, but private readings and recitations, for which each tragedy could be easily adapted; extracts could even have been used as sung accompaniments to pantomimic dances.[98] Like their Republican antecedents, these plays reach back to fifth-century models in their plots, but overlay them with contemporarily relevant political themes and a wide variety of Latin intertexts, from Ennius' tragedies to Ovid's *Metamorphoses*.

Composed half a millennium after the time of Aeschylus, Seneca's plays seem far from the Greek models with which this chapter has been primarily occupied. Roman playwrights still looked to fifth-century tragedy for their source material, and for them classical tragedy was represented by the works of Aeschylus, Sophocles, and Euripides. In perhaps the ultimate demonstration of the genre's malleability, however, their cultural appropriation of tragedy also transformed it into a distinctly Roman art form. Though Senecan drama continues to be performed today, we too usually look to classical Athens for ideas of what tragedy was or should be—partly as a result of the influence of Aristotle's *Poetics*, partly because the vast majority of surviving tragedies come from that era. As we have seen, however, the particular survival of thirty-three complete plays by the three giants of Athenian tragedy is not accidental, but instead reflects a process of classicization of the tragic genre that had already began by the end of the fifth century BCE. All too often we approach tragedy through the lens of Aristotle, viewing it in terms of set patterns of plot, style, and performance. But not only did it spread far beyond classical Athens, tragedy also continued to be an extraordinarily flexible genre, adapting to different political and cultural climates and adopting many different forms and modes of performance.

CHAPTER TWO

Sites of Performance and Circulation

ROSA ANDÚJAR

It is a truth universally acknowledged that tragedy was born in classical Athens. For much of the fifth century BCE it was performed in the Theater of Dionysus on the southern slope of the Acropolis during festivals honoring the god.[1] The genre was closely connected to the Athenian democracy of the fifth century.[2] Athenian dramatic festivals were elaborate multi-day events in which all official business was suspended. Their organization and financing formed a fundamental part of the public service institution of *leitourgia* (civic/public service). Each year, the city's eponymous archon appointed six wealthy Athenian citizens to fund the choruses for each of the three tragic and three comic playwrights that would compete in the upcoming Great Dionysia festival. This task, *chorēgia*, was a major civic duty in Athens, on a par with paying for a troop of soldiers or equipping a trireme.[3]

But despite its origins as an Athenian invention, and despite its centrality to Athenian civic identity, tragedy quickly became "Greek," spreading to other venues beyond Attica as early as the late fifth century BCE, including many across the Mediterranean, from Sicily to the Black Sea.[4] Scholars have shown how and where tragedy spread, and the process through which it was transformed into an international and Panhellenic art form.[5] Here, I outline certain key moments that led to tragedy's rapid rise to importance in Greek and Roman cultural and political life. I argue that we should rethink what counts as a site of performance beyond literal theatrical spaces and instead consider the myriad places in which tragedy re-emerges.

ANCIENT GREEK WORLD

Tragedy in fifth-century autocracies

As early as the fifth century BCE, various accounts report tragic performances outside Attica, and under the sponsorship of tyrants.[6] Aeschylus, we are told, visited the island of Sicily, and Euripides spent time in Macedon.[7] In both places, the tragedians were based at the court of autocrats: they apparently accepted the patronage of these rulers, and even composed new tragedies that celebrated their exploits. I will provide a brief review of the evidence available about these visits to illustrate tragedy's early appeal to a non-Athenian audience. My focus is on tragedy's immediate potential as a valuable export and as a tool for propaganda. As I show, autocrats, particularly those on the periphery of the Greek world, sought to link themselves to Athens and to the wider Greek world through tragedy.

Aeschylus in Sicily In a passage describing the Palici gods of Sicily, the late antique writer Macrobius reports that their presence in literature is first attested in Aeschylus, who was, "a truly Sicilian man" (*Sat.* 5.19.17).[8] This intimate association between Aeschylus and Sicily might seem outlandish, were it not that fourteen different sources report that Aeschylus left Athens at least once to visit Sicily at the invitation of the tyrant Hieron.[9] The *Life of Aeschylus* 9 (=*TrGF*[3] T1.33–4) specifically links his visit with the production of a new play, *Women of Aetna*, composed in honor of Hieron's founding of the city (476/5 BCE). It states that for the new inhabitants the play was "to be regarded as an omen of good life." The language employed here clearly indicates that the play was meant to celebrate the recent establishment of the city, which was a fundamental part of Hieron's colonialist enterprise.[10]

According to the first-century BCE historian Diodorus, Hieron's founding of Aetna in 476 BCE was a bloody affair, since Hieron founded the new city by driving out Naxians and Catanians and then importing his own people.[11] Seen in this context, Aeschylus' composition of *Women of Aetna* raises difficult questions that challenge our perception of the Athenian poet. Why would Aeschylus, whose *Persians* celebrated the victory of Greece against an invading army, accept a commission to praise a colonialist enterprise involving the occupation of a city?[12] Why would Hieron wish to celebrate his new city by means of a foreign genre? And how was tragedy received on Sicilian soil? Unfortunately, the play's murky remains make it difficult to answer the tantalizing questions. Not much is known regarding the characters of the play or even its basic plot. Macrobius (*Sat.* 5.19.16–31) suggests that the story involved a nymph of mount Aetna named Thaleia who was impregnated by Zeus. However, scholars surmise that the play's central myth "had to be invented more or less *ex novo*."[13] Macrobius includes a four-line fragmentary dialogue that discusses a new genealogy for the Palici gods of Sicily; scholars deduce from this that the play may Hellenize Sicilian life.[14] It therefore appears that Aeschylus stretched Greek mythical narratives in order to accommodate Sicilian characters, such as its autochthonous gods and its traditions. Other surviving testimonies raise further questions about Sicilian stagecraft. The fragmentary hypothesis of the play, which survives on a papyrus (*P.Oxy.* 2257 fr. 1 = *TrGF*[3] 126–7), reveals that it had an impressive number of scene changes involving five locations across Sicily, including Aetna, Leontini, and Syracuse.[15] That a tragedy at this early historical point could feature so many scenic changes has raised new questions about the dramaturgical technology available in Sicily at this date.[16] One area of speculation is whether the chorus would have been less anchored to the dramatic plot, to allow for so many scene changes.[17] The *mēchanē* may have been used, suggesting that theaters outside Athens may have had sophisticated equipment at their disposal.[18]

More evidence suggests that Aeschylus visited Sicily a second time for a second play. The *Life of Aeschylus* 18 (=*TrGF*[3] T1.37) states that Hieron let him stage *Persians* in Sicily. Scholars believe that this event occurred most likely around 470, two years after the play's Athenian premiere.[19] If this is correct, it would be the earliest reperformance of any Athenian tragedy, perhaps one of very few occurring in the fifth century.[20] Why would such a play be restaged on Sicilian soil? Oliver Taplin suggests one possible solution: that *Persians* was a vital part of the "celebration culture of the 470s" which commemorated and communicated the victories against the Persians to a broad audience of Greeks, including those beyond the mainland.[21] These victories, he posits, led to a general aspiration towards, "coherent Hellenicity."[22] Perhaps victory in the Persian Wars also had a particular resonance in Sicily. Citing Herodotus, who claims that the Sicilians' defeat of

Carthage at Himera occurred on the very same day that Athens destroyed the Persians at Salamis, Rush Rehm discusses the "synchronicity of greatness" that connected Athens and Syracuse.[23] The performance of *Persians* may have effectively connected and reframed Hieron's victories in wider Panhellenic terms. In both these Aeschylean performances on Sicily, we can see tragedy's potential as a Panhellenic telescope, able to focus and bring to light what was previously thought to be distant and foreign.

Aeschylus, who ultimately died at Gela,[24] paid perhaps three visits to Sicily, which was an early and important site of circulation for tragedy.[25] Moreover, Aeschylus was not the first tragic poet to visit Sicily: Phrynichus the tragedian had already visited, and Aeschylus may have been following in his footsteps.[26] It would appear that Sicily was already in the early fifth century BCE a recognized venue for tragedy, with an audience already receptive to the genre. This is certainly the case by the end of the century: in *the Life of Nicias* 29.2, Plutarch recounts the story of Athenians imprisoned on the island after the failed Sicilian expedition who were freed by their Sicilian captors simply because they recited excerpts from Euripides' plays.[27] Certainly, Athenian tragedy's impact on the development of theater on the island was enormous,[28] continuing well into the fourth century. Tragedy was a genre sponsored by autocrats: Dionysius I of Syracuse, who reportedly bought Euripides' harp, pen, and tablet from the poet's heirs, produced many tragedies in Athens and even won first place at the Lenaea festival of 367 BCE with a play entitled the *Ransom of Hector*.[29] Aeschylus' presence must have been a major catalyst for this enthusiasm, perhaps even helping with the eventual spread of Athenian theater to South Italy.[30] From its early days, then, tragedy's appeal was broad and international, reaching the farthest extremes of the Greek West, from where it would travel to Rome.

Euripides in Macedon The biographical accounts of Euripides' life similarly report that the poet spent time away from Athens, moving in his old age to Magnesia and Macedonia and spending some years there until his death in 406 BCE.[31] As with his predecessor Aeschylus, Euripides was reportedly based at the court of an autocrat, Archelaus, and even wrote a play in his honor.[32] The anecdotes of his time in Macedon are plentiful and attested by many sources: Aristotle mentions a story that Euripides flogged a certain Decamnichus who later plotted against Archelaus (*Pol.* 1311b30), Plutarch cites a famous cup that Archelaus gifted him (*Mor.* 177a, 531d-e), and the late antique writer Diomedes Grammaticus states that the poet taught an ignorant Archelaus about tragedy (Diom. 488). There are further stories relating to his death; we are told that Athenian delegates traveled to Macedon to claim his remains (Gell. *NA* 15.20.9-10).[33] While we may debate the reliability of these anecdotes, the evidence for Euripides' presence in Macedon and his close relationship to the tyrant is much more wide-ranging than for Aeschylus' visits to Sicily. We cannot doubt that tragedy seems to have thrived in Macedonian autocratic soil.[34]

Archelaus' reasons for inviting the Athenian poet to his court are clearer than Hieron's. In offering his patronage to Euripides, Archelaus was following in the philhellenic footsteps of his grandfather, Alexander I, who, in an effort to establish close ties with the wider Greek world after the Persian Wars, had invited known poets such as Pindar and Bacchylides to his court, so Macedon was already an established site for the performance of poetry.[35] Greek sources from the classical period testify to a general sense of Macedonian "otherness"; such efforts to court Greek poets with an international reputation would have helped improve the Macedonian public image.[36] However, the fragments of the eponymous play that Euripides wrote for the ruler reveal that Archelaus was not just interested in connecting with the rest of the Greek world by embracing its artistic trends, but he also sought to be recognized as a fellow Greek. One of the principal fragments of the *Archelaus* relates an impressive genealogy of the Macedonian royal family (*TrGF*[5.1] F 228). According to Eoghan Moloney, Euripides introduced two crucial elements to this genealogy: the poet identifies a mythical Archelaus responsible for founding the Macedonian royal line, and at the same time extends the legacy of the children of Heracles to Macedon by making Archelaus the son of Temenus.[37] The summary by Hyginus (*Fab.* 219) likewise mentions this new genealogy manufactured by Euripides and illustrates the new connection to Heracles that the Macedonian kings have as a result. Euripides develops a prestigious Greek lineage for this mythical Archelaus, which extends to the contemporary Archelaus.[38] Annette Harder points out that this echoes other evidence that also connects the Macedonian royal line to Heracles, such as Macedonian coins showing the head and attributes of Heracles (Figure 2.1).[39]

While Aeschylus composed a myth *ex novo* to celebrate the exploits of Hieron and Sicilian life in general, Euripides adapts existing mythical narratives about the children of Heracles to include contemporary Macedonians. Throughout his extant corpus, Euripides alters traditional myths to suit his dramatic needs: in *Medea* the children die at their mother's hands and are not killed by the Corinthians; in the second (and surviving) version of *Hippolytus* he rewrites the role of Phaedra so that she is no longer just a shameless woman who propositions her stepson. The freedom with which he adapts these myths is widely recognized, but it appears in a new light when we encounter it in an alternative site of performance—the autocratic venue. According to Plato (*Grg.* 471), Archelaus was "the greatest criminal," responsible for having killed three people. Perhaps the ruler sought to counter such condemnations in the wider Greek-speaking world, through tragedy.[40] The *Life of Euripides* does not explain Euripides' motives in creating the *Archelaus*; it simply states that Euripides wished to "please" (*charizomenos*) the

FIGURE 2.1: Silver coin minted in the reign of Alexander III of Macedon, showing the head of Herakles on its obverse, *c.* 336–323 BCE. Collection of the American Numismatic Society NNM.19 (1923).

tyrant.⁴¹ Looking ahead, however, we can see that tragedy was indeed an effective means of legitimization: a few decades later, Isocrates was able to praise Philip's direct connection to and descent from Heracles (Figure 2.1).⁴² By the time of Alexander, the Macedonian royal line was clearly connected with Heracles, an association which the ruler exploited.⁴³ Tragedy formed part of a larger public relations strategy for the autocratic ruler.

Despite the abundance of anecdotes about Euripides in Macedon, we do not know anything about the performance conditions or staging of *Archelaus*, or its immediate reception or circulation beyond the city. What we can see, however, is its impact on the Greek international stage. Euripides' plays "were absorbed to an extraordinary depth" in Macedon as a result of the poet's time there,⁴⁴ to the point that several decades later, Alexander and his courtiers displayed an easy familiarity with Euripidean texts, and, according to various anecdotes, quoted liberally from them.⁴⁵

In *Republic* 568a-b Plato discusses the compelling connection between tragic poets and tyrants, singling out tragedians as "men who sing the praises of tyranny" (*tyrannidos hymnētas*);⁴⁶ he may have been thinking of Aeschylus and Euripides. The origins of tragedy, murky as they are, point to a genre that arose in the time of the Peisistratid tyrants in sixth century BCE Athens; perhaps, then, autocracies can even be seen as a natural venue for tragic performance.

Greek tragedy in the footsteps of Alexander

For Archelaus' most famous fourth-century successors, Philip and his son Alexander, there is even stronger evidence for the Macedonian use and promotion of tragedy. Philip established a permanent theater at the Macedonian capital of Aigai, and his death reportedly took place there, moments before the performance of a tragic ode.⁴⁷ Both kings organized dramatic competitions for significant occasions, such as the destruction of Olynthus in 348 BCE.⁴⁸ Alexander was particularly fascinated with theater; he quoted tragic excerpts by Euripides, and even arranged for a dramatic contest to take place before his departure for Asia.⁴⁹ Athenaeus reports that he had so many actors in his entourage that they were referred to as "Alexander-flatterers" (*Alexandrokolakes*) instead of "Dionysus-flatterers" (*Dionusokolakes*).⁵⁰ He repeatedly sponsored dramatic performances while on campaign, which helped disseminate tragedy across a number of new venues, from the Balkans to places in Asia such as Ai Khanoum, in modern day Afghanistan.⁵¹ With Alexander, tragedy not only continues to flourish under the direct sponsorship of an autocrat but also becomes a ready-made symbol of Hellenic culture for transplantation anywhere. Alexander created new public festivals and celebrations in which tragedy could be performed and consumed by a wide and varied audience.

Vesa Vahtikari identifies a tripartite pattern from the extant sources which summarizes Alexander's engagement with theater during his campaigns: "1) Alexander is coming back from somewhere, 2) he rests with his troops, and 3) he holds a festival / a dramatic contest / a drinking party / a Dionysiac revel."⁵² Arrian, for example, reports that in 324, upon reaching Ecbatana (in modern-day Iran), Alexander hosted such athletic and musical contests,⁵³ and Plutarch clarifies that in this same event Alexander was involved "in theaters and festivals."⁵⁴ At his own wedding to the Persian King's daughter, also in 324, he reportedly hosted five days of dramatic and musical competitions in Susa.⁵⁵ Alexander thus helped spread tragedy by including it in large public festivals that celebrated his arrival in a new location or the success of a military campaign. The sources unanimously attest that Alexander himself ordered these festivals: dramatic performance thus became a royally-decreed occasion. Plutarch says that three thousand artists arrived from Greece to Ecbatana for the event; apparently Alexander invited them as a visible display of his power.[56] The king transformed himself into a champion of Greek culture, promoting two venues long connected with the city of Athens: the theater and the gymnasium.[57] Both had a huge impact on his soldiers and their conception of leisure.[58] Further, these performances promoted tragedy to local populations who might have never encountered tragedy before.

The problematic nature of the sources relating Alexander's theatrical activities and his enthusiasm for tragedy has been widely discussed.[59] Martin Revermann nevertheless argues that these stories about Alexander's enthusiasm for theater must "originate in an authentic and widely-known familiarity of the king with drama."[60] These stories may also have another historical basis: the king went to great lengths to associate himself with the god Dionysus, particularly after his arrival on Indian soil.[61] This historical self-association with the god is a crucial part of Alexander's legacy: later Hellenistic monarchs decided to follow in his footsteps, appropriating the image of Dionysus as an official part of royal ideology and promoting theater to emphasize this new connection.[62] In either case, it is easy to see the authority that tragedy carries, both as a means of further solidifying ruler's connection with Dionysus, and as an effective literary strategy for an ancient biographer.

Throughout the Hellenistic period, Alexander's successors continued this intimate connection with theater, sponsoring many festivals featuring drama, often naming them after themselves, or attaching their name to an existing festival.[63] Tragedy was an established and effective tool of royal propaganda.[64] It is in this context that the Associations of the Artists (*technitai*) of Dionysus were able to flourish; these, professional associations of musicians, poets, and performers were thus likewise crucial in spreading theater.[65] As independent city-states yielded to larger autocratic spheres of influence, these artists flocked to the festivals sponsored by Hellenistic rulers across the Mediterranean, and their participation in them was crucial in promoting the new ruler-cults and thus in affirming royal power.[66] These festivals also functioned as important sites in which Hellenic values could be performed and articulated, specifically helping new cities celebrate and advertise their Greekness. In this context, we can see tragedy as a transportable and accessible declaration of Greek identity. Alexander thus set up a framework within which tragedy continued to circulate through the centuries in diverse geographical locations.

Tragedy in Hellenistic democracies

After Alexander the Great we continue to see accounts of festivals featuring dramatic performances (the islands of Chios, Lemnos, and Paros, for example, held a Dionysia),[67] and reports of the people involved with theater, such as the Associations of Artists of Dionysus.[68] The evidence for theatrical activity begins to include more epigraphical and archaeological material. Although the scant and fragmentary nature of this evidence prevents a systematic analysis, the sheer fact that it was widespread shows that drama continued to play an important role in many different contexts across the Hellenistic world.

As we saw in the previous section, dramatic performances were often a vital part of the larger celebratory culture for Hellenistic rulers, and were an important means by which the ruler displayed his power to the wider public. However, not all Hellenistic venues for

FIGURE 2.2: Detail of a Ptolemaic marble relief, showing a ceremony in which Ptolemy as Chronos (Time) and his queen as Oikumene (The Inhabited World), crown Homer's living statue from behind in the Homereion (Homeric temple) that Ptolemy erected in Alexandria; signed Archelaos of Priene, c. 225–205 BCE. The British Museum 1819,0812.1 © The Trustees of the British Museum. All rights reserved.

the performance of tragedy were autocratic. Here, I consider two non-autocratic contexts which appear to have embraced the older Athenian tradition of tragedy in the Hellenistic period: Cos and Rhodes, two autonomous islands that were "democratic" in a time of monarchs and had a system of *chorēgia* in place for various religious festivals featuring dramatic contests.[69] In the late fourth century, the city of Athens reformed the institution of *chorēgia*, replacing it with *agnothesia*, i.e., a single elected official (*agnothetēs*) responsible for overseeing contests and organizing choruses on behalf of the city.[70] The choregic system, formerly a hallmark of Athenian drama, began to flourish far away from Attica.

FIGURE 2.3: Greek (Sicilian) terracotta mask of a satyr, *c.* 200–100 BCE. J. Paul Getty Museum 96.AD.305. Digital image courtesy of the Getty's Open Content Program.

From the late fourth century onwards, there were at least two festivals for Dionysus in Cos.[71] These festivals appear to have featured substantial choregic activity, as evidenced by various victor lists naming the winning *chorēgoi* in both dramatic and choral contests held there.[72] Inscription *ED* 234 demonstrates their extent: it lists processions by boys (l. 2), *chorēgoi* for cyclic *pyrrhikha* (10–11 and 22–3), comic actors (15), and *chorēgoi* for tragedy (34–5).[73] The lists of victors also include professional actors not from Cos, which suggests that this was an international festival.[74] From 242 BCE onward there also appears to have been another major international festival on the island, the Great Asclepieia, which also featured dramatic and musical competitions.[75] Other decrees and inscriptions testify to the presence of a guild of non-local Dionysiac artists who visited the festival.[76] Inscriptional evidence on Rhodes also shows that, from the third to first centuries BCE, the island played host to a variety of festivals, including an Alexandreia festival in honor of Alexander. It too featured a choregic system facilitating dramatic performances.[77] Multiple literary sources indicate that Rhodes had several theaters,[78] which is not surprising given the island's cultural importance as a site for the performance of Greek poetry.[79] In both cases, it appears that the choregic system functioned much as it had in Athens, allowing for wealthy and aristocratic citizens to take up a large portion of the expense in producing these dramatic and musical contests. Given this similarity, it is assumed that they were modeled on the Athenian system.

These festivals seemed to have attracted benefactors beyond the local aristocrats who participated in the system of *chorēgia*.[80] Gabrielsen notes that after the earthquake of 227 BCE, the Rhodians received a donation of 60,000 drachmas from the Syracusan ruler Hieron and his son Gelon, which was earmarked for the "enrichment (*epauxēsis*) of the citizens"; for the same occasion Ptolemy III Euergetes donated an impressive amount of Egyptian grain to Rhodes, to be used for entertainment.[81] While these festivals appear to have been organized locally, they nevertheless attracted powerful international patrons who may have had some say in their administration. This also applies to the islands themselves: despite their independent nature as islands free to govern themselves, they nevertheless seem to have been under the spheres of influence of monarchs. In fact, both islands had arrangements with Antigonous and the later Ptolemies.[82] Though built around a choregic framework that clearly evoked classical Athens, the festivals themselves took place in a complex world in which "democratic" islands had to grapple with powerful monarchs.

Other cities well beyond Athens appear to have had a system of *chorēgia* as early as the fifth century BCE. One such is the city of Mytilene on Lesbos. Antiphon's *On the Murder of Herodes* includes testimony from a Mytilenean named Euxitheus, who, when providing a defense of his father in connection with the revolt of Mytilene from Athens in 428 BCE, mentions furnishing choruses in local festivals at Mytilene in a context of public service (*lēitourgia*).[83] This evidence suggests that a choregic system similar to that of Athens may have been in place as early as the fifth century; perhaps the city of Mytilene had a framework in place which was amenable to the circulation and production of drama. There are various epigraphic records which mention that Dionysia continued to occur in Lesbos at the end of the third century BCE.[84] Despite the patchiness of the evidence, the continued presence of theatrical activity in the third century might be reasonably ascribed to a long-established choregic system. Moreover, if we consider these islands' strategic position in the Mediterranean, with direct connections to Egypt, Asia Minor, and other eastern points, we can see the importance of such festivals in promoting tragedy further afield. Rhodes' early alliance with Rome in 164 BCE makes it a suggestive space for the spread of tragedy to a Roman market; after all, we know that important figures such as Cicero visited Rhodes as part of their education.[85] In any case, it is clear that tragedy was firmly established in a variety of venues across the Hellenistic world, and as such well positioned for further spread as the Greek world expanded and came into contact with other cultures.

ROME

In the Roman period, tragedy continues to develop and transform. Given the wide-ranging nature of its impact and dissemination, in this section I discuss "sites of performance and circulation" in a broader sense: rather than outlining the genre's importance in geographical locations, I now consider a "site" as a textual and imaginative entity. This shift in conceptual framework is necessary for the understanding of tragedy's movements across the Roman world and beyond, since tragedy for the Romans was often understood and experienced as a literary phenomenon, divorced from performative contexts. When tragedy is primarily mediated by and experienced through texts, an account of these sites of circulation and performance must therefore consider multiple receptions, primary, secondary, and beyond.

Greek and Roman tragedy

Though my focus in the remainder of this chapter is on the circulation of *Greek* tragedy in Rome, a note on Roman tragedy is warranted, given that Roman readers would have had access to both Greek and Roman tragic texts. Roman tragedy originates in the direct transposition of a Greek play into Latin:[86] Livius Andronicus' production which was adapted from a Greek model at the *Ludi Romani* of 240 BCE in honor of Jupiter Optimus Maximus.[87] Though there existed many local and independent performance traditions before this event,[88] Greek-style drama heavily influenced the definition and composition of Roman plays.[89] There were other Roman dramatic genres, such as the *fabula praetexta* and *fabula togata*, but the scant nature of the surviving evidence suggests that they were far fewer than the tragedies and comedies adapted from Greek originals.[90] We must, therefore, acknowledge one of the critical issues at the heart of what we have come to know as "Roman" drama, namely, its nature as a subgenre that is modeled after its Greek forebear, and we must consider how this complicates the understanding of tragedy in Rome and its circulation.

The early figures of Roman theater—Livius Andronicus, Naevius, and Ennius—were familiar with Greek dramatic traditions and had access to the various theatrical performances and representations of Greek drama in South Italy that emerged from the fourth century BCE onward.[91] That their "translations" led to the establishment of a new Roman genre illustrates the general popularity and appeal that Greek drama had beyond Greek shores, and also the importance of translation and adaptation as a route of circulation. When compared to comedy, a genre that also borrowed from its Greek model, Republican adaptations or "translations" of Greek tragedy in Rome appear not to have been as successful as its popular comic counterpart precisely because of its same "derivative" nature. We have no single Roman Republican tragic play that has survived complete; instead we possess a series of value judgments on the worthlessness of Roman tragedy.[92] Part of the reason for this low estimation was the elevated place that Greek texts held in Roman education. The formal teaching of rhetoric included analysis of poetic texts, often in both Greek and Latin, and a public career in oratory involved memorization and recitation of tragic excerpts seen to contain examples of persuasive argumentation (Figure 2.4).[93] In this way Greek tragedy was circulated along with Roman tragedy for an educated and elite audience.

Given this model of parallel circulation, Roman tragedy was likely not appreciated on its own terms, always existing under the shadow of its Greek counterpart. In Roman Republican tragedy, the Greek imprint is so powerful that it even helps construct a history of the genre: Cicero, for example, proposes the tragic triad of Ennius, Pacuvius, and Accius to match their Athenian predecessors Aeschylus, Sophocles, and Euripides (*De Or.* 3.27).

There is evidence for the popularity of tragedy in Republican Rome as a performed event: the period between April and November was filled with *ludi*, religious festivals which incorporated dramatic performances.[94]

Despite this tradition of performance, beginning in the early Augustan period, tragedy was not always granted full scale stage performance.[95] Instead, reading plays became the main method of experiencing tragedy.[96] Evidence for this shift is already evident in Cicero's time, and his writings further testify to the parallel circulation of Greek and Roman texts. In an opening discussion justifying the rendering of Greek philosophy into Latin, (*Fin.* 1.2.4), Cicero cites the trend towards translating of Greek plays almost verbatim:

FIGURE 2.4: Roman terracotta figurine of a boy in Greek attire holding a tragic mask, possibly representing the learning of Greek drama as part of Roman education, c. 100–200 CE. The British Museum, London, 1756,0101.962 © The Trustees of the British Museum. All rights reserved.

FIGURE 2.5: Roman carnelian cameo, engraved with the god Pan gazing at a theatrical mask, as though he were an actor preparing for a role, c. first century CE. J. Paul Getty Museum, 2001.28.2. Digital image courtesy of the Getty's Open Content Program.

Why should they dislike their native language for serious and important subjects, when they are quite willing to read Latin plays translated word for word from the Greek? Who has such a hatred, one might almost say for the very name of Roman, as to despise and reject the *Medea* of Ennius or the *Antiope* of Pacuvius, and give as his reason that though he enjoys the corresponding plays of Euripides he cannot endure books written in Latin? What, he cries, am I to read *The Young Comrades* of Caecilius, or Terence's *Maid of Andros*, when I might be reading the same two comedies of Menander? With this sort of person I disagree so strongly, that, admitting the *Electra* of Sophocles to be a masterpiece, I yet think Atilius's poor translation of it worth my while to read.[97]

This passage makes clear that readers such as Cicero had easy access to both the Greek and Roman versions of dramatic texts. It also encapsulates the ambiguities of these "new" Roman texts: should they be seen as verbatim translations or autonomous texts in their own right? The passage further reveals that the mode of parallel circulation contributes to a poor understanding and devaluation of what is seen as a Roman copy in favor of the Greek original. As the passage continues, Cicero insists that Roman versions go beyond mere translation, and that Roman writers like himself "add to them our own opinions and style of composition."[98]

The shift in the first century CE from experiencing tragedy as performed event to a largely internalized experience on the page complicates our understanding of the reception of tragedy. The only examples of Roman tragedy which survive complete—the tragedies of Seneca—may have been performed or even intended for performance, although many scholars doubt it; the texts themselves contain no indications of stagecraft and performance history.[99] However, scholars also recognize the theatricality of Seneca's plays.[100] Annette Baertschi reminds us that Seneca routinely included graphic messenger scenes at the very heart of his tragedies and that the messenger can "recreate for the audience an otherwise irretrievable scene."[101] In giving messenger speeches such a central place, Seneca foregrounds a key element of tragedy. His emphasis on reporting violent and spectacular action transforms drama from a performed and public event to an internal and private experience. Secondary and imaginary receptions of tragedy cannot be ignored: with the rise of reading they themselves become critical contexts for circulation, and a different kind of site of performance.

Quotations of tragedy in philosophical texts

One of the most important "sites of circulation" in Rome was education. Evidence for tragedy's crucial role in Roman Republican education can be seen throughout the writings of Cicero.[102] His letters include many direct quotations from extant Greek tragedy.[103] For example, in a letter to Atticus dated January 49 BCE (*Att.* 7.11.1), Cicero applies a verse from Euripides' *Phoenician Women* (506), in which Eteocles praises tyranny, to the recent actions of Caesar.[104] According to Gildenhard, by means of this single quotation Cicero effectively transforms Caesar "into a Greek tragic monster lusting for absolute power."[105] For this transformation to be effective, however, the reader of the letter must be able to recognize the context of the quotation. According to Goldberg, the educational common ground between Cicero and his readers is always emphasized, since Cicero's tastes in quotation generally correspond to "school texts and cultural landmarks."[106]

Cicero is an extraordinary case: he was extremely well-educated, and especially knowledgeable about Greek and Latin drama,[107] although Cicero does not mention attending theatrical performances. His quotations are drawn from reading rather than performance.[108]

Cicero's philosophic dialogues illustrate how a single individual reader can act as a site of circulation. Cicero "circulates" tragedy by using quotations and references in philosophical dialogues like *The Tusculan Disputations*, which contains more quotations from Greek and Roman poetry than any other Ciceronian dialogue.[109] In this text, Cicero incorporates tragic references in discussions about emotions. The second book, devoted to pain and how to endure it, utilizes the tragic figures of Philoctetes, Heracles, and Prometheus (15–31a). In order to draw attention to their suffering, Cicero quotes the sounds of pain which they emit in tragedy: at 2.19, for example, he cites six verses in Latin uttered by the groaning Philoctetes from Accius' eponymous play.[110] He then moves to a fuller consideration of the portrayal of pain in two Greek tragic texts related to Heracles and Prometheus, quoting them far more extensively than he did Accius: in 2.20–22, he loosely translates forty-five verses from Heracles' first speech in Sophocles' *Trachiniae* (1046–1103)—the majority of this speech—followed by twenty-eight lines spoken by Prometheus in 2.23–25 from the lost play *Prometheus Luomenos* (*Prometheus Unbound*), attributed to Aeschylus.[111] This is a rare instance in which we find the translation of a passage whose original verses are completely lost.[112]

Why does he quote so extensively from these Greek source texts and provide his own Latin translation? The focus on Heracles can be explained by his importance for the representation of pain in Latin poetry: later, Ovid would also draw from the *Trachiniae* in depicting the suffering of Heracles (*Met.* 9.159–229) as would Seneca in his *Hercules Oetaeus*.[113] In Cicero, however, quotations from drama are directly employed to support philosophical arguments.[114] Here, drama does more than simply provide clear examples of suffering and emotion. The direct parroting of its language transforms both the prose text and the philosophical argument contained in it. Tragic theater becomes a sort of universal language which can easily be called upon to testify to any account of suffering. As such, it can be reperformed in pithy excerpts, which themselves instantly possess the power to lend credence to any narrative and argument.

Novel receptions

The performance of tragedy in the Roman imperial period is notoriously difficult and ambiguous to determine. It is clear, however, that tragedy was a prominent feature of contemporary cultural life.[115] Tragic imprints appear in numerous literary texts, including in the emerging genre of prose fiction. Tragedy is one of many genres featured in the ancient novel, which famously collapses and synthesizes a variety of genres,[116] producing a unique hybrid text which Mikhail Bakhtin called polyglossic or heteroglossic.[117] As I will illustrate in the following sketch of Apuleius' *Metamorphoses* and Heliodorus' *Aethiopica*, the presence and integration of tragic imagery, themes, and allusions in the ancient novel not only demonstrates the widespread nature of tragedy's dissemination at the period but also its overall unwieldiness as a genre that is uber-present.

May has recently shown Apuleius' wide-ranging interest in the dramatic genres of tragedy, comedy, and pantomime, and how he integrates them into his novel.[118] Comic motifs and frameworks are particularly prevalent throughout the *Metamorphoses*.[119] Tragedy is more difficult to trace, given that it is often modeled after a lost Greek original,[120] but it is nevertheless noticeable as a general theme in the inserted tales.[121] Though it features in other parts of the novel,[122] it is given special attention in book 10, when the narrator marks his new tale as especially tragic:

> So now, excellent reader, know that you are reading a tragedy, and no light tale, and that you are rising from the lowly slipper to the lofty buskin.
>
> —*Met.* 10.2[123]

This shift in tone is followed by sketch of a story involving a stepmother in love with her chaste stepson, immediately bringing to mind the story of Phaedra. Though there are many sources of it, including Latin literary texts such as Ovid's *Metamorphoses* and Labrius' Belonistria mime,[124] the mention of the buskin (*coturnus*) immediately signals that we should understand its tragic iteration as the main intertext. The story of Phaedra, however, had multiple tragic formulations both Greek and Roman: the two famous *Hippolytoi* of Euripides (*Kalyptomenos* and *Stephanephoros*), and Sophocles' *Phaedra*, and Seneca's.[125] Given the multiplicity of tragic sources, it is impossible to tell whether Apuleius was privileging a particular version, or the entire tragic tradition. The parallel circulation of these different versions, as well as their multiple invocations in non-tragic texts, compounds the difficulty, because a knowledge of these texts could be gleaned from other sources. We cannot therefore automatically assume that Apuleius had personal experience with these tragedies. There is also an unexpected reversal at the end of the tale as Apuleius tells it, which subverts the expectations of the reader who, primed to expect a tragedy, now finds herself faced with a comedy.[126] The co-existence of tragic with comic elements testifies to the rich literary texture of the novel and the manner in which it can blend a variety of genres to produce a unique mix.

If we turn to the Greek novel, we can similarly detect the pervasive role of tragic references. In Heliodorus' *Aethiopica*, tragedy also features in the inserted tales of minor characters and in subplots.[127] The tragic specter of Hippolytus is invoked by name in Cnemon's story about his stepmother (at 1.10.2), and in the scene where Theagenes is pursued by Arsace and her nurse Cybele.[128] The novel teems with figures from the world of tragedy: Thyamis and Petosiris are versions of the warring brothers Eteocles and Polynices, a comparison which immediately transforms Calasiris into Oedipus.[129] In an article on Heliodorus' use of the *Iphigenia* plays of Euripides, Leftratou writes that the role of tragedy in the novel is beyond intertextual: in her view, it is "hypertextual," as "the Heliodoran transposition of Euripides' drama is realized through both plot and genre."[130] This notion of tragedy's hypertextuality encapsulates the new ways in which literary texts at the close of antiquity had become sites for the performance of tragedy in their own right. Tragedy had become a genre so internalized and embedded in the larger culture that it could be experienced and re-performed in parts, since mere fragments of it could readily assemble an entire tragic structure.

CHAPTER THREE

Communities of Production and Consumption

EIRENE VISVARDI

This chapter focuses on the role of ancient tragedy in civic life. The plays, the theater industry, and discourses around them became central to the self-perception and interactions of communities across different periods. The production and consumption of tragedy helped to mold collective thinking, feeling, and acting inside and beyond the confines of the theater.

COLLECTIVE ENGAGEMENTS IN THE FIFTH CENTURY BCE: TRAGEDY AND ATHENIAN DEMOCRACY

Fifth-century Athenian democracy operated within a robust performance culture.[1] Citizens participated in the law courts and the Assembly to reach collective decisions in public. The official production of tragedy was embedded in state religious festivals and was in this sense, a political institution.[2] The state involved the community in all aspects of production and consumption. Watching tragedy was a political act in itself.[3]

Three tragedians staged their plays in the dramatic competition of the Great Dionysia, the major venue for new productions. They were selected by the state official (*archôn epônymos*) in charge of the festival.[4] The city-state was likely responsible for the protagonists (chief actors);[5] it also allotted a *chorêgos* ("chorus funder") to each poet. The institution of the *chorêgia* was vital to the financial organization of the festival and the production of the plays.[6] Service as a dramatic *chorêgos* depended on two conditions: Athenian citizenship and great wealth. Responsibilities included recruiting the best possible chorus members, finding a professional trainer and possibly other men to assist the poet, providing the training space, housing, and food for the chorus throughout their preparation, and paying for production materials such as costumes and masks. The chorus defined the genre in terms of both content and occasion and was key to the community's engagement with tragedy. The collective choral voice and action were fundamental to the meaning of each play. Chorus members, moreover, were required to be Athenian citizens, and the chorus was the most expensive component of the production, thereby diverting private wealth to public consumption and enjoyment. Chorality encapsulated the participatory dynamics of both tragedy and the democracy that sponsored it.

The spectators at the City Dionysia were mostly citizen Athenian men. Resident aliens (metics) and out-of-state visitors also attended, while slaves, women, and underage boys were very likely, but not certainly, present.⁷ The effect of the prevalent female and/or enslaved characters and choruses in tragedy would have been different, depending on whether or not there were women and slaves in the audience. Although performed by men for an audience consisting primarily of male citizens, Athenian tragedy also invited empathy for disenfranchised characters and generated ideas about collective prosperity that spread in the community.⁸

Tragedy explored and redefined the private and public domains—the household (*oikos*) and the *polis*—and thus affected private temperament and social temper.⁹ For example, Aeschylus' *Eumenides* (458 BCE) and Euripides' *Hecuba* (420s BCE) explore the integration of individual and community in enacting justice. The *Oresteia*, the trilogy in which the *Eumenides* is the final play, moves from a cycle of intrafamilial murder to the mythic foundation of the Areopagus, the homicide court that operated in Athens at the time of the play's production; in the play it also represents the legal process at large. The trilogy traces a transition from individual revenge to institutionalized anger: the ideal judges of the new court in the *Eumenides* are described as "quick to anger" (l.705), an attribute which will secure the citizens' reverence for justice.¹⁰ Yet the play suggests that such anger will be calibrated through the structure of the court and the exceptional

FIGURE 3.1: Paestan mixing vessel depicting Orestes seeking sanctuary from the Furies at the temple of Apollo at Delphi and Apollo and Athena purifying him of matricide, possibly influenced by Aeschylus' *Eumenides* and attributed to the Python painter, *c.* 360–320 BCE. The British Museum, London, 1917,1210.1. © The Trustees of the British Museum. All rights reserved.

morality of the jurors. Large numbers of citizens served as jurors in Athens every year. They also initiated legal procedures.[11] The presentation of the Areopagus in the play invites citizens' trust in their legal system's capacity to render private attachments conducive to collective well-being.[12]

Euripides' *Hecuba*, on the other hand, foregrounds the dangers of the abuse of power by institutional representatives. Having saved his life in the past, Hecuba entreats Odysseus to prevent her daughter's sacrifice by the Greeks, to no avail. She also discovers that her guest-friend Polymestor murdered her youngest son and she supplicates Agamemnon to punish this brutal violation of guest-friendship. But the Greek lords reject her pleas. The play ends with violent revenge exacted on Polymestor by Hecuba and her fellow slave-women and a mock trial overseen by Agamemnon. The Greek leaders fail to listen to the needs of the disenfranchised even as they offer them a hearing: Hecuba turns wrathful precisely because the representatives of Greek institutions refuse to get angry on her behalf. If processes of accountability are to be inclusive and effective, the play seems to suggest, the agents of justice ought to be continuously self-aware and adaptable.

The *Hecuba* was produced in the 420s BCE. In 427 BCE the Athenians held an Assembly to reconsider a political decision they had made the previous day: to kill Mytilene's male population and enslave its women and children because the *polis* had revolted from the Athenian alliance. One of the public speakers, Cleon, insisted that they must hold onto their initial anger, which reflected an accurate assessment of the offense and hence a righteous rationale for punishment. Criticizing the demos for being unable to think and feel responsibly, he calls them "spectators of speeches and listeners of deeds," slaves of pleasant paradoxes, and unconcerned with facts as a trustworthy basis for judgment (Thuc. 3.38.4–5). According to Cleon, by passively indulging in a kind of collective pleasure, similar to what uncritical spectators experience watching theatrical and sophistic competitions, the Athenians avoid the real engagement that produces effective policy.

The habits cultivated in the consumption of spectacles, Cleon suggests, become habits of feeling and thinking in political decision-making. The issues debated in the plays, the Assembly, and the courts are shared—and so is their discourse.[13] Cleon rebukes the Athenians for the pleasure they take in passive spectatorship. But, in reality, tragedies invited audience members to empathize with both individual heroes and collective bodies. They also provided the venue for citizen-men to enact and thus inhabit these perspectives, especially when participating in the chorus. Citizens were not merely spectators of tragedy.

In 405 BCE, Aristophanes' comedy the *Frogs* had Dionysus, god of theater, worry that after the death of Aeschylus, Sophocles, and Euripides, tragedy itself may be dead. Dionysus eventually sets up an underworld contest between Euripides and Aeschylus: the two poets weigh verses like cheese, compare lyrics, and contrast the effects of their poetry on the citizen soul and mind. Aeschylus' characters inspire military valor and heroism; Euripides' engage in endless democratic contestation and undermine the common good. Dionysus directly asks the poets to advise the *polis* about the controversial politician Alcibiades. When that fails, he chooses the poet that his soul now prefers: Aeschylus. Off the comic stage, tragedians of course do not advise their audiences directly. Yet the Aristophanic Euripides defines the poet's role as making citizens better through skill (*dexiotês*) and advice (*nouthesia*) (ll.1009–10), a claim no one contests. While the *Frogs* cannot be seen as a straightforward template for the aesthetics and politics of tragedy, it confirms that tragedy cultivated habits of thinking and feeling and played a crucial civic role beyond the theater.

TRAGEDY IN THE FOURTH CENTURY: ATHENS AND BEYOND

Partly because there are no extant tragedies from the fourth century, a narrative of decline has arisen. Nonetheless, the festivals of the Great and Rural Dionysia and the Lenaia (another festival in honor of Dionysus), as well as festivals outside Athens, continued; there were new playwrights and plays, and actors' status and popularity increased.[14] In Athens, comedy engaged extensively with tragedy's authors, aesthetics, and impact; philosophical works evince a preoccupation with the genre's effects on the community; political initiatives claimed tragedy as an Athenian achievement and trademark; and tragic paradigms permeated legal speeches. Such a pervasive engagement with tragedy in the theater itself, and in philosophical, political, and legal discourses makes sense only if a theater industry was thriving in the background.[15] The vitality of the production and consumption of tragedy becomes apparent in the ways it was embraced, exploited, or even opposed, because of its perceived power to shape individual and collective mentality.

Philosophizing the tragic product: states of perilous consumption

Any consideration of how tragedy may affect community life in classical antiquity cannot bypass the Platonic "quarrel between philosophy and poetry," which culminates in the expulsion of tragedy and other poetic genres from the semi-ideal states envisioned in the *Republic* and the *Laws*.[16] These texts show how the emotional effect of tragedy—its effect on the individual—morphs into collective sentiment. In the *Republic* tragedy is presented as a form of imitation that, by misconceiving reality, necessarily misrepresents ethical values. One of its fundamental misconceptions, for instance, is the representation of death as dreadful and a source of overpowering grief. By encouraging deep empathy and lamentation, tragedy skews the spectators' judgment and emotional inclinations. It thus cultivates a manner of thinking (believing in appearances) and feeling (indulgence in non-justifiable emotions) that corrupts the soul and irrevocably compromises the spectators' potential for a good and just life outside the theater. This effect is all the more powerful and insidious because of the pleasurable trappings of theatrical production. Tragedy corrupts the soul and thereby corrupts the *polis*.[17]

The *Laws*, in turn, offers insights into the effects of both choral performance (*choreia*) and theater. Identified with *paideia* (education/acculturation) itself, *choreia* is seen as tapping into our natural inclination to move and imitate. Giving humans profound pleasure, *choreia* forms habits of thinking and feeling that stay with us: the positions we inhabit as performers—first, unconsciously as children and, subsequently, by choosing our performances as adults—become second nature.[18] With tragedy as a form of adult *choreia*, moreover, the focus shifts to tragedians, as the producers, and audiences, as the consumers. Eager to be innovative and crowd-pleasing without acquiring any true expertise, playwrights compose licentious works that provide easy gratification and render audiences lawless, bold, and unaware of their own ignorance. This results in disobedience outside the theater: defiance of rulers, parents, and elders, and eventually laws and the gods themselves. The theater thus becomes the site of formation for species of collective thinking and feeling that turn into habits of political participation. In a democracy that gives equal power to all, the ignorant included, such pernicious effects are exacerbated. The habits of the theater become the habits of the *polis*, and vice versa.[19] This is why the tragedians must be displaced by the philosophers, who will provide "the finest drama" for the just city.

Plato's reflections convey the potentially all-pervasive effect of Athenian tragedy as popular culture. Plato also suggests that the collective enjoyment of tragedy cultivates audience members who, while reacting in concert in the theater, are essentially divided. As empathy with tragic suffering habituates them to indulge their private grief in real life, they grow unable to collaborate toward true collective prosperity.

Cultural industry, collective memory, and public life: tragedy in the Lycurgan era

In the fourth century, new initiatives used tragedy to promote the community's cohesion: theater culture aimed to enhance and reflect economic and social stability; the history of the genre was constructed so as to redefine collective memory and affirm Athenian cultural superiority; and examples from tragedies permeated different public forums that negotiated collective values. Theater assumed great importance especially during 355–324 BCE, when the politicians Eubulus, Lycurgus, and their circle became particularly invested in developing Athens' cultural industry.[20]

Certain initiatives reveal a concerted effort to support theater and to link drama, especially tragedy, to Athenian identity. The Theoric Fund, the "Lycurgan" theater, the statues of the three tragedians, and the establishment and safekeeping of official scripts of their plays—along with the requisite economic strategies to support them—stand out among such initiatives. The Theoric Fund was a central treasury for surplus revenues which were then disbursed toward public ends, such as money-distribution to citizens for festival-spending, for instance covering admission to the theater. Even Lycurgus' rival Demades called these disbursements "the glue of democracy," emphasizing their contribution to political consensus and social stability.[21] The construction of the so-called Lycurgan theater of Dionysus was supported also through the lease of public and sacred lands and transfer of lands on security as well as by private donations and dedications.[22] The latter were encouraged through civic honors and even the award of citizenship. The range of supporters is revealing: talented actors, prosperous foreign benefactors, Athenian officials, and grain traders.[23] The economic and cultural regeneration of Athens was thus seen as a single process and integral to a program that aimed to build social stability. Theater became the locus to build community and advertise its cohesion.

The decision that most vividly illustrates the leadership's attempt to identify Athens with the achievement of tragedy is Lycurgus' law to erect a statue-group of Aeschylus, Sophocles, and Euripides in the eastern side-entry (*parodos*) of the new stone theater and to commission official state copies of their plays against which actors were required to test their scripts. By choosing to monumentalize these three tragedians, Lycurgus selected the parts of Athens' cultural past that were to have a bearing on the present. The Golden Age of history corresponded with the Golden Age of Athenian Tragedy. Moreover, by preserving authoritative scripts, Lycurgus established Athens as the "capital and rightful home of the theater."[24] The Lycurgan law could be enforced only within Athens, and so it amounted to a powerful claim of ownership of the original texts, which would be preserved in their original and legitimate home.[25] Alongside the ongoing festivals, this program attempted to define "classical" tragedy and to insist on Athens' entitlement to it during a period when theater was spreading outside Athens and was strongly claimed by other regimes and political elites such as the Macedonians.[26] Athenian leaders strategically devoted significant resources to canonize Athenian theatrical heritage and to motivate the Athenian community to embrace it along with the cultural supremacy and political power it conveyed.[27]

It is also in the fourth century that tragedy, for the first time in our evidence, becomes embedded in the discourses of different public forums, such as the law courts. Lycurgus' own use of Euripides in the court may be an answer to the Platonic challenge against the tragedians.[28] In his speech *Against Leocrates*, Lycurgus extensively quotes a Euripidean character (Praxithea, from the lost play *Erechtheus*) as a paradigm of patriotism who expresses values worth emulating.[29] Earlier in the century, Aeschines—an actor and politician—had used multiple quotations from Euripides in his speech *Against Timarchus*, the latter allegedly having been a decadent prostitute who broke the law by taking political office.[30] In one instance, Aeschines invited the jurors to judge Timarchus by using Euripides' character Phoenix (from the lost play of the same name) as an example: to judge him, that is, according to his habits and company. Phoenix suggests that a man manages the affairs of his *polis* just as he manages himself and his household.[31] Aeschines' opponent Demosthenes struck back by also drawing on tragedy. He accused Aeschines of being inadequate as an actor and unable to judge which examples from tragedy are appropriate for the demos' judgment: his lack of talent in the theater overlaps with his failures as a citizen in the court and in state affairs.[32] On a different occasion, the two opponents debated the appropriateness of crowning citizens in the theater, before the plays.[33] As was the case in the fifth century, the festival context remained a high-visibility public event.[34] According to Demosthenes, it offered the ideal occasion for honoring benefactors: by gazing upon them, the citizens became motivated to emulate them.[35] Whether to promote one's own collective spirit and good judgment, or to pinpoint an opponent's lack thereof, it was tragedy as a genre and theater as a public space that provided the testing ground for citizen mentality and responsibility.

In political rhetoric, tragedy became the source for examples of good and bad types of behavior: it dramatized the individual's position in the public realm and consistently broke down the divide between private and public.[36] Public speakers selected, manipulated, or distorted such paradigms, in the act of contesting what was lawful and beneficial for the *polis*. While there could be both good use and abuse of tragedy, its relevance was not disputed. Thus in the theater itself, the "classics" became defined, honored, and owned. In the courts, litigants reproduced tragedy for a different kind of consumption. They reaffirmed shared cultural references and values and invited the jurors to take responsibility as individuals who define their community's well-being.

Shifting philosophical politics: tragedy without theater and state?

While the Lycurgan program tied tragedy to Athens, Aristotle's account of tragedy in the *Poetics* seems to present a significant shift, which has influenced the perception and reception of tragedy by individuals and communities alike.[37] Produced between 367 and 322 BCE, the treatise traces the development of the genre and attempts to define what constitutes good tragedy. Aeschylus, Sophocles, and Euripides delineate the arc of creativity that brings the genre to its maturity, while references to fourth-century poets such as Astydamas II, Theodectes, Carcinus the Younger, and Chaeremon—authors from whom we only have fragments—point to the continuous production of new plays in the fourth century. Descriptive and normative, Aristotle's account has often been seen as a response to Plato's expulsion of tragedy from the ideal state, but Aristotle presents no civic context for tragedy. Some scholars have argued that Aristotle pointedly eliminates both democratic Athens and even the abstract notion of a *polis* from his *Poetics*.[38] By presenting poetry as a self-sufficient art with rules of correctness that do not pertain to other spheres of human activity, he also sidesteps the Platonic demand that poetry combine pleasure and political usefulness.[39] The particular philosophical undertaking of the treatise, however, may justify the absence of a *polis*: by offering an understanding of poetry as a universal human activity that is autonomous within its own sphere of competence, the *Poetics* separates it from any particular community. Even though there is no activity not answerable to politics, according to Aristotle, the value of tragedy is not defined by social and political contingency.[40]

Nevertheless, we can try to read the *Poetics* for evidence of communities of tragic consumers in the fourth century. The absence of specific references to Athens may indicate the broad dissemination and (re)production of tragedy outside Athens.[41] At the same time, Aristotle suggests that tragedy can perform its most important emotional and intellectual effects by being read, not performed. Even though he includes spectacle (*opsis*) in the elements that define the genre, and refers to audiences and theatrical production, he casts tragedy as an art which may not need the theater space to perform its ideal function.[42] He also all but ignores the role of the chorus, the element in the plays that is both collective and more performance-oriented.[43]

Aristotle is likely not opposing performance itself, which he views as the appropriate embodiment of tragic poetry, but a fourth-century dominance of actors and producers.[44] On the one hand, the poet is encouraged to compose his plays by envisioning or even implying the physical movements and behaviors necessary for the staging of his plots.[45] On the other, the plots should instigate the proper cognitive and emotional experience without depending on production. Solitary reading, moreover, allows for dispensing with a collective audience.[46] Collective engagement is no longer presumed as the primary or even preferred kind of consumption. When tragedy's role as a collective experience becomes optional, so does the incentive to envision its contribution to a collective mentality.

Shifting theater and community relations: actors in the fourth century

From the fourth century on, we have increasing evidence about actors. Within Athens, the city took on the responsibility to choose and (likely) pay actors, probably in an attempt to attract the best performers for its Dionysia, which now competed for them with festivals at other places.[47] The revival of "old tragedy" was institutionalized in 386 BCE, another development that acknowledged the importance of acting troupes.[48] Actors' income and prestige both increased throughout the century. Most importantly, actors participated in the elite gift economy that official representations had earlier reserved for the "voluntary" contributions of citizen *chorêgoi*, choral dancers, and poets. As an exercise in public relations, this constitutes a "watershed in the relationship between actors and other actors, between actors and poets, and between actors and their public."[49] The Athenian actor Theodoros, for instance, contributed seventy drachmas for the rebuilding of the Temple of Apollo at Delphi. An actor told Demosthenes or Demades that he earned the vast amount of one talent for two days' competition. With the internationalization of theater, moreover, and as they became more mobile, actors acquired high status as ambassadors and intermediaries between states.[50] Emerging celebrities became influential diplomats. They also gradually organized in what would become the guilds of the "*technitai* of Dionysus" in the Hellenistic period.

By the end of the fourth century, public discourses including philosophy and oratory expanded on the role of the tragedians and pointed to what actors can do as well. Star

FIGURE 3.2: Gold ring engraved with an actor holding a theater mask, c. 325–300 BCE. J. Paul Getty Museum, 85.AM.276. Digital image courtesy of the Getty's Open Content Program.

actors created new possibilities for empathy through their acting and their personalities.[51] They also moved theater itself in new directions through the negotiations they facilitated with local rulers. By straddling the world of entertainment and politics, they slowly altered the nature of theater as an institution and especially the ways in which different leaders used it for community building. A look at the Macedonian kings sheds significant light on this shift.

A thriving theatrical market: the Macedonians

Theater figured prominently in the cultural politics of the Macedonian court. Archelaus already in the fifth century drew tragedians to his court, partly to compose plays that supported his political agenda. Theater-occasions changed in the fourth century. Philip and Alexander seem to have been the first ones to attach drama to ad hoc festivals celebrating their alliances and achievements.[52] Private theater also became popular. While the notion of "private" requires caution because it may still imply large audiences, the diversification of performative occasions renders tragedy a cultural product that mediates the private and public in novel ways.[53]

A celebration at Aegae in 336 BCE, an event well-known for combining public and "private" theater, is worth mentioning in some detail. During a private banquet before the celebration of his daughter's wedding, Philip asked the actor Neoptolemus to sing something relevant to his campaign against the Persians. Neoptolemus obliged with tragic odes on the potential obliteration of the Persian king's wealth. The next day, the statues of the twelve gods were brought into the theater followed by a statue of Philip—godlike himself. Certain of divine protection, the king then entered without his bodyguard and was soon assassinated in front of the gathered audience. The meaning of the actor's words transcended their original context, as the theater of real life took over and provided the tragic spectacle before the plays even began.[54] Neoptolemus himself was a captivating celebrity. A native of Skyros, he either enjoyed high standing in Athens or was granted citizenship after winning first prize in 341 BCE. Growing closer to Philip, he acted as a diplomat and reported to the Athenians on Philip's policy. He eventually sold his Athenian property to move to Macedonia.[55] When asked what he liked from the tragedians, he chose the "drama" of Philip's assassination instead. Stories like the one about Neoptolemus bring out "the particularly close analogies between theatrical and political power and the way in which drama and life, particularly the lives of famous people, were felt to interact and to shape one another."[56] Both Philip and Alexander contributed to the ascendancy of actors partly, if not primarily, for political reasons: they capitalized on the mobility, charm, and speaking skills that rendered actors ideal ambassadors and negotiators.[57]

With Alexander, the adaptation of theater to benefit Macedonian rule on multiple levels—military, political, cultural—became even more apparent. Alexander kept artists in his court on a more or less long-term basis even during campaigning, and he enlarged his semi-permanent circle by inviting actors and other artists from Greece. His organization of scenic contests seems to have followed the model of the Great Dionysia.[58] Men in his army may have provided chorus members, though plays may also have been performed without a chorus. Eager to draw the best performers, he cultivated close relationships with actors by granting them financial benefits and favors that enhanced both their fame and their loyalty to him. One such actor, Athenodorus, despite his commitment to perform in Athens, decided instead to appear at Alexander's festival at Tyre and thus to incur a high fine from Athens which the king paid off.[59] By offering competing venues for talent from far and wide at large-scale events, Alexander presented himself as a champion of Greek culture and influenced the cultural production of places like Athens itself. He was particularly invested in tragedy: he quoted Euripides, asked for the texts of the three "classics" while on campaign, and set up tragic contests.[60] On his return from India, moreover, he presented himself as Dionysus on earth.[61] He has thus been seen as extending his war into the arena of culture to demonstrate his all-encompassing capacities as a leader.[62]

Incorporating theater in the royal banquet created a "form of relation of fealty between a lord and his retainer," whether he be an actor or guest.[63] On a collective level, festivals consolidated communities around and for the king who orchestrated these occasions. Our sources point to the growing professionalization of actors and a cosmopolitanism of tragedy that affected the ways in which audiences viewed themselves as participants in changing political and social environments. As performances became larger and more spectacular, and performers more famous and specialized, audiences may have become more passive consumers of cultural and political ideology.

CONSPICUOUS PRODUCTION AND THE THEATRICS OF PUBLIC LIFE: HELLENISTIC AND ROMAN TRAGEDY

The Hellenistic period

The cultural and political dynamics around the production of tragedy in the Hellenistic period have been extensively debated, because of the genre's growing cosmopolitanism, the diversification of festivals that is already apparent with the Macedonians, and the full professionalization of actors. There are no extant plays from the Hellenistic age, but a consideration of actors' corporations allows us to see how fundamentally they contributed to the circulation of tragedy and its role in the community.

The *technitai* (artists or artisans) of Dionysus included all kinds of practitioners that made production possible: actors, poets, musicians, mask- and costume-makers, and more. These guilds secured protections and privileges for their traveling members: for example, sacred status, immunity from aggression, exemption from taxation and military service, and protection of property.[64] They thus operated both as religious associations and as communities that issued decrees and appointed their own officials and representatives. One guild referred to itself as a *techiteuma*: "just as a *politeuma* is a self-governing body of citizens, the *technê* has its own political existence, its own rights of self-determination, as a *polis*."[65] Specifying only the number of leading actors, contracts between guilds and states indicate that actors played a central role in the negotiations. Artists associated specifically with tragedy seem to have received positions of delegation more often than others.[66]

This professionalization, along with the likelihood that choruses also became professionals, has been seen as evincing a decline in the civic spirit of theater.[67] But it is political communities themselves that were changing. Both in Athens and in other cities, the *chorêgoi* were gradually replaced by a new official called the *agônothetês*, an institution likely used for royal propaganda.[68] Festivals combined the celebration of divinities with ruler cult and guilds became involved in different parts of these festivals that asserted royal power and city-cohesion.[69] Theater, in other words, remained part of how political influence was negotiated and showcased.

The Hellenistic kings seem to have used the dramatic medium to reach their mass audiences.[70] Alongside mythic themes, tragedy now dramatized events of recent history while the theater space was still used for both dramatic performances and other public gatherings and political announcements.[71] The imbrication of dramatic performance and politics, therefore, continued and often became more transparent and more conspicuous. Mass entertainment itself need not imply lack of sophistication on the part of the audience. Audiences were consistently exposed to both old and new plays. Scripts were available for solitary reading. Competition between guilds may have raised performance standards and the sophistication of at least segments of different populations.[72] What remained a constant was that rulers used the production and consumption of tragedy to support their power and consolidate audiences around it.

There seems, however, to be a shift in audience engagement. Hellenistic urban centers have been characterized as "cities of onlookers," in which the dichotomy between specialized performers and spectators grew stark: "[the individual] went to the theater not to admire his own son as a member of a chorus or his neighbor as an actor, but to applaud the foreign professional. In the assembly, or in other public events he was an onlooker as well, even when he was actively engaged in the spectacle."[73] The political "actors" that orchestrated the theatrics of public life attempted to maintain this separation of roles between performers and spectators along with the mentality and power dynamic that resulted from it. In the Hellenistic period, even though the demos remained active, the rule of the people has come to be seen as a fiction maintained by statesmen who were skillful performers of political manipulation.[74]

Roman tragedy: contexts of production and the politics of collective engagement

The theatricality of Roman life has become a truism. The role that tragedy played in such theatrics poses a challenging question primarily because of the nature of our evidence: mostly fragments of plays, Seneca's extant corpus, and references to plays, events, and theater culture in historical, rhetorical, and philosophical works. By the early Empire, moreover, tragedy was not performed in full production, while other genres (such as the pantomime) and arena performances appropriated tragic elements and commanded popular attention. But tragedy still reflected and contributed to the expression of individual and community in the late Republic and early Empire.

First attested in 240 BCE, tragedy in Rome was produced as part of dramatic performances (*ludi scaenici*) during public festivals in honor of the gods.[75] Other occasions included triumphs, funerals, dedications of temples, and great votive *ludi* in honor of Jupiter (*ludi magni votivi*) offered by military commanders or consuls. While the state allocated a grant to the shows, the magistrates in charge contributed their own funds, which seems to reflect their intent to win the people's good will both at the time of the *ludi* and for future election to higher offices.[76] In imperial times, the emperor restricted the magistrates' role and expanded his control over public spectacles, dramatic shows included. Theatrical spectacle was thus seen as having the potential of winning the people's support.

At the same time, the absence of permanent theaters reflected an attempt on the part of elites to limit popular power. As Cicero attests, "the opinion and feeling of the Roman People in public affairs can be most clearly expressed on three occasions, at a meeting, at an Assembly, at a gathering for plays and gladiatorial shows."[77] It was not until 55 BCE that the first permanent theater was built, that of Pompey. Even after that, temporary wooden structures continued to host the *ludi scaenici*. Sometimes they were as elaborate as Curio's double theater, which was set up for drama in the morning and rotated in the afternoon to form an amphitheater for gladiatorial games.[78] This alternation interestingly captures Cicero's equation of plays and gladiatorial shows. Within the theater, while admission was free, seating was highly regulated, mirroring class and status and allowing officials to discern the origins of the audience's reactions.[79] Yet seating arrangements also left the elites in the first rows vulnerable to attacks from both actors and audience.[80]

Roman drama begins with Livius Andronicus, originally a Greek slave, who wrote plays with mythological subjects, a number of them from the Trojan cycle. Gnaeus Naevius subsequently founded the *fabula praetexta*, a type of serious play that dramatized ancient or recent moments of Roman history.[81] The second wave of tragedians—Quintus Ennius, Marcus Pacuvius, and Lucius Accius—produced both kinds of plays. Mythological plays likely carried topical significance in a manner similar to that of Greek tragedy. Language and rhetorical style drawn from contemporary discourses helped render myth resonant with current political and ethical issues. Political allusions could also be added.[82] *Praetextae*, in turn, resonated partly through their production context: at triumphs or funerals the plays would be celebratory or commemorative. During special votive *ludi* in honor of Jupiter or dedications of temples, drama would showcase a god's favor toward the Roman people while also celebrating the patron or general.[83] Because of the patrons' control over their content, *praetextae* may have been controversial and not frequently staged.[84] Even so, as political circumstances changed, the balance between such control, the political nuances of the plays, and the audience's perception may also have shifted.[85] In the *Octavia*, for instance, our only extant *praetexta* from the Empire, the heroine's exile and execution likely communicated a critique of Nero and of imperial "tyranny" more broadly. It thus expressed political opposition and contributed to historical consciousness.[86] The *praetexta* of the early Empire was thus a form of tragedy that encouraged ethical and political critique.

Another set of venues added to the diverse dynamics of audience engagement. At least from 107 BCE onward, powerful members of the Roman elite hosted private banquets that incorporated dramatic performance.[87] As with the Macedonian court, the notion of "private" is problematic. In some instances, the *triclinium* (dining room) in private residences was reshaped to resemble a theatrical space.[88] Starting in the late Republic, elite men, such as Agrippa, Caligula, Nero, and Hadrian, also built private stages and whole theaters in their villas and palaces with a capacity ranging from 150–200 to approximately 1,500 guests.[89] The line between private and public drama was thus blurred depending on the magnificence and inclusiveness of the occasion.[90]

Given the scale of productions, the influence on and by the communities involved became significant. Both public and private drama remained highly political. "Tragedians, comedians and pantomimes were the mass media of the day—as tragedians and comedians were indeed in Athens—but with the difference that the masses were larger and the politics more openly contested."[91] The role of actors in creating community is particularly interesting, especially when compared with the mobility and status of the *technitai* of Dionysus. In Rome, actors were often slaves. Even when free-born, they belonged to the group of *infames*, a status that imposed on them an array of legal disabilities.[92] Elites often owned them, rendering actors a status symbol and a guarantee that they would be readily available to perform in a manner serving the owners' cause.[93] When on stage, however, actors' freedom may not have been as circumscribed. For instance, while acting in a mythological tragedy, Aesopus addressed the audience by applying lines to Cicero's exile. As he pleaded Cicero's case, the Roman people lamented and applauded, in hopes of his recall.[94] Aesopus went as far as to interpolate a line from a *praetexta*, Accius' *Brutus*, to mention Cicero by name. The people expressed their collective sentiment, as the line was encored "a thousand times."[95]

The actor himself most likely "did not wield political power; vast networks of patronage wielded power through him."[96] Even so, actors could isolate or interpolate lines and create the conditions for the audience to define the text's meaning.[97] In addition, before the plays started, audiences could react to their leaders' arrival, rendering the theater a testing ground for the elites' assessment of their popularity with the community.[98] Public applause, it has been suggested, signaled the community's assent. Being "an active instrument of participation," it was valuable because it was free.[99]

Cicero's accounts thus show theater to be a microcosm of Rome.[100] In the late Republic tragedy seems still to play some part in interrogating and celebrating the values of this microcosm.[101] But this dynamic was built on a strict role separation between acting *infames* and spectators who reacted en masse. This separation affected tragedy's role in cultivating empathy and in shaping conceptions of responsibility and justice. In later Roman periods, the popularity of tragedy itself waned and other spectacles of justice absorbed tragic elements, in a changing political climate.

FIGURE 3.3: Detail of a Roman mosaic from the House of the Tragic Poet in Pompeii, depicting actors and an *aulos* player, perhaps preparing for the performance of a tragedy, c. first century CE. Museo Archeologico Nazionale di Napoli, Naples, Italy. Photo by Marie-Lan Nguyen. Courtesy of Wikimedia.

Alternative modes of production and consumption: private and collective engagement with tragedy and "the tragic"

From the late Republic onward, we see a growing preference for spectacular action along with diverse modes of engaging with tragedy.[102] Members of the elite turned to tragedy partly as intellectual exercise. Cicero, for instance, translated [Aeschylus'] *Prometheus* and his brother Quintus wrote four tragedies in sixteen days; Julius Caesar wrote an *Oedipus*, and Augustus wrote an *Ajax* that he did not wish to share. By the second century CE tragedy seems to have lost its popular appeal.[103] Already before that, different types of performance had diversified or replaced full production. Tragedies were published and read. They were recited in theaters, private houses, or recitation halls either as autonomous events or as a preliminary to fuller performance or publication. Recitations could focus on a single speech, episode, or tragic aria instead of presenting full plays.[104]

Emperors influenced public theater on all levels: authorial output, administration, and production. They restricted the capacity of officials to organize and participate in spectacles in order to capitalize on theater's influence themselves.¹⁰⁵ Although new writers and tragedies did appear, it was primarily older plays that were revived and the pantomime gradually displaced tragedy.¹⁰⁶ Under Caligula, no new tragedies appear in our evidence. Performances including tragedy most likely occurred in private.¹⁰⁷ Under Nero, the *imperator scaenicus*,¹⁰⁸ theatricality was taken to a new level of extravagant self-consciousness. Drama and real life became consistently conflated.¹⁰⁹ This most "tragic" emperor, a matricide whose reign was a continuous dramatic act, took the stage himself. Often wearing masks that replicated his own features or those of his mistresses, Nero impersonated tragic characters such as Orestes, Oedipus, and Heracles. Real violence took place during staged performances. Nero also instituted new festivals, both private (Juvenalia) and public (Neronia), acted in them, forced applause in his favor, and despite his subversive behavior, seems to have remained popular.¹¹⁰ Yet with spectacular acts becoming the primary attraction, tragedy as a literary dramatic genre lost its cultural centrality.

Seneca's plays, some composed under Nero's reign, combine linguistic and physical violence with a declamatory mode, epigrammatic pronouncements, and a complex engagement with the ideas and tropes of Stoic philosophy.¹¹¹ They also draw attention to their own theatricality.¹¹² Scholars have debated whether Seneca's plays were meant exclusively for recitation or private reading, rather than public performance.¹¹³ In either case, the plays fit the cultural dynamics of the time, in which declamation habituated audiences to overlook the distinction between person and persona,¹¹⁴ role-playing was imperative on the social and political stage, and theater and amphitheater collapsed the distinction between reality and illusion. Senecan rhetoric controls both the spectacle of violence and suffering and its interpretation: his characters showcase an (in)ability to "read," recognize, and engage with the tragic scripts that inform their lives.¹¹⁵

Seneca's plays invited critical self-awareness of all spectacle that incorporated tragic elements. The pantomime, for instance, adopted tragic episodes and plots: a solo dancer enacted them to music and narration, eliminating the element of debate and thus the interaction of individual and collective voices that are central to the tragic genre.¹¹⁶ Conversely, the chorus in Senecan tragedy may be influenced by pantomime, perhaps in a deliberate attempt to counteract the effects of this new popular genre.¹¹⁷ Moreover, the Senecan reliance on language reverses the cultural tendency toward spectacle and invigorates tragedy as "a vehicle for serious literary endeavor" in private halls.¹¹⁸

Tragedy thus became primarily a medium for elite self-reflection, while the pantomime and the spectacles of justice in the arena attracted the masses. In the amphitheater, Greco-Roman mythology and tragedy itself offered creative examples for public executions.¹¹⁹ As audiences grew familiar with violence and craved greater creativity, each generation of Romans seems to have competed with their predecessors for more gripping spectacles.¹²⁰ To convey a compelling message in public, the spectacular presentation of punishment and justice had to surpass even myth.¹²¹ The amphitheater's separation between performers and audience is particularly significant. The pleasure of the (quasi-tragic) spectacle of suffering and violent punishment in the amphitheater was built on a lack of empathy and the righteous power of the spectating collective to endorse and relish the public punishment of criminals.

In one of his letters, Seneca invites us to reflect on spectacular justice, tragedy, and community building:

But nothing is so damaging to good character as the habit of lounging at the games; for then it is that vice steals subtly upon one through the avenue of pleasure. What do you think I mean? I mean that I come home more greedy, more ambitious, more voluptuous, and even more cruel and inhuman – because I have been among human beings [. . .] In the morning they throw men to the lions and the bears; at noon, they throw them to the spectators. [. . .] The outcome of every fight is death, and the means are fire and sword. . . You may retort: "But he was a highway robber; he killed a man!" And what of it? Granted that, as a murderer, he deserved this punishment, what crime have you committed, poor fellow, that you should deserve to sit and see this show?[122]

Seneca portrays the act of watching cruel punishment as itself a cruel punishment of the spectators, because it insidiously creates a community of inhumane humans.[123] We saw how Thucydides' Cleon and Plato claimed, from different perspectives, that the habits cultivated in the consumption of spectacles necessarily become the habits of thinking and feeling outside the theater. The consumption of new engrossing spectacles of justice continued to affect spectators in their ability to think, emote, and act, both as individuals and as community members.

ACKNOWLEDGMENTS

Many thanks to Anastasia-Erasmia Peponi, Andy Szegedy-Maszak, and Richard Martin for their insights and feedback on this chapter. I am also thankful to Emily Wilson for her thorough reading and editing of this work.

CHAPTER FOUR

Philosophy and Social Theory

AUSTIN BUSCH

In classical antiquity, "philosophy" encompassed a range of intellectual interests broader than those normally associated with the term today, including language and hermeneutics, metaphysics and epistemology, theology and ethics, but also natural science, psychology, rhetoric, and more. Of the two ancient tragic oeuvres that survive (a collection of fifth-century BCE Athenian plays by Aeschylus, Sophocles, and Euripides and a smaller collection of first-century CE Roman tragedies written by or attributed to Seneca), the less familiar Senecan dramatic corpus evinces more sustained and systematic interaction with philosophical ideas.

Complete works survive of almost none of the philosophers who would have influenced extant Greek tragedy. Our knowledge of earlier Greek philosophy relies on citations, paraphrases, or quotations of earlier writings in the works of Plato, Aristotle, and other later authors, but since they quote selectively and interpret tendentiously, reconstructing the philosophical project or even general intellectual outlook of, say, the leading sophistic philosopher Protagoras is a challenging endeavor. Protagoras might have publicly read one of his books at Euripides' home (Diogenes Laertius 9.54) and Athenaeus, among others, called Euripides "the Philosopher of the stage" (4.158e), so it comes as no surprise that we find connections between the plays of Euripides in particular and ideas from early philosophical fragments.[1] But determining how Euripides understands and evaluates, for instance, Protagoras' epistemology is fraught with difficulty.

Some have attempted the feat, with reference to Euripides' *Helen*, for example. According to Plato's *Theaetetus*, Protagoras wrote "man is the measure of all things: of those which are, that they are, and of those which are not, that they are not" (152a).[2] Plato's Socrates interprets the line to suggest that Protagoras equated knowledge with perception and judgment (152a-e), perhaps as mediated by social convention (cf. 167c-d). Protagoras may have proposed a subjective conception of truth that eschewed absolute judgments and metaphysical abstractions in favor of discrete empirical encounters. This would explain the claim elsewhere attributed to him that "there are two possible accounts about every question, opposed to each other" (Diogenes Laertius 9.51), as well as why Protagoras could simultaneously argue that "contradiction is impossible" (Diogenes Laertius 9.53). Such "accounts" might correspond to reports uttered from different perspectival positions, which are opposed insofar as they are irreducibly different, but evade contradiction because they reflect independent subjective experiences.[3] Didymus the Blind apparently understood Protagoras to argue for negative dogmatism: if one cannot refer to ultimate, objective truth in order to resolve perspectival conflicts, then one cannot declare anything true at all, including God.[4] By some analyses, Plato's refutation of Protagoras in the *Theaetetus* is similar, insofar as the disclosed shortcomings of his subjective empiricism could open up space for a presupposed doctrine of the Forms.[5] But Protagoras himself may not have been concerned with the metaphysical implications of his views; perhaps he instead leveraged his arguments to urge people to focus on the immanent world, to use the things their lives touch productively and to shape for the better the communities in which they live.[6] This would explain his well-attested interest in ethical and political improvement,[7] as well as his agnosticism regarding divinity (Diogenes Laertius 9.51).

Integrating early sophistic fragments into coherent philosophical systems is necessarily speculative, but if this assessment of Protagoras' ideas is credible,[8] then it seems likely that Euripides' *Helen* engages with them substantially. In this play, Euripides develops an account of Helen perhaps first put forth by Stesichorus (cf. Plato, *Phaedrus* 243a–b) and closely analogous to Helen's defense as undertaken by the Sophist Gorgias in his *Encomium*. According to Euripides, Helen is innocent of abandoning Menelaus and eloping with Paris, for Hermes hid the real Helen away in Egypt, with a divinely made simulacrum departing to Troy in her place. In Euripides' play, the existence of two identical heroines makes it difficult for characters to determine which is genuine and which counterfeit—a difficulty evident in the inability of even the messenger who viewed the simulacrum's dissolution to distinguish the authentic Helen from the false, and precisely as he recounts the latter's disappearance to the supposedly real one (605–21)![9] Helen herself encourages this confusion, by professing to feel guilt for what the simulacrum has done (52–3, 196–202 [esp. 198]) and by exhorting Menelaus to accept uncritically the evidence of his eyes when he sees her (574–82), despite the fact that she knows he has just left behind an identical replica (570–3; cf. 33–5).[10] Beyond the perplexity the simulacrum introduces, the play also features contradictory accounts of Helen's parentage (16–19) and of her brothers' deaths (137–42), as well as the same character arguing one thing (e.g., that recounting sufferings is easy and brings pleasure; 663, 665) and then, without batting an eye, precisely the opposite (recounting suffering is difficult and brings pain; 769–71).[11] Finally, cultural differences between Greek and Egyptian burial practices create confusion (798–802), which provides opportunity for deceptive persuasion (1065–6) leading to Helen and Menelaus' escape.

Scholars have observed these and other points of contact between the *Helen* and the epistemological ideas attributed to Protagoras (and other Sophists) in extant quotations and *testimonia*,[12] but in light of the fragmentary nature of the intertexts and necessarily speculative reconstructions of the underlying philosophy, interpretive confidence regarding what work Protagoras does for Euripides remains elusive. Does the *Helen* stage the failure of Protagoras' subjectivist epistemological propositions to account for the sure acquisition of knowledge—e.g., about the true Helen's identity—or, on the contrary, does it shrewdly display the erratic, tumultuous reality revealed by Protagoras' equation of truth with appearance and culturally mediated judgment, perhaps even highlighting the dangerous power of persuasion in a world wherein reality is the same as façade? Chris Willis argues that the play resists resolving the question of which "Helen" is real and which is simulated—arguably a meaningless question for Protagoras.[13] Not all will be convinced, though, and Conacher sees in the play not a sympathetic exploration of Protagoras' ideas, but their sending up.[14] For others, Euripides is using quasi-philosophical ideas for different cultural and dramatic purposes—for instance, to suggest that the constructions of feminine virtue the play seems to privilege actually amount to ideologically coercive fabrications.[15]

With Roman tragedy's philosophical engagement, we are on firmer interpretive ground. Seneca wrote at least eight of the ten Roman tragedies extant, and he was a philosopher as well as a dramatist, many of whose philosophical writings survive. In Senecan tragedy, we can discern specific philosophical ideas with certainty, and interpret the work they do in their dramatic contexts with reference to the Senecan philosophical corpus and its Stoic framework. We can also analyze the broader relationship that obtains between Seneca's imaginative dramas and his discursive philosophical prose.

Seneca's philosophy, like Roman imperial philosophy in general, is not so interested in the questions of epistemology that animated the Sophists and Plato. Perhaps this is because understanding the theoretical basis of persuasion—how to convince someone that something is true—is less urgent when public policy is determined by an absolute ruler and a small cadre of advisors than in a democracy like Athens', where any free male citizen had an opportunity to persuade the *polis* of a particular course of action. In any case, Senecan philosophy focuses on ethics and personal morality, advising readers how they should understand, evaluate, and govern their own feelings and behaviors. It features two distinct conceptions of the ethical self: one involving independence from external forces impinging on it; the other postulating the self's cosmic embeddedness, its interdependence with the external world. While these theories complement one another in the philosophical prose, in Senecan tragedy they stand in frequent tension, which can become especially severe when the tragic hero imagines or experiences his or her self being physically penetrated. Penetration serves as the key synecdochal trope by which Senecan tragedy evokes human beings' vulnerability to the external world. These vivid and visceral moments—more than displays of gory violence—become something like dialogical allegories, figuring contentious debate between the distinct self-conceptions described above.

STOIC CONCEPTIONS OF THE ETHICAL SELF

In *Epistle* 66, Seneca advances the ideal self's radical independence from all that is external to it. An imagined interlocutor asks "is there no difference between joy and unbending endurance of pain?" (66.14), to which the dominant authorial voice responds:

> None as concerns the virtues themselves; but there is a great deal of difference in the manner in which each is displayed, for in the one instance there is a natural relaxation and expansion of the mind; in the other pain, which is contrary to nature.[16]
>
> —*Ep.* 66.14

Later in the letter Seneca explains his position by identifying virtue with reason ("for virtue is nothing other than right reason. All the virtues are reasoning processes": 66.32), which forms judgments about sense perception's immediate experiences of external impingements on the self: "Sensation makes no judgment concerning goods and evils; it does not know what is useful and what is not. . . . Reason, then, is the arbiter of what is good and bad, and reason holds cheap whatever is external and not its own" (66.35).[17] The differences in virtue's appearance within radically dissimilar social and physical contexts are superficial and incidental, for virtue itself is a rational mental judgment independent of, albeit directed at, external impingements on the self that are insignificant apart from this evaluation (66.15).

For Seneca, to cultivate the self's virtue means enhancing the independence of rational judgment from external coercion. This is evident in Seneca's acceptance of one of the more controversial features of Stoic ethical theory, namely its hostility toward affective experiences that overlap with our conception of emotion, such as anger, sorrow, or desire.[18] Scholars rightly qualify this hostility by labeling the emotions Stoics reject "passions" and distinguishing them from "good" emotions, such as joy or reverence.[19] Stoics only rejected emotions that could be analyzed as affective responses based on irrational judgments. But the Stoic notion of what counts as a rational or irrational judgment was quite different from most people's "common sense" assumptions, either in antiquity or today. For the Stoics, grief and anger are always based on a misperception, since what really matters—a person's virtue—cannot be harmed by any external circumstances, even the death of a loved one or an apparently terrible humiliation.

Seneca devotes two epistles (85 and 116) and virtually the entirety of his treatise *On Anger* to explaining the opposition between external circumstances and the self. He insists in *Epistle 85*,

> If reason is of any use, then emotions [*adfectus*] will not even begin: if they begin without the acquiescence of reason, they will continue without it. It is easier to forestall their beginnings than to govern the impulse [*impetum*]. Hence the notion of "moderation" is false and of no utility.... If you grant any scope to sadness, fear, desire, and the other depraved emotions [*motibus pravis*], they will not be in our power. Why? Because the causes by which they are incited are external to us. Hence they will increase in proportion to lesser or greater stimuli.[20]
>
> —*Ep.* 85.9–11

Though Seneca can closely link emotions with externals, as he does here, they nonetheless remain an aspect of the self, stimulated by externals, to be sure, but constituting internal mental dispositions toward them, much like the virtuous judgments Seneca discusses in *Epistle* 66.35, quoted above. In *On Anger*, Seneca goes a step further in his analysis of affective response, distinguishing between emotion and "that first mental jolt," an involuntary registration of an external's minor impingement on the self.

> That first mental jolt produced by the impression of an injury is no more "anger" than the impression of injury itself. The impulse [*impetus*] that follows, which has not only taken the impression of injury but approved it, that's anger: the arousal of a mind that moves willingly and deliberately toward a goal of vengeance.[21]
>
> —*Anger* 2.3.5

Even a Stoic sage, Seneca concedes, will experience a shudder upon encountering something startling (*Anger* 2.3.3). Such responses are of no ethical consequence. Passion, on the other hand, develops through a process of false reasoning about externals that inverts virtue. Recall that virtue involves a rational judgment on external impingements that denies them significance and authority. Reason determines or even constitutes a proper mental disposition manifested with reference to externals, but fundamentally independent of them. Emotions such as anger, on the contrary, amount to irrational judgments regarding external impingements on the self that begin to grant them the persuasive authority that reason denies. They emerge when a person chooses to subordinate his or her mental dispositions to these externals' prompting. Emotions, in other words, constitute judgments on externals impinging on the self that fail to acknowledge the self's autonomy from them. They result from a false belief that the self is under the control of these externals, or perhaps fail to differentiate the self from externals to begin with—by allowing the jolting shudder occasioned by a startling encounter to engender anxiety that begins to characterize a self's actions and whole orientation to the external world. Since passions signify the self's enslavement to always impinging externalities, they must be prohibited and, if they surface, ruthlessly expurgated: "Our people [the Stoics] drive emotions out [*adfectus . . . expellunt*]" (*Ep.* 116.1).

Even as Seneca cultivates a conception of the virtuous self as rationally independent of external circumstances, he acknowledges that the judgments the rational self makes about externals are based on something that transcends that interior mental space, namely nature. Seneca articulates this understanding in *Epistle* 66:

> The material of the good is sometimes contrary to nature; but the good never is, since there is no good without reason, and reason follows nature. What, then, is reason? The imitation of nature. What is the highest good of the human being? Behaving in accordance with nature's will.[22]
>
> —*Ep.* 66.39

Nature in Stoic philosophy and ethics is a notoriously complex topic, into which it is impossible to delve deeply here. But it is important to recognize that throughout his writings, Seneca links natural law—or, more broadly, "nature" understood as an abstract standard of ethical evaluation—to the Stoic physical principles governing the universe. The connection is especially relevant to Stoic conceptions of fate, understood as a complex but still comprehensible cosmic chain of events in which seemingly independent phenomena are causally interrelated in ways theoretically accessible to rational investigation (cf. *NQ* 2.32). Seneca's analysis of nature as such a grand cosmic chain implies a significant obligation (although not an absolute one) to remain contentedly in the site wherein one has been situated by fate.

> The good man . . . will calmly tolerate anything that happens to him, for he knows that it has happened through the divine law by which all events advance. If that is the case, then in his eyes honorable conduct will be the sole good; for that includes . . . accepting one's fate with patience and acting as commanded.[23]
>
> —*Ep.* 76.23

I will have more to say about this later. Here, I merely observe that Seneca conceives of the self as at once rationally rejecting the influence of discrete external impingements, and at the same time as implicated in a grand cosmic system that transcends the self, making forceful demands on its judgments and constraining its actions from the outside, like the military discipline into which a soldier's individual actions are subsumed. While this is broadly analogous to the way nature's laws are habitually understood to constrain the self even today—e.g., one avoids stepping off a cliff because of gravity—the Stoics went beyond this conventional view to discern an ethical dimension in nature. They perceived the pressure nature exerts as moral as well as physical and pragmatic.

While the two Stoic views of the ethical self that I have delineated stand in some tension, they are successfully integrated in Seneca's philosophical writings. For instance, the good person's obligation to submit to fate in *Epistle* 76.23 complements the discussion of the ethical self's freedom from externals in *Epistle* 66: if external circumstances are ultimately insignificant, as *Epistle* 66 argues, then the self's efforts are better directed at cultivating a rational (i.e., virtuous) disposition toward them than at trying to alter or evade externals, and that is much the same thing as submitting to fate. As Brad Inwood's analysis of natural law in Seneca shows, the philosopher's elevation of suicide to a position of prominence bridges the gap between the self's radical autonomy from externals and its dependence on nature as the standard by which it rejects externals' significance. Suicide, for Seneca, is the means by which one can escape the laws of nature and the suffering they may occasion, over which one has no control but to which staying alive constitutes voluntary submission.[24]

We should note that Seneca and other Stoics regularly gendered the ethical self as male. "Virtue" (Lat. *virtus*)—the ethical quality at stake in the wise person's adoption of an attitude of independence from rather than enslavement to external circumstances—has as its root *vir*, the Latin word for "man," and can also be translated as "courage" or even "manliness." This linguistic fact is integral to understanding Seneca's philosophical discourse. For Seneca, virtuous freedom from external circumstances is an important element of masculinity. Complementarily, appropriate submission to fate is not passive acquiescence or servile submission, but rather good military order—a related manifestation of ideal manliness (cf. *Ep* 76.23).[25]

Not coincidentally, as the ethically upright Stoic sage was conceived of as masculine, so was the sexually penetrable body figured as feminine. As the Ovidian story of Caenis/Caeneus suggests, an impenetrable woman was understood to be a contradiction in terms;[26] likewise, a penetrated male could cease to be recognized as *vir* in a Roman cultural context.[27] It therefore comes as no surprise that when Seneca explores bodily penetration as a philosophically resonant trope in the tragedies, female characters such as Medea and Polyxena occupy prominent positions, especially when the penetration imagined or dramatized has a sexual component. Yet just as Senecan tragedy leverages penetration to expose and exploit tensions latent in Stoic philosophy, as I will show, it also employs the theme to complicate Roman ideologies defining and policing gender. It is significant that Medea, in a passage whose philosophical implications I will explore, imagines sexually penetrating herself at precisely the moment she gloats over her husband in a violent victory that, from a Stoic philosophical perspective at least, turns out to be self-defeating. Similarly, the self-penetration Thyestes proposes as a response to being duped and dominated by his brother Atreus may be interpreted as subversively reconfiguring conception and childbirth. Though the limited scope of this essay prevents me from addressing in a sustained way the gendered dynamics of such scenes, I want to signal their presence in the Senecan corpus and invite readers to explore them on their own, in the service of complicating the philosophically engaged interpretations I present or of generating new readings altogether.

Senecan tragedy employs the trope of corporeal penetration philosophically to explore the possibility that the two conceptions of the ethical self featured in the discursive prose might destructively collide, or else pull the self in violently opposing directions so as to damage it beyond repair. In what follows, I consider examples of tragic characters' embodied selves being breached by the external world, or of characters attempting to extirpate from themselves external invaders of their corporeal space. These figures of destructive confrontation between the interior self and the exterior world—images of penetration proposed, attempted, effected, resisted, or overcome—stand in suggestive and contentious intertextual relationships to the philosophical writings, pressing questions about the costs and viability of key aspects of the Stoic ethical system, including emotional expurgation (*Medea* and *Thyestes*), suicide as a means of liberation from passionate suffering (*Troades*), and the self's alignment with nature (*Oedipus*).

MEDEA AND *THYESTES*

In a provocative interpretation of the *Medea* against the backdrop of ancient Stoicism, which has influenced my understanding of the figure of corporeal penetration throughout Senecan tragedy, Martha Nussbaum argues that "Medea's emotions—love, grief, anger—fundamentally involve the assignment of high value to external objects and situations," foremost among which is Jason and her marriage.[28] From the moment he comes to Colchis, Seneca's Medea says she has acted entirely in Jason's interests, and repeatedly recalls all that she has abandoned or destroyed for his sake: "my fatherland gave way to you; father, brother, modesty as well. / This was the dowry I married with. Give the fugitive back what is hers!" (488–9).[29] Medea is ravaged by disappointed love, wrath, and sorrow when Jason abandons her for a new wife. As the play draws to its close and she determines to act on the wrath into which her love for Jason has devolved, she kills their children (Figure 4.1).

FIGURE 4.1: Roman fresco from Pompeii, depicting Medea planning the murder of her children as they play a game of knucklebones, *c.* first century CE. Museo Archeologico Nazionale di Napoli, Naples, Italy. Photo by Marie-Lan Nguyen. Courtesy of Wikimedia.

This is more than revenge. Seneca's Medea seeks to regain what she has given up for love. In a speech she makes to Jason after killing their first child, she reclaims what she had earlier yielded:

> Now, now I have regained my throne, my brother, and my father.
> The Colchians keep the treasure of the Golden Ram.
> My kingdom comes back to me, my stolen virginity returns.[30]
>
> —Medea 982–4

Medea murders her children to nullify her relationship with Jason and cancel out all she has experienced as its result, including her loss of virginity. This explains why she forcefully disowns her offspring ("I disown, forswear, repudiate them!"; 507) at the same time as she insists that Jason take responsibility for the crimes she had committed: "They are yours, yours! The one whom a crime benefits / has committed it" (500–1).[31] In Medea's fantasy, eliminating evidence of her love for Jason will restore her integrity, ethical as well as corporeal. In killing their children, she hopes not only to restore her physical integrity (virginity), but also her religious purity and perhaps even her moral probity, for she aims to make amends for the murder of her brother by sacrificing those whom she most loves: "Leave me to myself and use this hand, my brother, / which has drawn the sword: we appease your spirit now, / with this sacrificial victim" (969–71).[32]

That Medea's infanticide aims at restoring the integrity violated by the love that had so calamitously gained entrance explains why she recalls her children's origin within her womb at the same time as she finally determines to destroy them (954–7). A few lines later, Medea actually imagines burrowing into her womb: "if some love pledge [*pignus*] is hiding even now in my mothering body, / I shall probe my innards with a blade and extricate it with a sword" (1012–13).[33] Medea kills her children in order to eliminate all evidence of her love for Jason, and discursively locates them within her body, so that her act of infanticide becomes a self-administered abortion. Nussbaum perceptively interprets this troubling image with reference to the Stoic urge to extirpate emotions: Medea hopes that her own imagined self-penetration, "ridding her body of love's tumorlike growth, will restore her to the health of self-sufficiency."[34] Her analysis brings to mind a vivid passage from the *Consolation to Marcia*, where Seneca compares the expurgation of Marcia's grief for a deceased child to a physician reopening, probing, and cauterizing an infected wound:

> I should have wished to begin treating your grief in its earliest stages. . . . This is also true of wounds: while they are still freshly inflicted and bloody, they can be easily treated; the time when they are subjected to cautery and opened up to the bottom and investigated by probing fingers is when they have turned septic and become dangerous sores.[35]
>
> —Marcia 1.8

Lines 1012–13 constitute an extension of this sort of violent medical imagery, disturbingly applied to a potentially life-bringing pregnancy rather than to a dangerously infected wound.

Medea's plan is obviously immoral, insofar as it sacrifices innocent lives in order to restore the integrity of the violated. Beyond that, it may be imaginatively incoherent, at least as a figure of Stoic emotional expurgation. Medea twice calls the children she will destroy "pledges" (*pignora*) of her and Jason's love (145, 1012). A pledge is by definition a token, an evident sign guaranteeing something that it would otherwise be difficult to trust, and the term was conventionally used of children as a guarantee of marital love.[36]

But from a Stoic perspective, Medea's problem is precisely the internal reality to which the external sign can only testify, namely the love resulting from Jason's psychical penetration of her and the extremely high value she has irrationally assigned to their relationship. Medea can no more expurgate this love by destroying its sign than one can remedy a wound by burning its bandage. She imagines the children inside herself, but she needs to address something hidden even deeper within—namely her feelings for Jason, which cannot be extricated with a sword, no matter how deeply it cuts.

One might object that this places too much pressure on Seneca's attempt to figure in vivid tragic language a Stoic idea familiar from the philosophical prose, namely that the only way one can restore integrity violated by passion is to expurgate all internal traces of it. But even granting the broad figurative coherence of Medea's proposal, conceptual problems remain, for in the play's symbolic economy Seneca's Medea aims to restore her "stolen virginity" (984) and undo her marriage (986) by penetrating her womb with a sword (1012–13)—a self-evidently absurd plan, as well as a gross one. Stoic ethics may promise something just as absurd, and hardly less disturbing. Aggressive policing of the self is required to maintain its inviolability, and only radical surgical intervention can restore the self once it has been emotionally penetrated. All this violence may not only fail to address the underlying problem, but may in addition violate the self's integrity no less injuriously than the original invasion.[37] The treatment might be worse than the disease.

Though they resonate with Stoic arguments urging emotional expulsion as a way to preserve the integrity of the self, Medea's fantasies about undoing her marriage, restoring her virginity, and atoning for her crimes by infanticide reveal themselves to be incoherent, with her final speech succinctly acknowledging that the violent expurgatory actions she takes fail to restore her physical or ethical integrity. Immediately after she kills her second son, Medea identifies herself not as a newly restored virgin, nor as a faithful daughter or filial sister, but rather as precisely Jason's wife, fleeing from Corinth as a murderer just as she had earlier fled from Colchis and Iolcus after having betrayed her family and committed murder on his behalf: "Ungrateful Jason, do you recognize your wife? / This is the way I always leave a country" (1021–2).[38] The failure is especially poignant, for Medea does manage a kind of restoration, though not of her integrity; ironically, she has returned only to the moment her passionate violence began.

A similar figurative complex surfaces in Seneca's *Thyestes*, where the titular character's son Tantalus urges his father's assent to the value of externals such as power and ease. As Thyestes ponders whether to remain content with his rustic existence as an exile or to accept the invitation Atreus offers him to return to Argos' luxury (404–28), Tantalus urges reconciliation with Atreus and a return home (429–90). Thyestes, against his better judgment, accepts his advice (488–9), and soon he is gorging on a lavish banquet Atreus has thrown, which unbeknownst to him includes his sons, slaughtered by Atreus. At the meal's conclusion, Thyestes cries "What is this turmoil that shakes my guts? / What trembles inside me? I feel a restless burden, / and my breast groans with a groaning not my own" (999–1001).[39] Dramatizing the logic of Stoic ethical psychology, Tantalus' voice, which had persuasively demanded that Thyestes highly value Argos and all it offers, literally comes to be located within Thyestes after he assents by entering the city and partaking in its indulgences.

Thyestes' response to the desire for external objects that has taken root within him upon irrational assent to their value is to attempt extirpation. The impulse to expel desire is figured by Thyestes' plan to penetrate his body and extricate his sons' remains: "The blade must give my children a path. / You refuse the sword? Let me batter my chest / smash resounding blows against it" (1044–6).⁴⁰ The frantic, hyperbolic image of a father gouging his gut or smashing open his torso to access his sons' consumed bodies rapidly gives way to an even more extreme image of corporeal penetration in Thyestes' prayer to Jupiter:

> Let your trident pierce
> my chest with fire. If I want to bury my sons
> as father and cremate them with due rites,
> then I myself must burn.⁴¹
>
> —*Thyestes* 1089–92

Against the backdrop of Seneca's discursive prose, which figures such violence as psychically beneficial surgery and cauterization, the imagined corporeal expurgations in this play come into relief as symbols of the impossibility of expelling emotion. As Thyestes' prayer to Jupiter admits, Tantalus and the gratified desire he represented cannot be expelled from Thyestes without Thyestes' own incineration.

TROADES

The *Troades* too contains an image of penetration that materializes and implicitly interrogates Stoic conceptions of the self's deliverance from passion occasioned by violent external impingements, but it resonates with a different ethical concern: the self's willingness to embrace death as a last resort for maintaining its autonomy from passion.

The deaths of Astyanax and Polyxena at the end of the *Troades* resemble the exemplary suicides Seneca rhetorically showcases throughout the philosophical prose.⁴² While Polyxena does not technically kill herself, as does her nephew (1102–3), various details assimilate her willing destruction to Seneca's famous depiction of his hero Cato's suicide in *On Providence* 2.9–12, including the specific method of her demise (a sword thrust, 1155–7), the emphatic theatricality of its report (esp. *theatri more*, 1125; cf. 1123–9), and the suggestion that her death constitutes resistance to political oppressors (1157–9). It is especially important that Polyxena is bolder in confronting death than Pyrrhus is in killing her (1151–9) and that she shows herself happy to die from the moment she learns of her impending sacrifice to Achilles' shade (945–8):⁴³

> See! Her great soul is glad to hear of her death.
> She wants the fancy royal clothes, and lets
> the hand comb through her hair. She used to think
> the marriage death; now she thinks death is marriage.⁴⁴
>
> —*Troades* 945–8

Polyxena's joyful response to learning she will die assimilates her death to a marriage, as does the fact that her sacrifice on Achilles' tomb is carried out "so that [Achilles] may be a bridegroom in the Elysian fields" (944).⁴⁵ Polyxena's initial response naturally leads to her death's eroticization, with her modesty and physical beauty impressing the observers as she walks to the site of her execution (1137–47), like a bride processing to her groom's home on a wedding night: "The whole crowd was astounded. . . . / Some notice her beauty, / others her youth" (1143–5).⁴⁶ The imagery of violent physical penetration with which Seneca describes Polyxena's death alludes to Lucretius' famous depiction of sex in *On the Nature of Things* (compare 1155–9 and Lucretius 4.1049–57), but even for a reader unfamiliar with that intertext, it is not difficult to see how the image of Pyrrhus driving his sword deep into Polyxena's body, leading to a sudden burst of blood from the wound and the bride's collapse upon her bridegroom, perversely evokes the experience of a bride on her wedding night. Thus, while Seneca assimilates Polyxena's death to an idealized Stoic suicide, in particular his hero Cato's, he at the same time presents her death as a violent erotic encounter.

Seneca's conflation of Polyxena's death with her wedding develops a well-known tragic trope,[47] and it provides an obvious way to express her desperation. Yet Polyxena's passion for her death/union with the dead Achilles remains shocking. As she is penetrated, she collapses upon her groom, not with love or desire for her beloved Hector's killer, but with an emotion no less intense: "she fell face down with furious impulse [*impetu*] / as if to burden the earth that buries Achilles" (1158–9).[48] This final burst of passion complicates any interpretation of Polyxena's self-willed death against the Stoic philosophical background that Seneca's presentation of her elsewhere invokes.

In *On Anger*, Seneca denies that fury or rage is an acceptable response to any circumstance at all, even to one as extreme as a man witnessing his father being murdered, his mother raped (1.12.1–2), or his sons slaughtered and served to their father on a platter by tyrants (3.14–15). Although Seneca acknowledges that acts of defense and vengeance may be called for in such situations, he insists they be pursued because they are reasonable and not out of angry grievance (1.12.2). Yet while Seneca resists rage, he is also disgusted by attempts to hide it in the cause of submission to or rapprochement with unjust political authority oppressing oneself or one's familiars (3.15.1–3). Some situations, Seneca seems to acknowledge, are genuinely enraging, though rage is not available as a response to the wise person whose rational disposition is determined independently of them.

Seneca resolves this problem by invoking suicide: if an oppressed self cannot avoid a supplementary internal victimization at the hands of *ira*, if it risks enslavement to grievous passions in connection with what amounts to primary enslavement to tyrannical forces, then self-destruction is an appropriate option (3.15.4). In these situations, Seneca has a strong imaginative preference for physical self-penetration. Not only is this the method Cato employed when confronted with such slavery, but, after surveying a number of ways in which one might bring one's life to an end in order to avoid suffering from wrath, Seneca himself asks in *On Anger*, "Do you ask what path leads to freedom? Any vein in your body" (3.15.4).[49]

If Polyxena were a proper Stoic sage, her self-willed death should be a means of liberating herself not only from the external oppression of the Greek army that has enslaved her people, but also from her own psychically destructive emotions. Yet as she collapses on her groom Achilles' body, his grave thirstily consumes her blood (1162–4), which imaginatively suggests that Polyxena's death has not actually freed her from slavery to her Greek captors, but on the contrary has prolonged her enslavement to them. As I have elsewhere argued, the *Troades* explores a number of competing visions of what happens to the self upon death that line up with various views Seneca presents at one point or another throughout the philosophical prose, including annihilation (e.g., 371–408) and a postmortem existence in Hades—perhaps a happy one (142–63, on Priam), but more often disconsolate (190–4, on angry Achilles; 448–50, on wretched Hector).[50] Other characters in the play report seeing Achilles' (168–202) woeful shade, and it is supposedly at the will of dead Achilles (195–6) as much as at her own that Polyxena dies. All of this suggests that Polyxena is condemned by her death to precisely the kind of forced marriage with a Greek captor she dies in order to avoid. Even more importantly, since she dies consumed by the angry grief she should by dying avoid (*irato impetu*,

1159), Polyxena's self-willed death consummates her passion rather than extirpating it. Her passionate death challenges a notion that Seneca articulates throughout the discursive prose, namely that one can readily be freed from passion, if not initially through self-control (*Epistle* 116.1), then secondarily through emotional expurgation (*Consolation to Marcia* 1.1), or, as a last resort, by embracing a liberating death (*Anger* 3.15.4). Polyxena's death entails neither emotional expurgation nor liberation; on the contrary, it incinerates her in a conflagration of passion, and it may as well extend into an attenuated afterlife her self's enslavement to Achilles and the passion he provokes.

OEDIPUS

In gouging out his eyes, Oedipus—like Medea imagining her self-administered abortion—figures a failed attempt at repudiating destructive passions. But in other ways his gruesome self-penetration more closely resembles Polyxena's. Like that heroine's self-willed demise, Oedipus' de-oculation concedes violability in the face of external impingements. Through it, Oedipus makes a desperate but arguably futile attempt to salvage his rational autonomy, even while acknowledging his embeddedness within a cosmic context (*natura*) that influences, if not determines, his destiny.[51]

Oedipus' self-blinding represents the culmination of a rational process. He thinks at first, impetuously, of killing himself, but then recognizes that death would not be an appropriate punishment for his crimes (915–42). He proceeds to deliberate about what retribution his unique transgressions deserve, offering various reasons for avoiding one punishment or another (942–51).[52] In this context, Oedipus' decision to blind himself makes a good deal of sense (952–64), as I will show. Thus, Oedipus does not so much wildly rip out his eyes—although there is ferocity in the deed—as meticulously and thoroughly remove every bit of ocular tissue from the sockets (see 965–70), showing the same careful determination in carrying out his punishment that he demonstrates in choosing it.

The punishment Oedipus selects is appropriate for a variety of reasons, many of which have to do with the play's thematization of natural portents. Oedipus has been confronted with these again and again throughout the tragedy. They frequently signify his guilt, which must be expiated in order for Thebes to be saved, yet the hero never interprets them correctly. For instance, the plague, which constitutes a physical effect of Oedipus' transgression on the natural cosmos, registers the familial confusion resulting from the hero's incest with various examples of unnatural familial conflation in the destruction it brings (e.g., the ashes of sons and fathers mingle in a single cremation, 52–70, cf. 872–5).[53] Yet Oedipus never suspects that this points to his own "wretched ties of kinship" (19) fulfilled in his own destructive conflation with his father in the bed of his mother. His blindness persists despite the fact that he knows he has been prophesied to commit these crimes (see 15–26) and doubts himself accordingly: "I am afraid of everything, I do not trust myself" (27).[54] Fearful self-doubt originating in this prophecy is a central characteristic Seneca's Oedipus displays, and it likely would have surprised the original audience, for Oedipus from Sophocles' famous tragedy was characterized not by trepidation, but by the kind of self-confidence bordering on hubris that commonly leads to Greek tragic heroes' destruction.

For Seneca's Oedipus, though, the plague and its disastrous effects constitute not a challenge for his impressive intellect, but dreadful circumstances he would rather flee than comprehend—perhaps because he unconsciously fears that he is responsible for them (e.g., 77–81). The same might be said of the *extispicium* (inspection of animal innards for purposes of divination) that Oedipus orders to discover the party responsible for Laius' murder, in which the beasts' entrails register in an almost woodenly allegorical manner Oedipus' transgressions and the future transgressions springing from them (299–392).[55] In the face of these dreadful portents, Oedipus struggles to maintain his composure (384–6), as Tiresias concludes from what little even he understands that Oedipus "will envy these troubles for which [he] now seek[s] help" (388).[56] Oedipus confronts portents in nature all throughout the play, but never succeeds in interpreting them rationally. Paralyzing terror is his dominant response, to which he either succumbs, as in the play's opening lines (15–27), or, at best, barely manages to hold up under, as in the passage cited just above (384–6).

Oedipus' self-blinding in part represents an attempt to free himself from this debilitating fear. He thinks of removing his eyes immediately after he senses himself weeping (954–5), which implies that his chosen punishment repudiates the despairing fear that has characterized his response to natural portents throughout the play. Moreover, immediately after Oedipus removes his eyes, "he lifts his head, / scanning the vault of heaven with empty sockets, / testing his new night" (971–3).[57] This image recalls the beginning of the *Natural Questions*, where Seneca insists that natural philosophy "is not satisfied with the eyes; it suspects that there is something greater and more beautiful that nature has placed beyond its sight" (1 praef. 1).[58] Elsewhere in that preface, Seneca elaborates on the mind's ability to occupy the inaccessible heavenly regions so that it can study the stars (NQ 1 praef. 11–12), which a later passage of the treatise (2.32) identifies as natural portents alongside birds and animal entrails. In a related vein, Seneca in book 6 speculates about why people view nature with fear, and understand themselves at the mercy of arbitrary gods who punish out of wrath (NQ 6.3.1):

> Because we grasp nature with our eyes, not with reason, and we do not consider what nature can do but only what it has done. So we are punished for this carelessness when we are terrified as if by something new, when it is not new but unusual.[59]
>
> —NQ 6.3.2

Against this philosophical backdrop, Oedipus' self-blinding and subsequent gaze at the night sky may be interpreted as an admission that he had been unable to comprehend the terrifying natural portents he has seen, and for that reason found himself debilitated by the anguished terror to which they initially gave rise. By violently removing his eyes and looking up toward the sky, he signals his readiness to examine the portentous heavens with reason alone and discover their true causes, precisely as Seneca Philosophus advises.

The potentially frightful natural phenomena whose rational understanding Seneca advocates in the *Natural Questions* were understood by the Stoics to include portents such as the bovine entrails that Tiresias and Manto examine:

> Birds do not move in order to be seen by us, yet they produce favorable or unfavorable auspices. . . . Those things are just as much the results of divine agency if birds' wings are not guided by god, and the entrails of cattle are not formed under the very axe. By another rationale does the sequence of fated events unfold, sending out signs of the future at every point, some of them familiar to us, some unknown. Everything that happens is a sign of some future event. . . . The orderly series to which a thing belongs is also its means of prediction.[60]
>
> —NQ 2.32.3–4

The entire natural cosmos is systematically structured, so that all phenomena are perspicuous to rational inquiry insofar as all exist in casual relationships with other phenomena, even if a particular secondary phenomenon's cause is not self-evident and it is therefore superficially astounding—as in the disordered bovine innards that Tiresias and Manto inspect, and the Theban plague itself.[61] Since the signifying power of omens is not arbitrarily divine, but cogently emerges from their situation in a grand, God-infused causal structure, the appropriate response to the mysteries they present is not passionate terror but thorough rational inquiry into their location within this complex causal scheme.[62] As Seneca goes on to declare, "There is no living creature that does not foretell something by its movement and by an encounter with us. But, to be sure, not everything gets noticed" (NQ 2.32.5).[63]

Though rife with images of nature out of order, Seneca's tragedy confirms the Stoic view of the cosmos as a grand, causally ordered structure, for nature insistently registers Oedipus' crimes throughout the play, with the portentous plague and animal entrails constituting effects clearly signifying their original causes (e.g., the virgin heifer's perverse fetus recalls Jocasta's children of incest with Oedipus; cf. 373–5), and at the same time pointing to future effects of those causes (e.g., certain distortions in the animals entrails predict the war between Oedipus' sons over the kingship of Thebes, 358–64).[64] Oedipus cannot unravel this bewilderingly complex "sequence of fated events" (NQ 2.32.4), for he always responds with confused dread and incapacitating depression rather than with effective inquiry into the omens' portentous regularity. His self-blinding, in the symbolic economy suggested by the *Natural Questions*, signals a repudiation of not only his fear, but also his attempts at analysis and interpretation as superficial and inadequate. By gouging out his eyes, Oedipus eliminates both his weeping and his sight, metaphorically extirpating passionate terror and at the same time committing himself to the more vigorous rational analysis of apparent (but not genuine) anomalies in nature—analysis that the *Natural Questions* figures as a privileging of the mind over sight, of reason over terror.[65]

Oedipus' cry to the gods as he "scans the vault of heaven with empty sockets, / testing his new night" (972–3) is, then, both a prayer and a certain expectation on the basis of a rational conclusion he draws regarding the expiatory implications of his self-blinding. Though he cannot observe them, Oedipus infers and boldly expects that portentous signs in the sky will register his sins' just expiation. Thus, he cries:

> Now spare my homeland, I implore you!
> Now I have done right, I have accepted my proper punishment.
> I found at last a night appropriate for my marriage.[66]
>
> —*Oedipus* 975–7

While Oedipus' self-inflicted blinding does in discrete ways answer for Oedipus' initial crimes (see, e.g., 977, and perhaps 939–40), these crimes were fated and he arguably had limited control over them.[67] Much more significant is how it addresses and attempts to remediate Oedipus' inappropriate response of fear and debilitating depression about the portents with which his crimes are linked in the cosmic chain, as well as his failure rationally to discern the fated sequence's signifying structure. Oedipus' self-blinding carefully poises him between the two complementary impulses that animate the ethical self in Seneca's philosophy: a drive for autonomy from the irrational emotions (debilitating fear) occasioned by external impingements on the self (natural portents), and acknowledgment of the self's embeddedness within the natural cosmos, which makes rationally discernable and morally binding claims on it from the outside.

Yet Oedipus' position here is far from stable. Despite the rational deliberation the hero demonstrates in choosing to remove his eyes, and the thorough care with which he rips them out, Oedipus' self-blinding is still furious (see, e.g., 957). Joe Park Poe captures the odd admixture of rationality and rage in the self-blinding with the incongruity "reasoning mania."[68] As in the *Troades*, so in the *Oedipus*, rage disrupts the philosophical resonance of the violence that the self willingly suffers.[69] Viewing Oedipus' self-blinding against the *Natural Questions*' discursive background, one might think that Oedipus' self-blinding would sharpen his discernment of natural order in the animal entrails and other regular natural portents. But in the play, self-blinding actually assimilates Oedipus to Tiresias, the blind *haruspex* on whom the hero relies for help interpreting the *extispicium*. Tiresias is hardly a more effective interpreter than the sighted Oedipus, and is no less fearful an investigator (see 328–30, 351). In this light, Oedipus' cry to the gods, which accompanies his sightless scan of the heavens in 974–8, may be interpreted as a frantic, superstitious response to his circumstances, such as those that Seneca disparages in the *Natural Questions* (6.3.1–2). Oedipus may presume that the gods arbitrarily dispense wrath, instead of overseeing a natural causal order in which effects follow causes in a rationally discernable way. Indeed, if one emphasizes his prayer to the gods (*precor*, 975) rather than

FIGURE 4.2: Hellenistic, Megarian pottery relief in the form of a bearded blind man, possibly Oedipus, *c.* 300–100 BCE. British Museum, London, 1856,1004.148. © The Trustees of the British Museum. All rights reserved.

his cry of triumph (974–5), Oedipus seems to plead with them to display evidence that their wrath has somehow been placated by his desperate, bloody deed. Since this is precisely the sort of religious superstition blind Tiresias showed while futilely evaluating the innards (see esp. 330–4), by gouging out his eyes Oedipus may be doubling down on his terrified failure to discern causal order and rationality in the cosmos, rather than repudiating it. Instead of examining nature with increasing rationality, he may be fearfully refusing to look at all.

This ambiguity raises a related philosophical question implicit in Seneca's tragedy: if one really is embedded within the natural cosmos in the way Stoics believed, and if one's actions are in some way determined by their location in a cosmic causal chain, does it matter whether or not one acknowledges this embeddedness? Would not ignorance and discernment be interchangeable, since fate necessarily implies the self's lack of autonomy?[70] That possibility occupies a central position in the Oedipus myth Seneca adopts, according to which the hero's cautious response to a prophetic warning results in precisely his fulfillment of the prophecy he sought to avoid. While by gouging out his eyes and forcing himself to rely solely on reason instead of sense perception, Seneca's Oedipus comes to resemble the ideal investigator from the *Natural Questions*, he by the very same deed is assimilated to the failed and frightened *haruspex* Tiresias. His self-blinding thus constitutes either an admission of his inability and refusal to discern what he needed to see or—surely more troubling—a declaration that sight and blindness, insight and ignorance do not meaningfully differ in a world in which the self's actions are not finally in its control.

TRAGEDY AS PHILOSOPHICAL DIALOGUE

My analysis of discrete scenes and images from Seneca's plays suggests that a comprehensive understanding of Senecan tragedy's relationship with Senecan philosophy must come to terms with both correspondences and tensions between them. Scholars have proposed several interpretive models that attempt this. For instance, Gordon Braden views Senecan Stoicism as "one manifestation of drives that, swerving in another direction, lead to the rage of Seneca's [tragic] madmen."[71] The solipsism inherent in the self's valuing of its own virtue over all things external to it in the philosophical prose surprisingly manifests itself in tragic villains like the *Thyestes'* Atreus, with his drive to conquer all external threats to his own self's integrity, both real and imagined, and whose rhetoric encompasses the dissolution of the cosmos external to the self. Alternatively, David Wray understands the passionate insanity Seneca's tragic characters vocalize in a way that complements and advances Stoic philosophy's therapeutic goal of eradicating passion: "Until I hear Medea's voice singing . . ., my soul cannot be satisfied that when the Stoic philosopher reasons about *ira* ["anger"], that signifier adequately represents everything that the passion of anger has ever felt like to anyone in its thrall."[72]

Wray's analysis implies a dialogic approach to the Senecan literary corpus that seems to me hermeneutically productive, though requiring modification.[73] Seneca's philosophical writings habitually introduce imagined interlocutors that rhetorically challenge the dominant authorial voice, forcing it to confront important questions. Sometimes, the voices Seneca Philosophus introduces make compelling cases. In *Epistle* 116.2, for instance, an imagined interlocutor resists Seneca's argument in favor of extirpating emotion by urgently pleading, "It's natural for me to suffer torment because of ardent desire for a friend. Allow my justified tears the right to fall!"[74] The interlocutive voice suggests that Seneca's ethical advice does not enhance but rather assault its humanity. Nonetheless, while Seneca Philosophus gives opposing views their say and sometimes allows them to speak with affective eloquence, he always allows his dominant authorial voice to have the final word. In fact, the "interlocutors" tend to raise precisely the problems that Seneca aims to resolve, and they raise them in ways amenable to the solutions Seneca presents.

In Senecan tragedy, this dialogue continues, but the interlocutors become far more determined interrogators of Seneca's Stoic philosophy. For example, Medea does not merely insist that it is natural for her to suffer because of love of another, as does the interlocutive voice from *Epistle* 116, but demonstrates that an attempt to remediate such suffering by emotional extirpation will actually damage the self (and others as well) more severely than the original external impingement and the passionate attachments her love occasioned. Seneca's *Medea* does not vividly present a problem that Seneca's philosophy solves (*pace* Nussbaum, at times). Although she stands in continuity with the imagined interlocutor from *Epistle* 116, Medea cannot be reduced to that voice. On the contrary, the *Medea* imaginatively wrestles with Senecan philosophy, pointing to a problem with the solution Seneca offered to the problem the epistle's interlocutor posed. Senecan tragedy pursues the same sort of dialogical questioning that the philosophical writings habitually feature, but with increased intensity, persistence, and imagination.

If Senecan tragedy gives the interlocutive voices from the philosophical prose a wider scope in which to pursue their questioning of Stoic philosophy, then one might ask how Senecan drama tends to make use of that opportunity. Frequently, Senecan tragedy materializes Stoic ethical precepts. That is, if Seneca Philosophus urges emotional expurgation, as in the *Consolation to Marcia* and elsewhere, then Medea, for instance, disturbingly and incoherently contemplates penetrating herself to extirpate a fetus to restore the self-integrity violated by her and her husband's mutual love. If he urges self-willed death as a means of escape from suffering occasioned by otherwise unavoidable passion, as in *On Anger*, then the *Troades*' Polyxena dramatizes that sort of death so as to call into question its ability to deliver what was promised. Or if Seneca Philosophus privileges evidence inferred from rational inquiry into nature over the senses' sometimes terrifying perceptions of ominous natural phenomena, as in the *Natural Questions*, then Oedipus' self-blinding implicitly questions to what extent such an epistemological strategy really can remediate fearful confusion.

In this dialogic interpretive context, the tragic images of penetration and self-mutilation which I have explored make an important point about Seneca's philosophy. As the imagined interlocutor in *Epistle* 116.2 suggests, Seneca's Stoic ethical project seems aimed at separating people from things that many intuitively believe are essential to their humanity: especially passionate emotion, but also reliance on sense perception—even an attachment to life itself! That tragic characters who figure or materialize Stoic ethical doctrine frequently become, or threaten to become, mutilated or disfigured furthers this suggestion, implying that Seneca's philosophy will not so much make people superior human beings as it will make them other (less? more?) than human.[75] One may become better than one was before embracing Stoicism (arguably, Oedipus), or one may become worse (Medea), or one may even cease to exist at all (perhaps Polyxena)—but is one who sincerely attempts to live according to Stoic ethical precepts an authentic, fully functioning human being? This seems to me the most pressing question the dramatic scenarios and characters I have considered above raise about Senecan philosophy. Significantly, it is a question familiar from the philosophical writing itself, though articulated there with nothing approaching the urgency, let alone the imaginative vividness, of Senecan tragedy.

CHAPTER FIVE

Religion, Ritual and Myth

ISABELLE TORRANCE

Athenian tragedy developed within a ritual context: an annual spring festival in honor of the god Dionysus. This festival was attended by thousands of Athenian citizens, and was open to non-citizen residents and visitors from around the Greek world.[1] The extant tragedies of Aeschylus, Sophocles, and Euripides share a broad preoccupation with the relationship of humans and the divine. Tragedy sometimes shows divine will working in tandem with unwise or unknowing human actions to bring about destruction; sometimes, the gods intervene to assist human characters and to provide benefits for the community at large. Tragedy often echoes and distorts the norms of Greek ritual practice for theatrical effect. There are also some differences in the details of the ways each of the three major Greek tragedians treats religious issues. Both Aeschylus and Sophocles tend to characterize the divine by a particular inscrutability. The action in plays such as Aeschylus' *Persians* and Sophocles' *Oedipus Tyrannos* is driven by (mostly nameless) "gods," or oracles and prophecies, whose meaning is unclear to the human characters. All three tragedians bring gods onstage at times (for instance, Aeschylus' *Eumenides*, Sophocles' *Ajax* and *Philoctetes*, or Euripides' *Bacchae*); but Euripides includes gods onstage most frequently. All three tragedians include divinities at the end of certain plays, and have them prescribe the foundation of some form of commemorative ritual worship; these aetiologies, as they are called, serve as an explanation (*aition*) for a recognized form of contemporary worship and link the mythological past to the Athenian present. Euripides uses the device most frequently. Most strikingly, characters in Euripides sometimes reject traditional beliefs in the anthropomorphic gods and propose highly intellectualized rational alternatives—even in plays which also feature anthropomorphic gods as characters (such as *Trojan Women* or *Heracles*).

Roman tragedy may also have had religious or ritual origins. According to Livy (7.2.3–13), the Romans instituted theatrical shows to appease the gods during difficult times, and the *fabula praetexta*, an early form of historical drama and a precursor to surviving Roman tragedy, was likely produced in a religious context. The official shows (*ludi*) at which dramatic performances took place in early Rome were held in honor of various divine patrons.[2] However, our only surviving Roman tragedies, which are from a much later period, written by Seneca, were certainly not produced at a religious festival. We know frustratingly little about their performance contexts.[3] The discussion of Senecan tragedy here will therefore not include speculation on the staging of religious rituals. It is clear from Seneca's dramas that aspects of Roman religion, particularly sacrifice and augury, are important to his tragic world. The gruesome violence of his dramas reflects the violent and dangerous period of Roman history during which he lived in the first century CE, under the emperors Tiberius, Caligula, Claudius, and Nero. Seneca was closely associated with Stoicism, and the diseased natural world in his tragedies seems to provide a dark counterpart to the concept of Nature as a divine force in Stoic thought. Stoicism advises the elimination of one's "passions" (emotions based on false ideas about the world). In Senecan tragedy, the passions are dangerously unleashed, and natural phenomena respond with alarming aberrations. The anthropomorphic gods are far more distant than in Greek tragedy, while the forces of the Underworld play a more significant role. Any connection between the world of mythology and that of contemporary Rome comes not through religious aetiologies of any kind, but through the implication that Rome's increasingly corrupt emperors should consider the fate of figures like Hercules who is laid low as he strives to conquer heaven (in *Hercules*).

ATHENIAN TRAGEDY

Aristotle in his *Poetics* (1449a9) suggests that tragedy developed from the dithyramb, a choral song and dance performed by men or boys in honor of Dionysus, and most scholars trace the origins of Athenian tragedy to ritual contexts involving the worship of Dionysus.[4] Certainly, by the fifth century BCE, Dionysus was the patron god of the dramatic festivals

FIGURE 5.1: Attic wine vessel depicting Pompe, the female personification of a procession, between Eros and Dionysos. This likely represents the Anthesteria festival, in which a sacred marriage took place between the god and the wife of the archon basileus, a high official who represented ancient Athenian kings, *c*. mid-fourth century BCE. The Metropolitan Museum of Art, NY, 25.190.

at Athens. The Great or City Dionysia was the most significant of these, and it lasted several days. Immediately preceding the festival, a procession took place commemorating the first arrival of the god Dionysus to Athens. The cult statue was taken from the temple on the southern slope of the Acropolis to a grove outside the city where hymns were sung and sacrifices made in honor of the god. Once these proceedings had concluded, the statue was returned to the theater with a torch-lit parade. A second procession opened the official festival and included representatives from different categories of Athenian life carrying provisions for the sacrifice and feast. It was led by a virgin of aristocratic background holding a golden basket with sacrificial offerings. Male citizens carried wine and bread. Metics (resident aliens) also carried provisions and their daughters carried water jugs. Ephebes (young men of military age) led a bull, which was the main sacrificial animal. Groups of men sang hymns and carried large phalluses, indicative of Dionysus' fertility.

Dithyrambic competitions were held, with each of the ten tribes of Athens supplying choruses of fifty men and fifty boys. The competitive dramatic performances followed over the course of several days. These were preceded by the ritual purification of the theater and a libation of wine offered by the ten generals of Athens. Several ceremonial actions of civic importance also took place, including the naming of distinguished citizens and benefactors, the display of tribute sent to Athens by allied states, and the honoring of war orphans.[5]

Although tragedy was performed at a festival in honor of Dionysus, and religious themes are of central importance to the genre, some scholars have questioned the extent to which Dionysiac worship was significant for actually experiencing tragedy.[6] Attending the festival was not in itself an act of worship. Nevertheless, it remains incontestable that all Greek tragedy is saturated with references to religious language and ritual.[7] Moreover, the importance of Dionysus was reasserted in the satyr drama that followed each tragic trilogy. This type of play, of which Euripides' *Cyclops* is the only surviving example, was characterized by a chorus of satyrs (half man, half horse, in the classical period) who are in the service of the god Dionysus.[8]

Abnormal sacrifices

Several Greek tragedies present horrifying distortions of normal sacrificial practice where the cultural language and imagery of animal sacrifice is applied to the murder of humans. In Aeschylus' *Oresteia*, Agamemnon, the leader of the Greek army, seals his own personal doom when he agrees to sacrifice his daughter Iphigenia to the goddess Artemis in order to gain good winds for his military fleet to set sail. This is reported in an extensive choral song (*Ag.* 104–257) where Iphigenia is compared to a sacrificial animal, but has to be gagged to prevent her from pleading for her life (228–47). In animal sacrifice, it was important that the animal should not struggle at the point of death. Iphigenia's death in *Agamemnon*, then, is seriously ill-omened, and the pattern of murder represented as animal sacrifice is repeated when Agamemnon's wife Clytemnestra "welcomes" her husband home after his long absence, and refers to the "sacrificial sheep" ready for slaughter before killing him and his concubine (1056–7).[9] In Euripides' *Iphigenia at Aulis*, Iphigenia eventually agrees to go willingly to her sacrificial death; but if she does not agree, she knows she will be dragged to the altar regardless (1365–6; Figure 5.2). Euripides conflates the language of sacrifice and marriage: Iphigenia is lured to the army camp on the pretense of marriage to Achilles and references to the imminent "sacrifices" take on a double and bitterly ironical meaning.[10]

FIGURE 5.2: Apulian mixing vessel, showing the sacrifice of Iphigeneia. Visible behind her are the head and legs of the hind for which she was substituted as a victim, *c.* 370–350 BCE. The British Museum, London, 1865,0103.21. © The Trustees of the British Museum. All rights reserved.

The motif of a "marriage to death" for young women occurs in several tragedies (cf. Cassandra in Aeschylus' *Agamemnon*, Antigone in Sophocles' *Antigone*, Evadne in Euripides' *Suppliant Women*, and Alcestis in his *Alcestis*).[11] Euripides often foregrounds a self-sacrificing young person, usually a woman, who agrees to die in order to ensure an army's success; Polyxena in Euripides' *Hecuba* (521–81) also goes willingly to her sacrificial death. Young women from aristocratic families sacrifice their lives for the salvation of their cities in the *Children of Heracles* and in the fragmentary *Erechtheus*. In *Phoenician Women*, it is a young man, Menoeceus, who offers his life as a sacrifice to save the city.[12] Actual human sacrifice was considered barbaric by the Greeks and Euripides plays on this irony particularly in his *Iphigenia among the Taurians*, where Iphigenia has been miraculously saved by Artemis and transported to a barbarian land on the fringes of the Greek world, where she must serve the goddess by presiding over the human sacrifices of others. The trope highlights the human cost of war and the waste of young lives as barbaric during a century when Athens was almost constantly at war.

Animal sacrifice also appears in Greek tragedy in inauspicious contexts. In Sophocles' *Antigone* (999–1022), Tiresias reports a sacrificial fire devoid of flames which smokes and sputters as the gods reject the offering because their altars are polluted by carrion from the dead and unburied son of Oedipus (Polynices) brought in by birds and dogs. Similarly, in Euripides' *Electra* (774–859), when Aegisthus examines the entrails of the calf he has sacrificed, which he has unwittingly allowed Orestes to butcher, he finds that the lobe of the liver is missing while the portal vein and the gall bladder are not as they should be. As Aegisthus bends over to examine the entrails more closely, Orestes slaughters him with a cleaver and he becomes the "sacrificial victim." Not all sacrifices involved live victims. In Sophocles' *Electra* (634–59), Clytemnestra makes an offering of fruits to the god Apollo and prays that he may grant her his favor. Since Apollo is the patron of Orestes who has been commanded to kill Clytemnestra, we know that her prayer will go unanswered and that her sacrifice will have no effect. Sacrificial rituals in tragedy, then, tend to draw attention to deep underlying problems relating both to the individuals who are involved in the rituals and their broader communities. Occasionally, previously distorted sacrificial rituals are returned to an auspicious context. This occurs at the end of Aeschylus' *Oresteia*, where the Furies will be appeased with sacrifices of first fruits, and sacrifices before childbirth and before the completion of marriage (*Eum.* 834–6). In *Iphigenia among the Taurians*, Iphigenia escapes from her involvement with human sacrifice and Athena intervenes to end the practice among the Taurians.

Religious settings and stage properties

The temple setting of *Iphigenia among the Taurians* probably represented severed human heads or skulls in place of animal skulls.[13] These would have adorned the otherwise recognizable backdrop of a Doric-style Greek temple, housing the cult statue of Artemis, which is carried off by Iphigenia in the final scenes. The temple seemingly corresponds to a real location for a temple of Artemis in the Crimea,[14] and imagery of this temple from the *Iphigenia among the Taurians* story was popular on Greek vase paintings.[15] Several other tragedies are set at temple locations, including Delphi (the opening of Aeschylus' *Eumenides*, Euripides' *Ion*), and the temple of Zeus Agoraios at Marathon (Euripides' *Children of Heracles*); both would have been familiar locations for most audience members. The *Children of Heracles* is a suppliant drama, meaning that central characters have taken refuge in a sacred place in the hope of gaining asylum from their persecutors with the local community. Supplication was a divinely protected ritual and could also take place without any formal religious context. The suppliant typically appealed through physical contact, touching the knees, hand, or chin of the person supplicated (as in *Medea* 709–18).[16] Significant suppliant tragedies include Aeschylus' *Suppliant Women* and Euripides' *Suppliant Women*. The latter is set at the temple of Demeter and Kore (Persephone) at Eleusis, close to Athens, and features the mothers of the dead champions from the Argive-sponsored war against Thebes which generated the fratricidal battle between the sons of Oedipus. Aeschylus' *Suppliant Women* dramatizes a different myth and is set at a shrine in Argos with altars and images of the major gods of the city. The suppliants are the fugitive former king of Egypt, Danaus, and his daughters who form the chorus. Suppliants often carried olive branches wrapped with wool to indicate their divinely protected status (A. *Supp.* 21–2; E. *Supp.* 36; S. *OT* 3).

Statues, shrines and other religious equipment onstage serve to emphasize the humans' dependence on and hope for divine aid. Orestes in *Eumenides* clasps the statue of Athena after arriving in Athens pursued by the Furies. The goddess herself will later appear and adjudicate in his favor. Andromache, the concubine of Achilles' son Neoptolemus, seeks protection with their son at the shrine of Thetis when her child's life is threatened by Neoptolemus' legitimate wife Hermione in Euripides' *Andromache*. The tombs of mortals can also have particular powers. In Euripides' *Helen*, the title character has taken refuge

FIGURE 5.3: Paestan mixing vessel depicting Alcmene seated on an altar, entreating Zeus for aid against her angry husband Amphitryon. Zeus responds by sending rain to quench the pyre Amphitryon has built and lighted beneath Alcmene, attributed to the Python painter, c. 360–320 BCE. The British Museum, London, 1890,0210.1. © The Trustees of the British Museum. All rights reserved.

at the tomb of Proteus, the former king of Egypt, in protest against his son Theoclymenus' plans to marry her against her will. Aeschylus' *Persians* features the tomb of Darius from which his ghost is conjured; the opening of *Libation Bearers* is set at the tomb of Agamemnon; and in Sophocles' *Oedipus at Colonus*, the grove of the Eumenides where the action takes place will also become the location of Oedipus' secret burial spot from which he will posthumously exude benefaction on the land of Athens. Visits to tombs are normally accompanied by libations for the dead (A. *Pers.* 611–21, *LB* 23–4; S. *El.* 326–7, 404–8; E. *Or.* 112–25, *IT* 61–2). Statues of various kinds feature in different tragedies. In Aeschylus' *Seven against Thebes*, the chorus offer robes and garlands to the statues (101–2); in Aeschylus' *Suppliant Women*, the Danaids threaten to hang themselves from the statues if Pelasgus refuses their request for asylum (463–5). In Euripides' *Hippolytus*, the palace is flanked by statues of Aphrodite and Artemis, while the small cult statue of Artemis is carried off at the end of *Iphigenia among the Taurians*. The most impressive array of religious props comes in the form of the multiple accoutrements of the chorus of followers of Dionysus in Euripides' *Bacchae*. They appear equipped with drums (58–9, 156), and probably also most of the Dionysiac paraphernalia they mention in their entry song: *thyrsus* staffs of giant fennel covered in ivy and topped with pine cones (80, 113, 147), ivy crowns (81, 106), snakes (101–2), fawnskins (111, 137–8), and wool (112–13).

Epiphany, aetiology, prophecy

The gods frequently appear onstage in Greek tragedy, often suspended above the human action onstage on a kind of pulley known as a *mechane*. Most often, they appear at the beginning (in the prologue), or the end, or both. This is most common in Euripides, who ends many plays with a divine epiphany (literally, a *deus ex machina*— a god from the *mechane*): Athena in *Ion*, *Iphigenia among the Taurians*, and *Suppliant Women*; Thetis in *Andromache*; Castor and Polydeuces in *Electra* and *Helen*; Artemis in *Hippolytus*; Apollo in *Orestes*; Medea as a quasi-divine figure in *Medea*. The device also features in Sophocles' *Philoctetes* where the divine Heracles closes the play. In *Philoctetes* and *Orestes*, both late plays, events which threatened to derail established mythology are put back on course by the commands of the divinities. In many Euripidean dramas, the deity prescribes the establishment of an enduring religious cultic association for one or more characters at the drama's conclusion (*Andr.* 1239–40, *Hel.* 1666–75, *Hipp.* 1423–30, *IT* 1442–67, *Med.* 1381–3, *Or.* 1684–90, *Supp.* 1188–204).

Scholars disagree over the extent to which these cult aetiologies reflected actual rituals, but certainly the gods in Greek tragedy regularly refer to real locations and recognizable types of ritual.[17] We know, for example, that a temple to Artemis existed at Brauron and that Iphigenia was connected with the location.[18] Not all aetiologies given by the gods are strictly related to rituals. At the end of *Ion*, for example, Athena explains how the Ionians Greeks will be descended from Ion (1573–88). At the same time, not all religious aetiologies are communicated by deities. Orestes explains the connection between his pollution of matricide and the foundation of the Pitcher Festival (Choes), a drinking festival in honor of Dionysus featuring individual pitchers (*IT* 947–60). Eurystheus in Euripides' *Children of Heracles* (1026–44) and Oedipus in Sophocles' *Oedipus at Colonus* (1518–34, 1760–7) both predict the location of their own burials and the posthumous benefaction of their presence for Athenians. The fourth-century BCE tragedian Carcinus the Younger includes an aetiology for the cult of Demeter and Persephone at Syracuse in a lost play, where the speaker is not identified (*TrGF* 1.70 F5).

Gods appearing in an opening scene predict the oncoming mayhem. In Euripides this occurs in five surviving plays—Apollo and Death in *Alcestis*, Dionysus in *Bacchae*, Aphrodite in *Hippolytus*, Hermes in *Ion*, and Athena and Poseidon in *Trojan Women*. In the prologue of Sophocles' *Ajax*, also, Athena appears to describe the madness she has inflicted on Ajax. Like Ajax, Heracles in Euripides suffers a divinely induced madness, but this happens spectacularly in the middle of the play, a structural point at which a divine epiphany is not normally expected. In *Heracles*, Iris (messenger of the gods) and Lyssa (personification of madness) appear to effect the will of Hera, albeit reluctantly. Three surviving Greek tragedies, Aeschylus' *Eumenides*, the *Prometheus Bound* attributed to Aeschylus, and Euripides' *Bacchae* are unique in their representations of gods onstage. *Eumenides* features a divine chorus of Furies as well as Apollo and Athena as major characters in the trial of Orestes. *Prometheus Bound* has an almost entirely divine cast, featuring Prometheus, who is onstage for the entire play, Hephaestus, Power and Violence (divine personifications), the Titan Oceanus, his daughters who form the chorus, and Hermes. The only mortal character is the long-suffering Io. Dionysus, by contrast, is the only divine character in the *Bacchae*, but his presence throughout the play is both constant and infectious. Moreover, the entire play can be read as an aetiology for the foundation of cult worship of Dionysus in Greece. The tragedy is a terrifying display of the power of Dionysus and a warning to those who reject him. Tales of the destructive power of

Dionysus were popular in Greek tragedy notably through the myth of Lycurgus, a Thracian king who, like Pentheus in the *Bacchae*, opposed Dionysus and was punished horrifically as a result. It was the subject of a lost trilogy by Aeschylus, the *Lycurgeia*, which influenced Euripides' *Bacchae*. *Edonians*, the first play of the trilogy dramatized the arrival of Dionysus and his followers to the kingdom of Lycurgus in Thrace and the king's attempts to suppress Dionysiac worship. After a series of miracles, Dionysus drives Lycurgus into a madness during which he kills his own son with an ax believing that he is cutting a vine-branch. In the second play, *Bassarids*, Orpheus is torn limb from limb by a group of Thracian women who are devotees of Dionysus as a punishment for rejecting the god and honoring Apollo instead. It has been argued that the trilogy reflected a rivalry between the Pythagoreans, for whom Apollo was the most significant deity, and Dionysiac mystery-cults, since both claimed Orpheus as their prophet.[19] Aeschylus may have been influenced also by the tragic *Lycurgeia* trilogy by Polyphrasmon, which was produced in 467 BCE, probably before Aeschylus' own trilogy. In Euripides, the destruction of Pentheus at the hands of a spurned god is similar to that of Hippolytus, who proudly neglects the worship of Aphrodite and devotes himself to Artemis, but is killed as punishment according to Aphrodite's predictions in the prologue of *Hippolytus*.

The function of divine epiphanies, then, is varied, although it is clear that divine characters always either drive or redirect the plot. The situation is more complicated in the Aeschylean *Eumenides* and *Prometheus Bound* plays, where there are divine characters with competing agenda. In both cases the dominant divine figure is the absent Zeus who exercises his will through Athena in *Eumenides*, and through Hephaestus and Hermes especially in *Prometheus Bound*. Similarly in *Hippolytus* (1331–4), Artemis cites her fear of Zeus as the reason she was unable to intervene in Aphrodite's destruction of Hippolytus, though she also announces her plans to kill Aphrodite's favorite in retaliation (1416–20). In Euripidean tragedy, divine epiphanies can sit uncomfortably alongside rational challenges to the concept of gods in their traditional forms expressed by the characters. In *Hippolytus* (120), for example, the Servant prays to Aphrodite to overlook Hippolytus' folly, suggesting that gods should be wiser than mortals, but we know from Aphrodite's appearance in the prologue that she has already planned Hippolytus' destruction.

Apollo is criticized for his behavior by characters in several plays: for remembering old quarrels like a base mortal (*Andr.* 1161–5), for commanding Orestes to commit matricide (*El.* 1245–6) and then deserting him (*Or.* 163–5, 191–3, 285–7, 595–6, 955–6, cf. 1666–8), for raping Creusa and abandoning her when she was pregnant (*Ion* 436–51). Nevertheless, Apollo never answers these criticisms and his will is imposed on mortals regardless. In *Iphigenia among the Taurians* (380–91), Iphigenia refuses to believe that Artemis could welcome human sacrifice in her honor while rejecting mortals who have had contact with blood or childbirth, or that the gods once ate the flesh of Pelops, but Athena confirms in the *exodus* that Artemis will continue to demand symbolic blood sacrifice (1458–61). Most pointed of these tensions is Heracles' refusal to believe that the gods have love affairs or try to gain mastery over each other (*Her.* 1340–6), when the entire premise of the plot and the divine interventions of Lyssa and Iris rest on Hera's jealous revenge for Zeus' affair with Heracles' mother.

How are we to reconcile such apparent contradictions within Euripides' representation of the gods? In Nietzsche's highly influential *The Birth of Tragedy*, first published in 1872, Euripides is condemned for his theatricality, his use of the *deus ex machina*, and his lack of religious reverence (among other things). Appropriating the classical teachings of the Schlegel brothers who traced their criticisms of Euripides back to the caricatures of his art found in the comedies of Aristophanes, Nietzsche's condemnation took root.[20] Late nineteenth- and early twentieth-century scholars viewed Euripides as a "rationalist," even if they defended the quality of his works.[21] More recently, several scholars have argued that the divine in Euripides is bleak and traditional.[22] It is also the case, as we have just seen, that the message of the god from the machine consistently fails to address the theological concerns raised in the play, or is at odds with challenges to divinity previously expressed. Moreover, the *deus ex machina* device is obviously artificial;[23] it was disliked by Aristotle for that reason (*Poetics* 1454b1–6), and mocked by the fourth-century BCE comic poet Antiphanes as a device used by tragedians who cannot figure out how to conclude their plots (fr. 189.13–16 Kassel Austin). However, it complements other self-conscious aspects of Euripides' dramatic art, such as his extensive use of metatheatricality and intertextuality. The main function of drawing attention to the artifice of the drama is to invite audience contemplation on its position within the literary and theatrical tradition. Arguably, the artifice of imposing gods onto the tragic plot is similarly designed to provoke audience reflection on the alternatives raised during the course of the play.[24]

Euripides was not the only fifth-century tragedian to present characters with views critical of traditional religion. A fragment in a tragedy attributed to Critias states that fear of the gods was invented by some clever human who introduced religion as a lie to the world in order to prevent crime and maintain social order (*TrGF* 1.43 F.19.1–26). Nevertheless, Euripidean drama contrasts starkly with the plays of Sophocles where the gods are rarely criticized by characters within the play.[25] In Sophocles, the gods are elusive and there is little interest in their rage against, or lust for, mortals. For this reason, Sophocles had a special appeal to nineteenth-century monotheistic Europeans. It is not useful, however, to judge the tragedians in terms of relative "piety." This culturally loaded term in the mainly monotheistic modern world does not apply itself comfortably to the flexible polytheistic religion of classical Greece. All the extant tragedies suggest that gods must receive appropriate worship. When humans make errors in judging the nature of that worship, consequences can be disastrous. Similarly, when humans disregard or misinterpret oracles and prophecies they bring terrible sufferings down on their families.

Forces of destiny, fate, unspecified "gods," and the *daimōn* (an unnamed deity) are important in all three tragedians, but most prominent in Sophocles, whose gods are usually more distant, present indirectly through oracles or omens. The natural landscape is also strongly connected with the divine in his plays. These forces cannot be appealed to in the same way as Olympian gods can through sacrificial offerings and prayers, since one cannot offer worship to an unspecific divinity.[26] Several tragedies deal with human resistance to oracles, and its disastrous consequences. In Aeschylus' *Seven against Thebes* (745–57) we learn that Laius had received an oracle that he should die without issue in order to save his city, but he disregards the oracle, fathers Oedipus, and seals the fate of Thebes to subsequent generations of warfare. In Euripides' *Phoenician Women* (21), Laius is overpowered by drunken lust and ignores the oracle as a result. The attempt to expose and kill the child is ineffective. The infant is saved and raised in ignorance of his biological identity. In Sophocles' *Oedipus Tyrannos* (183–4), Oedipus flees from his home in order to avoid fulfilling the prophecy that he will kill his father and marry his mother—only to embark on the journey during which he will fulfil the prophecy. Oedipus rejects the prophet Tiresias when he reveals the truth, assuming that he has financial motivations for his words, as does Creon in Sophocles' *Antigone*, and Pentheus in Euripides' *Bacchae*. Usually, prophetic knowledge or advice is communicated by gods or prophets, but sometimes more mystical figures have prophetic gifts, such as the omniscient Egyptian princess Theonoe, whose name means 'divine knowledge' (in Euripides' *Helen*), or the ghostly apparitions of Darius in Aeschylus' *Persians,* and Polydorus in Euripides' *Hecuba.* In all cases, the prophet turns out to be correct.

In Euripides' *Iphigenia at Aulis*, however, the prophecies of the seer Calchas are put under more serious scrutiny. He claims that Artemis demands the sacrifice of Iphigenia, but the characters within the play stress the army's role in making the decision, led by Calchas and the rabble-rouser Odysseus, rather than the demands of Artemis, who is only briefly mentioned. Unlike other sources for this myth, the demand is a conditional one. The sacrifice is required only if the fleet wishes to set sail (89–93). Elsewhere, Agamemnon had vowed to sacrifice to Artemis the finest thing the year would bear and Calchas determines that he must sacrifice Iphigenia (*IT* 15–24); alternatively Agamemnon had offended Artemis by killing her sacred stag and boasting about it (S. *El.* 563–76). In Aeschylus' *Agamemnon* (105–249), Calchas interprets the omen of two eagles feasting on a pregnant hare as signifying the future destruction of Troy by the sons of Atreus. Artemis is angry at the feast and demands a sacrifice. Calchas names Iphigenia as the sacrificial victim, and his prophecies are fulfilled. The representation of Calchas being in league with the deceptive and dangerously persuasive Odysseus in *Iphigenia at Aulis*, then, is unusual and disturbing, reflecting the play's broader concerns with the tensions between rhetoric and politics within a context of war weariness and crisis in late fifth-century BCE Athens.[27]

Curses, oaths, prayers

In Athenian tragedy, human actions and divine agency always work in tandem to bring events to their destined fulfillment. The oracles and prophecies that foretell the ruin of the house of Laius are accompanied by the curse of Oedipus on his sons, uttered as punishment for their mistreatment of him (A. *Se.* 720–33, E. *Pho.* 66–8, S. *OC* 421ff, 788–9, 1370–6). In Aeschylus' *Seven against Thebes*, the curse is personified as a Fury (a spirit of vengeance) which drives Eteocles to the decision of facing his brother in battle. Not yet understanding the true meaning of Oedipus' riddling curse, Eteocles appeals to the "Almighty Curse and Fury of [his] father" in his opening prayer (*Seven* 70) in a formal but anomalous pattern that signals his doom, since the Fury is not an appropriate recipient of prayer or cult.[28] Moreover, the invocation of the Fury comes after a triad of divine addressees (Zeus, Earth, and the gods who hold the city), a unit which is normally complete. As the play progresses Eteocles becomes less measured as he falls under the power of his father's curse.[29] Human actions in Greek tragedy can be linked to the inherited guilt of a cursed dynasty. Aeschylus tends to focus on the agency of individual mortals, whereas Euripides often presents multiple members of a household acting in destructive ways (contrast Euripides' *Phoenician Women* with Aeschylus' *Seven*).[30] In Sophocles, inherited guilt is less significant.[31] For example, the Furies feature prominently in Aeschylus' *Oresteia*, and they are internalized but also important in Euripides (*El.*, *IT* and *Or.*), whereas in Sophocles' *Electra* they are barely mentioned.[32]

The *Oresteia* also features numerous oaths, which are by their nature an expression of conditional self-cursing. An oath calls on a divine witness to ensure the truth of a statement, assuming divine punishment as a consequence for any breach thereof. In the *Oresteia*, oaths form a linguistic counterpart to the imagery of nets and binding.[33] In the final play, *Eumenides*, a recognizable set of legalistic oaths is manipulated to heighten the dramatic suspense surrounding Orestes' trial for matricide.[34] The oaths of the *Oresteia* are conspiratorial or political. Conspiratorial oaths conform to the broader pattern of the trilogy where images and language that are perverted or inverted in the first play are returned to a normative and auspicious context in the last play. For example, in the first two tragedies natural enemies have come together in sworn conspiracies—Fire and Sea (*Ag.* 650), Clytemnestra and Aegisthus (*LB* 978). In the final play, the natural allies Sleep and Toil are an authoritative pair of conspirators who afflict the Furies (*Eum.* 127). Political oaths, however, remain anomalous throughout the trilogy. In the conclusion of *Eumenides* (287–91) the oath of alliance between Argos and Athens contains some unusual features. The alliance is sworn unilaterally by Argos without any corresponding commitment from the Athenian side. In addition, Orestes names his future ghost as guarantor of the Argive oath rather than an external divine power. These anomalous elements in an aetiology for the recent Athenian–Argive alliance of 462/1 BCE, between city-states that had never previously been allies, suggest the possibility of an ambiguous attitude towards that alliance, where Aeschylus has exploited religious language and ritual in order to comment on contemporary politics.[35]

The language of oaths is also used to surprising effect in Sophocles. Real oaths require a sanctifying witness and/or a self-curse. Within the corpus of surviving classical Greek literature, only a handful of statements referred to as oaths are not, and these occur almost exclusively in Sophocles. In five of his seven surviving plays, characters retroactively refer to unsworn statements as oaths, thus adding the implications of a religious contract, with divine penalties for perjury, to a previously non-binding agreement. As a result, the audience becomes involved in a process of assessing riddling language, which is a recurring literary strategy in Sophocles.[36] Oaths and deception are linked in *Women of Trachis*. The deceitful herald Lichas lies to Heracles' wife Deianeira about the identity of the captive woman he has brought home. When Deianeira discovers the truth, she denounces Lichas as a perjurer even though he had not sworn any oath (*Trach.* 378–9); Lichas then lies on oath and perjures himself soon thereafter after calling Zeus as his witness (*Trach.* 399–401). In *Philoctetes* and *Oedipus at Colonus* it is expressly stated that an oath is not required in an agreement, but the same agreement is subsequently treated as a sworn contract. In *Philoctetes*, it is the betrayal of trust that causes a retrospective reassessment of the agreement. When Philoctetes believed Neoptolemus to be his friend, he had asked not to be left on the island requesting a pledge and not an oath (*Phil.* 811–13). After discovering that Neoptolemus has deceived him, Philoctetes laments that Neoptolemus had sworn to bring him home (*Phil.* 941–2), treating the oathless pledge he received from a friend as the sworn statement he would have exacted from an enemy. In *Oedipus at Colonus* also, the shift in language reflects the changing dynamic of the relationship between two parties. When Theseus assures Oedipus that he will never betray him, Oedipus explicitly states that he does not require an oath (*OC* 650). Much later in the play, however, after coming to the aid of Oedipus' daughters, Theseus claims to have fulfilled what he had "sworn" to Oedipus (*OC* 1145). This reflects the growing power of Oedipus, since Theseus treats the unsworn agreement between equals as the sworn statement he would have made to a more powerful being.[37]

The dead (like the ghosts mentioned above) and the dying were believed to have prophetic powers, while the ability to curse could be accompanied by powers to bless. Sophocles' *Oedipus at Colonus* is set in the grove of the Eumenides, which is to be the location of Oedipus' mysterious resting place. The Eumenides, which means "Kindly Ones," are the positive manifestation of the Furies who feature prominently in the tragedies dealing with the descendants of Agamemnon and Clytemnestra. At the trial of

Orestes for matricide, the Furies of his mother demand blood for blood as payment for Clytemnestra's death. When the votes are tied and Orestes is acquitted, Athena must use all of her persuasive powers to appease the angry Furies by offering them honorific rites in exchange for their blessings on the land; they retain their powers to curse if they are not properly propitiated. In Aeschylus' *Eumenides*, the Furies form the chorus and appear onstage in terrifying form. Wearing dark robes and with serpents wreathed through their hair, they drip loathsome fluid from their eyes (*LB* 1049–50, 1058, *Eum.* 51–6). In Euripides' *Iphigenia among the Taurians* (939–72), the conclusion of *Eumenides* is challenged in relation to the appeasement of the Furies, since a faction remains unpersuaded by Athena and continue to hound Orestes.

Euripidean tragedies often raise theological and philosophical questions. One condensed example comes in a prayer from his *Trojan Women* (884–8). The distressed queen of Troy, Hecuba, addresses Zeus: "Earth's support, having your seat also upon the earth,| whoever you may be, so difficult to fathom,| Zeus, whether you are the necessity of nature or the mind of mortals I pray to you!" Menelaus, who hears her prayer, expresses surprise: "What does this mean? How you have innovated in your prayer to the gods!" (889) The novelty of the prayer here lies not in its form, which is fairly traditional, but in its references to three different philosophical ideas regarding the nature of Zeus— Zeus as Air (Earth's support and surrounding atmosphere), Zeus as natural compulsion (the necessity of nature), Zeus as the mind. The first concept refers to the notion of Zeus being coterminous with Air, which the philosopher Diogenes of Apollonia had argued was the source of all being.[38] The second possibility of Zeus representing the necessity of nature derives from the Atomist philosophy of Leucippus and Democritus.[39] Finally the concept that "mind" (*nous*) was the animating principle of the universe evokes the theories of Anaxagoras.[40] In typical Euripidean fashion, the play gives no specific answer on the nature of Zeus, except to confirm bleakly that the gods will punish the Greeks and will not alleviate the sufferings of the Trojans.

The power of the traditional gods and the sanctity of divinely protected rituals, such as supplication or oath-taking, are always ultimately upheld in Euripides. Those who threaten suppliants, such as Lycus in *Heracles*, and those who break their oaths like Jason in *Medea*, are punished severely. In spite of this, Euripides gained a reputation for promoting anomalous attitudes to the gods through parodies in the comedies of Aristophanes which influenced scholarly approaches to Euripidean tragedy. Most infamously, a line from Euripides' *Hippolytus* (612: "It was my tongue that swore but my heart remains unsworn") was quoted and appropriated out of context by Aristophanes to suggest that it was a clever loophole for perjury (*Thesm.* 275–6, *Frogs* 101–2, 1471). In the tragedy, Hippolytus is tricked into swearing a blind oath, agreeing in advance that he will not reveal the secret he is about to be told. When he discovers that he has sworn to keep his stepmother's lust for him a secret, he becomes enraged and makes the infamous exclamation. In fact, however, Hippolytus does not break his oath and is praised by Artemis in the tragedy's conclusion for keeping his oath even in the face of his father's slanderous accusations (*Hipp.* 1306–9). Similarly, we are not supposed to believe Theseus' charge that the skilled hunter Hippolytus practices vegetarianism as part of some Orphic beliefs (952–5). Rather, the insult suggests that Hippolytus is as suspicious and unreliable as members of this fringe cult in the classical period. Hippolytus dies a gruesome death, orchestrated by Aphrodite whom he has dishonored and set in motion by his father's invocation of a curse from his own father Poseidon (887–90). The punishment happens to be consistent also with the divinely ordained fate of perjurers or would-be perjurers, which is the extinction of their family line (as with the oath-breaker Jason in Euripides' *Medea*). In no way, then, does Euripides' play actually promote perjury; like Athenian tragedy in general, the play is theologically conservative. Nevertheless, line 612 apparently caused controversy. According to Aristotle, Euripides was charged with impiety on account of line 612 by a man called Hygiaenon, although the accusation went nowhere (*Rhetoric* 1416a31–2). Euripides had won a rare first prize in 428 BCE for the tetralogy in which *Hippolytus* appeared, so the judges clearly did not find it immoral. Moreover, the extraordinary proposition that the mind and the tongue might act independently of each other notably gained significant traction among the intellectual elite of classical Athens. This is evidenced not only by the references in Aristophanes but also in the dialogues of Plato, where the concept is invoked twice by Socrates (*Theaetetus* 154c-d, *Symposium* 199a).[41]

ROMAN TRAGEDY

Apart from the tragedies of Seneca, so little survives of Roman tragedy, even in fragments, that it is difficult to make general observations on the role of religion within the genre as a whole. It is clear that myths related to Bacchus (the Roman Dionysus) were popular as a subject. The poet Naevius wrote a *Lucurgus* tragedy in which the Roman god of vegetation and fertility, Liber, was associated with the ecstatic persona of Bacchus. The late third century BCE, when Naevius was writing, preceded a period in which the worship of Bacchus was aggressively suppressed by the Roman senate (186 BCE). Perhaps Naevius' choice of material was designed to advocate inclusiveness in Roman religion.[42] Bacchic worship also seems to have been at the core of Ennius' *Athamas*, Pacuvius' *Pentheus*, and Accius' *Bacchae* and *Liber's Trophy*, produced in this same social context.[43] We can also glean that the motif of augury was important. A fragment of Accius in which a character claims not to trust augurs (*Diomedes* fr.iii, Klotz) may well reflect the climate of suspicion of prophets in second-century BCE Rome.[44]

None of Seneca's surviving tragedies dramatize a Bacchic myth, but his *Oedipus* contains appeals to Bacchus as a patron divinity of Thebes. The chorus sing a hymn in his honor at the instruction of the prophet Tiresias as Thebes is ailing from the plague (401–508). As in Sophocles, the plague on Thebes is caused by Oedipus' pollution, but the emphasis on the abnormalities in nature is distinctly Senecan (2, 47, 41–3, 49–51). This aspect must be understood in light of Seneca's sympathy with Stoic philosophy. The Stoics believed in a universe with a single controlling power, Nature (or God), as a rational force, and Nature is named "mighty mother of the gods" in Seneca's *Phaedra* (959). We find manifestations of macabre and sinister omens in nature throughout Seneca's tragedies where horrors are taking place. This phenomenon extends itself particularly to the realms of sacrifice and augury. In *Oedipus*, the blind Tiresias presides over the sacrifice of a bull and a heifer, with the aid of his daughter Manto who relays what she sees. The sacrifice produces multiple disturbing signs representing the doom of the Theban dynasty. The flames of the sacrificial fire split in two, and the libation of wine changes into blood (321–4). The heifer thrusts herself on the sacrificial knife while the bull, struck twice, wanders erratically (341–4), here an obvious foreshadowing of Jocasta's suicide and Oedipus' self-blinding. The entrails are abnormal, featuring a diseased heart, sickly veins, missing innards, a rotten liver, misplaced organs, and an unnatural fetus in the heifer (353–83).

Like the Athenian tragedians, Seneca exploits the metaphor of sacrifice in the representation of human murders. Most gruesome is the description of Atreus acting as a demented priest in *Thyestes* (Act 4). He butchers his brother's children with macabre precision in a horrifyingly precise re-enactment of Roman sacrificial practice. He prepares the victims, examines the entrails once they have been killed, dismembers the bodies and cooks the limbs before feeding them to their unsuspecting father (in Act 5). Omens from the divine world demonstrate revulsion at this aberration. Statues weep in the temples (702), and the sacrificial fire does not burn properly but turns into a smothering smoke (772–5). Elsewhere, Polyxena in Seneca's *Trojan Women* (1132–64) goes bravely to her forced sacrificial death, in a perverted marriage ritual over the tomb of Achilles, while Medea refers ambiguously to slaughtering victims on a consecrated altar after sacrificial prayers (*Med.* 38–9). The first choral ode of *Medea*, a wedding hymn, picks up on this imagery and ambiguity, as the chorus pray for divine blessings at the impending wedding of Jason and Creusa. A "white-backed bull" must be sacrificed (60) and "a female of snow-white body" must be offered to Lucina (61–2), the Roman goddess of childbirth. These "sacrifices" will come in the form of Medea's victims Creusa (the female) and her father Creon (the bull).

In Stoicism, the wise person is supposed to submit to fate, and to ignore the fluctuations of fortune. Seneca's tragedies echo and distort these Stoic tropes. In *Oedipus*, the chorus proclaim that we are driven by fate and must yield to fate (980–94), a grim message when Oedipus' final words call the fates savage and equate them with disease, plague, and pain (1059–60). In *Thyestes*, where the ghost of Tantalus eventually yields to pressure from the Fury to bring havoc on the Penates (Roman household gods), the Fury functions as a force of destiny or fate (52–3, 98–100).[45] Fortuna, the Roman goddess of luck, is a negative force in Senecan tragedy. In *Agamemnon*, she causes the incest between Thyestes and his daughter (28–30) and is a beguiler who exalts men with unstable power and then brings them low (57–107; cf. 698). Similar sentiments are expressed in *Trojan Women*, where Fortuna is associated with fickle gods and the instability of royal power (1–6) as well as the humbling of men previously exalted (259–63). Kingly power in *Oedipus* is open to Fortuna's blows (6–11). In his *De Beneficiis* (4.7–8), Seneca considers nature, fate, fortune, and named gods such as Liber, Mercury (the Roman Hermes), and Hercules to be one and the same. But in other prose works, he distinguishes fate from fortune, suggesting that the Stoic sage should align himself with fate and nature but should resist fortune.[46] In Seneca's tragedies, the gods often seem to be distinct from fate; the chorus who proclaim the primacy of fate in *Oedipus* also say that not even a god can change a series of events set in motion by fate (989–90), implying that the two forces are separate. Seneca's impassioned, dangerously destructive characters—such as Medea, *Med.* 520, and Hercules, *Her.* 1271–2—often co-opt the language of the wise person who can hold out against fortune.[47] But clearly, their rage precludes a positive interpretation of these characters' behavior in Stoic terms. Fate is a positive force in Stoic philosophy, while in the tragedies it is difficult to find any positive meaning in the working out of fate.

Senecan tragedy blurs boundaries between mortals and deities, where human figures cast themselves as gods or seek to challenge the divine realm. Atreus in *Thyestes* sacrifices to himself (713), as if he were a god, imagines himself as one with the stars, and dismisses the gods since he considers that he has reached the pinnacle of his prayers (885–8). Medea claims to be sea and land, steel and fire, gods and thunderbolts (*Medea* 166–7), and plans to attack the gods (424; cf. 673). Indeed the gods literally frame this play since "gods" is both the first and last word of the tragedy. What is most disturbing about these figures is that they accomplish their goals unchecked and unpunished. When Jason delivers the famous closing line of *Medea* (1027), "bear witness where you ride that there are no gods," he is addressing a woman flying off in a divine chariot whose prayers to the gods have been unequivocally answered. The gods exist but, as in Euripides, they are on Medea's side and Jason is punished as an oath-breaker (7–8, 343–7). The existence of the gods is also vaguely questioned by Thyestes (*Thyestes* 407). He later prays they may give Atreus the rewards he deserves (503), but is forced to conclude after his discovery of Atreus' heinous crimes that the gods have fled (1021). This attitude to divinity is reflected in the play's choral odes which move from prayers and appeals for divine aid (122–75), to terror at the chaos of a world abandoned by the gods (789–884).

Hercules was an important character for the Stoics, as a representative of human virtue and self-control. He was also a mortal who was deified, and worshiped at Rome at the Ara Maxima ("Greatest Altar") and at the Temple of Hercules Victor.[48] Deceased emperors were worshiped as gods, and emperors like Caligula and Nero claimed divine status while they were still alive; so the issue of a mortal gaining divine status has profoundly contemporary implications. In Seneca's *Hercules*, the usurper Lycus and Amphitryon (Hercules' father) debate the issue of apotheosis for mortals (447–58). Lycus is unwilling

FIGURE 5.4: Marble bust of the Roman emperor Commodus dressed as the demigod Heracles, part of a statuary group illustrating Commodus' apotheosis, *c.* 192 CE. Commodus was following a tradition of earlier emperors who presented themselves as heroic or divine. Musei Capitolini, Rome, MC1120. Photo by Marie-Lan Nguyen. Courtesy of Wikimedia.

to admit that mortals can become gods, or that gods could be slaves or exiles, but mythology proves the opposite and Amphitryon is able to provide Bacchus (born of a mortal mother), and Apollo (who was punished by Zeus to serve the mortal Admetus) as counter-examples. Hercules himself, of course, is another example. His identity as the son of Jupiter (the Roman Zeus) is stressed throughout the play, and appeals to Hercules by both Amphitryon and Megara (Hercules' wife) contain elements of prayer implying that he is already semi-divine.[49] In *Hercules on Oeta*, attributed to Seneca, which dramatizes the death of Hercules, the apotheosis is made explicit. Hercules actively seeks a path to the gods in *Hercules* (64–74) but is brought low by the madness inflicted on him by Juno (the Roman Hera) which causes him to murder his wife and children. Rather than becoming a god within the play, Hercules recognizes himself as a "monster" (*Her.* 1280), an image repeated at the beginning of *Hercules on Oeta* (55–6). Monstrosity also characterizes Medea through her plans (*Med.* 395, 675). In *Thyestes*, only Atreus is unaffected by the monstrous creatures and omens that accompany his gruesome sacrifice (673, 703). The monstrosity that comes with seeking divinity or challenging divine order in Seneca echoes the biographer Suetonius' description of Caligula. Like Atreus who sacrifices to himself (*Thyestes* 713), Caligula instituted elaborate sacrifices in honor of his own divinity (Figure 5.4). He equipped himself with attributes of the gods such as a thunderbolt or a trident, thus becoming a monster rather than a man (*Caligula* 22, 52).[50]

Seneca's tragedies are marked by the physical absence of Olympian gods. With the exception of Juno who appears in the prologue of *Hercules*, the gods do not appear onstage. In *Phaedra* (modeled on *Hippolytus*) Seneca makes much of the inherited curse of Phaedra's family which predetermines events in accordance with fate (*Phaedra* 113–28, cf. 174–7, 242, 687–9), an emphasis entirely different from what we find in Euripides. Hippolytus worships Diana (the Roman Artemis) in *Phaedra*, while Venus (the Roman Aphrodite) afflicts Phaedra, as in the original, but the goddesses do not appear. Moreover, Diana and Venus are depicted in complementary rather than opposing terms, both representing aspects of nature's violence and savagery.[51] The Nurse's arguments that Venus and Cupid are fictions (195–203) are proved incorrect by the tragedy's conclusion. In *Trojan Women* (inspired by Euripides' play of the same title), there is no divine epiphany to predict the misery of the characters though the brutality depicted in the play generates the concept that death is a haven. Through death Priam is free from degradation (142–55), while the death of Astyanax is to be his freedom (790–1). Oedipus in *Phoenician Women* (80–181) also views death as a relief from troubles, and Hercules considers suicide (*Hercules* 1258–62).

The world of the dead and the powers that emanate from there are far more prominent than in Greek tragedy. *Thyestes* opens with the ghost of Tantalus accompanied by a Fury from the Underworld, while the ghost of Thyestes declares that the world of infernal Dis (the Roman Hades), for all its horrors, is preferable to life in the house of Atreus (*Ag.* 1–21). In an elaborate and terrifying ritual of necromancy, the ghost of Laius is conjured from among the shades to name his murderer in *Oedipus* (548–658). Medea invokes the dead and their powers in her complex incantations for success and sees the ghost of her dead brother attended by Furies (*Medea* 740–816, 959–66). Cassandra sees into the Underworld during her prophetic visions in which the Furies advance on the house (*Ag.* 741–74), and the ghost of Agrippina (Nero's mother) appears in *Octavia*, attributed to Seneca.

The absence of physical intervention from the Olympian gods in Seneca and the prominence given to the powers of the dead contribute to the sense of a chaotic and disordered universe in his tragedies.[52] It also speaks to Senecan tragedy's examination of interiority and the psychology of the self.⁵³ Representation of the divine in Seneca is disconcerting overall because we are left without a moral compass. In *Agamemnon*, Cassandra wisely abandons any attempt to placate the gods with prayer (696). It is a tragedy in which not only do prayers go unanswered, but they perversely seem to precipitate the kinds of disasters they seek to avert. The Greeks who pray for calm seas, for instance, are immediately shipwrecked on completion of their prayer (519–27).⁵⁴ The prayers of Theseus in *Phaedra* "do not move the gods" (1242). The gods flee from Atreus' crimes in *Thyestes*, as we have seen. Medea is god-like in her sinister ill-omened revenge (cf. *Med.* 680), while Juno, the only Olympian god to appear onstage is characterized by the destructive passion of rage (*ira*) in the same way as is her victim Hercules.⁵⁵ The universe of Senecan tragedy is one in which relationships between mortals and gods are deeply troubled. The world of the dead is caught up in the world of the living. The cosmos is filled with disease and in need of a cataclysmic cleansing.

CONCLUSION

Ancient tragedy is a genre that promotes polyphony and we cannot necessarily expect an entirely consistent theological message either across a playwright's oeuvre or even within a single play. Perhaps what is most striking, in comparison with more recent tragedies, is the deep pervasiveness of religious issues in ancient tragedy. In both the performance context of the ancient Athenian religious festivals, and in the thematic preoccupations, content, imagery, and language of the plays themselves, the relationship between gods and mortals is a fundamental and recurrent concern. Ancient tragedy grew out of, developed in parallel to, and, perhaps most importantly, served to examine the religious beliefs and practices of ancient Greece and Rome.

CHAPTER SIX

Politics of City and Nation

ROBERT COWAN

Tragedy was always political in the Graeco-Roman world, but not always in the same way.[1] It was born under tyranny but flowered under democracy, only to be appropriated by oligarchies and other tyrannies. Scholars disagree radically about tragic politics even in the period for which we have the most evidence, fifth-century Athens. Some believe that tragedy asserted the values of Athenian democracy, and shared the spirit of questioning and debate that were prominent in the political assembly.[2] Some argue that the political concerns of tragedy are those of any classical Greek *polis* rather than specific to those of democratic Athens.[3] Others argue that tragedy can, sometimes at least, serve as an apolitical exploration of the human condition.[4] Yet the definition of politics should not be limited to constitutional debates like that in Euripides' *Suppliant Women* or the (narrated) dramatizations of an assembly in session, as in his *Trojan Women* and *Orestes*. Politics is about how human beings relate to each other within a societal context, and how their ethical values impact upon themselves and their fellows; as such, politics is at the heart of tragedy.[5]

THE POLITICS OF FORM: TRAGEDY VERSUS EPIC AND LYRIC

Tragedy is political in its very form.[6] Earlier genres, notably epic and lyric, have a narrator who channels the divine discourse of the Muses and guides the audience's response to the story. In Pindar's *Nemean 8*, the lyric "I" asserts the superiority of aristocratic to democratic values by claiming that Ajax lost to Odysseus in the contest for the arms of Achilles as the result of deceit and corruption (*Nem.* 8.21–32).[7] Audiences can oppose or reject these assertions, and they may be undermined or questioned by other voices in the poem itself; but the existence of a narrator (in epic) or a lyric "I" provides an overwhelmingly authoritative guiding voice.

Tragedy, by contrast, has no authorial or authoritative voice. Opinions are asserted by individuals on the stage without gloss or commentary from a narrator, so that the audience is invited, or rather is required to assess those opinions using their own judgment. In Sophocles' *Ajax*, the same accusation about the contest of the arms is made as in *Nemean* 8:

> And yet I reckon this for sure: that if Achilles
> were alive, and going to award his armour
> as the prize for highest bravery,
> then no one else would bear it off but me.
> Instead, the Sons of Atreus have purveyed them

to a man who'll stop at nothing,
and pushed aside my powerful claim.

—Sophocles *Ajax* 441–6, tr. Taplin

Yet where the Pindaric persona's allegations of malpractice claim the authority of the Muses and enlist the consensus of the citizen chorus, the accusation in Sophocles is made by Ajax himself, a great hero, but one who has just attempted treacherously to slaughter his own fellow-soldiers, one voice among many as opposed to the only voice speaking.[8] Persuasive speech was of immense importance in fifth-century Athens, but it was also the object of immense suspicion. The ability of an individual to sway the jury or the assembly by the power of words, rather than by the weight of ancestral influence, lay at the heart of democratic ideology. Yet it also had the potential to be abused, to make the worse case the better, as the Sophists were accused of doing. Tragedy allows its characters to speak for themselves, to have the opportunity to persuade the pseudo-assembly of the audience, but it also subjects them to full scrutiny and skepticism, unprotected by the inspired endorsement of an omniscient narrator.[9] This is the Greek ideal of *isegoria*, equal right to speak, in action. Politics, and more specifically democratic politics, is both debated and enacted.

Of course, tragedians had mechanisms for shaping the audience's responses to characters and their opinions. Characters can be depicted as cruel, arrogant, or tyrannical, and their assertions accordingly undermined. Yet even here, the possibility remains, within the democracy of the stage, for their voice to persuade at least some of the audience. In Euripides' *Heracles*, the usurping Theban tyrant, Lycus, attempting to murder the helpless wife, elderly father, and young children of the absent hero, is about as close to an irredeemable villain as Attic tragedy can offer; but even he is given a potentially persuasive speech attacking archery in favor of the more traditionally Greek and ideologically-charged mode of hoplite warfare.[10] The audience is left to judge.

Political assertions in tragedy are contested, and it is this aspect of tragedy's form which is perhaps most overtly political. Though the origins of tragedy are endlessly controversial, it seems likely that we can accept the broad traditional outline whereby it started as a choral genre, whose chorus-leader became a separate actor who could interact with and confront the chorus. The addition of a second and later a third actor increased the potential for interactions and confrontations between individuals. Even in its most abstract form, this setting of an individual in polar opposition to the community, actor, and chorus, whether in antagonism, domination, or cooperation, dramatizes the essence of politics, the relationship between the political subject and the collective of which she or he both is and is not a part. Early tragedy shows this most clearly. In many of the plays of Aeschylus, the chorus interacts for the most part with one protagonist, as the Theban maidens do with Eteocles in the *Seven Against Thebes*, or with a series of individuals, as the Argive elders do in turn with Clytemnestra, the Messenger, Cassandra, and Aegisthus in the *Agamemnon*. In the *Suppliant Women*, the Chorus of Danaids are themselves the protagonist, asking for guidance from their father Danaus, seeking asylum from Pelasgus, and confronting the Egyptian herald, dramatizing the different ways in which a community can interact with powerful individuals and they with it.

Almost every tragedy features at least one passage of stichomythia, where two characters each deliver one line alternately.[11] Although such passages can feel intolerably strained and artificial to modern audiences, they perfectly embody the balanced juxtaposition of opposed points of view, the cut-and-thrust of debate, in marked contrast to the extended, single-voiced utterances of epic and lyric. Diametrically-opposed views are allowed one iambic trimeter each, responding to and capping each other. Politics are enacted as well as debated; they are both form and content.

As well as the back-and-forth of stichomythia, many tragedies include a more extended, formal debate, or *agon*, whose modes of argumentation have a great deal in common with the contemporary rhetorical techniques of the law courts and assembly.[12] Indeed, a recent radical re-evaluation of tragic rhetoric argues that forensic and political rhetoric might have been as much influenced by tragedy as vice versa.[13] As with stichomythia, two sides of the argument are balanced and the audience invited to respond. Such debates are inherently political—in their form regardless of their content—as can be seen from the *agon* in which Hippolytus defends himself to his father Theseus against the (false) charge of raping his stepmother Phaedra. He begins, "I lack the art of glib speech for addressing a crowd" (Euripides *Hippolytus* 986 tr. Morwood). Hippolytus is an anti-democratic figure, whose devotion to Artemis and virginity is bound up with a refusal to progress to manhood and to play a full part in the life of the *polis*.[14] His attack on "glib speech" is primarily an attack on the democratic nature of rhetoric and debate, and thus paradoxically a reassertion of their democratic nature. Euripides reinforces the political dimension of the *agon* even as his protagonist tries to undermine it. Form asserts meaning even in the face of opposing content.

THE POLITICS OF CONTEXT: TRAGEDY IN FIFTH-CENTURY ATHENS

The importance of tragedy within the fifth- and fourth-century Athenian democracy can be inferred from a number of aspects largely separate from the content of the plays themselves. The plays were financed by a combination of state funding and the semi-compulsory public benefactions known as liturgies. Actors were paid by the *polis*, which in itself argues for the genre's political significance. The funding and training of the chorus (*khoregia*) were undertaken as a liturgy by sufficiently wealthy Athenian citizens.[15] More controversially, the Theoric Fund enabled poor Athenians to pay the entrance fee to the dramatic festival of the Great Dionysia. The dating and even existence of this fund has been much debated, though there is some consensus that it was a feature of the fourth century. In any case, state funds enabled a wide cross-section of the demos to attend the dramatic festivals. Tragedy was publicly funded in Athens not to broaden the mind but, like Dionysus bringing back Aeschylus from the Underworld in Aristophanes' *Frogs*, to save the city by creating good citizens.

Tragedy was performed at festivals of the wine-god, Dionysus, the Lenaea, and above all the Great or City Dionysia.[16] The latter festival was a flagship event for the Athenian *polis*, celebrating and reinforcing its own values among its citizenry, while at the same time advertising its power and prestige in front of visiting non-Athenians, who, in late March (the festival ran from 10th–14th Elaphebolion), would have recently arrived following the early spring re-opening of the sailing season.[17] The various activities that preceded the performance of the plays fit into this picture. The ten "generals" (who were political as much as military leaders) performed a sacrifice on behalf of the city. Tribute from Athens' erstwhile allies in the Delian League, who in the second half of the fifth century were almost unambiguously subjects in her empire, was paraded before the audience. A list of those who had benefited the *polis* was read out and honors bestowed on them. Finally, boys and young men who had been orphaned when their fathers died fighting for Athens were paraded in the full hoplite panoply, a set of infantry armor and weapons, which the *polis* paid for in such cases. It seems inevitable that the performance of the tragedies following these parades should serve comparable political ends, and that the political import of the parades should color the reception of the plays and vice versa. Yet it is not at all clear what precisely that political import was.

One clear political effect of the Dionysia's pre-play rituals is that they were aimed at glorifying Athens. Religion and politics were rarely separated in the classical Greek world, but the choice of Athens' political leaders to perform the sacrifice to Dionysus emphatically reinforced the *polis*' claim to peculiar divine favor, a claim for which there is much other evidence.[18] The parade of tribute could be presented as a celebration of Athens' role in leading other Greek cities in their continued defense against Persian attack. More importantly, it was a declaration of Athenian naval and hence political power, wealth, and prestige. However, the remaining two turned the focus from Athens' military and financial glory to moral and civic excellence. The practice of rewarding benefactions celebrated the reciprocal relationship between citizen and *polis*. It emphasized that prominent individuals are needed within the egalitarian collective, but that they must be properly integrated in such a way that they serve rather than threaten the *polis*.[19] Similarly with the parade of war-orphans, the self-sacrifice of the one for the many, of the hoplite for the *polis*, is valorized but also inextricably linked with the reciprocal nurturing of the one by the many, of the orphan by the *polis*.

The pre-play rituals find echoes in the action of the tragedies. The role of the "great man" as, like those rewarded in the festival, potential benefactor but also potential threat to the wider community is a recurrent motif in plays such as *Ajax*, *Oedipus Tyrannos*, *Oedipus at Colonus*, and *Heracles*, where the tension between benefit and threat is often only resolved through insulating the great man in the safe space of hero-cult.[20] The metaphorical self-sacrifice in battle performed by the fathers of the war-orphans finds its mythological analog in the literal self-sacrifice to save the community by Menoeceus in the *Phoenician Women*, Macaria in the *Children of Heracles*, and the daughters of the eponymous hero of *Erechtheus*.[21] Finally, the treatment of war-orphans themselves is foregrounded in the depiction of Eurysaces in *Ajax*, who will be deprived of his warrior father, though in rather different circumstances.[22] Audience response to these motifs would have been shaped by the political context of the City Dionysia.

But we should not assume that all audience members would respond in the same way. Athenians and non-Athenians, the latter including other Greeks and non-Greeks, would surely have different responses, as would men and women, if the latter were indeed in the audience, and spectators of different social statuses. Responses to the politics of tragedy would also have varied according to spectators' diverse attitudes towards the relative merits of democracy, tyranny, or oligarchy.[23] We can plausibly imagine different responses even from different individuals of roughly the same socio-political status.[24] Moreover, even this complex contextual picture only applies to the first performances of tragedies in the fifth-century Great Dionysia in Athens.[25]

THE POLITICS OF ANACHRONISM: TRAGEDIES SET IN ATHENS AND IN NOT-ATHENS

The political content of Attic tragedy ranges from explicit debates over constitutional theory and the depiction of governance in action to less overt explorations of interactions

FIGURE 6.1: Attic amphora showing Ajax and Achilles playing a board game in the presence of the goddess Athena, *c.* 510 BCE. This scene was popular in late sixth-century Athens and it has been suggested that it illustrates the value, within the contemporary political arena, of staying alert, since it was because the army was distracted that Peisistratos the tyrant had been able to take control of the city. Attributed to Leagros Group. J. Paul Getty Museum, 86.AE.81. Digital image courtesy of the Getty's Open Content Program.

between individuals and between individuals and the community. Nevertheless it almost all takes place a long time ago in a *polis* far, far away.[26] Its sister genre, Old Comedy, for all the fantasy of its flying dung-beetles and bird-cities in the clouds, was generally set in a recognizable version of contemporary Athens, peopled by recognizable contemporary types and even (parodic versions of) real contemporary figures, such as Lamachus, Socrates, and Cleon. By contrast, virtually all Attic tragedy is set in the mythical past, and the majority in locations other than Athens. Its political content is therefore less explicit than that of comedy. But tragedy does not try to reconstruct the Mycenaean Age or even to replicate the composite heroic world of Homeric epic. The introduction of deliberately anachronistic fifth-century ideas and institutions into the notionally heroic world of the plays repeatedly invites the spectator to draw parallels between her or his world and that of Eteocles, Orestes, and Hecabe.[27] At the same time, the plays insist on the otherness of the tragic world.[28] Tragedy is both mirror and foil to contemporary politics and society.

An example:[29] when the Argive assembly gathers in Euripides' *Orestes* to decide how to deal with the eponymous anti-hero and his sister, Electra, who have killed their mother, Clytemnestra, a Messenger reports the intervention of a rabble-rousing orator:

> Then there stood up a man with no check on his tongue, strong in his brashness;
> he was an Argive but no Argive, suborned,
> relying on noise from the crowd and the obtuse license of his tongue,
> persuasive enough to involve them in the future in some misfortune.
> When someone of pleasing speech but without sense persuades the people,
> it is a great misfortune for the city.
>
> —Euripides *Orestes* 902–10 tr. Kovacs

Would an Athenian spectator take this as a lightly-veiled critique of the Athenian assembly, which could similarly be swayed by demagogues towards self-destructive decisions? Or would audience members think such abuses were inevitable in a less politically enlightened age, in contrast to the superior constitutional set-up of Athens? These are, of course, crude extremes at the ends of a spectrum; but they demonstrate the range of possibilities open to modern interpreters of tragic politics, and also surely to the original audience. The various settings of the extant tragedies, Argos, Troy, and above all Thebes, serve as a sort of anti-Athens, an inversion and sometimes perversion of all the positive political and ethical qualities upon which Athens prided herself.[30] Yet such self-definition by antithesis also inevitably expresses anxieties about what Athens could become, or perhaps already is.

Despite the anachronistic introduction of democratically flavored elements, such as the Argive assembly, most cities in tragedy are set apart from fifth-century Athens by their constitutional status as monarchies. This contrast is made explicit in the *agon* between the pro-monarchic Theban Herald and the paradoxically democratic king Theseus in Euripides' *Suppliant Women*, the former mocking the gullibility of the ignorant mob and proclaiming the desirability of a single strong ruler, while the latter asserts that "There is nothing more hostile to a city than a tyrant" (429). The slippage between monarchy and tyranny is a significant one. Athenian citizens in general abhorred the idea of tyranny and celebrated the (historically dubious) ending of their own Peisistratid tyranny by the tyrannicides Harmodius and Aristogeiton as an aetiology of its democracy; but opposition to the institution was widespread in other Greek cities, including oligarchies and monarchies. Attic tragedy is distinctive, however, in depicting all monarchy as tending towards tyranny.[31]

In marked contrast to the concept of "the good king" so prominent in Hellenistic political philosophy, and already foreshadowed in Homer, Pindar, and Xenophon, in tragedy there is almost no such thing as a good king. Partial exceptions can be found in, significantly, the Athenian kings, Theseus, his son Demophoon in *The Children of Heracles*, and the eponymous Erechtheus, though even these have their critics.[32] Apart from weak kings like Pelasgus in Aeschylus' *Suppliants* and Aegeus (another Athenian) in Euripides' *Medea*, non-Athenian tragic kings dramatize the inevitability of monarchy's degeneration into tyranny. Even as sympathetic a figure as Sophocles' Oedipus, despite starting the play as the benevolent father of his people who has saved the city once and is trying to do so again, shows this tendency in his increasingly paranoid suspicion of Creon and Teiresias, and his threats of brutal violence towards the Shepherd. However, it is Creon himself, in *Antigone*, who most clearly dramatizes—and implies the inevitability of—the degeneration of kingship into tyranny.[33] Modern performances and receptions of this play often cast Antigone as a relatively straightforward resistance figure opposing the dictatorial Creon. A more nuanced reading is Hegel's famous assertion that the play is a clash of right against right: the assertion of personal and religious principles, against the rule of law in

FIGURE 6.2: Detail of a Lucanian nestoris (Lucania is a region of southern Italy, and a nestoris is a type of vase), possibly depicting the scene from Sophocles' *Antigone* in which Antigone is brought before Creon, who listens to the explanation of the guard; this interpretation is debatable, and the scene has also been understood as showing Helen and Priam. *c.* 390–380 BCE, attributed to the Dolon painter. The British Museum, London, 1867,0508.1330. © The Trustees of the British Museum. All rights reserved.

defense of the community. However, in many ways the play dramatizes the clash of wrong against wrong, or at least shows how rights can be perverted into wrongs. Antigone's defense of divine law by giving her brother Polynices due burial is increasingly shown to be motivated by her obsession with the rights of her own, royal family over those of the *polis*, the house of Oedipus, whose proclivities towards incest and fratricide embody the insularity and self-destructiveness of tyrannical monarchy.[34] Creon's defense of the law of the *polis* degenerates into an assertion of his own monarchical authority, the essence of tyranny. The fall of Creon shows what happens when a superficially democratic agenda is implemented by a monarch, who must inevitably become a tyrant.

It is no coincidence that such a perverted mirror of political process takes place in Athens' evil twin city of Thebes, but this in turn raises questions about the politics of tragedies set in Athens itself. As has been mentioned, tragedy, unlike comedy, almost always avoided the directly contemporary. The two known exceptions are the extant *Persians* by Aeschylus (472 BCE), which deals with the relatively recent Battle of Salamis (480) and the end of the Persian Wars, but maintains maximum geographical distance and cultural difference by being set in the Persian capital of Susa and having a cast of Persian characters (for a roughly-contemporary visual depiction of the conflict between Greeks and Persians, see Figure 6.3). Contemporary Greek and especially Athenian achievements could thus be celebrated while maintaining a "tragic" depiction of the downfall of the royal house, a downfall explicitly resulting from the political (as well as cultural, ethnic, and moral) inferiority of Xerxes and the Persian Empire.[35] The other example is only known from its mention in Herodotus' *Histories* in relation to the sack by the Persians of the Greek city of Miletus in 499 BCE:[36] for the Athenians, besides that they signified in many other ways their deep grief for the taking of Miletus, did this especial when:

> Phrynichus having written a play entitled *The Fall of Miletus* and set it on the stage, the whole theater broke into weeping; and they fined Phrynichus a thousand drachmae for bringing to mind a calamity that touched them so nearly, and forbade forever the acting of that play.
>
> —Herodotus 6.21, tr. Godley

The "calamity that touched them so nearly" (*oikeia kaka*) could also be translated as "their own misfortunes," which more sharply delineates the distinction between what Athenian audiences felt was and was not appropriate for tragic representation. Distance and difference must be maintained: if misfortunes are depicted, they must not be Athenian; if Athens is depicted it must not be suffering misfortunes, or at least not deserved and unmitigated ones.[37] Tragedies set in Athens do show crises, threats, and suffering, but always overcome, usually by the political and moral excellence of Athens, often in defense of the weak and oppressed. This pattern can be seen in Euripides' *Suppliant Women* and *Children of Heracles*, where Argive widows and refugee Heraclids respectively are

FIGURE 6.3: Attic amphora showing a rare scene of a Greek warrior fighting a Persian warrior, *c.* 480–470 BCE. The Metropolitan Museum of Art, NY, 06.1021.117.

championed and defended by the Athenian *polis*. Some scholars still raise questions about aspects of Athenian policy in these plays, such as the vengeful execution of the surprisingly pitiful defeated oppressor Eurystheus in the latter tragedy. Yet even here the moral and political opprobrium is heaped upon Alcmene and her Spartan descendants, and Athens, so far from being criticized for conniving at Eurystheus' death, is promised his protection against Sparta as the recipient of hero-cult. Athenian judicial procedure ends the Argive cycle of blood-feud in Aeschylus' *Eumenides* by acquitting Orestes of culpability for killing his mother, Clytemnestra. When Athens herself is threatened in Euripides' *Erechtheus*, the self-sacrifice of the royal family—the literal human sacrifice of the king's daughters and his own death in battle—shows the subordination of the individual, even the most powerful individual, to the good of the community. Again, critics have expressed unease at this sacrifice, especially the sentiments expressed by the girls' mother, Praxithea.[38] But Athens is saved and Praxithea's sacrifice is efficacious; because it inverts the natural and social norms of motherhood, the sequence dramatizes democracy's valuation of the community's good over the preservation of the royal family. While we should not argue for an exclusively pro-Athenian interpretation, many Attic tragedies do seem to celebrate the city of Athens and Athenian democratic values, and offer a critique of non-democratic modes of government.

THE POLITICS OF APPROPRIATION: TRAGEDY COMES TO ROME

Tragedy was reinvented for Sicilian tyrants and oligarchic colonies in Magna Graecia, and for Macedonian kings and Hellenistic cities, in recomposition and in reperformance; each of these new contexts required tragedy to take on a different political identity. Yet the most radical transformation of tragedy—and of what we can conveniently call Greek literature as a whole—was its appropriation by Rome in the third century BCE.[39] It is easy to forget just how radical a move this was. The composition of works in a genre which originated in another culture—haikus in English, tragedies in Hausa—is commonplace in modern societies. However, there is no earlier or contemporary parallel for the way in which Rome took the Greek genres of epic, comedy, and above all tragedy, and appropriated them by writing works in the Latin language to be performed to Roman audiences using conceptual terms comprehensible to their new public. Attic tragedies took on a new meaning when reperformed in Syracuse or Heracleia, but they still retained their place within a wider Panhellenic linguistic, cultural, ethnic, and in the broadest sense political system. The Romanization of tragedy was an altogether more revolutionary political act.

Almost two and a half centuries later, at the end of the first century BCE, the poet Horace neatly encapsulated the paradox, writing that "captured Greece captured its savage conqueror" (*Epistles* 2.1.156). On one level, appropriating Greek tragedy was indeed a gesture of cultural submission, suggesting that this foreign genre was superior to Italy's native dramatic traditions. Nevertheless, it was also an assertive and aggressive act of conquest, analogous to the plundering and transport of vases and statues from Corinth to Rome. In the course of the second century, Rome would conquer the territory of mainland Greece itself, rendering Greek soil and Greek culture Roman. It is no coincidence that the first "Greek" plays in Latin, by Livius Andronicus, who also transformed Homer's *Odyssey* into a Latin version in Italian Saturnians, were performed in 240 BCE to celebrate

Rome's victory over Carthage in the First Punic War and the acquisition of her first overseas colony, Sicily. Victory, colony, and tragedy all signaled Rome's new status as a world power and one whose destiny was conquest.

Tragedy never entirely lost its flavor of "Greekness" and at least some of its cultural cachet derived from this sense of incomplete naturalization. The alterity of tragedy also contributed to its political function within a Roman context, as the feeling of distance and difference between audience and stageworld, already detectable between fifth-century Athens and heroic Thebes, was given another dimension when Roman audiences were invited both to identify with and differentiate themselves from the even more remote Greek heroes onstage. Some scholars have tried to find significance in the depiction of the Romans' mythical ancestors, the Trojans, but the evidence is unconvincing.[40] Indeed, the interpretation of Republican tragic politics is made very difficult by the loss of all but fragments from the plays themselves and of almost all contemporary accounts of their performance context. What evidence does survive risks distorting our interpretation, since we are forced to view the politics of tragedy in the third and second centuries through the lens of the very different political conditions of the late Republic, and in particular the writings of Cicero.[41] However, with due caution, some sense of the politics of mid-Republican tragedy can be reconstructed.

The performance context of Republican tragedy was very different from that of fifth-century Athens, and this has massive implications for its political connotations.[42] Plays were performed at religious festivals, *ludi scaenici*, in honor of gods such as Jupiter, Apollo, Ceres, and Cybele, just as Attic tragedies were performed at festivals of Dionysus, but the similarities end there. Performances were indeed subject to the organization, control, and funding of public officials, the curule aedile, plebeian aedile, or city praetor, depending on the festival, but the political connection was more with the individual magistrate himself than with the *res publica* as a whole. The production of lavish performances may have contributed to the advancement of political careers, but the situation was very different from the Dionysia, where archons and strategoi represented the *polis* as a whole and thus forged a close connection between *polis* and performance.[43]

Roman tragedies were further separated from the body politic by the identity of their composers and performers. Unlike the Athenian Aeschylus, Sophocles, and Euripides, and their citizen choruses, Rome's tragedians and their players were largely non-citizens from outside Rome: Livius Andronicus, a freed slave from the South Italian Greek colony of Tarentum; the Messapian Ennius, who claimed to have three hearts because he spoke three languages, Latin, Greek, and Oscan; and Accius, a freedman's son from the newly-founded colony of Pisaurum. These tragedians, like the tragedies they composed, embodied the liminal status of a cultural transaction between Greek and Roman culture, and of a political position at the heart of Rome's most important public festivals but still carefully demarcated as coming from outside. Rome's actors were not citizens performing a civic act analogous to their roles in the assembly, the law courts, the temples, and the navy, but outsiders whose very status as actors denied them citizen rights, branding them *infames*. Even the performance space was very different from the Theater of Dionysus, a permanent space on the lower slopes of the Acropolis at the heart of Athens. Rome had no permanent theater until 55 BCE and numerous attempts to build one failed.[44] Tragedies (and comedies) were instead staged on temporary structures at various locations throughout the city, such as the Forum and the Circus Maximus, which were constructed for and dismantled after each festival. Even on a physical level, tragedy was something set apart, confined not only to festival time but to a space which ceased to exist when the performance ended.

This careful segregation of tragedy at Rome, especially when contrasted with Athens, could be thought to deprive it of political significance.[45] Instead, we should see the politics of Republican tragedy as transformed not merely in its meaning but in its mode of dramatization. Tragedy ceases to be embedded within the *polis*. Tragedy is now set apart as a cultural artifact, controlled by an aristocratic elite and performed by non-citizen outsiders, a political performance for but not by the *res publica*. Once more, the transformation of tragic politics reflects the transformation of politics offstage. The Roman Republic had democratic elements within its mixed constitution, but the dominance of its aristocratic elite made it far closer to Spartan oligarchy than to Athenian radical democracy. Tragedy still had the potential to challenge and question, but its dominant tendency to reinforce the status quo by dramatizing the self-destruction of alternative political scenarios held as true in Republican Rome as in democratic Athens. The peculiarly Roman phenomenon of *fabulae praetextae*, tragedies on Roman themes, offers a close parallel to Athenian tragedies set in Athens, as distance and difference are partially collapsed to offer a celebration of Rome and a denigration of threats to its political values.[46]

The fragmentary nature of the plays, more exiguous than those of even lost Athenian plays that are often supplemented by papyrus finds, makes it very hard to reconstruct the specific political content of the plays; but the insistence on aristocratic values is pervasive. So too is the hatred of tyranny, as deep-seated in Rome as in Athens, and possessing its own foundational place in the Republic's birth with the expulsion of the kings. Some have seen the depiction of Accius' tyrants, such as Tereus and especially Atreus, with his notorious slogan "let them hate so long as they fear," as targeted particularly at the populist politicians of the late second century, in particular the revolutionary brothers Tiberius and Gaius Gracchus.[47] While such coded allusions can be seductive, it is more likely that such tragic tyrants are responses to a broader anxiety about monarchical politics and its threat to Rome's constitutional stability, in particular the preservation of its political elite's position of dominance. In the absence of more evidence we cannot be certain, but it seems overwhelmingly likely that Republican tragedy was as intricately bound to the ideology of the Roman Republic as Attic tragedy was to that of democratic Athens.

THE POLITICS OF REPERFORMANCE: TRAGEDY IN THE LATE REPUBLIC

The great period of Republican tragedy ended with the death of Accius around the start of the first century BCE, but the great plays continued to be reperformed. Several late Republican performances show a particularly radical reshaping of political meaning in reperformance.[48]

The first and probably most radical reshaping by reperformance was the manipulation, by actors and by audience, of individual lines, largely deracinated from their wider context within the play, to yield a specific, topical significance. Cicero writes to his friend Atticus of an incident in 59 BCE when the actor Diphilus used an existing line of tragedy to attack Pompey the Great: "To our misfortune you are Great (*nostra miseria tu es magnus/ Magnus*)," punning on Pompey's cognomen *Magnus* "The Great," an attack which led to multiple encores.[49] We do not know what play the line came from and whether any of the force of the attack derived from a constructed parallelism between Pompey and a character onstage, as opposed to resting solely on the wordplay, but in either case the tragedy, or at least one line from it, was given a new political meaning generated entirely by the context of its reperformance. Indeed, Cicero's remark that "these lines might seem to have been written for the occasion by an enemy of Pompey" underlines the way in which reperformance mimics the effect of composition, producing a meaning which is as new as if it had just been written. A similar but even more complex effect was produced, if we can trust Cicero's own understandably partial account, when the actor Aesopus used lines from a reperformance of Accius' *Eurysaces*, with further lines interpolated from Ennius' *Andromacha*, to lament Cicero's exile and support his recall, to (allegedly) great acclaim by the audience.[50] Here the manipulation of the original script is more overt, since lines from another play are introduced, but there is also a clearer sense that the cumulative effect of numerous lines and perhaps even of a scene or the play as a whole was made into a political allegory. Such manipulations are significant for what they tell us about the political meaning which could be generated by the reperformances themselves, but also because they show that audiences were already predisposed to interpret tragedy as having a political meaning.

An intriguing test case for this is the opening of Pompey's theater in 55 BCE and the tragedies staged, alongside other entertainments, to mark the occasion.[51] This was the first permanent theater in Rome, a significant moment in itself for the political history of tragedy, but its main interest for our purposes lies in Pompey's attempt to harness tragic spectacle for political self-glorification. Again, our evidence is from Cicero, whose emphasis is on the vulgarity of the spectacle and its lack of cultural merit, rhetorically asking his friend Marcus Marius "What pleasure is there in getting a *Clytemnestra* with six hundred mules or a *Trojan Horse* with three thousand mixing bowls?"[52] Through the cultural snobbery (Cicero also sneers at the public's gaping wonder at the spectacle) can be seen the political significance of Pompey's performance. The victor over Mithridates and over the pirates of the Eastern Mediterranean was depicting himself as a new Agamemnon, king of kings, and conqueror of a great eastern power. It is tempting to speculate that the mixing bowls might have been actual booty from Pompey's eastern campaigns, further blurring the distinction between onstage action and offstage reality. This hyperbolic aggrandizement of Pompey was obviously very well-suited to his great act of public munificence, the building of the theater whose existence and opening performance both celebrated the great man.

Although we know nothing about the *Trojan Horse*, not even whether it was Livius' or Naevius' tragedy of that name, the dramatization of the Sack of Troy would doubtless suit Pompey's allegorical program reasonably well, provided it did not focus too much on the impious excesses of Cassandra's rape and Priam's murder. Accius' *Clytemnestra*, however, must surely have followed the glorious, pseudo-triumphal procession of the returning Agamemnon, complete with six hundred mules, with his ignominious murder by his eponymous wife and her lover Aegisthus. How should an audience cope with the equivalence of Agamemnon and Pompey as the plot continued? It seems most likely that they were intended to compartmentalize their reactions, associating Pompey with the conquering hero but not with the butchered cuckold. That such mental division was considered possible is significant in itself. Nevertheless, reception is notoriously hard to control and it is attractive to wonder whether at least some in the audience saw Pompey not only in Agamemnon triumphant but also in Agamemnon dead.

THE POLITICS OF INTERIORITY: SENECAN TRAGEDY AND THE PRINCIPATE

The politics of Senecan tragedy, like that of the monarchical principate in which it was composed and performed, is marked by a turn inwards and upwards.[53] In performance, in theme, and in form, it moves away from the public interrelations of citizens within the body politic to focus on the internalized conflicts of the passions within the often-mutilated physical body of the individual. The loss of opportunities for elites to compete and perform in the agonistic forum of public life led them to look inwards into the petty republics of their villas and their psyches. The remaining concerns of politics were centered on one man, the princeps. So in Seneca's plays, politics is either sublimated into the metaphorical state of the soul, present only in its absence as an exhortation to withdraw from the perils of public life, or concentrated on the single figure of the monarch, be he good king or tyrant.

Caution is always needed when using an artist's life to interpret their work, but it is virtually impossible to separate the dramatic career of Seneca the Younger from his dramatic writings.[54] Mediating between the two are his philosophical dialogues and letters, which reflect more formally on the political questions which were the stuff of their author's life and of his tragedies. He was born into a distinguished provincial family from Spain, which included his father (Seneca the Elder), the famous writer on declamation, and in the next generation, his nephew, the epic poet, Lucan. Yet it was his contacts with the imperial family which most shaped his life and career. Mistrusted by Caligula, he was exiled to the island of Corsica by Claudius and then recalled by the latter's new wife, Agrippina, to be the tutor of Nero. He continued in this role after Claudius' death and Nero's accession, and is generally credited, along with the praetorian prefect Burrus, with keeping the young princeps' worse excesses in check and producing the relatively prosperous first five years of his reign. After Burrus' death, Seneca withdrew from public life but was implicated in the Pisonian conspiracy and compelled to commit suicide in 65 CE. Seneca was a man who benefited and suffered from the exercise of absolute power, who tried with temporary success to guide and control it, and who was ultimately destroyed by it. Even if we stop short of seeing flashes of self-portrait in his tragedies' many doomed victims and impotent advisors, the political ideas explored and dramatized in them were undeniably rooted in his lived experience.

Alongside—many would say in spite of—his great wealth and involvement in politics, Seneca was, perhaps above all, a Stoic philosopher. This chapter is not the place to discuss the larger question of the relationship between Stoicism and Senecan tragedy, but philosophy is another site of contact between the tragedies and Seneca's life, and one which shares much territory with politics. Stoicism was by no means a quietist or antipolitical philosophy like Epicureanism, with its key doctrines of not being involved in politics and living without anyone noticing. Indeed, a modified form of Stoicism tallied so well with elite Roman political values that its language of excellence (*uirtus*) and steadfastness (*constantia*) pervades the political discourse of the late Republic. Under the principate, the same philosophy offered a model of passive resistance, the autonomy of the individual who can withdraw from a political system which is uncongenial and even from a life which is unlivable. Seneca's prose writings reflect on and try to shape the political landscape through which he was traveling, examining them through a philosophical lens which more implicitly colors the worldview of the tragedies. The late *Letters to Lucilius* reflect the inward turn of Seneca's own last years, and the failure of tragic figures like Thyestes to do likewise. The *On Clemency* (*De Clementia*) offers a positive model of kingship for the young Nero, but one pervaded by the shadow of its dark opposite, tyranny. The inward and upward turn fuse in *On Anger* (*De Ira*), as Seneca meditates on the way that anger tyrannizes over the soul and is externalized in the way the angry tyrant oppresses his subjects. All of these elements, political in their rejection of conventional politics, recur in the tragedies.

Performance context, as ever, is key, though here we enter once more an area of controversy which is beyond the scope of this chapter.[55] No one knows for certain what the original performance context of Senecan tragedy was and possibilities range from fully-staged public performance to private reading, with a small majority favoring the idea of unstaged recitation, by several or, more probably, a single performer. Tragedy was no longer the popular public (and political) spectacle of Cicero's day, a position then filled by pantomime, a sort of solo ballet with choral accompaniment, and gladiatorial shows, both of which had an impact on Seneca's dramaturgy.[56] Full public staging of Senecan tragedy in stone theaters is the least likely scenario, which is by no means to deny the intense theatricality of the plays, even if that theatricality may have been realized primarily in the mind's eye of a reader or listener, rather than of a spectator. Whether the plays were staged in small, private theatrical spaces, recited in recitation halls, or read privately in a domestic environment, the move away from tragedy as a popular, public performance towards the elite gathering, the imperial court, and the reader's mind parallels the movement of tragic politics away from the people and the *res publica* to the court, the emperor, and the soul.

It is tempting—and it is a temptation to which many scholars have succumbed—to see codes and allegories for specific emperors and their entourages in the plays:[57] Nero or Claudius in the incestuous and parricidal Oedipus, Caligula in the tyrannical Atreus. Such interpretations cannot be disproven and there is evidence that other imperial tragedies were taken in this way, even by emperors themselves, as when Tiberius is claimed to have executed a tragedian for slandering Agamemnon in a play, presumably because of the implied identification with the princeps.[58] Indeed, an earlier imitator of Seneca's tragic style implicitly read his models in this way when he depicted Nero's incestuous, matricidal, and tyrannical behavior very much in the Senecan manner in the (probably early Flavian) historical drama *Octavia*. However, it is safer and arguably more satisfying to see the plays as reflecting wider political concerns about the principate and the massive power of one man as opposed to the specific flaws of individuals.

Tyranny is even more prominent in Senecan tragedy than in its predecessors. Not only the more obvious despots like Atreus in *Thyestes* and Lycus in *Hercules Furens*, but characters who are largely depicted more neutrally as kings in Attic tragedy, like the eponymous Agamemnon and Creon in *Medea*, become outright and even self-conscious tyrants. Tragedy here shows the influence of centuries of Roman political discourse, itself informed by Attic and Hellenistic depictions of tragic tyrants, and also the prominence of tyrants in declamation, the rhetorical training exercises central to Roman elite education.[59] However, it is their self-consciousness about their tyranny which sets Seneca's tyrants apart. The most self-conscious of all is Atreus in *Thyestes*, who revels in his wickedness, plotting to transgress all boundaries, ethical and political, in his revenge, wittily twisting and capping the "good king" platitudes with which his attendant tries to restrain him:[60]

> ATREUS: This is the greatest value of kingship: that the people are compelled to praise as well as endure their master's actions.

ASSISTANT: When fear compels them to praise, fear also turns them into enemies. But one who seeks the tribute of sincere support will want praise from the heart rather than the tongue.
ATREUS: Sincere praise often comes even to a lowly man; false praise comes only to the mighty. They must want what they do not want!
ASSISTANT: Let a king want what is honorable: everyone will want the same.
ATREUS: Where a sovereign is permitted only what is honorable, he rules on sufferance.
ASSISTANT: Where there is no shame, no concern for the law, no righteousness, goodness, loyalty, rule is unstable.
ATREUS: Righteousness, goodness, loyalty are private values: kings should go where they please.

—Seneca *Thyestes* 205–18 tr. Fitch

Seneca here offers almost a parody of tyranny, an extreme, limiting case which can be taken as a mirror which presents the opposite of the desirable good king, or as an expression of anxiety about what a monarch can, perhaps must, become. The people are mentioned, but purely as the most debased of subjects, lacking all agency—political or otherwise—of their own. Not only all political power but all political agency, all politics, is concentrated in the person of the monarch. The most troubling aspect of Senecan tragedy is its tendency to show evil triumphant. Like his Medea, Seneca's Atreus ends the play in a state of gloating victory over his brother Thyestes and in total control of kingdom, cosmos, and even language. The absence of the reassuring closural downfall of the politically (as well as morally) deprecated anti-hero leaves the audience stuck in a Stoic nightmare where tyranny reigns in perpetuity. Whether they could detect any distance and difference from their lived reality is the unanswerable question at the heart of the politics of Senecan tragedy.

The one area in which Atreus', like Medea's, triumph can be seen to be incomplete is in their failure to exert dominion over their own souls. Although Atreus is depicted as a dark perversion of the Stoic wise man (*sapiens*), self-controlling and self-controlled, his excessive anger and his insatiable appetite to move beyond all human boundaries mark him out as a political failure in the kingdom of his own psyche.[61] When politics, in the conventional sense of the exercise of power in the interactions between individuals and communities, is impossible or at most limited to the caprices of one individual, a different politics must be practiced, a politics which denies politics and turns inwards. Atreus may dominate the world outside, but the wise man can be king in himself. These are the sentiments expressed by the chorus which immediately follows Atreus' disquisition on tyranny:

> A king is one rid of fear
> and the evil of an ugly heart;
> one that no willful ambition
> or the ever shifting favor
> of the hasty mob can affect . . .
>
> Set in an obscure place
> let me bask in gentle leisure;
> known to no Quirites
> let my life flow on through peace.

> So, when my days have passed
> without turmoil, let me die
> an old plebeian man.
>
> —Seneca *Thyestes* 348–52, 381–403

This passage is notable for anachronisms unparalleled in Attic tragedy or even elsewhere in Seneca, as the chorus of old men in mythical Argos sing of Rome's contemporary enemies, the Parthians, refer to their fellow-citizens by the distinctively Roman civic term of Quirites and to themselves by the scarcely less Roman "plebeian." Nowhere does any classical tragedian do more to obliterate the distance and difference between the worlds of play and audience, to demand that his audience interpret the tragedy as politically meaningful to its own age. Yet the politics it advocates is no politics and its king no king. The politics of Senecan tragedy, as of imperial Rome, was the avoidance of politics in favor of the kingship of the self, a sovereignty which no tyrant could take away and few could achieve.

CHAPTER SEVEN

Society and Family

MARCEL WIDZISZ

Literary-critical comments on the family in Greek tragedy begin with Aristotle's discussion in the *Poetics*.[1] His observations concern the prevalence given to certain families in the plays to which he had access (far more extensive, of course, for him than for us): Aristotle notices that the "best" tragedies are composed using stories drawn from relatively few families, a fact especially noteworthy given the vast store of mythological material available for the playwrights to use. The families he mentions (specifically, those of Oedipus, Orestes, Meleager, Thyestes, and Telephus)[2] prominently suffer some form of intra-familial violence and are well-known enough that, in some cases, nothing need be mentioned beyond the name of one of these principal figures for their whole story to be remembered.

Aristotle also juxtaposes the generic qualities of Homer to those of tragedy, especially as epic material contributes so significantly to the substance of tragic plots.[3] This comparison of the two types of poetry, epic and tragedy, however, is not only central to many of Aristotle's arguments, but has also laid the foundation for a continuing critical engagement which seeks to elucidate elements of both genres by contrasting them with one another. One of the central modern arguments has it that Homer, in his idealized presentation of the prerogatives and privileges of the aristocratic family, downplays the more objectionable elements or infamous episodes associated with these clans of the heroic age—exactly those that tragedy takes up and explores with such tenacity.[4] Furthermore, on this argument, both genres betray, in their differing presentations of the family, interests and emphases that are shaped by historical forces of the developing city-state, or *polis*.[5]

While it is clear that Homer knows of stories of violence within the family (e.g., by way of the several mentions of Orestes' revenge in the *Odyssey* at 1.40–3 and 3.306–8, the reference to Oedipus at 11.271–4, and the naming of Eriphyle, who would be killed by her son Alcmaeon, at 11.326), the extant poems that go by Homer's name, the *Iliad* and the *Odyssey*, do not, as a rule, go into details.[6] The Homeric family is rather depicted as committed to maintaining its own integrity against outside threats; witness Agamemnon's willingness to help reassert his brother's rightful claim upon Helen, or Telemachus' efforts to preserve his (i.e., Odysseus') household despite the uncertain fate of his father.[7] Marriage takes place, at least among aristocrats, between members of different communities.[8] Although powerful alliances can be sought through marriage ties, aristocratic families are depicted as largely self-sufficient.[9]

With the development of the *polis*, however, the erstwhile prerogatives of the aristocrats, the narrative focus of Homeric poetry, become progressively curtailed. Law courts, not heads of households, prescribe punishments for wrong-doing,[10] sumptuary laws restrict extravagant displays of familial wealth and power at funerals,[11] and the hero-cult—not especially stressed by Homer[12]—was encouraged as a means to build fellow-feeling among the citizens.[13] The *polis* in general appropriates familial language and family traditions to pull loyalty away from clan-based associations into a *polis*-identified citizen body.[14] Indeed, such was the centripetal pull of pro-*polis* ideology in its various ramifications that its force (despite what seems to be the case with more modern, liberal democracies) may well surprise us.[15]

SOCIO-CULTURAL REALITIES OF THE FIFTH CENTURY

All extant drama that can be safely attributed to one of the three classical tragedians can be assigned to a year or date range within the fifth century BCE.[16] From this same period, we are fortunate to possess a number of documents and other testimonia of the status of the family, which allow for a greater delineation of the transition from the Homeric worldview to the more *polis*-oriented literature of tragedy, comedy, epinician, philosophical prose, history, and—critical for an appreciation of the family—forensic oratory.[17] One of the more important phenomena is the peculiar position of the wife within the family, a position that betrays a potential conflict within the creation of every new household out of a pre-existing one.[18]

Wives and their families

In the fifth century, the *polis* was ideologically and legally invested in the preservation of the individual household (*oikos*);[19] families without a male heir to continue the bloodline received special attention in the form of regulations concerning a surviving female, called an *epikleros*.[20] This brother-less woman was to be married off to a relative on her father's side even if she was married to someone else and, indeed, even if her husband-to-be was already married.[21] Due to the relatively high mortality rate of men from warfare,[22] the phenomenon of the *epikleros* was not a rare one and surviving accounts from court cases explore some of the difficulties raised by the families finding themselves in such unenviable circumstances. While some particulars, such as whether a divorce might be obligatory in the case of an *epikleros*, are less clear, what is a constant is the interest the city-state had in the preservation of the individual household against the vicissitudes of existence in the fifth century.[23] Moreover, the institution of such a practice opens the space for a potential contradiction in the creation of one family from two separate groups, inasmuch as the *epikleros* may well be required to leave her current familial role for an entirely new one: such a policy demonstrates what kind of hold the natal family could exert upon even those of its members who had been married to different families.[24]

Another important way the city-state articulated the contours of the family, again in contrast to the Homeric examples, is the much-discussed Periclean marriage legislation of 451 BCE. By this law, Pericles, the great statesman of the Athenian democracy, had it established that *both* parents must be of verifiable Athenian extraction in order for their progeny to be considered proper Athenians themselves.[25] Although the precise reasons for restricting marriage in this way are debated,[26] the practical effects would have been most keenly felt by the upper classes for whom marriage ties beyond the confines of the *polis* were heretofore a possibility, if not a desideratum.[27] Paradoxically, while the new importance given to the citizenship status of the mother would seem to confer a concomitantly improved circumstance to women as a whole, the *polis* itself may have been the primary beneficiary of such laws.[28]

Women occupied intermediary positions in both their marital and their natal households:[29] we find Pythagoras advocating that wives be treated as "suppliants" at the hearth of their marital home,[30] while it has been argued that one of the factors that facilitated the transfer of a bride to her new home was the relatively tenuous position she occupied in her natal family.[31]

Moreover, the dowry itself was a potentially unstable element within the creation of the marital household, for, although it was never in the woman's power to spend it as she saw fit, it was nevertheless not inalienably part of the husband's property and always potentially something to be restored following divorce or the like.[32] Finally, in the event of her husband's death, there was, legally speaking, not an automatic way for the widow to be given a new *kyrios* or "legal representative."[33]

Fathers and sons at home and in society

The evidence for the relationship between males within the same family is more abundant, as we might expect for a patriarchal society such as the one Athens had during the classical period.[34] Not only does the literature of the period preserve perspectives on these relationships, but also contemporary inscriptions bear witness to the important connections between father and son.[35] Yet here too contradiction, tension, and instability abound, given the dynamics of a society that enjoined and promoted filial loyalty but, at

FIGURE 7.1: Attic pyxis showing preparations for a marriage, *c.* 440–415 BCE. The British Museum, London, 1874,0512.1. © The Trustees of the British Museum. All rights reserved.

the same time, expected young men to show spirit and independence of mind and activity.[36] Indeed, such is the evidence on this score that some argue[37] that we can even go so far as to trace a parabolic rise and descent of the "son" during the course of the fifth century in the tumultuous times of the Peloponnesian War (431–404 BCE) and its aftermath,[38] the time during which almost all of Euripides' extant plays and probably half of Sophocles' surviving tragedies (*Philoctetes* and *Oedipus at Colonus*, and possibly *Oedipus Rex* and *Electra*) were performed.

THE FAMILY OF GREEK TRAGEDY

Fathers and sons on the stage

Both direct and indirect confrontations between fathers and sons are dramatized from the very first surviving play of the fifth century, Aeschylus' *Persians* (472 BCE), to one of its last, Sophocles' *Oedipus at Colonus* (401 BCE);[39] and despite the years intervening between them, both plays depict the struggles of sons to manage familial and political affairs in the shadow of powerful fathers whose gaze sits uncomfortably upon the shoulders of their younger iterations.[40] Almost every encounter between father and son is fraught with misunderstanding and argument (*O.C., Pers., Ant. Phoen., Alc., Hipp.*) if not outright violence (*Her., Hipp., Ant.*, and presupposed in *O.T.*). More often than not the son wilts under the pressures of paternal expectations and will end up dead or greatly diminished in attempting to manage his own and his household's affairs apart from the father's direction. Thus, Xerxes will have to live with a circumscribed ambit for Persian power, just as Polynices' designs for a resumption of power at Thebes will end with his death instead of his (re)installation. In Euripides' *Alcestis*, we find Admetus formalizing a complete rupture with his father, Pheres, who was not willing to die on behalf of his son. The difficulties of interpreting such material can be gauged by how some scholars have read in such encounters either a mythologizing that depicts the fall of the aristocratic household and thus confirms the power of the *polis*, while others have seen in the same plays a continued and largely supportive interest in the prerogatives of the powerful (aristocratic) families to run the affairs of the state.[41]

Case study: Sophocles' Ajax

In Sophocles' *Ajax*, we see both direct and indirect encounters between sons and fathers who struggle with the enduring paternal order. This play treats the aftermath of Ajax trying to wreak revenge upon the Greek army for awarding the arms of Achilles to Odysseus and not to himself. Deluded by Athena into thinking he is killing his human enemies, in reality he is slaughtering the army's cattle.

Recovering from delusion and confronted with his handiwork, Ajax reviews his options (*Aj.* 457–80). Should he return home, he would have to face his father, whom Teucer, Ajax's half-brother, will describe later in the play as particularly mirthless and severe (*Aj.* 1006–18). We know that Telamon, Ajax's father, served in a prior, successful campaign against Troy and expected no less of his son. The account of Telamon's instructions to Ajax gives a clear instance of the tension between father and son in the matter of accruing honor, for while Telamon is insistent that Ajax give credit to the gods for any success (*Aj.* 764–5), Ajax, for his part, is so confident of his own abilities that he boasts of being able to gain victories even without the help of any divinity (*Aj.* 767–9). The son, it seems, aims to do as well or better than the father without the traditional tutelage, a striking claim which was to resonate, as Barry Strauss has shown, in the course of Athenian father–son relations.[42]

Although Ajax rejects some of his father's directives, he does not ignore his own status as a father of Eurysaces, his son by Tecmessa, a "spear-won" bride. Indeed, the first person Ajax calls for as he comes out of his brief coma is his son (*Aj.* 349), whom Tecmessa wisely hid during the hero's bout of madness. Later, after Ajax publicly resolves upon suicide as the best expedient for his (shameful) situation, he calls again for his son. Although his child is too young to understand any of what is said to him (*Aj.* 553; 558–9), Ajax enjoins Eurysaces to be in all respects like his father, only, if possible, luckier (*Aj.* 550–1). Furthermore, his education is to commence immediately, what with the boy looking fearlessly upon the blood-spattered Ajax, since it is necessary to "break him in" (*pōlodamnein*, literally, "to break a horse in")[43] to the "raw tenets" of his ferocious parent (*Aj.* 548–9)—if, that is, the boy really is his father's son (*Aj.* 547).

Apart from the direct patrilineal line of Telamon–Ajax–Eurysaces, the gaze and expectations of the father are felt by Teucer as well, who appears onstage too late to save his half-brother but does all he can for Tecmessa, Eurysaces, and especially for Ajax's corpse, which ought to be buried with all due rites. Looming over Teucer's decision-making process is what Telamon will think of him upon his return to Salamis (*Aj.* 1008–21). By contrast, he only devotes a couple of lines to thoughts of what more immediately awaits him at Troy now that his protector is gone. Teucer's worries reveal the latent problems in the status of a bastard. He fears that he may be suspected of letting Ajax die in order to usurp his position within Telamon's household (*Aj.* 1015–16) and that Telamon may, in response, drive him into exile and render him more a slave than a free-born man.[44]

Within this nexus of stern fathers and sons strongly incentivized to protect and add to familial *timê* (honor), women seem to occupy ambiguous roles. Tecmessa, for one, is met with brusque commands from the outset (e.g., "woman, for women silence brings adornment!" *Aj.* 293; cf. *Aj.* 527–8), and her pleas that Ajax consider herself and her son as primary concerns at Troy do not, of course, prevail.[45] While she is called a "spear-won bedmate" (e.g., 211) and appropriates for herself the *recherché* term *homeneutis*, "bed partner,"[46] she comes closest to the status of a true wife when Ajax, during the Deception Speech, considers her lot as a widow (a *chéra* at line 653)—albeit in a speech where it is exceptionally difficult to discern Ajax's true intent.[47]

Eriboea, Ajax's mother, is mentioned three times. Tecmessa asks Ajax to show proper regard for her, given both her old age and her prayers for his safe return (*Aj.* 507–9). Ajax brings up his mother only when charging Teucer to take Eurysaces to be sent in his stead to take care of his aged parents (*Aj.* 567–70). In deputizing Eurysaces to act as his surrogate, Ajax once again evinces his desire to make his son an iteration of himself.[48] Later, the chorus imagines that Eriboea, upon hearing of her son's "sickness" (*Aj.* 625–6), will preemptively begin wailing a dirge over him, tearing her white hair in grief. However, this song of the chorus ends not with a sustained inquiry into Eriboea's plight, but rather ensconces Ajax into the succession of sons descended from Aeacus and finds in his lot an unexampled instance of a "ruin" (an *atê*), a burden which his father will have to bear.

In the end, Ajax decides upon a course of action that will least threaten what is left of his personal, and by extension, his birth family's honor. Moreover, suicide will prevent him from meeting his father's gaze, and also deprive the Greeks of any further service from his sword. The predicament in which this arrangement leaves his "family-at-Troy" (concubine, half-brother, and bastard child) is well illustrated by their desperate attempt to safeguard his body for a proper burial, the success of which is only guaranteed by the intervention of none other than Odysseus, his enemy, who prevails upon the Atreidae to relent in their desire to deny Ajax funeral rites. Ajax's own actions, while imperiling one set of relations, may, it has been argued, ring in sympathy with a patriarchal audience who could see in him the all-important, authoritative general without whom they would cower like the chorus.[49]

Amidst such concerns, the fate of Tecmessa is largely ignored. In the second half of the play she, along with Teucer and Eurysaces, supplicates at Ajax's corpse in a scene that may reflect hero-cult.[50] Her status as a spear-won bride and her son's as a bastard, however, have analogs with Teucer's own condition, which Agamemnon exploits (*Aj.* 1228–30; 1260) when he comes to declare that Ajax is to be denied a proper burial. Agamemnon goes so far as to say that Teucer's very words lack authority because he is not free-born and that, as such, he stands in need of someone of legitimate birth, a *kyrios* in effect, to speak on his behalf (1261). Scholars have seen in such emphasis upon matrilineal qualifications a reflection of the ideology of Periclean marriage legislation, although this point of view has not gone uncontested.[51]

FIGURE 7.2: Attic drinking cup showing Tecmessa covering the body of her husband Ajax after he has committed suicide, in what is probably an allusion to Sophocles' *Ajax*. Attributed to the Brygos Painter, *c.* 490–470 BCE. J. Paul Getty Museum, 86.AE.286. Digital image courtesy of the Getty's Open Content Program.

Case study: Euripides' Phoenissae

While *Ajax* shows a particular emphasis on fathers and sons, Euripides' *Phoenissae* ("Phoenician Women," so named after the composition of the chorus) depicts the widest range of intra- and interfamilial relationships of any of the extant dramas.[52] Nearly every scene foregrounds a new familial permutation: mother and son (Jocasta and Polynices), brothers (Polynices and Eteocles), uncle and nephew (Eteocles and Creon), father and daughter (Teiresias and his daughter),[53] father and son (Creon and Menoeceus), aunt and nephew (Jocasta and Menoeceus), mother and daughter (Jocasta and Antigone), brothers-in-law (Creon and Oedipus), and niece and uncle (Creon and Antigone)[54] take the stage in a sequence only interrupted, apart from choral song, by the reports of messengers—all of this in addition to accounts of exogamous marriage alliances, such as those between the house of Adrastos and Polynices (*Phoen.* 337–49; 580–2). Unlike *Ajax*, however, here the paternal gaze is quite literally blinded in the figure of Oedipus, whose curse upon his sons to divide their patrimony by the sword is less a deliberate attempt to mold the character of his male progeny than a belated reaction to their decision, as they came of age, to keep him shut away in the palace (*Phoen.* 63–8). Nor is figurative or literal paternal blindness confined to Oedipus, as later developments make clear.

The action of *Phoenissae* begins after the rupture between the sons of Oedipus, Eteocles, and Polynices and then depicts the abortive attempt to reconcile them, and, finally, deals with the aftermath of their mutual slaughter on the battlefield. This play, beyond presenting a wide variety of familial relationships, also highlights the often interwoven lines of family and politics. It is Jocasta, the mother, who brings Polynices into the city under a military truce so he can face his brother in words before confronting him on the battlefield—the men in charge of Thebes, both the former ruler (Oedipus) and the future one (Creon), have nothing to do with such an arrangement. Jocasta seems to have conceived the stratagem on her own. In an opening address to her sons, she focuses only fleetingly upon their blood-relationship (*Phoen.* 455–8), but expatiates in gnomic *sententiae* on how friends should reconcile (460–4), comments in the abstract upon the differences between the young and the old (528–30), and delivers a speech against Ambition in favor of Equality (*Isotēs*) as they relate to statehood, economics, and the cosmos (531–48). The issue is, moreover, one that pulls at one of the core difficulties of the *polis* experience: zero-sum honor is at a premium, but so too is the alternation of ruling and being ruled.[55] The mother, old enough to be her sons' grandmother,[56] rehearses newfangled democratic values; by contrast, the new generation operates on the basis of a more traditional, aristocratic prerogative.

The challenge of this play centers on how to harmonize competing claims. Some, such as Eteocles, seems oblivious to familial considerations, focusing instead upon political power, a univocal allegiance which seems to make Eteocles a less sympathetic character, while the more endearing members of the ensemble, such as Menoeceus, Creon's son, make decisions based upon what is best for family and *polis* alike.[57] When Teiresias prophesies that Creon must sacrifice his son to guarantee the city's safety, the latter is faced with a choice between preserving the *polis* or a member of his family. While Creon schemes to spirit his son out of the city to safety, his son Menoeceus reasons that such a course of action amounts to a betrayal of "father, brother, and city" (*Phoen.* 1002–4) and so resolves upon suicide in order to save all three. Menoeceus, the youngest male to come onstage during the action of the play, manages to find a principle of action which satisfies duties to family and state, while Jocasta can only plead the same to her sons who refuse to countenance the possibility.

The principal figures of Greek tragedy struggle to maintain balance upon shifting ground, on the mingling and colliding concerns of the *polis* and those of the *oikos*, and this perhaps nowhere so broadly true as in *Phoenissae*. Such a confrontation is the hallmark of every scene and nearly every chorus: just as Jocasta tries to find a voice persuasive to the ears of her sons in order to save family and city-state alike, so too do others in the play attempt much the same. Thus, we find even Eteocles speaking in a separate scene with his uncle Creon first about how to manage the war (*Phoen.* 705–56), then how to make provisions for his sister, Antigone, and her upcoming marriage to Creon's son (757–65), next why Teiresias needs to be summoned (766–74), and finally what to do with Polynices' corpse: the decisions taken in each of these areas will have particularly cruel repercussions for the families involved, all of which highlight Eteocles' inability to reconcile familial and political realities at Thebes.[58] But, as *Phoenissae* demonstrates, different groups comprise the totality of the *polis*; accordingly, the stage is commanded by different families not limited to the nuclear unit.

TRAGIC FAMILIES

A synoptic consideration of the families featured in Greek tragedy reveals that, in the main, we are witnessing not the trials and travails of one family in its nuclear form, but rather, in effect, of two. Moreover, these two families are so closely conjoined as to share members in ways that are mutually exclusive. In what follows I will argue that much of the explosive power of Greek tragedy derives from the attempts to reconcile the contradiction over improperly shared memberships between two competing, but nevertheless overlapping households.

An especially clear case of such contested and contradictory familial dynamics is dramatized in Euripides' *Medea*, in which disaster erupts from Jason's attempted bigamy. Despite the anomalous circumstances of their liaison, Medea believes that she and Jason are married, as she avows repeatedly (she calls him her *posis* [spouse] at 161, 229, 261, etc.). Jason, however, is recently engaged to the daughter of the ruler, Creon, and expects to produce legitimate children from this new union, perhaps with some benefit to the sons he has begotten with Medea (563–5). The chorus and Aegeus, the Athenian king who makes an appearance midway through the play, deplore alike Jason's decision to marry again (576–8; 695). Infamously, Medea kills not only the king and princess, the members of Jason's new family, but also her sons by Jason in outrage over her mistreatment. Jason cannot be shared, inasmuch as he cannot be the husband of two women at once. Furthermore, we notice here what will be a recurring theme: the first or original household reasserts its prerogatives over against the emergent one with consequences devastating not only for the latter but for the former as well.

A similar configuration, that of the bigamist husband and the ramifications his choice has for his first household, is also the focal point of Sophocles' *Trachinian Women*. In this play, Heracles returns to Trachis, the home he has made with his wife Deianeira and their children. His long absence worries his wife who, on the advice of the chorus, urges her eldest son Hyllus to go out in search of his father's whereabouts. Soon after Lichas, Heracles' associate, joyously announces his imminent return, Deianeira learns that all will not be as it ought: an informant reveals that Heracles has indeed arrived but with a "spear-won" bride, Iolê, in tow. Deianeira fears that Heracles will be called her "spouse" (*posis*) but the "husband" (*anêr*, literally "man") of Iolê (*Trach.* 550–1). In response, Deianeira decides to regain Heracles' affections through a (poisoned) love-

FIGURE 7.3: Lucanian mixing vessel, showing a scene possibly inspired by Euripides' *Medea*, in which Medea rides off in a chariot, leaving behind Jason and the bodies of her murdered sons. Attributed to "near the Policoro Painter," *c.* 400 BCE. The Cleveland Museum of Art, 1991.1.

potion, which ends up, of course, effecting the opposite, destroying both Heracles and herself.

Euripides' *Andromache* varies the theme of the twice-married husband (here embodied in the character of Neoptolemus, the son of Achilles) by shifting perspectives: this play features the first wife in the person of a spear-won bride (Andromache) who gives birth to a boy while the second, but more legitimately-born wife, Hermione (daughter of Menelaus and Helen) suffers from childlessness, a condition she blames upon the concubine Andromache. Neoptolemus' decision to keep two women under the same roof is censured by the chorus, Hermione, and Orestes: the arrangement is called a "double-marriage" (123–4; 465–6; 908) whereby the husband, who improperly "holds the reins" of two women (177–8), is "held in common" between them (*epikoinos*, 124).

Andromache's condition goes from wretched to worse from the outset. Despite already being given as a prize to the son of her first husband's killer, we learn, as the play opens, that she is seeking refuge at an altar after being accused of administering prophylactic drugs to Hermione. Unlike *Medea* and *Trachinian Women*, however, in *Andromache* the two women confront each other directly, with Hermione threatening to kill the offending (male) child and woman over the insult they present to her position within the household.

Furthermore, there is latent instability in the relationships Neoptolemus has contracted with the two women: Hermione not only flaunts the size of her dowry and thereby her connection to her natal household (147–53), but also emphasizes that Andromache deserves censure for acquiescing to a union with Neoptolemus, the son of the Achilles (170–3) who had slain her first husband, Hector.[59] Neoptolemus himself is absent from the action of the play, leaving open the question of who is *kyrios* over his wives. Capitalizing on this ambiguity, Menelaus takes up his daughter's cause, while Peleus, Neoptolemus' grandfather, intervenes no less confidently into his grandson's affairs. Although Peleus forestalls the deaths of Andromache and her son, he hears too late about a plot, conceived and put into motion by Orestes, to have Neoptolemus killed in Delphi. Compounding Peleus' predicament is the fact that Orestes has already spirited away Hermione on the claim that she was originally betrothed to him (967–8). Thus, once again, a prior/original familial claim reasserts itself in the course of the drama, the re-establishment of which spells disaster for the secondary/later household arrangement.[60]

The *Oresteia* makes much of the confrontation between mutually exclusive familial arrangements before suggesting a novel expedient for disentangling the confused lines of blood relations. In the parodos of the first play, the chorus describes how King Agamemnon chose to honor his brother's request for aid in retrieving the wayward Helen from Paris and the Trojans. Calchas, the Greek seer, informs the army that due to Artemis' interference they cannot set out for Troy until Agamemnon's daughter Iphigeneia is sacrificed to appease her rage.[61] Agamemnon's choice is starkly set in familial terms: should he avoid staining his hands with the pollution from his shedding his own daughter's blood (*Ag.* 206–7), or should he help his brother recover his wife Helen?[62] The choice is between preserving his brother's interests or those of his more recent family. With Agamemnon's decision to sacrifice his daughter, the goddess Artemis is appeased, permitting the Greeks to sail for Troy.[63]

The great confrontation between Clytemnestra, Iphigeneia's mother, and Agamemnon occurs midway through the first play of the trilogy (*Ag.* 810–974) in a scene which allows Aeschylus to double the theme of improperly shared family members. On the one hand, Agamemnon approaches his palace with Cassandra (another "spear-won" woman, the daughter of Hecuba and Priam) on a chariot, in what visually represents the approach of newlyweds to their home.[64] Within his palace, however, Clytemnestra has a paramour herself in Agamemnon's cousin Aegisthus,[65] whom she deems her conspirator in planning her rightful husband's death. Agamemnon's choice both to sacrifice his daughter, thus proving himself to be more part of his brother's family, and to bring a concubine into the household (brazenly at that), contribute directly to the murder Clytemnestra has prepared for him within the palace walls.[66] In effect, king and queen are already married to other parties while still nominally retaining the status of husband and wife with one another.

After Agamemnon's murder, Clytemnestra and Aegisthus stop hiding their affair and now rule openly over Argos. A complication is, of course, the survival of Agamemnon's and Clytemnestra's son Orestes, who is himself exercised by a set of incompatible claims of familial loyalty. As he makes clear he must avenge his father and so show himself to be the dutiful son;[67] yet how, he asks, is he to become his mother's killer (*Cho.* 899; Figure 7.4)? On the quick response from Pylades, his stalwart friend, and with the prior sanction of no less a divine authority than Apollo, Orestes commits matricide only to be pursued by the Furies in whose jurisdiction it lies to torment, kill, and torture even in the Underworld those guilty of shedding kindred blood.

FIGURE 7.4: Amphora depicting Orestes murdering his mother, Clytemnestra, as a Fury observes from above, *c.* 340 BCE. It is probably inspired by the scene in Aeschylus' *Libation Bearers* in which Clytemnestra pleads with Orestes "Easy my son, take pity on this breast . . . ." J. Paul Getty Museum, 80.AE.155.1. Digital image courtesy of the Getty's Open Content Program.

The *Oresteia* thus develops the tangled and mutually exclusive allegiances found within the house of Atreus; the resolution, at least to the conflicting loyalties of son to mother and father, finds a novel expression in a controversial argument put forward by Apollo at Orestes' trial in Athens during the action of the final play of the trilogy. Apollo, as Orestes' advocate, argues that the mother is not in fact a blood relation to her children but rather only a nurse of the newly-implanted seed (*Eum.* 658–9).[68] On the analogy of what is in effect an agricultural view of the matter, Apollo argues that the father sows the seed and thus ought to be deemed the true parent, while the mother merely provides sustenance to what has been sown. Given this view of reproduction, the issue of mutually exclusive familial loyalties disappears and leaves Orestes with a clear conscience, at least insofar as Apollo and his defendant are concerned.[69]

While the *Oresteia* differentiates within the nuclear family, Sophocles' *Oedipus Rex* provides an example of a royal family seemingly composed of two separate lines (Oedipus is initially assumed to be of Corinthian extraction). Furthermore, to the extent that the royal Theban family has incorporated an outstanding and unaffiliated male into its line, it appears to have employed one of the successful strategies of maintaining its continuity despite the lack of male issue.[70] The impossibility of shared membership here violates generational lines insofar as Oedipus ought not, of course, be both the son and husband of Jocasta nor again both the father and sibling of his children. Thus, instead of the more common horizontal problematic found between different families, the Oedipus story effects the same by a more vertical collapsing of different generations of the family into itself by means of the improperly doubled son/husband.

In the next generation of the same family, Sophocles dramatizes reduplicated instances of impossibly shared memberships across and within *oikoi*. Creon, the current ruler of Thebes and *kyrios* of Oedipus' daughters, declares that, in the matter of Oedipus' dead sons, one is to be honored for having defended the city, while the other is to be left unburied for threatening his city of birth with war and worse (*Ant.* 192–206). In response, Antigone sees it as her duty to oppose Creon, her uncle, just as Ismene sides with him against her sister. In Antigone's definition of kinship, only those who act as she does can be considered a legitimately well-born member of the family (*Ant.* 37–8). Ismene, on this understanding, cannot be both her sister's true sibling and her uncle's dutiful niece. Later in the play, Haemon finds it impossible to be both a loyal son to his father, Creon, and a devoted fiancé to Antigone; he goes so far as to attack his father (*Ant.* 1231–4) out of rage over his betrothed, whose suicide precipitates his own. Creon's very actions create mutually exclusive familial claims, causing members of his own household to choose against him as father (in the case of Haemon) and husband (in the case of Eurydice, his wife, who commits suicide when she hears of the death of her son [*Ant.* 1282–3]).

Despite the extreme reactions of Haemon (for his fiancée) and Eurydice (for her son), Antigone, for her part, argues in this play that spouses and children are, in comparison to siblings and parents, replaceable and would not elicit the same response on her part if one of them had died and not her brother (*Ant.* 905–15).[71] In effect Antigone confirms the substance of Apollo's argument in the *Oresteia*, for she too indicates that marriage and children, at least as the mother is concerned, do not rank as highly as the blood relations found in brothers and sisters.

Variations on the problematic of the doubled-family reverberate throughout the corpus of Greek tragedy. While it lies beyond the scope of the present study to bring out this theme in every play, a few other treatments deserve attention here. *Alcestis* (438 BCE), often termed proto-satyric,[72] depicts the confrontation between different generations over the extension of Admetus' life. Admetus will disown his parents for their refusal to die for him (*Alc.* 734ff); by contrast, in recognition of Alcestis' self-sacrifice he promises never to marry another. The tragic exigency results in Admetus choosing categorically between his marital and natal families.

In *Bacchae*, Dionysus himself is the point of overlap between his mortal and immortal family. Semele's sisters deny that her child was born of Zeus and is thereby divine; for them that story seeks to conceal the shame of an affair, which led to her destruction for impiety (*Bac.* 26–31). Pentheus too denies that his aunt had lain with Zeus (245)—his grandfather adjures him to accept the affair as a white lie (*Bac.* 334–6)—and resists the importation of his cult, all to a disastrous result. Thus at the root of *Bacchae* is a familial problem that serves as an initial catalyst and only later becomes complicated by matters of cult, gender, and sexuality.

In *Orestes*, Menelaus is forced to choose between allegiances to his nephew and to his father-in-law Tyndareus, who wants revenge upon Orestes for killing his daughter

Clytemnestra. Orestes counters that he was put in the unenviable position of having to choose between his mother and father, reproducing (*Or.* 552ff.) Apollo's argument from *Eumenides*. Later the play pivots when Menelaus is confronted by an Orestes who holds his daughter hostage, threatening to kill her unless he is rescued by his uncle. Thus Menelaus must choose again between two familial connections, but whereas in the first instance it was between his father-in-law and his nephew, the issue is now driven into even sharper relief when the latter is no longer his brother's child but his own.

Beyond the extant plays, we may see in those adduced by Aristotle as particularly good examples of the tragic genre, similarly convoluted family dynamics. Aristotle offers the following (*Poetics* 1453a 16–22) on the development of tragic mythology:

> Originally, the poets recounted any and every story, but nowadays the finest tragedies are composed about only a few families, such as Alcmaeon, Oedipus, Orestes, Meleager, Thyestes, Telephus, and as many others as have suffered or perpetrated terrible things.
>
> —trans. Halliwell

The tragic treatment of the stories of Oedipus and Orestes we have already had occasion to consider; the main lines of the others can be reconstructed from later sources.

Alcmaeon prefigures the Orestes story; in this "original" instance of matricide, Alcmaeon gains revenge for his father, Amphiaraus, by killing his mother, Eriphyle, who betrayed the latter for a necklace.[73] Also like Orestes, Alcmaeon is pursued by the Furies until he seeks an initial purification at the hands of king Phegeus of Psophis. The king marries his daughter to Alcmaeon, but when a plague arises, Alcmaeon is sent by an oracle to the court of Acheloüs for another round of purification. Once again, however, Alcmaeon must marry the king's daughter who asks for items he had given to his first, and still current, wife back in Psophis. Upon his return there, Alcmaeon's bigamy is discovered, and he is killed by Phegeus and his sons. Both parts of this figure's story display the implosion of the family under divided loyalties and mutually exclusive memberships: Alcmaeon, like Orestes, cannot be both a son to his mother and his father at the same time; like Jason, Alcmaeon brings calamity upon himself for being married to two women at the same time.

First mentioned in the *Iliad* (9.529–99), Meleager was part of the Calydonian boar hunt, a successful enterprise until a division of the spoils resulted in Meleager killing one or more of his maternal uncles. His mother, Althaea, is so grieved by the loss of her brother(s) that she throws into a fire a sacred brand that was to be coeval with Meleager's own life. The outlines of the story suggest that here too much could be made of mutually exclusive contradictions between natal and married ties, the result of which ends in the destruction of the offending relation.

The story of Thyestes is the subject of repeated allusion in extant drama (e.g., Aes. *Ag.* 1191–3; Eur. *El.* 699–746; Sen. *Thy.*). We hear that he seduced his brother's wife, Aeropê, and in so doing gained control over Argos/Mycenae. Such a transgression is, of course, a repeated one in the house of Atreus: the seduction of a spouse by a member of the same family makes for an impossibly convoluted state of affairs. It is, in effect, a combination of the tragic themes of bigamy, as in *Medea*, and incest, as in *Oedipus Tyrannus*.

For the story of Telephus we have fewer indications of exactly which mythological variant each tragedian chose to dramatize.[74] One version has it that he killed some of his uncles in a Meleager-like episode.[75]

CONCLUSION

All happy families are alike; every unhappy family is unhappy in its own way.

—Tolstoy, *Anna Karenina*

Pace Tolstoy, in dramatizing the repercussions of the improperly shared member, the Attic tragedians introduced at least one consistent element into their depiction of the unhappier sort.[76] At the heart of the matter may lie an instability inherent in every marriage and particularly pronounced in ancient Greek culture: two who become one by ritual and in law but remain subject to summary dissolution, as in the case of divorce, widowhood, or the *epiklerate*. Tragedy often assumes the fusion of the two as the center of the *oikos*, but then quickly explores the contrary motion occasioned by prior betrothals, new betrothals, concubines, uncles, fathers, mothers, brothers, and sisters, all of whom—from outside the marriage—pull away at the integrity of the unit and expose the fault lines seemingly effaced by ceremony, civilization, and the creation of offspring.[77] Particularly powerful amidst all these forces is the claim of the natal family upon its erstwhile member: thus, whereas society presupposes fixed identities for the members of the eternal *oikos*, tragedy reveals the gravitational pull of prior allegiances cutting across *oikoi*.

And yet the anxiety over maintaining the integrity of familial relations is not, of course, confined to the genre of tragedy. It is in Homer that we first find the theme *in utero*: the Achaeans are at Troy to rectify a case of bigamy (whether Helen went willingly or not with Paris). Again at the beginning of the *Iliad* proper, Agamemnon explicitly compares his current tent-mate, the spear-won Chryseis, to his wife Clytemnestra (*Il.* 1.113–15) in words which cannot fail to elicit worry for their impropriety.[78] In the *Odyssey*, Calypso, comparing herself to Penelope (and even reprising Agamemnon's language!), enjoins Odysseus to be her (eternal) mate as he, contrariwise, openly pines for his mortal wife. The ambiguous status of the wife while her husband is away recalls one of Telemachus' major concerns in the *Odyssey* about his mother Penelope: if she is married off, as many urge him to allow, and his father returns, what then? Should Penelope be restored to her natal family, as some suggest, or is she to wait indefinitely for the return of her current *kyrios* and *anêr* Odysseus?[79] Seen in this way, the tragedians' depiction of the family follows from Homeric precedent and shows again the dependency of the former on the latter despite both the many years separating their composition and contexts of performance.

CHAPTER EIGHT

Gender and Sexuality

KIRK ORMAND

Sexuality and gender in antiquity require some preliminary definition. First, the sources suggest that the fifth-century Greeks had a keen sense of gender as a fluid, and in some ways dangerous, form of identity.[1] Although there is little evidence of awareness of ambiguous sexual identity or intersexed individuals, the province of masculinity was not guaranteed by genitalia. Citizen men were expected to display mastery over themselves and others in a variety of spheres. Indeed, self-control was arguably the identifying feature of masculinity in both ancient Athens and ancient Rome: a real man displayed courage in the face of battle; appropriately controlled his household; was restrained in his expenditures so as not to waste his inheritance; and perhaps most importantly, kept his own desires—for sex, for food, for wine—under control.

Part of this set of expectations, as Michel Foucault, David Halperin, and others have shown, was the understanding that citizen men, once they reached adulthood, should not allow themselves to be sexually penetrated. Somewhat contrary to modern expectations, it seems that wishing to be so penetrated was thought of as a real temptation, not just for a particular subset of the population, but for most men. To act on that inclination, however, was in effect to abdicate masculinity and slide into an effeminate, though still male, gender identity.[2] Femininity was, then, not the exclusive province of women.[3]

Expectations about the proper gender roles for women, and about the proper expression of their sexual desires, were somewhat contradictory. Women were assumed not to be in control of their desires, and could not be trusted, if left alone and unattended, to remain chaste. In this regard, women appear at times to be thought of as inadequate men; they are men without autonomy or self-control.[4] On the other hand, in some contexts and some texts (tragedy among them) women are depicted not simply as imperfect men, but as a species apart, inscrutable to men, dangerous in their ability to disrupt men's orderly, which is to say, patriarchal and self-validating, mode of control.

Perhaps more difficult and more disputed is the ancient conception of sexual identities.[5] The ancient Greeks and Romans do not seem to have had a notion of heterosexuality and homosexuality identical with ours. Any normal Athenian man was assumed to be interested in sex either with women or with younger men, particularly those in the highly desirable ages of roughly fourteen to twenty. To have sexual desire for such a young man in no way impugned a man's masculinity, nor did it define him as a type of individual; indeed, such desire was not conceived of as different in kind from the desire a "normal" man might have for a woman. What was considered abnormal and perhaps a bit shameful (though not, in comparison to the modern West, particularly serious) was for a man to desire to be the "passive" or penetrated partner in a male–male relationship. This, again, was a form of abandoning self-control, and with it, masculinity. It is less clear what would have counted, for a male elite Athenian, as "normal" female sexual desire. Outside of the poems of Sappho, there is virtual silence about the possibility of female homoerotic relationships in the archaic and classical periods.[6] The Greeks, then, did not have a notion of "sexuality" in the modern sense of sexual identity, and to the extent that sexual behavior defined personal identity, it seems to have done so primarily through the structures of gender. That is, attaining masculinity (for men) and behaving within the bounds of femininity (for women) was of greater import than notions of sexual identity or erotic object choice, and for the remainder of this essay, I use the term "sexuality" in its more general sense of a person's embodiment of sexual desire.

Two curiosities confront us when we consider the depiction of gender and sexuality in the tragedies of fifth-century Athens. The first is that tragedy, at least as far as we can tell, avoided almost entirely depictions of homoerotic desire.[7] This fact is puzzling, not least because homoerotic relations between older men and younger men were a part of the daily life of Athens, and the subject of erotic poetry, philosophical discourse, and legal disputes. For reasons that remain mysterious, however, these relations do not seem to have occupied a central role in the conflicts of tragedy. The second is that a large number of tragedies are centered around domestic disputes between a husband and wife. This has become so much the norm in Western drama that it may not surprise, but it is far from inevitable. The Athenian playwrights, as we will see, seem to have gone out of their way to introduce familial disputes into stories that often had been, in the earlier mythic tradition, depicted as conflicts between men. Greek tragedy shifts the locus of the political disputes of aristocratic heroes to the *oikos*, the household—and often in an atmosphere of supercharged eroticism, in which women are presented as active, powerful, and sexually dangerous.[8] This characteristic of tragedy has presented a serious problem for scholars of antiquity, because it conflicts with our understanding of the status and role of real women in everyday life. I suggest that these conflicts carry particular resonance in fifth-century Athens in part because of ongoing shifts in the relations between household (*oikos*) and the political state (*polis*) during the century in which all extant tragedies were produced.

FROM LEGAL STATUS TO TRAGEDY

Though tragedy is supposed to have begun in the last quarter of the sixth century, when Athens was still under the rule of the Peisistratid tyrants, we have no extant texts of tragedy before the production of Aeschylus' *Persians* in 472—some thirty years after the establishment of the democracy. It is often asserted that the lives of citizen women in particular became more restricted under the democracy than before, though in fact we know precious little about the lives of citizen women in the archaic period. Our sources for the earlier period are primarily poetic (the epics of Homer, the lyric poetry of poets from various city-states). It is true that women in the Homeric epics seem at times to have more public and political independence than in fifth-century Athens, though extrapolating a picture of women's lives from such sources is particularly fraught.[9]

But certainly under democracy, the role of women as citizens played an increasingly important role, and consequently citizen women's lives, and sexual access to citizen women, came under greater public scrutiny and legal controls. Citizen women were, for their entire lives, under the "guardianship" of an adult male citizen, known as a woman's *kurios*: before marriage, a woman's *kurios* was her father; after marriage, her husband. If widowed or divorced she would normally return to control and protection of her natal family. It is a commonly stated social ideal that a woman would not venture out-of-doors without a guardian present, however frequently that ideal may have been violated. Legally, a woman was limited in the size of economic transactions she could undertake; she could not participate in any of the functions of government (voting, speaking in the Assembly, serving as a juror, etc.); citizen women were not even supposed to be mentioned by name in a court of law. We have very little evidence about the education of women; it seems unlikely that they had the same opportunities for formal education as did men, but it is clear that some women could read and write. Some texts—most often cited is Xenophon's *Oikonomikos*, or "Household Management"—make it clear that husbands could expect their wives to learn to administer the economic resources of their households. As a matter of principle, however, women's lives were, in fundamental ways, private.[10]

But in Athenian tragedies, women are often not private: they engage in public, political actions, and not infrequently call attention to the fact that they are doing so.[11] The tragedies of Aeschylus, Sophocles, and Euripides not only treat women with considerable

FIGURE 8.1: Attic wedding bowl, showing preparations for a wedding, attributed to the Naples painter, *c*. 420 BCE. The Metropolitan Museum of Art, NY, 06.1021.298.

sympathy, they ascribe to them social and even political power. Indeed, the figures of Clytemnestra, Electra, Antigone, Jocasta, Alcestis, Medea, Phaedra, and Helen (among many others) present women as independent actors, intellectually and emotionally capable, formidable opponents of men. The question for social historians, then, is to identify the relationship between the women of the Attic stage and the real women of classical Athens.[12]

Recent scholars have been hesitant to grant much credence to the portrayal of women in tragedy as an unmediated expression of their place in society. These characters' actions are often circumscribed, and when they do take on public actions, they sometimes call attention to the fact that in doing so they are breaking the usual rules.[13] More forcefully, Froma Zeitlin points out that, however powerful the woman onstage, the focus of tragedy remains relentlessly on the male subject: "*Functionally* women are never an end in themselves, and nothing changes for them once they have lived out their drama onstage. Rather, they play the roles of catalysts, agents, instruments, blockers, spoilers, destroyers, and sometimes helpers or saviors for the male characters."[14] We can see the tragic portrayal of women as not so much a representation of women's lives as one mode of working out the proper way to be a male Athenian citizen. The women of Athenian drama can be seen as representing public tensions in the Athenian state, for instance between nature and culture, household and city, or insiders and outsiders.[15]

Tragedy does often use women in precisely this way. But I also want to link the representation of women in Athenian tragedy specifically to the social structures of fifth-century Athens. I see not a direct conflict between the legal sources and the tragedies, but rather a set of related discourses about a common set of real, sometimes institutionalized, social conflicts.[16] I argue that the domestic conflicts of Greek tragedy stem from particular social and historical rifts and currents in fifth-century Athens. One reason for the increase in scrutiny of women with the development of the democracy was the importance placed on women as producers of citizens. Citizenship was a matter of birth: citizen women were born from citizen parents, and as such, had the ability to marry citizen men, produce citizen children, and take part in important civic rituals, many of which were restricted to citizens. They also could give birth to sons who would be expected to serve as soldiers in the Athenian army and who could inherit property. Daughters of citizen women also were understood as holding specific familial obligations and were guaranteed specific inheritance rights.[17] With the advent of the Athenian democracy, therefore, the state began to place increased emphasis on marriage to citizen women, and in the year 451/50, the Athenian statesman Pericles passed a law stating that only the offspring of two *astoi*— that is, Athenian citizens—would be citizens themselves. Marriage outside of the Athenian citizenry was still possible, but children born from such a union would not be considered Athenian citizens, could not inherit, and could not fully participate in public life.[18] These structures gave citizen women important legal and social status, and nourished anxieties about protecting their sexual integrity, and about their loyalties to natal and marital households.

Despite their exclusion from political life, women were valued in a variety of cultural and social venues. Women played an important role in the religious life of the city, and evidence from legal speeches suggests that these roles, limited to citizen women, were jealously guarded.[19] The ritual role of women is often reflected in tragedies, as in Antigone's insistence on her responsibility to bury her brother, even if he is defined as a political traitor, or in the not-infrequent references to the establishment of cults at the ends of plays.[20]

There were, of course, many non-citizen women in Athens: resident aliens (known as "metics") as well as slaves. Metics obtained significant legal status and protections, and could become quite wealthy, though they could not participate in the processes of Athenian government, and female metics could not give birth to citizens or participate with citizen women in certain religious rites; at a certain point it appears that citizen men were restricted from marriage to non-citizen women.[21] Slaves of course, both female and male, had no standing as subjects under the law, and literally did not control access to, or use of, their bodies. Characters who are non-citizen women (metics and slaves) appear in significant numbers in Greek tragedy, and deserve a fuller treatment than I can give them here; but such characters are often defined as much by their legal status as their gender. In this essay I focus only on the social conflicts that concern citizen women.

In what follows, I compare the events of Athenian tragedy to roughly parallel narratives in the legal speeches of the fourth century. I am not claiming that the legal speeches present a neutral, factual ground against which the fictional world of tragedy should be read. Rather, the legal speeches provide another discourse about women, rhetorical in nature and creating their own vision of the role of women in society, against which the relatively public and active women of tragedy can be read. While I do not want to suggest that the average Athenian man expected his daughter to be an Antigone, I do want to demonstrate that the tensions between men and women in tragedy often appear to have specific counterparts in contemporary Athenian society.

In the latter half of the fifth century in particular, we see an increased anxiety surrounding sexual access to Athenian citizen women, and a variety of concerns about their familial loyalties. I suggest that this partially explains why Greek tragedies—all the extant texts of which date from the period of 472–401 BCE—frequently center around familial conflicts, and especially conflicts arising from a woman's relation to her husband. This is not true of every Greek tragedy—Sophocles' *Philoctetes* has no female characters in it at all—but many tragedies of Aeschylus, Sophocles, and Euripides present a conflict in which women's sexual desires are either central to the conflict of the play, or lurk broodingly in the wings, threatening to overturn the civic space that is represented. In what follows, I analyze different sets of social anxieties about women's status and the way that they are represented as potential disruptors of society at large.

THE PROBLEMS OF DESIRE

Many women in tragedy present a threat to their husbands through an active and uncontrolled sexual desire. Perhaps the starkest example of this idea can be seen in Aeschylus' *Agamemnon*, in the character of Clytemnestra, Agamemnon's wife. As the play opens, Agamemnon is returning from the Trojan War, where he has been for the last ten years. While Agamemnon was away, Clytemnestra has taken up with his cousin, Aegisthus, and when her husband returns, Clytemnestra lures him into the house, wraps him in some sort of cloth—she compares it to fishermen's nets—and kills him in the bath. The play is suffused with erotic imagery, but perhaps no passage is as disturbingly sexy as that of Agamemnon's death, described by Clytemnestra herself after the fact:

I struck him twice, and with two cries,
his knees collapsed, and then, when he had fallen
I struck a third blow, with prayer and thanks
to underground Zeus, the savior of the dead.

> Thus, falling, he gasped out his life,
> and blew forth a sharp gush of blood,
> and spattered me with dark drops of bloody dew,
> and I rejoiced no less than the grain rejoices, in god-given
> joy, at the budding of flowers.
>
> —Aesch. *Ag.* 1384–92[22]

Here Clytemnestra appropriates a common poetic trope in which women are likened to the fertile earth, and men to rain.[23] But her moment of fertility has been perverted, and the rain that she receives gladly is the life-blood of the husband she has just slaughtered. Clytemnestra is the nightmare version of a proper wife: sexual and fertile, but unfaithful and murderous in that sexualized fertility.

This version of Agamemnon's death, emphasizing Clytemnestra's active and gleeful role as murderer, belongs to the world of tragedy and is not the inevitable result of a static myth. In the *Iliad*, for example, Clytemnestra and Aegisthus are indeed lovers, but it is Aegisthus who is blamed for the killing of Agamemnon.[24] The dynastic politics of the epic past have been moved explicitly into the household and recast as a domestic dispute. The narrative also demonstrates anxiety about women reversing gender roles: Clytemnestra is described early on as having a "man-counseling heart" (Aesch. *Ag.* 11), and in lines 1125–8 she metaphorically penetrates her husband. Her actions are simultaneously sexualized and gender-inverted.[25]

While the dangers of a Clytemnestra are easily understood, the force of erotic desire is depicted as potentially devastating in tragedy even when not combined with infidelity and gender-blur. Sophocles' *Trachiniae* presents the story of Herakles' wife, Deianeira, with considerable empathy. Deianeira spends most of the play talking about her marriage to Herakles, a moment in her life that she seems unable to move beyond.[26] When Herakles returns after a long absence, bringing with him a war-captive named Iole, Deianeira fears that Iole will replace her in Herakles' household. In this regard, she is directly parallel to Clytemnestra, some of whose resentment against Agamemnon can be chalked up to resentment against the war-captive Cassandra whom he brings home. Deianeira, however, responds differently: rather than deliberately killing her husband, she resolves to try to win him back by means of a love charm, blood from a centaur who assured her that this charm would make her husband "never look at another woman/ and fall in love, in place of you" (Soph. *Trach.* 576–7). As often with such pronouncements, these instructions do not mean what they seem: the lines turn out to be a prediction of Herakles' death. Though Deianeira might have been perspicacious enough not to trust the centaur, who was her husband's mortal enemy, and to see the ambiguity, these are innocent mistakes, and her deadly act is motivated by the most passive and innocuous of desires: she simply wants to remain the object of Herakles' desire. As she says, "I would not know how to do evil acts of boldness/ nor would I learn to; and I hate bold women" (Soph. *Trach.* 582–3). In the end, however, that does not matter: the blood proves to be a particularly nasty poison that, spread on a robe and sent to Herakles, consumes him alive (Figure 8.2). Too late, Deianeira recognizes her error, and goes offstage to kill herself; in the next scene, Herakles, raving with pain, is carried onstage and rages against the wife who, as he thinks, killed her. This play, perhaps more than any other, figures female desire, no matter how innocent, as a dangerous force for the tragic hero.

Somewhere between the active, violent desire of Clytemnestra and the misdirected wifely concern of Deianeira is the figure of Phaedra in Euripides' *Hippolytus*. In the

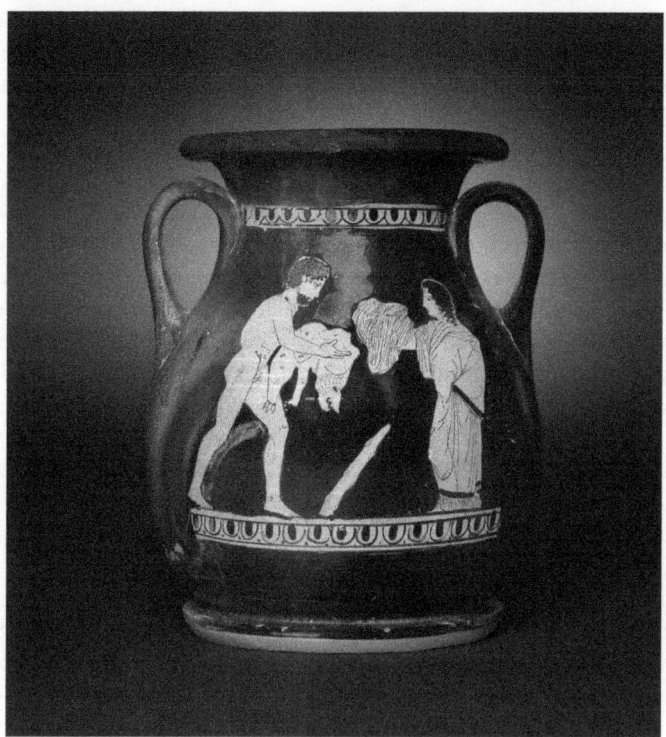

FIGURE 8.2: Attic *pelike* showing Heracles about to receive the poisoned garment that his wife Deianeira has innocently sent to him as a love charm, *c.* 430 BCE. The British Museum, London, 1851,0416.16. © The Trustees of the British Museum. All rights reserved.

extant version of this play, Phaedra is married to Theseus, but falls hopelessly in love with her stepson, Hippolytus. This passion is forced upon her by the goddess Aphrodite explicitly in order to punish Hippolytus; Phaedra struggles to control her passion through the exercise of self-control, and when that does not work, considers killing herself.[27] Even so, when she first appears onstage, her passion is so overwhelming that she is in a state of acute physical and mental distress, unable even to lift her head. She is a prime example of the presumption that women, unlike fully masculine men, are incapable of controlling their desires. In the course of the play, Phaedra is tricked into allowing her nurse to confess her passion to Hippolytus, who responds with horrified anger, and threatens to tell Theseus, his father and Phaedra's husband. Phaedra's fear of the resulting damage to her reputation and concern for her own children leads her to commit suicide, leaving behind a note that falsely accuses Hippolytus of rape. Theseus, on the evidence of the note, curses Hippolytus, who dies horribly in a chariot accident. Phaedra thus embodies the danger of erotic desire, and demonstrates what happens when that desire overwhelms its subject. Despite her good intentions, Phaedra becomes what men fear most: a woman who is not sufficiently controlled (either externally or by her own emotional fortitude), and who as a result becomes deceitful and destructive, threatening the personal bond between father and son.

All of this seems to be the natural stuff of tragedy, and few modern readers, I suspect, worry about similar events in their own lives. I suggest, however, that these tragedies are refractions of real anxieties, and in some ways not so far from historical events. To name only two examples: a legal speech of Isaeus (Isaeus 6) concerns the estate of a man named Euctemon. Euctemon died without legitimate sons, but had legitimate daughters; their husbands (who are their legal guardians) sued for his estate. His estate had been claimed by the sons of a woman named Alce, who, according to Euctemon's sons-in-law, was a freedwoman who ran a brothel. These sons of Alce claim to have been formally adopted by Euctemon and therefore to be his legal heirs (though this would clearly contradict the law concerning *epikleroi*, discussed below). The plaintiffs refer to Euctemon's entanglement with Alce as "a great disaster, which abused his whole household and consumed much property and created a conflict between him and those who were closest to him" (Isaeus 6.18). The cause of this great disaster is clearly the force of Alce's sexual attraction; a little later in the speech, the plaintiffs describe how Euctemon spent increasing amounts of time in the apartment building that Alce managed, eventually living there full time over the protests of his family, and was convinced to introduce Alce's sons to his phratry (thus formally adopting them) "having been reduced to such a state either by drugs or illness or by *something else*" (Isaeus 6.21, emphasis added). Seen in comparison to this apparently historical situation, Deianeira's fears about Iole being introduced into her own home take on a more realistic sheen. As Hall points out, in tragedy, every man who brings a concubine home to his wife ends up dead;[28] we can see this tragic trope as a reflection of real and present anxieties concerning wives' unstable positions in their husbands' households, and the dangers to the *oikos* of a husband's affections led astray.

Even more directly to the point, we have the text of a legal case in which a woman is accused of accidentally having poisoned her husband with what she thought was a love charm.[29] Antiphon 1 is a prosecution of a stepmother who, the speaker claims, deliberately killed his father. According to the prosecution, the deceased father had a friend named Phileonus, and this Phileonus had a concubine, with whom he was planning to end his relations. The stepmother, according to the plaintiff, convinced this concubine to administer a "love potion" to both Phileonus and to the accused's husband, suggesting that in this way both women would keep the affections of their men. What the concubine did not know, the speaker alleges, is that this was not a love potion at all, but poison, designed to kill the stepmother's husband (and speaker's father). Phileonus would be, apparently, collateral damage. The concubine followed the stepmother's instructions, giving a larger dose to Phileonus; Phileonus died immediately, and the wealthy father died after an illness some weeks later. In the course of the speech, the plaintiff refers to his stepmother as "this Clytemnestra, my stepmother" (Ant. 1.17), an example of the way that tragedies could be used to inform everyday speech. We will never know the truth of this case; it is possible that the poison really was meant as a love potion (as in the case of Deianeira), or it may be that the stepmother really was as deliberately murderous as the plaintiff claims (which would make her more like Medea, who uses drugs to brutally murder her husband's new fiancée). But in any case, the unsuspecting concubine, who was tortured for evidence and then put to death, seems to have believed that she was administering a love potion. In this respect, tragedy is remarkably close to an historical event. Both legal discourse and tragic drama figure female desire as dangerous, disruptive, and—accidentally or purposefully—sometimes deadly.

THE WIFE'S DIVIDED LOYALTY

Women in Athens had specific responsibilities to their households, and these responsibilities frequently put women in the position of acting in public. Perhaps one of the most important public functions in which women engaged was that of mourning for the dead (Figure 8.3). As Margaret Alexiou and Helene Foley have shown, we cannot easily separate acts of public mourning from politics: a lamentation can also be a form of protest, and the emotions stirred up can lead to direct political action.[30] Indeed, over the course of the sixth and fifth centuries, laws were repeatedly passed limiting the amount of public display that could take place at funerals, and limiting the mourners to the immediate family. As Alexiou argues, this legislation is reactionary: it is passed because of the state's concern with dramatic displays of overwhelming emotion.[31]

FIGURE 8.3: Attic *loutrophoros* (ceremonial water vase) depicting a deceased young man surrounded by female mourners (relatives and possibly professional mourners, as well), c. late sixth century BCE. The Metropolitan Museum of Art, NY, 27.228.

These concerns seem to be reflected directly in a number of tragedies, perhaps none more forcefully than Sophocles' *Electra*.[32] In this play Electra, the daughter of Agamemnon, has grown up at home under the not-very-friendly eyes of her mother and Aegisthus, her fathers' killers. As the play opens, she is waiting for the return of her brother Orestes, so that the two of them can enact revenge. In the meantime, however, Electra has done one thing consistently: she has lamented her father's death. The chorus comments that this constant, long-running lament is excessive, and even Electra realizes that it may appear so: she refers to her behavior as "terrible," "bad," and "shameful" (Soph. *El*. 221, 223, 308–9, 621).[33] But she engages in this behavior because it has a morally justifiable political purpose: to "cause them pain" (Soph. *El*. 355).[34] By refusing to give up on her publicly-sanctioned role as a lamenting woman, Electra keeps alive the memory of her father's death, and keeps visible the need for vengeance against Clytemnestra and Aegisthus. Tragedy can directly reflect contemporary male anxieties about women's display of grief, and the inter- and intra-familial feuds that they might foment.

Some tragedies, on the other hand, speak to a different set of anxieties, about a woman's primary loyalty. Again, some legal background is useful. When a woman in Athens married, she transferred households from that of her father to that of her new husband. But she never entirely severed her ties with her natal family. Her father or brothers could be called on to support her if her marriage was not going well; her dowry, which she brought to her new household, had to be returned to her natal family in the case of divorce; even the language used to describe the transaction suggests that she was being entrusted to her husband, but not alienated from her natal family.[35] This state of divided loyalty was acutely manifest in cases of inheritance. Under fifth-century Athenian law, if a man died without male heirs, his property went to his daughter on the condition that she then marry her nearest male relative, beginning with those on her father's side— so, typically, a paternal uncle or his son. Such a woman was known as an *epikleros*, and we have numerous legal speeches contesting the right of various family members to marry an *epikleros* and arguing the property rights that might result. Our sources agree that a woman who is already married might be forced to divorce her husband in order to marry as an *epikleros*, thus ensuring the continuation of her natal household.[36] A woman, then, held an institutionally unstable position in her husband's home, an idea that several tragedies reflect.[37]

No tragic heroine is ever explicitly named an *epikleros*, and it is a matter of some debate whether the Athenians, seeing a play set in the mythical past, would think of Antigone or Electra as *epikleroi*.[38] But tragedy frequently positions wives as outsiders in their husbands' homes.[39] We have already seen an example of this phenomenon in the character of Deianeira, who mistakenly trusted the centaur Nessos—her husband's enemy—in her attempt to win Herakles' affections back. Even as virtuous a wife as Euripides' Alcestis, who offers to die in place of her husband Admetus, is figured as a "stranger" in her husband's household (Eu. *Alc*. 533).[40]

In some dramas this tension between natal and marital loyalty is brought to the fore. In the trilogy that contained Aeschylus' *Suppliants*, for example, the fifty daughters of Danaos flee with their father from their Egyptian cousins, who pursue them to Argos in hopes of marrying them. Once in Argos, Danaos convinces the Argives to repel the Egyptians and accept his daughters into the community, and in the second and third plays of the trilogy (of which we have only fragments), the fifty daughters are married to men of Argos. Danaos, however, orders his daughters to murder their husbands on their wedding night, and forty-nine follow their fathers' instructions. The one who does not, Hypermestra, appears to have been somehow put on trial for failing in her filial duties, but is acquitted, possibly after a speech made in defense of marriage and fertility by Aphrodite herself. As Froma Zeitlin and others have argued, in Hypermestra's vindication we are given a foundation story for the institution of human marriage, but also a terrifying, exaggerated view of the potential conflict between the bride's father and her new husband.[41]

Other plays are more subtle in their treatment of a woman's ambiguous place in the family, and I have argued elsewhere that some plays deliberately invoke a young unmarried woman's status as an *epikleros*.[42] In the *Electra* of Sophocles—which in the myth of the house of Atreus follows the events that were treated in Aeschylus' *Libation Bearers*—Electra believes at a certain point that her brother Orestes is dead. Since her father, Agamemnon, had been killed by Aegisthus and her mother Clytemnestra, that leaves Electra in the position of an *epikleros*: she is a female descendant of her father, and she has no living brothers. Under Athenian law, she would inherit Agamemnon's estate, but only on the condition that she marry a relative from Agamemnon's line of inheritance, beginning with paternal relatives (i.e., her paternal uncle or his son). Up until this point in the play, Electra has been relatively passive: though she constantly mourns her father, thereby aggravating Clytemnestra and Aegisthus, she has taken no direct action. On hearing the (false) information that Orestes is dead, however, she begins without explanation to take on a more active role, and proposes to her sister Chrysomethis that the two of them should kill their father's murderers. At the high point of her political passion, she imagines how this action will be received:

> For what citizen or stranger, when they saw us,
> would not receive us with these sorts of praises:
> Look, friends, at these two sisters
> who saved their paternal household . . .
> we must all honor them in festivals
> and throughout the city, on account of their courage.
>
> —Soph. *El.* 975–83

As it turns out, Electra is wrong; her brother is not dead, and in this play, he will do the killing and Electra will be relegated to a supporting role. But it is significant that when she thinks Orestes dead, Electra imagines herself in a politically active mode, and moreover receiving public praise for that role and for her dedication to her paternal household. At the moment that her bloodline becomes active in that she would inherit under Athenian law, she becomes politically active in defense of her natal family. Most Athenian men would not, of course, marry an Electra; but every Athenian woman had a father, and a natal household, to whom she felt some responsibility and obligation. This is not to suggest, as Freud did, a universal "Electra complex." Rather, it is to insist on the historical conditions in fifth-century Athens that shaped and conditioned a daughter's social relation to her father's house.

Finally, we should consider the character of Euripides' *Medea*, who embodies many of the anxieties in the discussion above. Medea is the daughter of the king of Colchis, far to the north on the Black Sea, married to Jason, a Greek from Iolkos. As the play opens, Medea and Jason have moved to Corinth, and Medea learns that Jason plans to abandon her and marry the daughter of the king of Corinth (named Glauke in the later tradition). This is one of the best-known of Greek tragedies in modern times, because Medea famously enacts revenge on Jason not only by killing his future bride (and, incidentally, the king), but also by turning the sword to kill her own children. With this brutal act she eliminates both Jason's children with her and any hope for future progeny. It is a play that has struck readers since the late nineteenth century as timeless. But it is inextricably linked to the concerns that Athenians had regarding women and sexual desire. To start with, Medea is literally a foreigner, an exotic woman with magical powers (Figure 8.4), who proves herself fully capable of manipulating the men around her when her desires have been thwarted.

We can see this as an exaggerated form of the typical portrayal of a wife as an outsider to the husband's home. Though her foreign birth and magical powers put her out of the realm of the normal, Medea generalizes from her marriage to marriage in general:

FIGURE 8.4: Attic *hydria* showing Medea demonstrating her capacities as a sorceress by brewing a potion to renew Pelias' youth, attributed to the Copenhagen Painter, *c.* 480–470 BCE. The British Museum, London, 1843,1103.76. © The Trustees of the British Museum. All rights reserved.

> Of all creatures who are alive and can think rationally,
> we women are the most wretched in nature.
> First, it is required that we buy a husband
> with an overabundance of wealth,
> to acquire a master over our bodies;
> for this is a worse evil than the one before.
> And in this is the greatest contest, either to get a bad husband
> or a good one. For a woman cannot avoid marriage and keep a good reputation
> nor can she refuse a husband.
>
> —Eu. *Med.* 230–8

Medea's generalizations are not, strictly speaking, logical. To begin with, her reference to "buying a husband" refers to the fifth-century practice of dowry, a practice that did not apply in the mythical period of Medea's story, and in any case did not apply to Medea.[43] The rest of the speech is also curiously normalizing: though Medea will turn out to be a powerful enchantress, she speaks here of her experience of marriage as if she were an inexperienced and frightened bride, entirely at the mercy of her new *despotês* ("master"), her husband. Though a little later Medea will emphasize that she is different from the women of Corinth, in that she has no (natal) citizen family to look after her, all the language in this speech regularizes her as a typical young bride, allowing the Athenian audience to think of her in these terms.

At the same time, Medea is obviously not typical. One of the ways that the play brings this out is that she, like Clytemnestra, adopts language more regularly associated with male heroes. She speaks confidently of "becoming beautifully victorious over my enemies," (Eu. *Med.* 765–6), and wants to be thought of as "heavy to my enemies and gracious to my friends" (Eu. *Med.* 809). This latter phrase is a slight variant on a standard heroic code, to "help my friends and harm my enemies," embraced by numerous male heroes in the epic and tragic tradition. Finally, Medea is deeply concerned that her enemies not laugh at her (Eu. *Med.* 405, 1050, 1355), again a typically male concern. Part of what makes Medea terrifying is her appropriation of a male competitive ethic.

If masculine in her desire for victory, however, Medea remains nightmarishly feminine in her methods. She deliberately tricks the king (Creon) into giving her more time in Corinth to enact her revenge, playing on his pity for her children, and she speaks seductively and persuasively to Aegeus, the king of Athens, in order to secure safe harbor before she kills Glauke. When deciding how to respond to Jason's betrayal, she speaks of herself—and all women—as fundamentally deceitful:[44]

> And in addition, we were born
> women, most helpless of all for noble deeds,
> but the cleverest architects of every evil.
>
> —Eu. *Med.* 407–9

Medea is a quiet, confused young bride; a masculine monster of aggressive ambition; and a secretive, deceitful woman who might poison her husband out of an excess of desire. She is thus the perfect version of Athenian male anxieties about their wives: dangerously desiring, deceitful, and driven—a literal stranger whose presence in the husband's house is never entirely secure or entirely safe, whose very dedication to that household can become murderous if threatened.

THE COSTS OF MANHOOD

On the other side of the gender divide, the tragedies sometimes see masculinity itself as an unstable category, subject to internal as well as external assault. A man who demonstrated insufficient control over his own bodily desires might be portrayed as effeminate, and this in itself constitutes a threat not only to his own status, but to the larger society.

For the Athenians, sexual desire was a dangerous force that needed to be mastered. Perhaps even more importantly, mastery of one's own desires was seen as analogous to mastery over social structures: a man should control himself, just as a husband controlled his wife and household, just as he played his proper role in the affairs of the *polis*.[45] For a man to lose control over his own sexual desires, or over the use of his own body, was to fail in the arena of *enkrateia* ("self-control"), with broad social and political consequences. We have already seen one aspect of such a loss of self-control, in the text of Isaeus 6 (discussed above); there the father whose estate is contested is said to have fallen under the charms of a freedwoman, to the destruction of his family and estate, "having been reduced to such a state either by drugs or illness or by *something else*" (Isaeus 6.21).

In several tragedies, however, a male hero loses control over his body, whether through pain, sexual desire, or something else. At this moment, he is portrayed as having lost his manhood. As Froma Zeitlin noted, it is the condition of being aware of having a body that results in a hero's emasculation: ". . . at those moments when a male finds himself in a condition of weakness, he too becomes acutely aware that he has a body. Then, at the limits of pain, is when he perceives himself to be most like a woman."[46] To take one fairly straightforward example, after Herakles has put on the poisoned robe in Sophocles' *Trachiniae*, he is brought on to stage raving mad, incoherent in pain. At this point, he asks his son to pity him in pointed terms:

> Pity me,
> who am pitied by many, I who have roared,
> crying like a girl; and this is something that no one
> would ever say that they saw this man do before,
> but always I held myself without groaning in the face of evils,
> but now, in this circumstance, I have been revealed as female, alas.
> —Soph. *Trach.* 1070–5[47]

Herakles has been a representative of ideal self-control and masculinity, but in the moment of his abasement, he suggests that he is "revealed as female," as if femininity were the baseline to which all people risk descending when they are weak or disempowered. Although women can be crafty, dangerous, and masculine in their activity, when tragic heroes experience femininity it is as a form of abjection.

Similar moments occur in several plays. In Euripides's *Bacchae* we see an extended moment of feminization of the hero. The play dramatizes the entry of the cult of Dionysus into Thebes. Pentheus, the young king, is deeply suspicious of the stranger (Dionysus himself, claiming to be a priest of Dionysus) who has introduced Dionysian rites and led the women of the town out into the wilds, where they are engaging in typically masculine behavior, such as hunting. Though there is no evidence in the play that it happens, Pentheus also suspects them of drinking and engaging in indiscriminate sex (Eu. *Bacch.* 221–5). He is determined to put an end to these behaviors, and threatens to "hunt down" the women and trap them (Eu. *Bacch.* 230–1).

In the central tragic scene of the play, the god Dionysus convinces Pentheus that he should dress as a woman to spy on the women engaged in these rites. Pentheus is initially appalled by the idea of dressing as a woman, and then reluctantly agrees to it, so long as he can get out of town without being seen. But then, during a choral ode in which the female followers of Dionysus warn that the god punishes those who ignore him, a psychological change seems to take place in Pentheus. When we see him next, he is not in his right mind, and he is obsessively concerned with the success of his disguise as a woman (Eu. *Bacch.* 928–38). It is impossible to convey the sense of dread that hangs over this scene; Pentheus is not only dressing as a woman, but also seems to have adopted an almost parodically feminine mindset. In the scene that follows, as we learn from a messenger, he will encounter unmitigated disaster: while he is spying on the women, they spot him, and, under the influence of the god themselves, they rip him apart, believing that they are hunting a lion. His mother will be among his killers, and will carry his head back to Thebes. But this grotesque end to Pentheus' life is already signaled by his internal feminization.[48] Through this feminization Pentheus experiences what Medea feared—to be laughed at—and in the process he undergoes a total fall from political, social, and sartorial masculinity. He is rendered passive by the god, "controlled rather than controlling, viewed rather than viewing, powerless, helpless, a victim."[49]

Euripides shows that Pentheus' transformation is not only physical and visible, but psychological. In the highly competitive, public world of fifth-century Athens, masculinity was not a stable state, but a hard-won status, which any action, gesture, or mode of dress could put at risk. We can see this trope in our legal sources, as when Aeschines taunts the orator Demosthenes:

> Demosthenes, if someone should strip off those exquisite, pretty mantles of yours, and the soft, pretty shorts that you wear while you are writing speeches against your friends, and should pass them around among the jurors, I think, unless they were informed beforehand, that they would be at a loss to say whether they were holding the clothing of a man or of a woman.
>
> —Aesch. *Against Timarchos* 131

Aeschines deftly suggests that Demosthenes is less than a man because of the clothes that he wears, and in the process invites the jurors to mentally undress him. He subjects him to exactly the kind of ridicule that Dionysus planned—successfully—for Pentheus. We see in both legal and tragic texts the fear that a man might slip all too easily into a debased state of femininity.

THE ROMAN TURN

The social norms that governed Roman sexual life are, in many respects, similar to those that we saw in ancient Athens. Adult men were assumed to be erotically interested in younger men as well as women. Romans were, however, more strict about penetration in the highest social class than were the ancient Athenians: there was no situation in which it was considered legal or acceptable for a man to penetrate a citizen boy, and numerous texts express disdain for the Athenian practice of pederasty, in which such penetration was, though problematic, allowable.[50] (Penetration of male or female slaves by a Roman citizen was, however, allowed and considered within the bounds of normal desire.) Adult men in Rome were fundamentally defined by their impenetrability, and men who were penetrated were said to *muliebria pati* ("suffer womanly things").[51] Men who willingly allowed themselves to be penetrated were sexually non-normative, and the subject of ridicule and invective.

As in ancient Athens, Roman men's lives were more public than those of women, and women were, in most cases, under the guardianship of a man, either a father, husband, or brother. Women were less strictly sequestered than in Athens, however, and in some cases elite women achieved a level of financial, social, and even sexual freedom that would not have been imaginable at any point in the Athenian democracy. Particularly in the period of the Roman Empire, women at the highest levels of elite society—and especially wives and mothers of the emperor—became both wealthy and socially very powerful.[52]

All our extant Roman tragedies were written by Seneca (except *Octavia*). Seneca was a wealthy man closely involved with the imperial courts of Claudius and Nero. He was a proponent of Stoicism, which taught that Nature, properly interpreted, provides us with all the information that we need to lead an ethical and happy life.[53] Stoics believed that a good life required elimination of "passions" (obsessive emotions based on false beliefs), and a corresponding refusal to be unduly affected by external events or stimuli.[54] They argued that by cultivating a rigorous relation with his own soul, the philosopher could experience a form of *gaudium* (happiness) which is to be distinguished from *voluptas* (pleasure).[55] Seneca primarily defines *virtus*, "virtue," as this exercise of self-control leading to self-sufficient *gaudium*.

The Roman word for virtue is linguistically related to the word *vir*, the standard word for citizen men. Virtue is, in a sense, manliness, and linguistically it encompasses both bodily impenetrability and mental and emotional steadfastness—although Seneca did believe some women capable of achieving *virtus*.[56]

One of the primary threats to Stoic self-control is the experience of sexual desire (*cupido*), which even the most virtuous person might find overwhelming. Seneca's *Phaedra*, based in part on the *Hippolytus* of Euripides, provides an extended representation of the ethical problems of sexual desire, and a brief analysis of the play will show how Seneca refracted those problems through a Stoic lens, and in response to a specifically Roman imperial set of cultural conditions and artistic conventions.

In Seneca's play, Phaedra is the character who experiences the greatest degree of ethical conflict, again in the form of having to deal with her unnatural passion for her stepson. As in other Senecan tragedies, each of the characters fails as a Stoic, with gruesome results. The point is not to demonstrate Stoicism itself as a failure, but to show that ethical principles must be properly enacted in order to be effective in the face of the emotional force of sexual desire.

Several characters, most notably the Nurse, espouse clear Stoic doctrines. Early in the play, when Phaedra is struggling with her passion, the Nurse advises: "Whoever first resists / and rejects love, he is safe, and a victor" (Sen. *Phae*. 132–3; Figure 8.5). Here the Nurse gives good, if difficult, advice: simply reject passion from the start. But there is also a suggestion that Phaedra is responsible for her own passion, having "nursed it with sweet indulgence" (line 134)—and once a passion has taken hold of her soul, it is all the more difficult to banish. Later, the Nurse warns that Phaedra must not rely on external judges to determine the proper course of her actions: "Some women have borne crime safely; but none securely" (Sen. *Phae*. 164). Phaedra might, the Nurse suggests, get away with sleeping with her stepson, without punishment from the gods or detection by her husband. Women, here as always subject to suspicion of infidelity, have done so before. But if she does, Phaedra will be guilty, and will know it, and this in itself will destroy her happiness. Here, the Nurse articulates the Stoic idea that control of sexual desire must be internal;

FIGURE 8.5: Fragmentary Roman wall-painting from Pompeii showing Phaedra with her nurse, c. 20–60 CE. The British Museum, London, 1856,0625.5. © The Trustees of the British Museum. All rights reserved.

reliance on any external judge exposes the subject to the inconsistent enforcement, and the possibility of an unethical response.

As Roland Meyer points out, all three main characters are eventually ruled by *furor*, madness, and even the Nurse turns out not to steer on an even Stoic keel.[57] As in Euripides, the Nurse eventually recognizes the hopelessness of her mistress' passion, and she champions Phaedra's erotic cause. In Euripides' play the Nurse takes the disastrous step of telling Hippolytus about Phaedra's desire for him without Phaedra's permission. In Seneca, she lays the groundwork for an argument that Hippolytus should acknowledge Phaedra's passion; but, surprisingly, she frames her argument in strictly Stoic terms. She begins by arguing that Nature has assigned different behaviors to different times of life, and that it is natural for young men to enjoy love (Sen. *Phae.* 443–62). She concludes this speech with what looks like perfect Stoicism: "Follow Nature as your leader in life" (Sen. *Phae.* 481). In another context, this is exactly the sort of advice that Seneca *qua* philosopher might give; in his treatise *On the Happy Life*, he insists, "We must employ Nature as our guide . . ." (Sen. *de vita beata* 8). But in this context, what the Nurse means by "follow Nature," is "sleep with your stepmother."[58] Stoic doctrine is misinterpreted to argue for personal surrender to immoral passion, and the results, as the play runs its inevitable course, are catastrophic. Scholars frequently have a difficult time resolving the relationship between Seneca's tragedies and his prose works; it seems, at times, as if the tragedies serve only to demonstrate the failure of Stoic philosophy.[59] I argue that this play shows us, instead, a central tenet of Senecan Stoicism: that simple doctrine is not enough. Individuals must actively and habitually pursue the correct path. As in Euripides' play, sexual desire leads to social disaster. But in Euripides' version, the emphasis is on the destruction of familial relations through a female passion that is, in fact, beyond human control. In Seneca's version, Phaedra's desire is an ethical problem imperfectly addressed by Stoic-sounding characters, including Phaedra herself. Her downfall serves as a paradigm of the wrong way for individuals to respond to the overwhelming stimulus of erotic, or any, false and unethical desire. The proper way to achieve impenetrable *virtus*—the kind of ethical "masculinity" available to any true Stoic, female or male, if such a person exists—is to orient oneself only to the right, objectively desirable object of desire, which is virtue itself.

CONCLUSIONS

Ancient tragedy represents gender in ways that are familiar enough that they run the risk of seeming universal, or transhistorical. I have tried, however, to show that many of the fundamental aspects of gender and sexual desire in Athenian tragedy stem from specific social structures—and anxieties surrounding them—in fifth-century Athens. Female desire was always viewed as potentially dangerous, granting a personal subjectivity to citizens whose political life was thought of as in need of social control. A married woman was considered a stranger in her husband's household, the direct result of a system of marriage in which a woman maintained important ties to her natal family, and could, in fact, be called on to return to her father's household in order to remarry and produce heirs for her paternal bloodline. Her loyalty was thought of as necessarily divided. For men, femininity carried with it two threats. A man could find himself under the sway of a seductive woman, unable to control his desires, and thus destroy his home and family. Moreover, every man contained within himself the threat of accepting femininity both externally and internally, of being objectified, laughed at, and placed under the control of another. We see all of these anxieties played out in Athenian tragedy, sometimes in exaggerated form, but nonetheless, recognizable as having a firm basis in the cultural real.

Similarly, the Roman tragedies of Seneca are shaped by the intellectual movements of their time, as well as the philosophical interests of their author. Senecan Stoicism is itself an important response to the political chaos that the Roman senatorial class found in the Empire of the first century CE. That philosophical response is neither straightforwardly championed nor proven inadequate in the gruesome world of tragedy, but imperfectly enacted by characters who do not have the moral compass necessary to control their passions in the right way.

Both Roman and Athenian tragedy may be fun-house mirrors of the societies that produced them, but they are still mirrors: not transhistorical representations of human truth about gender or sexual desire, but media for refracted images, transferred to a tragic mode, of the fears and desires of the elite men of fifth-century BCE Athens and first-century CE Rome.

NOTES

Introduction

1. See Weiss this volume.
2. We have only one extant Athenian tragedy based on a historical, non-mythic story, Aeschylus' *Persians* (472 BCE: an early tragedy) and we learn from Herodotus (6.21.10) that another non-mythic tragedy, the *Capture of Miletos* by Phrynichus, was deemed by the audience too upsetting, and banned from reperformance; quoted and discussed by Cowan, in this volume.
3. Cf. the use of terms like "escape drama" or "problem play" to define the tragedies which seem un-tragic by modern standards; see A.P. Burnett, *Catastrophe Survived: Euripides' Plays of Mixed Reversal* (Oxford: Oxford University Press, 1971).
4. See M. Wright, *The Lost Plays of Greek Tragedy*, vol. 1: *Neglected Authors* (London: Bloomsbury, 2016) for an accessible and thorough account of our evidence for the many lost plays.
5. On the proportion of Athenian tragedies that survive, see also Weiss this volume.
6. J. Redford, *Nature and Culture in the Iliad: The tragedy of Hector* (Durham: Duke University Press, 1994); on Thucydides, cf. C. Macleod, "Thucydides and Tragedy," in *The Collected Essays of Colin Macleod*, ed. O. Taplin (Oxford: Clarendon Press, 1997).
7. For detailed analysis of the performance contexts of ancient tragedy, see Andújar, Weiss, and Visvardi, in this volume.
8. Attempts to bridge the gap include E. Jones, *The Origins of Shakespeare* (Oxford: Oxford University Press, 1977) which makes a strong case for Shakespeare's knowledge of Athenian tragedy in Latin translation. Cf. more recently the stimulating work of T. Pollard, *Greek Tragic Women on Shakespearean Stages* (Oxford: Oxford University Press, 2017).
9. M. de Unamuno, *The Tragic Sense of Life*, translated by J.E. Crawford Flitch (1921; reprint New York: Cosimo Classics, 2005).
10. L. Swift, *The Hidden Chorus: Echoes of genre in tragic lyric* (Oxford: Oxford University Press, 2010) teases out echoes of and allusions to various lyric genres within extant tragedy.
11. For good discussion of the importance of representations of foreigners or "barbarians" in tragedy, see E. Hall, *Inventing the Barbarian: Greek Self-Definition Through Tragedy* (Oxford: Oxford University Press, 1989); on slaves in tragedy, see E. Hall, *Greek Tragedy: Suffering under the sun* (Oxford: Oxford University Press, 2010).
12. The specific mechanics of dramaturgy for Athenian dramaturgy are well discussed by Naomi Weiss in this volume, while Andújar and Visvardi, in usefully different ways, provide insightful accounts of performance conditions and receptions of ancient tragedy.
13. On satyr plays, see further Weiss in this volume and M. Griffith, *Greek Satyr Play: Five Studies* (Berkeley and Los Angeles: University of California Press, 2013).
14. On cities: for instance Aeschylus' *Persians* contrasts Susa with Athens. On the relationship of households to each other, see Widzisz and Ormand in this volume. Sophocles' late tragedy *Philoctetes* is unusual in having a setting more reminiscent of a satyr play, outside a cave on a wild and remote island.

15. Men afraid of becoming women include Heracles in Sophocles' *Trachineae*; Pentheus dresses in women's clothes in Euripides' *Bacchae*; Clytemnestra in Aeschylus' *Agamemnon* is described as a masculine woman, a woman performing the role of a man. See Ormand in this volume, with bibliography, for more detailed discussion of ancient Athenian and Roman attitudes to gender.
16. There are good introductory essays on these issues in M. Fontaine and A. Scafuro, eds., *The Oxford Handbook of Greek and Roman Comedy* (Oxford: Oxford University Press, 2014); M. Revermann, ed., *The Cambridge Companion to Greek Comedy* (Cambridge: Cambridge University Press, 2014); M. Silk, *Aristophanes and the Definition of Comedy* (Oxford: Oxford University Press, 2002); E. Segal, "'The Comic Catastrophe': An Essay on Euripidean Comedy," *Bulletin of the Institute of Classical Studies*, Supplement 66 (1995): 46–55; O. Taplin, "Fifth-century Tragedy and Comedy: A *synkrisis*," *Journal of Hellenic Studies* 106 (1986): 163–74.
17. For instance, many scholars have tried to connect the plague at Athens to the plague at the start of Sophocles' *Oedipus Tyrannos*, and to associate Oedipus, the quick-thinking authoritative leader, with the great statesman Pericles; but this kind of connection remains debatable and controversial. On references to Alcibiades in Sophocles, and further discussion of the theoretical and methodological issues, see M. Vickers, *Sophocles and Alcibiades* (Ithaca: Cornell University Press, 2008).
18. On the latter, see Busch in this volume.
19. From *Die Fragmente der Vorsokratiker*, Hermann Diels and Walther Kranz (first published 1903; Weidmann, 6th edition, 1951–2, three volumes). The quotation appears in the writings of a Neo-Platonist from the sixth century CE, Simplicius, who describes the passage as poetical in phrasing.
20. On this, see further Cowan in this volume.
21. For more on tragedy and philosophy, see Busch in this volume, as well as (on Sophocles) J. Gregory, "Sophocles and Education," in *Brill's Companion to Sophocles*, ed. A. Markantonatos (Leiden: Brill, 2015) and E. Wilson, "Sophocles and Philosophy," in the same volume, and J. Dillon, "Euripides and the Philosophy of His Time," *Classics Ireland* 11 (2004): 47–73 on Euripides.
22. See further Visvardi, this volume, with bibliography.
23. Martha Nussbaum has influentially read Plato in terms of a resistance to a Homeric and tragic vision whereby human happiness is always precarious, and human life is inherently subject to luck or fortune. M. Nussbaum, *The Fragility of Goodness: Luck and ethics in Greek tragedy and philosophy* (Cambridge: Cambridge University Press, 1986; reprint 2001).
24. See Torrance's chapter in this volume.
25. See the seminal J.J. Winkler and F.I. Zeitlin, eds., *Nothing to do with Dionysus? Athenian Drama in its Social Context* (Princeton: Princeton University Press, 1992), which represented new wave in study of tragedy.
26. These questions are explored further in Andújar's and Cowan's essays, in this volume.
27. See Andújar in this volume, who emphasizes the range of different performance contexts for tragedy.
28. On this, see further Visvardi, in this volume.
29. See Cowan in this volume.
30. For instance by the Veterans Chorus at Aquila Theater: https://www.aquilatheatre.com/applied-theatre/ (accessed August 16, 2018).
31. Cf. Ormand's emphasis, in this volume, on the fact that male elite same-sex relationships were a central element in the lives of well-born fifth-century Athenian men, while ancient

Athenian tragedy seems to focus almost exclusively on sexual relationships between men and women. Athenian tragedy's focus on the household (the *oikos*) and the city-state (the *polis*) entails ignoring or at least sidelining other social structures that were prominent in contemporary Athenian culture, such as pederastic same-sex romances, the gymnasium, and all-male drinking clubs.

32. E. Wilson, *Mocked with Death: Tragic overliving from Sophocles to Milton* (Baltimore: Johns Hopkins University Press, 2004).

Chapter One

1. Aristophanes, *Clouds* 1361–78. On Hellenistic and Roman education, see esp. T. Morgan, *Literate Education in the Hellenistic and Roman Worlds* (Cambridge: Cambridge University Press, 1998).
2. The *Suda* (s.v. each tragedian) claims Aeschylus wrote ninety plays, Sophocles at least 123, and Euripides either seventy-five or ninety-two.
3. On tragic canonization, see P. E. Easterling, "From Repertoire to Canon," in *The Cambridge Companion to Greek Tragedy*, ed. P. E. Easterling (Cambridge: Cambridge University Press, 1997); J. Hanink, *Lycurgan Athens and the Making of Classical Tragedy* (Cambridge: Cambridge University Press, 2014); S. Nervegna, "Performing Classics: The Tragic Canon in the Fourth Century and Beyond," in *Greek Theatre in the Fourth Century B.C.*, ed. E. Csapo et al. (Berlin: De Gruyter, 2014).
4. Aristophanes, *Frogs* 1515–9.
5. On the transferal of the texts to Alexandria, see Hanink, *Lycurgan Athens*, 244–5.
6. For an overview of the *Poetics*' reception, see S. Halliwell, *Aristotle's Poetics* (London: Duckworth, 1986; reprint Chicago: University of Chicago Press, 1998), 286–323.
7. Aristotle, *Poetics* 1449b24-8. Translations of the *Poetics* are Halliwell (Cambridge, MA: Harvard University Press, 1995). Unless otherwise noted, all other translations are my own.
8. Euripides, *Electra* 508–84; Aeschylus, *Libation Bearers* 164–234.
9. On the "competence" of fifth-century audiences of Athenian tragedy, see M. Revermann, "The Competence of Theatre Audiences in Fifth- and Fourth-Century Athens," *Journal of Hellenic Studies* 126 (2006): 99–124.
10. Aristotle, *Poetics* 1454b8-9.
11. Ibid. 1149b33-4.
12. Ibid. 1458a18.
13. Ibid. 1456a29-32.
14. Plato, *Laws* 814e-17e.
15. Aristotle, *Poetics* 1450b16-7.
16. Aristotle, *Politics* 1339a11-42b35.
17. Plutarch, *Life of Nicias* 24.2-3
18. *Life of Aeschylus* 2, 7.
19. M. Schmidt, "Dionysien," *Antike Kunst* 10 (1967); M. C. Wellenbach, "The Iconography of Dionysiac Choroi: Dithyramb, Tragedy, and the Basel Krater," *Greek, Roman, and Byzantine Studies* 55 (2015): 72–103.
20. J. R. Green, "On Seeing and Depicting the Theatre in Classical Athens," *Greek, Roman, and Byzantine Studies* 32 (1991): 34–7.
21. On the professionalization of actors and auletes in the late fifth and early fourth centuries, see E. Hall, "Actor's Song in Tragedy," in *Performance Culture and Athenian Democracy*, ed. S. Goldhill and R. Osborne (Cambridge: Cambridge University Press, 1999); E. Hall, "The

Singing Actors of Antiquity," in *Greek and Roman Actors: Aspects of an Ancient Profession*, ed. P. E. Easterling and Edith Hall (Cambridge: Cambridge University Press, 2002); P. Wilson, "The *Aulos* in Athens," in Goldhill and Osborne, eds, *Performance Culture*, 74–5; P. Wilson, "The Musicians Among the Actors," in Easterling and Hall, eds, *Greek and Roman Actors*, 46–8.
22. P. Vienna G 2315, P. Leiden inv. P. 510. See E. Pöhlmann and M. L. West, *Documents of Ancient Greek Music* (Oxford: Clarendon Press, 2001), 12–21.
23. On Euripides' use of *melisma*, see the parody at Aristophanes, *Frogs* 1314.
24. A. D'Angour, "The New Music: So What's New?" in *Rethinking Revolutions through Ancient Greece*, ed. R. Osborne (Cambridge: Cambridge University Press, 2006).
25. Aeschylus, *Suppliants* 825–902.
26. Euripides, *Bacchae* 14–64; 114.
27. T. Power, "Sophocles and Music," in *Brill's Companion to Sophocles*, ed. A. Markantonatos (Leiden: Brill, 2012).
28. Athenaeus 1.20e; *Life of Sophocles* 5.
29. P. Wilson, "Thamyris the Thracian: The Archetypal Wandering Poet?" in *Wandering Poets in Ancient Greek Culture*, ed. R. Hunter and I. Rutherford (Cambridge: Cambridge University Press, 2009), 63–4.
30. Sophocles frag. 240 *TrGF*.
31. Sophocles, *Ajax* 701. See A. Henrichs, "'Why Should I Dance?': Choral Self-Referentiality in Greek Tragedy," *Arion* 3 (1994–5): 73–5.
32. N. Weiss, *The Music of Tragedy: Performance and Imagination in Euripidean Theater* (Oakland: University of California Press, 2018).
33. Aeschylus, *Eumenides* 372–4.
34. *Life of Aeschylus* 9; Pollux 4.110.
35. E. Hall, "Is There a *Polis* in Aristotle's *Poetics*?," in *Tragedy and the Tragic: Greek Theatre and Beyond*, ed. M. S. Silk (Oxford: Oxford University Press, 1996); M. Heath, "Should There Have Been a *Polis* in the *Poetics*," *The Classical Quarterly* 59 (2009): 389–402; Hanink, *Lycurgan Athens*, 215–20.
36. A.W. Pickard-Cambridge, *Dithyramb, Tragedy and Comedy*, 2nd edn., rev. T. B. L. Webster (Oxford: Clarendon Press, 1962), 16–18; W. Burkert, "Greek Tragedy and Sacrificial Ritual," *Greek, Roman, and Byzantine Studies* 7, no. 2 (1966): 87–121; C. Sourvinou-Inwood, *Tragedy and Athenian Religion* (Lanham: Lexington Books, 2003), 141–200.
37. *FrGHist* 239A 43.
38. *Anthologia Palatina* 7.410, trans. W. R. Paton (Cambridge, MA: Harvard University Press, 1917).
39. Horace, *Ars Poetica* 220.
40. On the festival's origins, see especially R. Rehm, *Greek Tragic Theatre* (London and New York: Routledge, 1992), 15–16; E. Csapo and W. J. Slater, *The Context of Ancient Drama* (Ann Arbor: University of Michigan Press, 1995), 104.
41. M. L. West, "The Early Chronology of Attic Tragedy," *The Classical Quarterly* 39, no. 1 (1989): 251–4.
42. Plutarch, *Life of Solon* 29.3–30.1.
43. Plutarch, *Life of Alcibiades* 32.3.
44. E. Irwin, *Solon and Early Greek Poetry: The Politics of Exhortation* (Cambridge: Cambridge University Press, 2005), 272–7.
45. On this issue see also discussions by Andújar, Visvardi, and especially Cowan in this volume with relevant bibliography.

46. P. Wilson, *The Athenian Institution of the Khoregia: The Chorus, the City and the Stage* (Cambridge: Cambridge University Press, 2000).
47. Hanink, *Lycurgan Athens*.
48. Plato, *Laws* 7.817b.
49. B. Kowalzig, "Changing Choral Worlds: Song-Dance and Society in Athens and Beyond," in *Music and the Muses: The Culture of "Mousikē" in the Classical Athenian City*, ed. P. Murray and P. Wilson (Oxford: Oxford University Press, 2004). On the Dionysian context of tragedy, see esp. J. J. Winkler and F. I. Zeitlin, eds., *Nothing to Do with Dionysus? Athenian Drama in its Social Context.* (Princeton: Princeton University Press, 1990).
50. Aristotle, *Poetics* 1449a9-11.
51. For a skeptical approach to Aristotle's account of tragedy's origins, see S. Scullion, "Tragedy and Religion: The Problem of Origins," in *A Companion to Greek Tragedy*, ed. Justina Gregory (Malden, MA/ Oxford: Blackwell, 2007).
52. Bacchylides 19. On the relationship between dithyramb and tragedy, see especially. L. Battezzato, "Dithyramb and Greek Tragedy," in *Dithyramb in Context*, eds. B. Kowalzig and P. Wilson (Oxford: Oxford University Press, 2013).
53. E. Csapo, "Later Euripidean Music," *Illinois Classical Studies* 24–5 (1999–2000): 399–426; Weiss, *Music of Tragedy*.
54. Aristotle, *Poetics* 1449a19-21.
55. M. Griffith, *Greek Satyr Play: Five Studies* (Berkeley and Los Angeles: University of California Press, 2013a).
56. On *Alcestis* as satyric, see esp. C. W. Marshall, "Alcestis and the Problem of Prosatyric Drama," *The Classical Journal* 95 (2000): 229–38; N. W. Slater, "Nothing to Do with Satyrs? *Alcestis* and the Concept of Prosatyric Drama," in *Satyr Drama: Tragedy at Play*, ed. G. W. M. Harrison (Swansea: The Classical Press of Wales, 2005); C. A. Shaw, *Satyric Play: The Evolution of Greek Comedy and Satyr Drama* (Oxford: Oxford University Press, 2014), 94–105.
57. On the synthesis of tragedy and satyr play on the Pronomos Vase, see Griffith, *Greek Satyr Play*, 129–45.
58. Euripides, *Helen* 1107–21; Aristophanes, *Birds* 209–14, 676–84. On Euripides' use of the Aristophanic passages, see W. Allan ed., *Euripides: Helen* (Cambridge: Cambridge University Press, 2008), 272; C. W. Marshall, *The Structure and Performance of Euripides'* Helen (Cambridge: Cambridge University Press, 2014), 213; Weiss, *Music of Tragedy*, 165-7.
59. On the influence of comedy in this and other Euripidean plays, see esp. E. Segal, "'The Comic Catastrophe': An Essay on Euripidean Comedy," *Bulletin of the Institute of Classical Studies. Supplement* 66 (1995): 46–55.
60. Pollux 4.111.
61. Weiss, *Music of Tragedy*.
62. E. Hall, *Inventing the Barbarian* (Oxford: Oxford University Press, 1989); N. Loraux, *The Invention of Athens: The Funeral Oration and the Classical City* (Cambridge, MA: The MIT Press, 1986); N. Loraux, *Mothers in Mourning* (Ithaca, NY: Cornell University Press, 1998); G. Holst-Warhaft, *Dangerous Voices: Women's Laments and Greek Literature* (London and New York: Routledge, 1992), 98–126.
63. On lament as a female and/or foreign activity in tragedy, see esp. Hall, "Actor's Song in Tragedy"; H. Foley, *Female Acts in Greek Tragedy* (Princeton: Princeton University Press, 2001); N. Loraux, *The Mourning Voice: An Essay on Greek Tragedy* (Ithaca, NY: Cornell University Press, 2002); N. Weiss, "Noise, Music, Speech: The Representation of Lament in Greek Tragedy," *American Journal of Philology* 138 (2017): 243–66.
64. Aeschylus, *Persians* 935–1076, 388–94.

65. Euripides, *Trojan Women* 308–40.
66. Ibid. 511–76.
67. Ibid. 565–7. On the mix of genres at play here, see especially N. Weiss, "Generic Hybridity in Athenian Tragedy," in *Genre in Archaic and Classical Greek Poetry: Theories and Models*, ed. M. Foster, L. Kurke, and N. Weiss (Leiden: Brill, forthcoming).
68. Euripides, *Trojan Women* 799–808.
69. L. Swift, *The Hidden Chorus: Echoes of Genre in Tragic Lyric* (Oxford: Oxford University Press, 2010), 156–70.
70. Aeschylus, *Eumenides* 321–96.
71. On the tragic *agōn*, see M. Lloyd, *The Agon in Euripides* (Oxford: Clarendon Press, 1992); E. T. E. Barker, *Entering the Agon: Dissent and Authority in Homer, Historiography, and Tragedy* (Oxford: Oxford University Press, 2009), 265–365.
72. Euripides, *Trojan Women* 915–1032.
73. Weiss, "Generic Hybridity."
74. Aristophanes, *Frogs* 1301–3.
75. Ibid. 1329–63.
76. M. Griffith, *Aristophanes' Frogs* (Cambridge: Cambridge University Press, 2013), 142–3.
77. On performances of Aeschylean tragedies in fourth-century Athens, see Nervegna, "Performing Classics," 166–72 with further bibliography.
78. Hanink, *Lycurgan Athens*, 207–11.
79. K. Bosher, ed., *Theater Outside Athens: Drama in Greek Sicily and South Italy* (Cambridge: Cambridge University Press, 2012); Csapo et al., *Greek Theatre*; also Andújar in this volume.
80. On Aeschylus in Sicily, see Andújar in this volume with further bibliography.
81. On Euripides in Macedon, see Andújar in this volume with further bibliography.
82. Arrian, *Anabasis* 6.3.1–2, 6.28.1–3, *Indica* 8.36.3, 17.107.4, 18.11–12; Athenaeus 13.586d–95e; see B. Le Guen, "Theatre, Religion and Politics at Alexander's Travelling Royal Court," in Csapo et al., *Greek Theatre*.
83. J. C. Moretti, "The Evolution of Theatre Architecture Outside Athens in the Fourth Century," in Csapo et al., *Greek Theatre*.
84. Aristotle, *Rhetoric* 1405a23–4.
85. See A. Kotlińska-Toma, *Hellenistic Tragedy: Texts, Translations and a Critical Survey* (London: Bloomsbury, 2015), 18–20 on Horace, *Ars Poetica* 189.
86. Kotlińska-Toma, *Hellenistic Tragedy*, 5.
87. Kotlińska-Toma, *Hellenistic Tragedy*, 13–14.
88. Galen, *In Hippocratis epidemiarum* iii 17a.607.7–17 Wenkebach.
89. On the "Romanness" of Republican tragedy, see R. Cowan, "240 BCE and All That: The Romanness of Republican Tragedy," in *Brill's Companion to Roman Tragedy*, ed. G.W. M. Harrison (Leiden: Brill, 2015).
90. Livy 7.2.3–8.
91. A. J. Boyle, *Introduction to Roman Tragedy* (London and New York: Routledge, 2006), 100–6.
92. See especially T. Moore, "Music in Roman Tragedy," in *Roman Drama and its Contexts*, ed. S. Frangoulidis, S. J. Harrison, and G. Manuwald (Berlin: De Gruyter, 2016).
93. Boyle, *Roman Tragedy*, 49–51; L.D. Ginsberg, "Tragic Rome? Roman Historical Drama and the Genre of Tragedy," in Harrison, *Roman Tragedy*.
94. Cicero, *Epistulae ad familiares* 7.1.2. See Boyle, *Roman Tragedy*, 156.
95. B. Zimmermann, "Seneca and Pantomime," in *New Directions in Ancient Pantomime*, ed. E. Hall and R. Wyles (Oxford: Oxford University Press, 2008); A. Zanobi, "The Influence of

Pantomime on Seneca's Tragedies," in Hall and Wyles, *Ancient Pantomime*; A. Zanobi, *Seneca's Tragedies and the Aesthetics of Pantomime* (London: Bloomsbury, 2014).
96. F. Leo, *De Senecae Tragoediis observationes criticae* (Berlin: Weidmann, 1878), 147–59.
97. See especially D. F. Sutton, *Seneca on Stage* (Leiden: Brill, 1986); M. Erasmo, *Roman Tragedy: Theatre to Theatricality* (Austin: University of Texas Press, 2004), 122–39.
98. Boyle, *Roman Tragedy*, 192, 208–18.

Chapter Two

1. The bibliography on this topic is extensive, but see, e.g., A.W. Pickard-Cambridge, *The dramatic festivals of Athens*, 2nd edn., rev. J. Gould and D.M. Lewis (Oxford: Clarendon Press, 1988); E. Csapo and W.J. Slater, *The Context of Ancient Drama* (Ann Arbor: University of Michigan Press, 1995); P. Cartledge, "'Deep plays': Theatre as process in Greek civic life," in *The Cambridge Companion to Greek Tragedy*, ed. P.E. Easterling (Cambridge: Cambridge University Press, 1997); P.E. Easterling, "A Show for Dionysus" in Easterling, ed. *Companion to Greek Tragedy*.
2. See the seminal J. Winkler and F. Zeitlin, eds., *Nothing to do with Dionysus*; cf. J.P. Vernant, "The Historical Moment of Tragedy in Greece: Some of the Social and Psychological Conditions," in *Myth and Tragedy in Ancient Greece*, trans. J. Lloyd, eds J.P. Vernant and P. Vidal Naquet (New York: Zone, 1988), which paved the way for much of this thinking. Tragedy, according to Cartledge, "Deep Plays," 3, was "itself an active ingredient, and a major one, of the political foreground, featuring in the everyday consciousness and even the nocturnal dreams of the Athenian citizen". See also S. Goldhill, "The audience of Athenian tragedy" in Easterling, ed. *Companion to Greek Tragedy*. For more discussion, see Cowan in this volume.
3. P. Wilson, *The Athenian Institution of the Khoregia: The Chorus, the City and the Stage* (Cambridge: Cambridge University Press, 2000).
4. Sicily: K. Bosher, ed., *Theater Outside Athens: Drama in Greek Sicily and South Italy* (Cambridge: Cambridge University Press, 2012). Black Sea: D. Braund and E. Hall, "Theatre in the fourth-century Black Sea Region," in *Greek Theatre in the Fourth Century BC*, ed. E. Csapo et al. (Berlin: De Gruyter, 2014); E. Stewart, *Greek Tragedy on the Move: The Birth of a Panhellenic Art Form c.500-300 B.C.* (Oxford: Oxford University Press, 2017), however, argues that the "Panhellenic" nature of tragedy is evident from its inception.
5. For some partial answers, see E. Csapo, "Some social and economic conditions behind the rise of the acting profession in the fifth and fourth centuries BC," in *Le statut de l'acteur dans l'Antiquité grecque et romaine: Actes du colloque qui s'est tenu à Tours les 3 et 4 mai 2002 organisé par l'UMR 5189 "Histoire et sources des mondes anciens,"* ed. C. Hugoniot, F. Hurlet, and S. Milanezi (Tours: Presse Universitaire François Rabelais, 2004); O. Taplin, "Spreading the word through performance," in *Performance Culture and Athenian Democracy*, eds S. Goldhill and R. Osborne (Cambridge: Cambridge University Press, 1999); O. Taplin, *Pots and Plays: Interactions between Tragedy and Greek Vase-Painting of the Fourth Century B.C.* (Los Angeles: Getty Publications, 2007); O. Taplin, "How was Athenian tragedy played in the Greek West?" in Bosher, ed. *Theater Outside Athens*; Csapo et al., eds., *Greek Theatre*; E. Csapo and P. Wilson, "Drama Outside Athens in the Fifth and Fourth Centuries BC," in *Reperformances of Drama in the Fifth and Fourth Centuries B.C.: Authors and Contexts*, ed. A Lamari (Berlin: De Gruyter, 2015); and Stewart, *Greek Tragedy on the Move*. J.R. Green, "Theatre Production: 1996–2006," *Lustram* 50 (2008): 97–8 contains a partial overview of recent scholarship.

6. For a more comprehensive account of the reperformances of tragedy in monarchies outside of Athens, see A. Duncan, "Political reperformances of tragedy in the fifth and fourth centuries BC," in Lamari, ed. *Reperformances*.
7. On the lives of poets as a source and genre, see M. Lefkowitz, *The Lives of the Greek Poets*, 2nd edn. (Baltimore: Johns Hopkins University Press, 2012) and R. Fletcher and J. Hanink, eds., *Creative Lives in Antiquity* (Cambridge: Cambridge University Press, 2016).
8. See also the scholiast to Ar. *Pax* 73b who describes Aeschylus in similar terms.
9. As E. Csapo, *Actors and Icons of the Ancient Theater* (Chichester: Blackwell, 2014), 96, elaborates, these fourteen sources "include some of our most trusted authorities: men like Eratosthenes and Plutarch. To reject such information offhand because of methodical or generic doubt is unreasonable." Scholars agree that Aeschylus most likely visited Sicily at least twice: see *TrGF*³ T 88–92 and K. Morgan, *Pindar and the Construction of Syracusan Monarchy in the Fifth Century B.C.* (Oxford: Oxford University Press, 2015), 96 n. 31.
10. C. Dougherty, "Linguistic colonialism in Aeschylus' *Aetnaeae*," *Greek, Roman, and Byzantine Studies* 32, no. 2 (1991): 119–32.
11. Diod. Sic. 11.49. See N. Luraghi, *Tirannidi archaiche in Sicilia e Magna Graecia: da Panezio di Leontini alla caduta dei Dinomenidi* (Firenze: Olschki, 1994), 335–46; and D.G. Smith, "Sicily and the identities of Xuthus: Stesichorus, Aeschylus' *Aetnaeae*, and Euripides' *Ion*," in Bosher, ed., *Theater Outside Athens*, 130–2.
12. The Theban poet Pindar likewise celebrates the founding of the city in his first *Pythian*, but epinician poetry, unlike tragedy, is by nature commissioned work, which at this time was almost exclusively produced within the framework of the *polis*; see A.D. Morrison, *Performance and Audiences in Pindar's Sicilian Victory Odes*, BICS Supplement 95 (London: Institute of Classical Studies, 2007) and Morgan, *Syracusan Monarchy*.
13. L. Poli-Palladini, "Some reflections on Aeschylus' *Aetnae(ae)*," *Rheinisches Museum für Philologie, Neue Folge* 144, no. 3–4 (2001): 296.
14. Ibid., 319–23. Dougherty, "Linguistic Colonialism" speaks of the "colonization" of the Palici, the autochthonous Sicel gods, into Greek mythology.
15. See Poli-Palladini, "Aeschylus' *Aetnae(ae)*," 289–96 for an overview.
16. As O. Taplin, *The Stagecraft of Aeschylus: the Dramatic Use of Exits and Entrances in Greek Tragedy* (Oxford: Clarendon Press, 1977), 416, comments, "the single change of scene in *Eum[enides]* is extraordinary enough: changes on the scale indicated in *Aitnaiai* were unknown before the publication of this fragment."
17. Ibid., 417.
18. Poli-Palladini "Aeschylus' *Aetnae(ae)*," 318. Recent research into theaters in Sicily suggests that fifth-century theaters there were advanced; for example, the theater at Syracuse which was rebuilt around 460 BCE included a low stage and three doors, which enabled sophisticated drama to be performed. For an overview of Sicilian theatrical culture in the classical period, see Csapo and Wilson, "Drama outside Athens," 328–44.
19. K. Morgan, *Syracusan Monarchy*, 96. Cf. K. Bosher, "Hieron's Aeschylus," in Bosher, ed., *Theater Outside Athens*, who suggests the play's *first* performance happened in Sicily.
20. The scholiast's comments on Ar. *Ran.* 1028–9 have been used to support the notion that *Persians* was reperformed in Sicily; see M. Broggiato, "Aristophanes and Aeschylos' *Persians*: Hellenistic Discussions of Ar. *Ran.* 1028f," *Rheinisches Museum für Philologie, Neue Folge* 157, no.1 (2014): 1–15. On the reperformance and revivals of old tragedies generally, see P.E. Easterling, "The end of an era? Tragedy in the early fourth century," in *Tragedy, Comedy*

and the Polis, eds A. Sommerstein et al. (Bari: Levante editori, 1993); P.E. Easterling, "Euripides outside Athens: A Speculative note," *Illinois Classical Studies* 19 (1994): 73–80; Taplin, "Spreading the Word"; J. Hanink, *Lycurgan Athens and the Making of Classical Tragedy* (Cambridge: Cambridge University Press, 2014); S. Nervegna, "Performing Classics: The Tragic Canon in the Fourth Century and Beyond," in Csapo et al., eds *Greek Theatre*; and Lamari, ed. *Reperformances*.

21. O. Taplin, "Aeschylus' *Persai*—The entry of tragedy into the celebration culture of the 470s?" in *Dionysalexandros: Essays on Aeschylus and his fellow tragedians, in honour of Alexander F. Garvie*, eds D. Cairns and V. Liapsis (Swansea: The Classical Press of Wales, 2006), 3.

22. Ibid., 4.

23. R. Rehm, "Aeschylus in Syracuse: The Commerce of Tragedy and Politics," in *Syracuse, the Fairest Greek City: Ancient Art from the Museo Archeologico "Paolo Orsi,"* ed. B. Daix Wescoat (Rome: de Luca, 1989), 31. See also R. Scodel, "The Poet's Career, the Rise of Tragedy, and Athenian Cultural Hegemony," in *Gab es das Griechische Wunder?: Griechenland zwischen dem Ende des 6. und der Mitte des 5. Jahrhunderts v. Chr.; Tagungsbeiträge des 16. Fachsymposiums der Alexander von Humboldt-Stiftung, veranstaltet vom 5. bis 9. April 1999 in Freiburg im Breisgau*, ed. D. Papenfuss and V.M. Strocka (Mainz: P. von Zabern, 2001).

24. *TrGF*^{3} T3. His tomb at Gela allegedly became a pilgrimage site, see *Life of Aeschylus* 11, *TrGF*^{3} T1.40–7. On the likelihood that Aeschylus was given the honor of a hero-cult, see P. Wilson, "Sicilian Choruses," in *Greek Theatre and Festivals, Documentary Studies*, ed. P. Wilson (Oxford: Oxford University Press, 2007), 357; L. Poli-Palladini, *Aeschylus at Gela: An Integrated Approach* (Alessandria: Edizioni dell'Orso, 2013), 284–316 and Nervegna, "Performing Classics," 172.

25. M. Griffith, "Aeschylus, Sicily and Prometheus," in *Dionysiaca: Nine Studies in Greek Poetry by Former Pupils Presented to Sir Denys Page on his Seventieth Birthday*, ed. R.D. Dawe, J. Diggle, and P.E. Easterling (Cambridge: Cambridge University Press, 1978), 106; cf. C.J. Herrington, "Aeschylus in Sicily," *Journal of Hellenic Studies* 87 (1967): 74–85.

26. *TrGF*^{1} 3 T6, D. Harvey, "Phrynichos and his Muses," in *The Rivals of Aristophanes: Studies in Athenian Old Comedy*, ed. D. Harvey and J. Wilkins (London: Duckworth, 2000), 114–15; K. Morgan, "A prolegomena to performance in the West," in Bosher, ed. *Theater Outside Athens*, 49; Nervegna, "Performing Classics," 172, n. 97.

27. A scholiast on Aristotle's *Rhetorica* later elaborated on this story, stating that Euripides himself was sent to Syracuse to negotiate the release of his fellow imprisoned Athenians: Schol. on Arist. *Rh*. 1417b.18.

28. As C.W. Dearden, "Fourth-Century Drama in Sicily," in *Greek Colonists and Native Populations: Proceedings of the First Australian Congress of Classical Archaeology held in honour of Emeritus Professor A. D. Trendall*, ed. J.-P. Descoeudres (Oxford: Clarendon Press, 1990), 232, writes, "in the opinion of ancient authorities, the poets who worked there in the 4th century BC were pale imitations of Aeschylus and Euripides."

29. J. Hanink, "The classical tragedians, from Athenian idols to wandering poets" in *Beyond the Fifth Century: Interactions with Greek Tragedy from the Fourth Century BCE to the Middle Ages*, ed. I. Gildenhard and M. Revermann (Berlin: De Gruyter, 2010), 46.

30. O. Taplin, *Comic Angels and Other Approaches to Greek Drama through Vase paintings* (Oxford: Clarendon Press: 1993); Taplin, *Pots and Plays*.

31. *Life of Euripides* 21–5.

32. The evidence found in the *Life of Euripides* can be supplemented by accounts found in Schol. Ar. *Ran*. 83 as well as Pl. *Symp*. 172c.

33. N.G.L. Hammond and G.T. Griffith, *A History of Macedonia, vol. 2: 550-336 B.C.* (Oxford: Clarendon Press, 1979), 162 and 391; M. Revermann, "Euripides, Tragedy, and Macedon: Some Conditions of Reception" in *Euripides and Tragic Theatre in the Late Fifth Century, ICS 24-25*, ed. M. Cropp, K. Lee, and D. Sansone (Champaign, IL: Stipes Publishing, 1999–2000), 454–5.
34. Though my discussion centers here on the *Archealus*, some scholars have also considered whether other Euripidean plays may have also been composed or performed at Archelaus' court, specifically *Bacchae* and *Iphigenia at Aulis* given their late composition and also *Andromache*, which contains some references to Macedonia (a scholion on line 445 moreover suggests it was not produced in Athens). See Revermann, "Euripides, Tragedy, and Macedon," 461–2 and W. Allan, *The Andromache and Euripidean Tragedy* (Oxford: Oxford University Press, 2000), 149–60.
35. E. Moloney, "*Philippus in acie tutior quam in theatro fuit* ... (Curtius 9.6.25): The Macedonian Kings and Greek Theatre," in Csapo et al., eds. *Greek Theater*, 235 and 240–48.
36. Demosthenes (10.31-4) would later call Archelaus' successor, Philip, a barbarian. See also E. Badian, "Greeks and Macedonians," in *Macedonia and Greece in Late Classical and Early Hellenistic Times, Studies in History of Art, 10*, ed. B. Barr-Sharrar and E.N. Borza (Washington: National Gallery of Art, 1982) and the first six essays in R.W. Wallace and E.M. Harris, eds, *Transitions to Empire: Essays in Greco-Roman History, 360-146 B.C., in honor of E. Badian* (Norman, OK: University of Oklahoma Press, 1996).
37. Moloney, "*Philippus in acie*," 238.
38. As Moloney (ibid.) states, in this manner Euripides endorses "the claims of the royal line that they are Temenidai in exile from Argos."
39. A. Harder, ed. *Euripides' Kresphontes and Archelaos* (Leiden: Brill, 1985), 130.
40. Revermann, "Euripides, Tragedy and Macedon," 454 discusses this as a deliberate strategy by the Macedonians, typically considered barbarians, which aimed "to dispel the stigma of cultural inferiority."
41. *TRGF*[5.1] T1.20.
42. See, e.g., Isoc. *Orat.* 5.95–105, 120–3, 132–6.
43. A.B. Bosworth, "Alexander, Euripides, and Dionysos: The Motivation for Apotheosis," in Wallace and Harris, eds, *Transitions to Empire,* 140–1.
44. Bosworth, "Alexander, Euripides, and Dionysos," 142.
45. Ibid., 142–6.
46. For this reason, according to Plato, they are to be excluded from the city. Cf. J. Adam, ed. *The Republic of Plato, edited text with critical notes, commentary and appendices,* with an introduction by D.A. Rees, 2nd edn, 2 vols. (Cambridge: Cambridge University Press, 1969) II, 260.
47. On the establishment of the theater, see Wiles, *Tragedy in Athens*, 38–9. On the tragic overtones of his death, see Duncan, "Political Re-Performances," 310–11.
48. Le Guen, "Theatre, Religion and Politics," 249.
49. Ath. 12 537d, Le Guen "Theatre, Religion and Politics," 249 and 270. Cf. B. Le Guen, "Théâtre et cités à l'époque hellénistique," *Revue des Études Greques* 108, no. 1 (1995): 60–1 who notes that stone theaters multiply in the aftermath of the new space created by the conquest of Alexander.
50. Ath. 12.539, cf. Duncan, "Political Re-Performances," 311.
51. Revermann, "Euripides, Tragedy, and Macedon," 456–61 and Le Guen, "Theatre, Religion and Politics."

52. V. Vahtikari, *Tragedy Performances Outside Athens in the Late Fifth and the Fourth Centuries BC, Papers and Monographs of the Finnish Institute at Athens 20* (Helsinki: Suomen Ateenan-Instituutin säätiö (Foundation of the Finnish Institute at Athens), 2014), 111.
53. Arr. *Anab.* 7, 14, 1.
54. Plut. *Vit. Alex.* 72.
55. Ath. 13, 538b-539a; see also Duncan, "Political Re-Performances," 311–13.
56. Plut. *Vit. Alex* 72.
57. As Le Guen, "Theatre, Religion and Politics," 269 states, "in laying claim to an area of supremacy long held by the city of Athens Alexander went far beyond the politics initiated by Archelaus."
58. Le Guen (ibid.) notes that these competitions "all shared the common aim of providing the soldiers, whether they participated or merely spectated, with relaxation and leisure and the chance to forget for a time the hard realities of combat."
59. By Le Guen, and Mossman, among others: Le Guen, "Theatre, Religion and Politics," 250; J. Mossman, "Tragedy and Epic in Plutarch's *Alexander*," *Journal of Hellenistic Studies* 108 (1988): 83–93; J. Mossman, "Tragedy and the Hero," in *A Companion to Plutarch*, ed. M. Beck (Chichester: Wiley-Blackwell, 2014), 438. See also C. Pelling, "Dionysiac Diagnostics: Some Hints of Dionysus in Plutarch's *Lives*," in *Plutarco, Dionisio y el vino*, ed. J.G. Montes, M. Sánchez, and R.J. Gallé (Madrid: Ediciones Clásicas, 1999), 365 who points out the theatrical motifs in the story.
60. Revermann, "Euripides, Tragedy, and Macedon," 455.
61. A.B. Bosworth, *Alexander and the East. The Tragedy of Triumph* (Oxford: Clarendon Press: 1996) and Le Guen "Theatre, Religion and Politics," 271.
62. Le Guen, "Theatre, Religion and Politics," 271.
63. J.L. Lightfoot, "Nothing to do with the technītai of Dionysus?" in *Greek and Roman Actors: Aspects of an Ancient Profession*, eds P.E. Easterling and E. Hall (Cambridge: Cambridge University Press, 2002), 221. See also K. Buraselis, "Appended Festivals: The Coordination and Combination of Traditional Civic and Ruler Cult Festivals in the Hellenistic and Roman East," in *Greek and Roman Festivals: Content, Meaning, and Practice*, ed. J. Rasmus Brandt and J.W. Iddeng (Oxford: Oxford University Press, 2012).
64. A. Kotlińska-Toma, *Hellenistic Tragedy: Texts, Translations and a Critical Survey* (London: Bloomsbury, 2015), 245–6. See Lightfoot, "Nothing to do with the technītai of Dionysus?", 221.
65. B. Le Guen, *Les associations de Technites dionysiaques à l'époques hellénistique* (Nancy: Association pour la diffusion de la recherché sur l'antiquité, 2001) and Lightfoot, "Nothing to do with the technītai of Dionysus?" For *technītai* in Athens, see Hanink, *Lycurgan Athens*, 231–4.
66. Lightfoot, "Nothing to do with the technītai of Dionysus?", 220–1.
67. Ibid., 267–76. See also Le Guen "Théâtre et cités" and P. Ceccarelli, "Tragedy in the civic and cultural life of Hellenistic city states," in Gildenhard and Revermann, eds. *Beyond the Fifth Century*.
68. See Le Guen, *Les associations de Technites* for an impressive account of these artists. It is important to note that dramatic representations also occurred under the auspices of other gods beyond Dionysus; see Le Guen, "Théâtre et cités," 65.
69. For an overview of *chorēgia* outside Attica, see Wilson, *Institution of the Khoregia*, 279–302.
70. Wilson, *Institution of the Khoregia*, 307–8; Kotlińska-Toma, *Hellenistic Tragedy*, 243–6; Hanink, *Lycurgan Athens*, 225–31
71. S.M. Sherwin-White, *Ancient Cos: An historical study from the Dorian settlement to the Imperial Period* (Göttingen: Vandenhoeck & Ruprecht, 1978), 315 and Csapo and Wilson, "Drama Outside Athens," 353.

72. Wilson, *Institution of the Khoregia,* 289–90 and Le Guen, "L'activité dramatique," 274.
73. M. Segre, ed. *Iscrizioni di Cos,* 2 vols (Roma: L'Erma di Bretschneider, 1993), 154–6 (*ED* 234); see also P. Ceccarelli, "Le Dithyrambe et la Pyrrhique: à propos de la nouvelle liste de vainqueurs aux Dionysies de Cos (Segre, *ED* 234)," *Zeitschrift für Papyrologie und Epigraphik* 108 (1995): 287–8.
74. E.g. *ED* 52, ll. 11–13 in Segre, ed., *Iscrizioni di Cos,* 46; *ED* 234 ll. 15–17 in ibid., 289.
75. Sherwin-White, *Ancient Cos,* 315 and 111–2.
76. Ibid., 315–6.
77. Wilson, *Institution of the Khoregia,* 290–2; Le Guen, "L'activité dramatique," 276; Csapo and Wilson, *Drama outside Athens,* 353. For the Alexandreia festival see C. Habicht, *Gottmenschentum und griechische Städte* (München: Beck, 1956), 26–8.
78. E.g. Diod. Sic. 20.98.6-8, Plut. *Mor.* 737c.
79. In a forthcoming chapter, T. Coward reviews the evidence both literary and epigraphic for the performance and composition of poetry across various genres in Hellenistic Rhodes. He also notes that there are many Rhodian actors and musicians winning competitions at home and abroad.
80. See V. Gabrielsen, *The Naval Aristocracy of Hellenistic Rhodes* (Aarhus/Oxford: Aarhus University Press, 1997), 33–6 and R.M. Berthold, *Rhodes in the Hellenistic Age* (Ithaca: Cornell University Press, 1984), 54.
81. Gabrielsen, *The Naval Aristocracy,* 35.
82. For Rhodes, see Berthold, *Rhodes.* For Cos, see Sherwin-White, *Ancient Cos,* 90–130. However, as Sherwin-White points out, "the island's status differed from that of Ptolemaic subject possessions in Asia Minor and the Greek islands. None of the trappings of Ptolemaic authority—governors, garrison and taxation—are attested in Hellenistic Cos" (93).
83. Antiph. *Herod.* 77.
84. E.g. *IG* XII 2, 15, 1.29; *IG* XII, 2, 18, 1.9; cf. Le Guen, "L'activité dramatique,": 268.
85. On Romans in Rhodes, see G.O. Hutchinson, *Greek to Latin: Frameworks and Contexts for Intertextuality* (Oxford: Oxford University Press, 2013), 101–8.
86. The debate about Roman genres deriving from Greek ones—and therefore Latin literature deriving from Greek—is old and extensive. For the most recent views, D. Feeney, *Beyond Greek: The Beginnings of Latin Literature* (Cambridge, MA: Harvard University Press, 2016). For the specific case of translations or adaptations of Greek drama into Latin, see A. Schiesaro, "Roman Tragedy," in *A Companion to Tragedy,* ed. R. Bushnell (Malden, MA: Blackwell Publishing, 2005), 269; I. Gildenhard, "Buskins and SPQR: Roman Receptions of Greek Tragedy," in Gildenhard and Revermann, *Beyond the Fifth Century,* especially 174–9; G. Manuwald, *Roman Republican Theatre* (Cambridge: Cambridge University Press, 2011), 282–92.
87. Livy 7.2; Gildenhard, "Buskins and SPQR," 156–60; Manuwald, *Roman Republican Theatre,* 34–7.
88. N.J. Lowe, *Comedy, Greece and Rome, New Surveys in the Classics,* 37 (Cambridge: Cambridge University Press, 2008), 85; Manuwald, *Roman Republican Theatre,* 22–30; C. Panayotakis, ed., *Decimus Laberius. The Fragments* (Cambridge: Cambridge University Press, 2010).
89. G. Manuwald and S. Frangoulidis, "Introduction: Roman Drama and its Contexts," in *Roman Drama and its Contexts, Trends in Classics Supplementary Volume 34,* ed. G. Manuwald and S. Frangoulidis (Berlin: De Gruyter, 2016), blame the perception of Greek-style genres as being "the more elevated and the more important dramatic genres" for the direction and focus of modern research that has devalued other Roman dramatic genres such as *fabula praetexta,* Atellana and mime.

NOTES   161

90. Gildenhard, "Buskins and SPQR," 157, citing G. Manuwald, *Fabulae Praetextae: Spurn einer literarishcen Gattung der Romer, Zetemata 108* (München: Beck, 2001). See also Manuwald and Frangoulidis, "Introduction."
91. B. Gentili, *Theatrical Performances in the Ancient World: Hellenistic and Early Roman Theatre* (Amsterdam: Gieben, 1979) and Nervegna, "Performing Classics," 159–60. On the representations of Greek theatrical scenes in South Italy, see Taplin, *Comic Angels* and *Pots and Plays*; also M. Revermann, "Situating the gaze of the recipient(s): theater-related vase paintings and their contexts of reception," in Gildenhard and Revermann, eds, *Beyond the Fifth Century*. According to Manuwald, *Roman Republican Theatre*, 22: Roman tragedies "seem to have followed classical fifth-century models with a preference for Euripides, whereas Roman comedies relied almost exclusively on Hellenistic models, particularly Menander." Romans may have also been exposed to Greek theater as soldiers as they traveled to Sicily during the First Punic War.
92. E.g. Cic. *Brut.* 71.
93. E. Fantham, "Orator and/et actor," in Easterling and Hall, eds, *Greek and Roman Actors*; Gildenhard, "Buskins and SPQR, 180. Cf. Cic. *De Opt. gen. or.* 14 and Quint. *Inst.* 1.4.2.
94. Manuwald, *Roman Republican Theatre*, 41–128.
95. We must acknowledge the lack of permanent dramatic structures in Republican Rome, since drama was always performed in a temporary wooden structure built for the particular festival. In fact, the first permanent theater in Rome was the Theater of Pompey, which was built in 55 BCE. See R.C. Beacham, *The Roman Theatre and its Audience* (London: Routledge, 1991), 56–85; C.P. Jones, "Greek Drama in the Roman Empire," in *Theater and Society in the Classical World*, ed. R. Scodel (Ann Arbor: University of Michigan Press, 1993); S. Goldberg, "The Fall and Rise of Roman Tragedy," *Transactions of the American Philological Association* 126 (1996): 265–86; and M. Erasmo, *Roman Tragedy: Theatre to Theatricality* (Austin: University of Texas Press, 2004), 83–91. Cf. Quint. *Inst.* 11.3.73.
96. Manuwald, *Roman Republican Theatre*, 124. cf. Quint. *Inst.* 11.3.4 and Gell. *NA* 2.23.1-3. Goldberg, "Fall and Rise," 272 blames the popularity of mimes and other public spectacles for audiences' lack of interest in performed tragedy.
97. Translation: H. Rackham, *Cicero, On Ends* (Cambridge, MA: Harvard University Press, 1914).
98. For a wider discussion of this passage, see Erasmo, *Roman Tragedy*, 1–2.
99. R.J. Tarrant, ed., *Seneca's Thyestes (American Philological Association Textbook Series)* (Atlanta: Scholar's Press, 1985), 14 notes that their text displays "a lack of concern for theatrical realities." For a consideration of this thorny issue, see the essays in G.W.M. Harrison, ed. *Seneca in Performance* (London: Duckworth, 2000).
100. E.g. essays in Harrison, ed. *Seneca in Performance* (especially J.G. Fitch, "Playing Seneca?" and J-A. Shelton, "The Spectacle of Death in Seneca's *Troades*") and Erasmo, *Roman Tragedy*, 122–39.
101. A. Baertschi, "Drama and epic narrative: the test case of messenger speech in Seneca's *Agamemnon*," in Gildenhard and Revermann, eds *Beyond the Fifth Century*, 251.
102. On Sophocles see L. Holford-Strevens, "Sophocles at Rome," in *Sophocles Revisited: Essays presented to Sir Hugh Lloyd-Jones*, ed. J. Griffin (Oxford: Oxford University Press, 1999).
103. See F.W. Wright, *Cicero and the Theater* (Northampton, MA: Smith College Classical Studies 11, 1931), 80–93.
104. I. Gildenhard, "Reckoning with Tyranny: Greek Thoughts on Caesar in Cicero's Letters to Atticus in Early 49," in *Ancient Tyranny*, ed. S. Lewis (Edinburgh: Edinburgh University Press, 2006), 197–9.

105. Gildenhard, "Buskins and SPQR," 181.
106. S. Goldberg, "Cicero and the Work of Tragedy," in *Identität und Alterität in der frührömischen Tragödie*, ed. G. Manuwald (Würzburg: Ergon Verlag, 2000), 52–3.
107. See also *Rep.* 4.11 and *Tusc.* 2.48
108. However, he is aware of basics of performance; see Wright, *Cicero and the Theater*, vii and E. Fantham, *The Roman World of Cicero's* De Oratore (Oxford: Oxford University Press, 2004).
109. H.D. Jocelyn, "Greek Poetry in Cicero's Prose Writings," *Yale Classical Studies* 23 (1973): 71; I. Gildenhard, *Paideia Romana: Cicero's Tusculan Disputations* (Cambridge: Cambridge Philological Society, 2007), 36; P. Schierl, "Roman Tragedy—Ciceronian Tragedy? Cicero's Influence on our Perception of Republican Tragedy," in *Brill's Companion to Roman Tragedy*, ed. G.W.M. Harrison (Leiden: Brill, 2015), 50 n. 28. Cf. S. Lundström, *Ein textkritisches Problem in den Tusculen* (Uppsala: Almqvist & Wiksell International, 1982), 7 for numbers. He also quotes Roman tragedies in philosophical arguments e.g., Accius' *Medea* and *Atreus* in *Nat. D.* 3.68.
110. A.E. Douglas, ed. and trans. *Tusculan Disputations 2 & 5, Cicero* (Warminster: Aris and Phillips, 1990), 64; cf. Cic. *Fin.* 2.94 which contains some of the same quotations.
111. *TrGF*^{3} 304–20; this is fr. 193 discussed on pp. 310–13.
112. Jocelyn, "Greek Poetry," 98 and Douglas, ed. *Tusculan Disputations*, 66. In fact the third book on grief contains various further quotations from plays which are otherwise lost: *Tusc.* 3.67 contains five translated lines from Sophocles' *Phrixus* (*TrGF* F. 821 Nauck), *Tusc.* 3.71 refers to Oileus' change of mind (Sophocles fr. 666 Nauck from unidentified tragedy).
113. On Ovid, see D. Curley, *Tragedy in Ovid: Theater, Metatheater, and the Transformation of a Genre* (Cambridge: Cambridge University Press, 2013), 115–21. On Seneca, see F. Budelmann, "The Reception of Sophocles' Representation of Physical Pain," *American Journal of Philology* 128, no.4 (2007): 443–67.
114. To some extent Cicero is following the model started by Plato and Aristotle; see Gildenhard *Paideia Romana*. On Cicero's taking over quotations from Greek philosophical sources, see Jocelyn, "Greek Poetry," 66, 77 and L. Spahlinger, *Tulliana simplicitas: zu Form und Funktion des Zitats in den philosophischen Dialogen Ciceros* (Göttingen: Vandenhoeck & Ruprecht, 2005), 13. For a view of the philosophical content of Roman tragedy, see C. Star, "Roman Tragedy and Philosophy," in Harrison, ed. *Companion to Roman Tragedy*.
115. J.R. Green, *Theatre in Ancient Greek Society*, (London: Routledge, 1994), 145.
116. S.J. Harrison, *Framing the Ass: Literary Texture in Apuleius'* Metamorphoses (Oxford: Oxford University Press, 2013). P. James, "*Apuleius' Metamorphoses*: A Hybrid Text?" in *A Companion to the Ancient Novel*, ed. E.P. Cueva and S.N. Byrne (Chichester: Blackwell, 2014).
117. M. Bakhtin, *The Dialogic Imagination: Four Essays*, trans. C. Emerson and M. Holquist (Austin: University of Texas Press, 1981).
118. R. May, *Apuleius and Drama: The Ass on Stage*, (Oxford: Oxford University Press, 2006).
119. The concluding words of his prologue, *lector intende: laetaberis*, recall prologues of Roman New Comedy. See H.J. Mason, "*Fabula Graecanica*: Apuleius and his Greek Sources," in *Aspects of Apuleius' Golden Ass: A Collection of Original Papers*, ed. B.L. Hijmans Jr. and R. Th. van de Paardt (Gronigen: Bouma's Boekhuis, 1978), 11. See also May, *Apuleius and Drama* for richness of Apuleius' comic intertexts and inspirations. On mime, see Mason, "*Fabula Graecanica*," 10–11.
120. Mason "*Fabula Graecanica*," and "The *Metamorphoses* of Apuleius and its Greek Sources," in *Latin Fiction: The Latin Novel in Context*, ed. H. Hofmann (London: Routledge, 1999).

121. J. Tatum, "The Tales in Apuleius' *Metamorphoses*," in *Oxford Readings in the Roman Novel*, ed. S.J. Harrison (Oxford: Oxford University Press, 1999).
122. E.g. A. Schiesaro, "La tragedia di Psiche: note ad Apuleio, *Met.* IV 28-35," *Maia* 40 (1988): 141–50 on tragic elements in the Cupid and Psyche novella; May, *Apuleius and Drama*, 250–2 on the old woman as a type of tragic nurse, and 307–28 on the *ex machina* elements of Isis' appearance.
123. The translation is that of J.A. Hanson, ed. and trans., *Apuleius.* Metamorphoses *Books 7-11* (Cambridge, MA: Harvard University Press, 1989).
124. May, *Apuleius and Drama*, 272–3.
125. O. Zwierlein, *Senecas* Phaedra *und ihre Vorbilder* (Stuttgart: Franz Steiner Verlag, 1987), 55–68 uses this to reconstruct the otherwise lost play by Sophocles.
126. M. Zimmerman, ed. *Apuleius Madaurensis*, Metamorphoses*: Book X* (Gronigen: Egbert Forsten, 2000), 68. Cf. May, *Apuleius and Drama*, 273–4.
127. S. Bartsch, *Decoding the Ancient Novel: The Reader and the Role of Description in Heliodorus and Achilles Tatius* (Princeton: Princeton University Press, 1989), 110 notes the language of spectacle and theater as well as instance of theater-related words appearing in other prominent places in the narrative.
128. J.R. Morgan, "The Story of Knemon in *Aethiopica*," *Journal of Hellenic Studies* 109 (1989): 99–113; and J. Pletcher, "Euripides in Heliodorus' *Aethiopiaka* 7–8," *Gronigen Colloquia on the Greek and Roman Novel* 9 (1998): 17–27. Hippolytus and Phaedra's story also appears in Xen *Eph.* 2.3; 3.2.
129. J.R. Morgan and S. Harrison, "Intertextuality," in *The Cambridge Companion to the Greek and Roman Novel*, ed. T. Whitmarsh (Cambridge: Cambridge University Press, 2008), 225.
130. A. Lefteratou, "Iphigenia Revisited: Heliodorus' *Aethiopiaca* and der Tod und das Mädchen pattern," in *Intende Lector—Echoes of Myth, Religion, and Ritual in the Ancient Novel*, ed. M.P. Futre Pinheiro, A. Bierl, and R. Beck (Berlin: De Gruyter, 2013), 201.

Chapter Three

1. See e.g., S. Goldhill and R. Osborne, eds., *Performance Culture and Athenian Democracy* (Cambridge: Cambridge University Press, 1999).
2. Work on the civic function of tragedy in Athens is extensive. See e.g., J.P. Vernant, "The Historical Moment of Tragedy in Greece: Some of the Social and Psychological Conditions," in *Myth and Tragedy in Ancient Greece*, eds J.P. Vernant and P. Vidal-Naquet, trans. J. Lloyd (New York: Zone, 1988), 23–8; J.J. Winkler and F. Zeitlin, eds., *Nothing to do with Dionysos? Athenian Drama in its Social Context* (Princeton: Princeton University Press, 1990); E. Seaford, *Reciprocity and Ritual. Homer and Tragedy in the Developing City-State*, (Oxford: Clarendon Press, 1994); H. Foley, *Female Acts in Greek Tragedy* (Princeton and Oxford: Princeton University Press, 2001).
3. S. Goldhill, "The audience of Athenian tragedy," in Easterling, *Cambridge Companion to Greek Tragedy*; N. Villacèque, *Spectateurs de paroles! Délibération démocratique et théâtre à Athènes à l'époque Classique* (Rennes: Presses Universitaires de Rennes, 2013).
4. On the City Dionysia, see A.W. Pickard-Cambridge, *The Dramatic Festivals of Athens*, 2nd ed. (Oxford: Clarendon Press, 1968), 57–125 and E. Csapo and W.J. Slater, *The Context of Ancient Drama* (Ann Arbor: University of Michigan Press, 1994), 103–21.
5. See Andújar in this volume. Firm evidence that the *archôn* allotted and likely paid for protagonists is later than the fifth century. Initially the poets were actors themselves and

responsible for hiring other actors, often from their own families. Sophocles abandoned acting purportedly because of his weak voice or, more likely, because of new professional standards. See Csapo and Slater, *The Context of Ancient Drama*, 222–3 and E. Csapo *Actors and Icons of the Ancient Theater* (Chichester: Wiley Blackwell, 2010), 88–9.

6. On the *chorêgia*, see P. Wilson, *The Athenian Institution of the Khoregia: The Chorus, the City and the Stage* (Cambridge: Cambridge University Press, 2000).
7. On the audience, see Csapo and Slater, *The Context of Ancient Drama*, 284–305; Goldhill, "The audience of Athenian Tragedy"; D.K. Roselli, *Theater of the People: Spectators and Society in Ancient Athens* (Austin: University of Texas Press, 2011).
8. See also F.I. Zeitlin, "Playing the Other: Theater, Theatricality, and the Feminine in Greek Drama," in *Nothing to do with Dionysos? Athenian Drama in its Social Context*, eds J.J. Winkler and F.I. Zeitlin (Princeton: Princeton University Press, 1990), 63–96.
9. Language by Ober and Straus, in Winkler and Zeitlin, *Nothing to do with Dionysus?*.
10. D.S. Allen, *The World of Prometheus: The Politics of Punishing in Democratic Athens* (Princeton: Princeton University Press, 2000), 21–4.
11. See D. MacDowell, *The Law in Classical Athens* (Ithaca: Cornell University Press, 1978), 24–40 and 53–66.
12. See also E. Visvardi, *Emotion in Action: Thucydides and the Tragic Chorus*, Mnemosyne Supplements 377 (Leiden: Brill, 2015), 98–120.
13. See also Villacèque, *Spectateurs de Paroles!*.
14. For fourth-century fragments and trends, see G. Xanthakis-Karamanos, *Studies in Fourth-century Tragedy* (Athens: Ακαδημία Αθηνών, 1980); Taplin uses papyri and vases to reassess fourth-century plays (O. Taplin, "How Pots and Papyri Might Prompt a Re-Evaluation of Fourth-Century Tragedy," in *Greek Theatre in the Fourth Century B.C.*, ed. E. Csapo, H.R. Goette, J.R. Green, and P. Wilson (Berlin: De Gruyter), 141–55.
15. J. Hanink, "Literary Evidence for New Tragic Production: The View from the Fourth Century," in E. Csapo et al., eds., *Greek Theatre in the Fourth Century BC*, 203 and *passim*.
16. *Rep*.10.607b5.
17. *Rep*. Bks 2, 3 (esp. 377b1–389b2) and 10. The bibliography on tragedy in the *Republic* is vast. See e.g., H.G. Gadamer, *Dialogue and Dialectic: Eight Hermeneutical Studies on Plato*, trans. P. C. Smith (New Haven: Yale, 1980), 39–72; E.S. Belfiore, "Plato's Greatest Accusation against Poetry," *Canadian Journal of Philosophy* 9 (1983): 39–62; T. Gould, *The Ancient Quarrel between Poetry and Philosophy* (Princeton: Princeton University Press, 1990); G.R.F. Ferrari, "Plato and Poetry," in *The Cambridge History of Literary Criticism*, ed. G.A. Kennedy (Cambridge: Cambridge University Press, 1993), 92–148; A.W. Nightingale, *Genres in Dialogue: Plato and the Construct of Philosophy* (Cambridge: Cambridge University Press, 1995), 60–92; A. Nehamas, *Virtues of Authenticity: Essays on Plato and Socrates* (Princeton: Princeton University Press, 1999), 251–99; J. Moss, "What is Imitative Poetry and Why is it Bad?," in *The Cambridge Companion to Plato's Republic*, ed. G.R.F. Ferrari (Cambridge: Cambridge University Press, 2007), 415–44; S. Halliwell, *The Aesthetics of Mimesis: Ancient Texts and Modern Problems* (Princeton: Princeton University Press, 2002), 37–147; and S. Halliwell, *Between Ecstasy and Truth: Interpretations of Greek Poetics from Homer to Longinus* (Oxford: Oxford University Press, 2011), 179–207.
18. Esp. *Laws*, 653c5–656c2.
19. *Laws* 700b7–701b4. On performance and politics in the *Laws*, see A.-E. Peponi, *Performance and Culture in Plato's Laws* (Cambridge: Cambridge University Press, 2013); L. Prauscello, *Performing Citizenship in Plato's Laws* (Cambridge: Cambridge University Press, 2014);

M. Folch, *The City and the Stage: Performance, Genre, and Gender in Plato's Laws* (Oxford: Oxford University Press, 2015).
20. For evidence and extensive analysis, see J. Hanink, *Lycurgan Athens and the Making of Classical Tragedy* (Cambridge: Cambridge University Press, 2014).
21. E. Csapo and P. Wilson, "The Finance and Organization of the Athenian Theater in the Time of Eubulus and Lycurgus," in E. Csapo et al., eds, *Greek Theatre in the Fourth Century B.C.*, 418.
22. On the construction of the theater, see C. Papastamati-von Moock, "The Theater of Dionysus Eleuthereus in Athens: New Data and Observations on its 'Lycurgan' Phase," in E. Csapo et al., eds, *Greek Theatre in the Fourth Century B.C.*, 15–76. On funding, see Csapo and Wilson, "The Finance and Organization of the Athenian Theater," 395–7.
23. See Csapo and Wilson, "The Finance and Organization of the Athenian Theater," 414: "the need to support the theater came second only to the need to secure the grain supply."
24. Hanink, *Lycurgan Athens*, 65. Hanink notes that the addition of Aeschylus, the poet of the Persian Wars, contributed to the glorifying chronology even though his plays were not frequently reperformed. On fourth-century reperformances of Aeschylus, see Hanink and Uhlig, "Aeschylus and his Afterlife in the Classical Period."
25. Ibid., 67.
26. For additional initiatives, see Csapo and Slater, *The Context of Ancient Drama*, 393–424.
27. See also R. Scodel, "Lycurgus and the State Text of Tragedy," in *Politics of Orality*, ed. C. Cooper (Leiden: Brill, 2006), 129–52.
28. Hanink, *Lycurgan Athens*, 86; E. Volonaki, "Euripides' *Erectheus* in Lycurgus' *Against Leocrates*," in *Theater World: Critical Perspectives on Greek Tragedy and Comedy* (Berlin: De Gruyter, 2017).
29. Lyc. 1.100.
30. While male prostitution was legal in Athens, citizens choosing to become prostitutes forfeited their (other) rights.
31. Aesch. 1.152-3.
32. Dem. 19.245–6 and Hanink, *Lycurgan Athens*, 144–51.
33. Dem. 18 and Aesch. 3. See Goldhill, "The Great Dionysia and Civic Ideology," 104–5.
34. On political ceremonies during the festival in the fifth century, see Goldhill, "The Great Dionysia and Civic Ideology," 100–14.
35. Dem.18.120.
36. See e.g., P.E. O' Connell, *The Rhetoric of Seeing in Attic Forensic Oratory* (Austin: University of Texas Press, 2017); and S. Papaioannou, A. Serafim, and B. da Vela, eds., *The Theatre of Justice: Aspects of Performance in Greco-Roman Oratory and Rhetoric* (Leiden: Brill, 2017).
37. For more on Aristotle's *Poetics*, see Weiss in this volume.
38. E. Hall, "Is There a *Polis* in Aristotle's *Poetics?*," in *Tragedy and the Tragic*, ed. M.S. Silk (Oxford: Oxford University Press, 1996), 296.
39. Ibid., 302–4.
40. From Heath's argument against the expectation of a *polis*-presence in the treatise (M. Heath, "Should There Have Been a *Polis* in Aristotle's *Poetics?*," *Classical Quarterly* 59.2 (2009): 468–85).
41. Hall, "Is There a *Polis* in Aristotle's *Poetics?*," 305; Hanink, *Lycurgan Athens*, 219–20.
42. *Poet.* 1449b31-32, 1450b17-20, 1453b1-13, 1461b-26-1462a18.
43. *Poet.* 1456a25-31.
44. S. Halliwell, *Aristotle's Poetics* (London: Duckworth, 1986; reprint Chicago: University of Chicago Press, 1998), 343.

45. G.M. Sifakis, "The Misunderstanding of Opsis in Aristotle's Poetics," in *Performance in Greek and Roman Theatre*, ed. G. Harrison and V. Liapis (Leiden: Brill, 2013), 60.
46. See also Hall, "Is There a *Polis* in Aristotle's *Poetics*?," 306.
47. Our evidence starts in 341 BCE. Csapo, however, contends that such competition had already started in the fifth century (Csapo, *Actors and Icons of the Ancient Theater*, 89). On actors, see also n.6.
48. P.E. Easterling, "Actor as Icon," in *Greek and Roman Actors: Aspects of an Ancient Profession*, ed. P.E. Easterling and E. Hall (Cambridge: Cambridge University Press, 2002), 332.
49. Csapo, *Actors and Icons of the Ancient Theater*, 107.
50. On connections between the developing acting profession and the spread of drama in both fifth and fourth centuries, see Lamari, *Reperforming Greek Tragedy, Theater, Politics, and Cultural Mobility in the Fifth and Fourth Centuries BC*, Trends in Classics 52 (Berlin: De Gruyter, 2017), 95–129.
51. See e.g., the story about Polos (Aulus Gellius 6.5) with Easterling, "Actor as Icon," 335–6.
52. Csapo, *Actors and Icons of the Ancient Theater*, 173; and A. Duncan, "Political Re-Performances of Tragedy in the Fifth and Fourth Centuries BC," in *Reperformances of Drama in the Fifth and Fourth Centuries BC: Authors and Contexts*, ed. A. Lamari (Berlin: De Gruyter, 2015), 310–13.
53. Csapo notes that the concept of private theater (*oikeion theatron*) appears for the first time in the Greek language (Csapo. *Actors and Icons of the Ancient Theater*, 172). He also shows that the Macedonian banquets followed a large-scale Persian model rather than an intimate Greek sympotic model. While on campaign, for instance, Alexander carried with him a symposium tent that held 100 couches (ibid., 175–7). Csapo's chapter provides a succinct history of the privatization of drama.
54. P.E. Easterling, "From Repertoire to Canon," in Easterling, *Cambridge Companion to Greek Tragedy*, 219.
55. Ibid., 217.
56. Ibid. Moloney adds that the elites use theater to consolidate their connections with each other through their shared taste in Hellenic culture and to make clear who the king's selected *hetairoi* are (E. Moloney, "Philippus in acie tutior quam in theatro fuit . . . (Curtius 9.6.25): The Macedonian Kings and Greek Theatre," in E. Csapo et al., eds, *Greek Theatre in the Fourth Century BC*, 246–8).
57. Csapo, *Actors and Icons of the Ancient Theater*, 172–3.
58. B. Le Guen, "Theatre, Religion, and Politics at Alexander's Travelling Royal Court," in *Greek Theatre in the Fourth Century BC*, ed. E. Csapo, H.R. Goette, J.R. Green and P. Wilson (Berlin: De Gruyter, 2014), 263–8; A. Fountoulakis, "When Dionysus Goes to the East: On the Dissemination of Greek Drama Beyond Athens," in *Theater World: Critical Perspectives on Greek Tragedy and Comedy: Studies in Honor of Georgia Xanthakis-Karamanos*, ed. A. Fountoulakis, A. Markantonatos, and G. Vasilaros (Berlin: De Gruyter, 2017), 80.
59. Plutarch, *Alex.* 29.5.
60. Alexander could also have been portrayed as able to apply his knowledge of drama in crucial political situations *post eventum*. See Le Guen, "Theater, Religion, and Politics," 270.
61. Bosworth traces the possible process and political motives leading to Alexander's association with Dionysus partly through Euripides (A.B. Bosworth, "Alexander, Euripides, and Dionysos: The Motivation for Apotheosis," in *Transitions to Empire: Essays in Greco-Roman History, 360-146 BC in Honor of E. Badian*, ed. R.W. Wallace and E.M. Harris (London: University of Oklahoma Press, 1996).

62. See Le Guen, "Theater, Religion and Politics," 273 and 268 on Alexander possibly commissioning the play *Agen* to serve his politics.
63. Csapo, *Actors and Icons of the Ancient Theater*, 177.
64. G. M. Sifakis, *Studies in the History of Hellenistic Drama* (London: The Athlone Press, 1967), 99–103.
65. J.L. Lightfoot, "Nothing to do with the technītai of Dionysus?," in *Greek and Roman Actors: Aspects of an Ancient Profession*, ed. P.E. Easterling and E. Hall (Cambridge: Cambridge University Press, 2002), 223.
66. A. Kotlińska-Toma, *Hellenistic Tragedy: Texts, Translations and a Critical Survey* (London: Bloomsbury, 2014), 212.
67. Alternatively, chorus trainers in the guilds may train locals at the cities they visit.
68. On the *agônothetês*, see Csapo and Slater, *The Context of Ancient Drama*, 143; Wilson, *The Athenian Institution of the Khoregia*, 272–6 and 307–8. On *chorêgia* and *agônothesia* used for royal propaganda, see Kotlińska-Toma, *Hellenistic Tragedy*, 192.
69. Lightfoot, "Nothing to do with the technītai of Dionysus?," 222. See also Andújar in this volume.
70. Fountoulakis also discusses the Hellenistic (and later) rulers' use of drama to dominate the consciousness of the community and promote their cultural and political hegemony (Fountoulakis, "When Dionysus Goes to the East," 70–110).
71. For examples, see Kotlińska-Toma, *Hellenistic Tragedy*, 28–30.
72. See Easterling, "The end of an era?," 569.
73. A. Chaniotis, "Theatricality Beyond the Theater: Staging Public Life in the Hellenistic World," in *De la scène aux gradins. Théâtre et représentations dramatiques après Alexandre le Grand*, ed. B. Le Guen (Toulouse : Presses Universitaires du Mirail 1997): 252.
74. Ibid. 253.
75. Starting in 364 BCE, *Ludi scaenici* included the *Ludi Romani, Florales, Plebeii, Apollinares, Megalenses, Ceriales*, and the *Liberalia*. See Csapo and Slater, *The Context of Ancient Drama*, 207–220. On interactions with theatrical life outside Rome, see E. Rawson, "Theatrical Life in Republican Rome and Italy," *Papers of the British School at Rome* 53 (1985): 97–113.
76. On the games as a means to control applause in the present, see H.N. Parker, "The Observed of all Observers: Spectacle, Applause, and Cultural Poetics in the Roman Theater Audience," in *The Art of Ancient Spectacle: Studies in the History of Art*, ed. B. Bergmann and C. Kondoleon (New Haven: Yale University Press, 2000), 168.
77. *Pro Sestio*, 106.
78. On early structures, see e.g., R.C. Beacham, *The Roman Theatre and its Audience* (London: Routledge, 1992), 56–85.
79. In 194 BCE, special seats in the orchestra—between stage and audience—were reserved for senate members. In 67 BCE the *Lex Roscia* gave the first fourteen rows of the auditorium to equestrian class members. Under Augustus the *Lex Iulia Theatralis* separated seats for soldiers, married plebeian men, and freeborn boys with their slave-tutors. Women were restricted to the back of the auditorium, except for Vestal Virgins who occupied a special section.
80. Parker, "The Observed of All Observers," 168.
81. Ancient grammarians saw *praetexta* as allied to tragedy; scholars discuss it along with or as a sub-genre of tragedy but also debate whether it should be seen as a different genre. Both could be performed in the same program slot. See H.I. Flower, "*Fabulae Praetextae* in context: when were plays on contemporary subjects performed in Republican Rome," *Classical Quarterly* 45 (1995): 170–90; G. Manuwald, *Roman Republican Theatre*

(Cambridge: Cambridge University Press, 2011), 140–4; L.D. Ginsberg, "Tragic Rome? Roman Historical Drama and the Genre of Tragedy," in *Brill's Companion to Roman Tragedy*, ed. G.W.M. Harrison (Leiden: Brill, 2015), 216–37.

82. C. Nicolet, *The World of the Citizen in Republican Rome*, trans. P. S. Falla (Los Angeles: University of California Press, 1980), 367; A. Schiesaro, "Roman Tragedy," in *A Companion to Tragedy*, ed. R. Bushnell (Malden, MA: Blackwell Publishing, 2005), 274–5.
83. Flower, "*Fabulae Praetextae* in Context," 182.
84. Ibid., 190.
85. Initially plays dramatized how the successes of Roman aristocrats benefited the Roman people. Under the Empire a new type of *praetexta* for recitation voiced political (especially Stoic) opposition. See Flower, "*Fabulae Praetextae* in Context," 172.
86. See A.J. Boyle, *Introduction to Roman Tragedy* (London: Routledge, 2006), 223–8; and L.D. Ginsberg, "History as Intertext and Intertext as History in the *Octavia*," in *Roman Drama and its Contexts*, eds S. Frangoulidis, S.J. Harrison, and G. Manuwald (Berlin: De Gruyter, 2016).
87. Funding of public banquets to accompany spectacles starts in the third century BCE. On dinner theater and theater dinner in the same system of benefaction, see C.P. Jones, "Dinner Theater," in *Dining in a Classical Context*, ed. W. J. Slater (Ann Arbor: University of Michigan Press, 1991).
88. Csapo, *Actors and Icons of the Ancient Theater*, 185; with K.M.D. Dunbabin, "Convivial Spaces: Dining and Entertainment in the Roman Villa," *Journal of Roman Archaeology* 9 (1996): 66–80; and K. M. D. Dunbabin, *The Roman Banquet* (New York: Cambridge University Press, 2003).
89. Ibid., 186.
90. By the end of the first century CE, however, tragedy is more often read than fully staged.
91. Ibid., 189.
92. T. Wiedemann, *Emperors and Gladiators* (London: Routledge, 1992); and Parker, "The Observed of All Observers," 162–6.
93. Csapo, *Actors and Icons of the Ancient Theater*, 184.
94. Cicero, *Pro Sestio*, 56–8. Aesopus inserted lines from Ennius' *Andromache* to Accius' *Eurysaces*.
95. The line "Tullius, qui libertatem civibus stabiliverat" about Servius Tullius was applied to Marcus Tullius Cicero.
96. Csapo, *Actors and Icons of the Ancient Theater*, 189.
97. Parker, "The Observed of All Observers," 172.
98. Nicolet, *The World of the Citizen in Republican Rome*, 364.
99. Parker, "The Observed of All Observers," 175–6.
100. Ibid., 170; W.F. Wright, "Cicero and the Theater," *Smith College Classical Studies* 11(1931): 1–9.
101. On the affinities and tensions between actors and orators, see W.A. Laidlaw, "Cicero and the Stage," *Hermathena* 94 (1960): 56–66; and E. Fantham, "Orator and/et actor," in *Greek and Roman Actors: Aspects of an Ancient Profession*, eds P.E. Easterling and E. Hall (Cambridge: Cambridge University Press, 2002), 362–76.
102. S.M. Goldberg, "The Fall and Rise of Roman Tragedy," in *Transactions of the American Philological Society* 126 (1996): 283.
103. On the "gentrification" or "ossification" of tragedy by the elites, see Ginsberg, "Tragic Rome?," 270–84; and Csapo, *Actors and Icons of the Ancient Theater*, 187–8.
104. Boyle, *Introduction to Roman Tragedy*, 186. See also Andújar's chapter on textual and imaginary "sites" of circulation.

105. E.g. under Augustus, a ban forbidding senators and their sons to appear on stage was reaffirmed and expanded to include their grandsons, if they belonged to the equestrian class.
106. For new writers, see Boyle, *Introduction to Roman Tragedy*, 166. On the "fall" of tragedy, see Goldberg, "The Fall and Rise of Roman Tragedy."
107. Boyle, *Introduction to Roman Tragedy*, 178.
108. Pliny, *Panegyricus* 46.4.
109. See e.g., C.A.J. Littlewood, "Theater and Theatricality in Seneca's World," in *The Cambridge Companion to Seneca*, eds S. Bartsch and A. Schiesaro (Cambridge: Cambridge University Press, 2015), 164–8. Bartsch applies her model of "theatricality" to both Nero and his audiences, because of their limited freedom of expression. She also analyzes "doublespeak" in literature during the early Empire; *Actors in the Audience* (Cambridge, MA: Harvard University Press, 1994).
110. M. Erasmo, *Roman Tragedy: Theatre to Theatricality* (Austin: University of Texas Press, 2004), 120.
111. On the relationship of the tragedies to Seneca's philosophical writing, see Busch in this volume.
112. Schiesaro discusses Seneca' plays as metaliterary (A. Schiesaro, "Roman Tragedy," 280–1). For a critical overview of Senecan tragedy, see C. Trinacty, "Senecan Tragedy," in *The Cambridge Companion to Seneca*, ed. S. Bartsch and A. Schiesaro (Cambridge: Cambridge University Press, 2015).
113. See also Andújar and Weiss in this volume. On the origins of the debate, see Schiesaro, "Roman Tragedy," 277–8. For an approach to performability with special focus on Seneca's *Troades*, see G.W.M. Harrison, *Seneca in Performance* (London: Duckworth, 2000).
114. On declamation and its effects, see also R.A. Kaster, "Controlling Reason: Declamation in Rhetorical Educations at Rome," in *Education in Greek and Roman Antiquity*, ed. Y. Lee Too (Leiden: Brill, 2001), 317–37.
115. A.J. Boyle, *Tragic Seneca: An Essay in the Theatrical Tradition* (London: Routledge, 1997), 136. See also G.A. Staley, *Seneca and the Idea of Tragedy* (New York: Oxford University Press, 2010). Schiesaro argues that the passions evoked by Senecan tragedy render the effect of the poet's utterances undetermined (A. Schiesaro, "Passion, Reason and Knowledge in Seneca's Tragedies," in *The Passions in Roman Thought and Literature*, ed. S.M. Braund and C. Gill (Cambridge: Cambridge University Press, 1997), 89–111).
116. On the pantomime, introduced in Rome in 22 BCE, see I. Lada-Richards, *Silent Eloquence: Lucian and Pantomime Dancing* (London: Duckworth, 2007); R. Webb, *Demons and Dancers: Performance in Late Antiquity* (Cambridge, MA: Harvard University Press, 2008); E. Hall and R. Wyles, eds, *New Directions in Ancient Pantomime* (Oxford: Oxford University Press, 2008).
117. B. Zimmermann, "Seneca and Pantomime," trans. E. Hall, in *New Directions in Ancient Pantomime*, ed. E. Hall and E. and R. Wyles (New York: Oxford University Press, 1990/2008); and A. Zanobi, "The Influence of Pantomime on Seneca's Tragedies," in *New Directions in Ancient Pantomime*, eds E. Hall and E. and R. Wyles (New York: Oxford University Press, 2008).
118. Goldberg, "The Fall and Rise of Roman Tragedy," 283.
119. Wiedemann, *Emperors and Gladiators*, 85; on criminals acting out parts of myth, see 81–91. See also K.M. Coleman, "Fatal Charades: Roman Executions Staged as Mythological Enactments," *Journal of Roman Studies* 80 (1990): 44–73.
120. Wiedemann, *Emperors and Gladiators*, 85–6.
121. W.J. Slater, "The Theatricality of Justice," *Classical Bulletin* 71 (1995): 154.
122. *Epistles* 7, 3–5; trans. R.M. Gummere.

123. See Coleman, "Fatal Charades," 72; and Boyle, *Tragic Seneca*, 135. Around 200 CE, Tertullian will give his fellow Christians a much more extensive warning against the corrupting effects of public shows with *De Spectaculis*.

Chapter Four

1. See, e.g., D. Conacher, *Euripides and the Sophists: Some Dramatic Treatments of Philosophical Ideas* (London: Duckworth, 1998); J. Dillon, "Euripides and the Philosophy of His Time," *Classics Ireland* 11 (2004): 47–73.
2. For quotations and *testimonia* of Protagoras, I quote J. Dillon and T. Gergel, trans., *The Greek Sophists* (London: Penguin, 2003), occasionally altered.
3. As Aristotle's discussion of Protagoras suggests; see *Metaphysics* IV 1009a7-16; XI 1062b11-19.
4. P. Woodruff, "Didymus on Protagoras and the Protagoreans," *Journal of the History of Philosophy* 23, no. 4 (1985): 490–1.
5. E.g., T. Chappell, *Reading Plato's Theaetetus* (Indianapolis: Hackett, 2005).
6. L. Versenyi, "Protagoras' Man-Measure Fragment," *The American Journal of Philology* 83, no. 2 (1962): 182.
7. As stressed by B.R. Donovan, "The Project of Protagoras," *Rhetoric Society Quarterly* 23, no. 1 (1993): 35–47.
8. Very different understandings of Protagoras' thought are plausible. See the relevant section in C.C.W. Taylor and M. Lee, "The Sophists," in *The Stanford Encyclopedia of Philosophy*, ed. E.N. Zalta, 2016, https://plato.stanford.edu/archives/win2016/entries/sophists/
9. C. Willis, "Conceptions of Language and Reality in Euripides' *Helen*," *Eras Journal* 5 (2003), http://artsonline.monash.edu.au/eras/1129-2/
10. Ibid.
11. Ibid.
12. See also, e.g., F. Solmsen, "Onoma and ΠΡΑΓΜΑ in Euripides' *Helen*," *The Classical Review* 48, no. 4 (1934): 119–21; Conacher, *Euripides and the Sophists*, 74–83.
13. Willis, "Conceptions of Language and Reality."
14. Conacher, *Euripides and the Sophists*, 77.
15. R. Blondell, *Helen of Troy: Beauty, Myth, Devastation* (Oxford: Oxford University Press, 2013), 202–21.
16. M. Graver and A.A. Long, trans., *Letters on Ethics* (Chicago: University of Chicago Press, 2015), 193. I quote standard translations of Seneca's works throughout, frequently altering them with reference to critical editions of the Latin: for *NQ*, H.M. Hine, ed., *Naturalium Quaestionum Libri* (Stuttgart: Teubner, 1996); for the *Epistles*, L.D. Reynolds, ed., *Ad Lucilium Epistulae Morales*, 2 vols. (Oxford: Clarendon Press, 1965); for the philosophical treatises, L.D. Reynolds, ed., *Dialogorum Libri Duodecim* (Oxford: Clarendon Press, 1977); for the tragedies, O. Zwierlein, ed., *Tragoediae* (Oxford: Clarendon Press, 1986).
17. Ibid., 196–7.
18. M. R. Graver, *Stoicism and Emotion* (Chicago: University of Chicago Press, 2007).
19. Ibid., 1–4.
20. Graver and Long, *Letters on Ethics*, 289 (altered).
21. R.A. Kaster and M.C. Nussbaum, trans., *Anger, Mercy, Revenge* (Chicago: University of Chicago Press, 2010), 36 (altered).
22. Graver and Long, *Letters on Ethics*, 198 (altered).
23. Ibid., 244 (altered).

24. B. Inwood, *Reading Seneca: Stoic Philosophy at Rome* (Oxford: Oxford University Press, 2005), 224–48.
25. This observation holds even though there is evidence that Roman Stoics viewed philosophy as relevant to women's lives, as well as to men's. See, for instance, Seneca's *Consolations to Helvia* and *Marcia*, the latter quoted below, and Musonius Rufus, who argued that women too should study philosophy in a treatise of that title.
26. After being raped by Neptune, Caenis asks to be a woman no longer so that she may never suffer such injury again. Neptune makes her a man (Caeneus) whose body is impenetrable (Ovid, *Met.* 12.189–209). For discussion, see A.M. Keith, *Engendering Rome: Women in Latin Epic* (Cambridge: Cambridge University Press, 2000), 82–5.
27. C.A. Williams, *Roman Homosexuality*, 2nd edn. (Oxford: Oxford University Press, 2010), 18–19, 137, and *passim*.
28. M.C. Nussbaum, *The Therapy of Desire: Theory and Practice in Hellenistic Ethics*, Martin Classical Lectures, new series, vol. 2 (Princeton: Princeton University Press, 1994), 449; cf. 455–7.
29. J.G. Fitch, ed. and trans., *Seneca VIII: Tragedies I: Hercules, Trojan Women, Phoenician Women, Medea, Phaedra* (Cambridge, MA: Harvard University Press, 2002), 387 (altered).
30. E. Wilson, trans., *Seneca: Six Tragedies* (Oxford: Oxford University Press, 2010), 100.
31. Fitch, *Seneca VIII*, 389 (altered).
32. Wilson, *Six Tragedies*, 100; cf. Nussbaum, *Therapy of Desire*, 440, 455–7.
33. Fitch, *Seneca VIII*, 431 (altered).
34. Nussbaum, *Therapy of Desire*, 440, though all of 439–58 is relevant.
35. J. Davie, trans., *Seneca: Dialogues and Essays*, with an introduction and notes by T. Reinhardt (Oxford: Oxford University Press, 2007), 54–5.
36. See *OLD pignus* 4.
37. See Nussbaum, *Therapy of Desire*, 456–7, though generally sympathetic to the Stoic approach.
38. Wilson, *Six Tragedies*, 101.
39. J.G. Fitch, ed. and trans., *Seneca IX: Tragedies II: Oedipus, Agamemnon, Thyestes, Hercules on Oeta, Octavia* (Cambridge, MA: Harvard University Press, 2004), 313.
40. Ibid., 317, 319; cf. Nussbaum, *Therapy of Desire*, 455–6.
41. Wilson, *Six Tragedies*, 211 (altered).
42. See A. Busch, "Dissolution of the Self in the Senecan Corpus," in *Seneca and the Self*, ed. S. Bartsch and D. Wray (Cambridge: Cambridge University Press, 2009), 278; also J. A. Shelton, "The Spectacle of Death in Seneca's *Troades*," in *Seneca in Performance*, ed. G.W.M. Harrison (London: Duckworth, 2000), especially 97–9, 107–12.
43. Busch, "Dissolution," 279–80.
44. Wilson, *Six Tragedies*, 130.
45. Ibid.
46. Ibid., 136 (altered).
47. E.g., R. Seaford, "The Tragic Wedding," *Journal of Hellenic Studies* 107 (1987): 106–30.
48. Wilson, *Six Tragedies*, 136 (altered).
49. Kaster and Nussbaum, *Anger, Mercy, Revenge*, 76.
50. Busch, "Dissolution," 255–66, 270–82. For discussion of Polyxena in this context, see ibid., 278–81.
51. This section summarizes, supplements and explores from a somewhat different interpretive angle ideas about Seneca's *Oedipus* originally and more thoroughly put forth in A. Busch, "*Versane Natura Est?* Natural and Linguistic Instability in the *Extispicium* and Self-Blinding

of Seneca's *Oedipus*," *The Classical Journal* 102, no. 3 (2007): 225–67, whose language it occasionally adapts.
52. Busch, "*Versane Natura Est?*", 254–9.
53. Ibid., 230, 258–9.
54. Wilson, *Six Tragedies*, 41; cf. Busch, "*Versane Natura Est?*", 261.
55. See Busch, "*Versane Natura Est?*", 228–9, and the works there cited.
56. Fitch, *Seneca IX*, 51 (altered).
57. Wilson, *Six Tragedies*, 67; on this as an image of penetration, see Nussbaum, *Therapy of Desire*, 455–6
58. H.M. Hine, trans., *Natural Questions* (Chicago: University of Chicago Press, 2010), 136.
59. Ibid., 91 (altered); for this link between *Oedipus* and *NQ*, see Busch, "*Versane Natura Est?*", 259–62.
60. Hine, *Natural Questions*, 178 (altered).
61. Busch, "*Versane Natura Est?*", 227–8.
62. I gloss over a host of complications in Stoic theories of divination, including precisely how omens' signifying power was related to the cosmos's grand causal structure. See Busch, "*Versane Natura Est?*", 228 n. 7 and S. Bobzien, *Determinism and Freedom in Stoic Philosophy* (Oxford: Oxford University Press, 1998), esp. chaps. 1, 2, and 4.
63. Hine, *Natural Questions*, 179.
64. Busch, "*Versane Natura Est?*", 228–31.
65. Ibid., 259–62.
66. Wilson, *Six Tragedies*, 67 (altered).
67. Jocasta makes this argument, echoing Chrysippus' analysis of the Oedipus myth. See Fr. 939, *SVF* 2.270–1, preserved at Eusebius, *Praep. Ev.* 4.3.12. For discussion, see Busch, "*Versane Natura Est?*", 255–9.
68. J.P. Poe, "The Sinful Nature of the Protagonist of Seneca's *Oedipus*," in *Seneca Tragicus: Ramus Essays on Senecan Drama*, ed. A.J. Boyle (Berwick: Aureal Publications, 1983), 154.
69. Busch, "*Versane Natura Est?*", 262–3.
70. This possibility was frequently debated by Hellenistic philosophers, and many resisted the conclusion. See Bobzien, *Determinism and Freedom*, 276–90 for a compelling reconstruction of how Chrysippus might have employed Stoic ethical ideas to preserve the rational self's autonomy from the causal chain in which it is embedded (perhaps with reference to the Oedipus myth; see ibid., 177–9, especially n. 84).
71. G. Braden, *Renaissance Tragedy and the Senecan Tradition: Anger's Privilege* (New Haven: Yale University Press, 1985), 30; cf. 28–62.
72. D. Wray, "Seneca and Tragedy's Reason," in *Seneca and the Self*, 250.
73. On the dialogic nature of Senecan tragedy, see also Busch, "*Versane Natura Est?*", 248.
74. Graver and Long, *Letters on Ethics*, 462.
75. See Nussbaum, *Therapy of Desire*, 402–5.

Chapter Five

1. See S. Dawson, "The Theatrical Audience in Fifth Century Athens: Numbers and Status," *Prudentia* 19 (1997): 1–14, E. Csapo, "The Men who Built Theatres: *Theatropolai, Theatronai*, and *Arkhitektones*," in *The Greek Theatre and Festivals: Documentary Studies*, ed. P. Wilson (Oxford: Oxford University Press, 2007), and H. Goette, "An Archaeological Appendix," in Wilson, ed. *The Greek Theatre and Festivals*.

NOTES 173

2. See A.J. Boyle, *Introduction to Roman Tragedy* (London and New York: Routledge, 2006), 8–9; 13–16.
3. For a brief overview, see C. Trinacty, "Senecan Tragedy," in *The Cambridge Companion to Seneca*, ed. S. Bartsch and A. Schiesaro (Cambridge: Cambridge University Press, 2015), 32–6; for more detail, see J.G. Fitch, "Playing Seneca?" in *Seneca in Performance*, ed. G.W.M. Harrison (Swansea: The Classical Press of Wales: 2000) and T. Kohn, *The Dramaturgy of Senecan Tragedy* (Ann Arbor: University of Michigan Press: 2013).
4. See e.g., A.W. Pickard-Cambridge, *Dithyramb, Tragedy and Comedy*, 2nd edn., rev. T.B.L. Webster (Oxford: Clarendon Press: 1962); W. Burkert, "Greek Tragedy and Sacrificial Ritual," *Greek, Roman, and Byzantine Studies*, 7, no.2 (1966): 87–121; A. Lesky, *Greek Tragic Poetry*, trans. M. Dillon (New Haven: Yale University Press, 1983), 1–24; C. Sourvinou-Inwood, *Tragedy and Athenian Religion* (Lanham: Lexington Books, 2003), especially 141–200.
5. On the dramatic festivals, see A.W. Pickard-Cambridge, *The Dramatic Festivals of Athens*, 2nd edn., rev. J. Gould and D.M. Lewis (Oxford: Clarendon Press, 1988) and E. Csapo and W.J. Slater, *The Context of Ancient Drama* (Ann Arbor: University of Michigan Press, 1995), 103–38.
6. For arguments against the importance of religion in the development of tragedy, see especially S. Scullion, "'Nothing to do with Dionysos': Tragedy Misconcieved as Ritual," *Classical Quarterly* 52, no.1 (2002): 102–37 and "Tragedy and Religion: The Problem of Origins," in *A Companion to Greek Tragedy*, ed. J. Gregory (Malden, MA/Oxford: Blackwell Publishing, 2005); and cf. E. Rozik, *The Roots of Theatre: Rethinking Ritual and Other Theories of Origin* (Iowa City: Iowa University Press, 2002).
7. Sourvinou-Inwood, *Tragedy and Athenian Religion* is a detailed survey of tragedy's engagement with Athenian religion.
8. See P.E. Easterling, "A Show for Dionyus," in *The Cambridge Companion to Greek Tragedy*, ed. P.E. Easterling (Cambridge: Cambridge University Press, 1997) on the important connection between satyr drama and Dionysus.
9. See F. Zeitlin, "The Motif of Corrupted Sacrifice in Aeschylus' *Oresteia*," *Transactions of the American Philological Association* 96 (1965): 463–508 and "Postscript to Sacrificial Imagery in the *Oresteia* (*Ag*. 1235–7)," *Transactions of the American Philological Association* 97 (1966): 645–53.
10. See H. Foley, *Ritual Irony: Poetry and Sacrifice in Euripides* (Ithaca: Cornell University Press, 1985), 65–105.
11. For full discussion of this motif in Greek tragedy, see R. Rehm, *Marriage to Death: The Conflation of Wedding and Funeral Rituals in Greek Tragedy* (Princeton: Princeton University Press, 1994).
12. On this motif in Euripides, see J. Wilkins, "The State and the Individual: Euripides' Plays of Voluntary Self-Sacrifice," in *Euripides, Women, and Sexuality*, ed. A. Powell (London: Routledge, 1990).
13. See I. Torrance, "Euripides' *IT* 72–5 and a *Skene* of Slaughter," *Hermes* 137 (2009): 23–7.
14. E. Hall, *Adventures with Iphigenia in Tauris: A Cultural History of Euripides' Black Sea Tragedy* (Oxford: Oxford University Press, 2013), 12–14; 17–20.
15. See O. Taplin, *Pots and Plays: Interactions between Tragedy and Greek Vase Painting of the Fourth Century BC* (Los Angeles: Getty Publications, 2007), 149–56.
16. For a detailed discussion of ritual supplication in antiquity, see F. Naiden, *Ancient Supplication* (Oxford: Oxford University Press, 2006).
17. S. Scullion, "Tradition and Invention in Euripidean Aitiology," *Illinois Classical Studies* 24–5 (1999–2000): 217–33 argues that cult aetiologies in tragedy are largely invented; R. Seaford, "Aitiologies of Cult in Euripides: A Response to Scott Scullion," in *The Play of Texts and*

Fragments: Essays in Honour of Martin Cropp, ed. J.R. Cousland and J.R. Hume (Leiden: Brill, 2009) argues, by contrast, that these aetiologies are significant in relation to the lived experiences of the audience.
18. Hall, *Adventures*, 30–2.
19. M.L. West, *Studies in Aeschylus* (Stuttgart: Teubner,1990), 26–50 and especially 32–46.
20. See further A. Henrichs, "The Last of the Detractors: Friedrich Nietzsche's Condemnation of Euripides," *Greek, Roman, and Byzantine Studies* 27 (1986): 369–87; E. Behler, "A.W. Schlegel and the Nineteenth Century *Damnatio* of Euripides," *Greek, Roman, and Byzantine Studies* 27 (1986): 335–67; and more generally M. Silk and J.P. Stern, *Nietzsche on Tragedy* (Cambridge: Cambridge University Press, 1981), 90–380.
21. E.g., A. Verrall, *Euripides the Rationalist: A Study in the History of Art and Religion* (Cambridge: Cambridge University Press, 1895).
22. T.W. Stinton, "'Si Credere Dignum Est': Some Expressios of Disbelief in Euripides and Others," *Proceedings of the Cambridge Philological Society* 22 (1976): 60–89; D. Mastronarde, "The Optimistic Rationalist in Euripides: Theseus, Jocasta, Teiresias," in *Greek Tragedy and its Legacy: Essays Presented to D.J. Conacher*, ed. M. Cropp, E. Fantham, and S.E. Scully (Calgary: The University of Calgary Press, 1986) and cf. D. Mastronarde, *The Art of Euripides: Dramatic Technique and Social Context* (Cambridge: Cambridge University Press, 2010), 205; M. Lefkowitz, "Impiety and Atheism in Euripides' Dramas," *Classical Quarterly* 39 (1989): 70–82 and *Euripides and the Gods* (Oxford: Oxford University Press, 2015); cf. also M. Wright, *Euripides' Escape Tragedies: A study of Helen, Andromeda, and Iphigenia among the Taurians* (Oxford: Oxford University Press, 2005), 387.
23. See F. Dunn, *Tragedy's End: Closure and Innovation in Euripidean Drama* (Oxford and New York: Oxford University Press, 1996), 26–44.
24. See I. Torrance, *Metapoetry in Euripides* (Oxford: Oxford University Press, 2013) on literary artifice in Euripides and *Euripides* (London: I.B. Tauris, 2019), Chapter 3, on the coexistence of traditional religion and rational philosophy in Euripides.
25. J. Mikalson, "Gods and Heroes in Sophocles," in *Brill's Companion to Sophocles*, ed. A. Markantonatos (Leiden: Brill, 2012), 432.
26. On the divine in Sophocles, see C. Segal, *Sophocles' Tragic World: Divinity, Nature, Society* (Cambridge, MA: Harvard University Press, 1995).
27. See P. Michelakis, *Euripides: Iphigenia at Aulis* (London: Duckworth, 2006), 73–81.
28. A. Henrichs, "Anonymity and Polarity: Unknown Gods and Nameless Altars at the Areopagus," *Illinois Classical Studies* 19 (1994): 27–58.
29. On curse and prayer in *Seven*, see E. Stehle, "Prayer and Curse in Aeschylus' *Seven Against Thebes*," *Classical Philology* 100, no. 2 (2005): 101–22.
30. See N. Sewell-Rutter, *Guilt by Descent: Moral Inheritance and Decision Making in Greek Tragedy* (Oxford: Oxford University Press, 2007), 15–48.
31. Sewell-Rutter, *Guilt by Descent*, 78–135.
32. Sewell-Rutter, *Guilt by Descent*, 78–109.
33. J. Fletcher, *Performing Oaths in Classical Greek Drama* (Cambridge: Cambridge University Press, 2012), 35–69.
34. See A. Sommerstein, "Orestes' Trial and Athenian Homicide Procedure," in *Law and Drama in Ancient Greece*, ed. E. Harris and D. Leão (London: Duckworth, 2010).
35. See I. Torrance, "Distorted Oaths in Aeschylus," *Illinois Classical Studies* 40, no. 2 (2015): 281–95.
36. See A. Long, *Language and Thought in Sophocles: A Study of Abstract Nouns and Poetic Technique* (London: Athlone Press, 1968) on abstractions and personifications; F. Budelmann,

The Language of Sophocles: Communality, Communication and Involvement (Cambridge: Cambridge University Press, 2000) on unpredictable sentence structure and ambiguous language; and S. Goldhill, *Sophocles and the Language of Tragedy* (Oxford: Oxford University Press, 2012) especially 13–133 on reading dramatic meaning in seemingly insignificant words and phrases.

37. On oaths in Sophocles, see I. Torrance, "The 'Sophoclean' Oath," in *Oaths and Swearing in Ancient Greece*, ed. A. Sommerstein and I Torrance (Berlin: de Gruyter, 2014).
38. Diels Kranz 64 B4–5 = Laks Most [28] DIOG. D9–10.
39. Diels Kranz 67 B2, 68, A1, A66 = Laks Most [27] ATOM. D13[45], 73, 74.
40. Diels Kranz 59 B13–14 = Laks Most [25] ANAXAG. D28, 29b.
41. See I. Torrance, "The Tongue and the Mind: Responses to Euripides *Hippolytus* 612," in Sommerstein and Torrance, eds., *Oaths and Swearing*.
42. See further Boyle, *Roman Tragedy*, 42–9.
43. Boyle, *Roman Tragedy*, 70; 98–9; 126.
44. Boyle, *Roman Tragedy*, 122; 126.
45. A. Schiesaro, "Seneca's *Thyestes* and the Morality of Tragic *Furor*," in *Reflections of Nero: Culture, History, and Representation*, ed. J. Elsner and J. Masters (London: Duckworth, 1994), 198–9.
46. See E. Asmis, "Seneca on Fortune and the Kingdom of God," in *Seneca and the Self*, ed. S. Bartsch and D. Wray (Cambridge: Cambridge University Press, 2009).
47. See A.J. Boyle, ed. and trans. *Seneca: Medea* (Oxford: Oxford University Press, 2014), 261–2.
48. On the worship of Hercules at Rome, see M. Beard, J. North, and S. Price, *Religions of Rome, Volume 1: A History* (Cambridge: Cambridge University Press, 1998), 2; 68; 90; 122; 173–4.
49. J.G. Fitch, ed. *Seneca's* Hercules Furens: *A Critical Text with Introduction and Commentary* (Ithaca: Cornell University Press, 1987), 22–3.
50. See also E. OKell, "*Hercules Furens* and Nero: The Didactic Purpose of Senecan Tragedy," in *Herakles and Hercules: Exploring a Graeco-Roman Divinity*, eds H. Bowden and L. Rawlings (Swansea: The Classical Press of Wales, 2005) who argues that Seneca's Hercules resembles the emperor Nero.
51. A.J. Boyle, *Tragic Seneca: An Essay in the Theatrical Tradition* (London: Routledge, 1997), 119–20.
52. Cf. C. Littlewood, *Self-Presentation and Illusion in Senecan Tragedy* (Oxford: Oxford University Press, 2004).
53. See further J.G. Fitch, ed. and trans. *Seneca VIII: Tragedies I: Hercules, Trojan Women, Phoenician Women, Medea, Phaedra* (Cambridge, MA: Harvard University Press, 2002), 5–10.
54. See Boyle, *Tragic Seneca*, 73 for elaboration on this pattern in *Agamemnon*.
55. Fitch, ed., *Seneca's* Hercules Furens, 33.

Chapter Six

1. A good, fairly recent survey of the politics of Greek tragedy, including earlier bibliography, is D.M. Carter, *The Politics of Greek Tragedy* (Liverpool: Liverpool University Press, 2007). There is no comparable overview of Roman tragic politics in English, but I. Gildenhard, "Buskins and SPQR: Roman Receptions of Greek Tragedy," in *Beyond the Fifth Century: Interactions with Greek Tragedy from the Fourth Century BCE to the Middle Ages*, ed.

I. Gildenhard and M. Revermann (Berlin: de Gruyter, 2010) covers the Republic and A.J. Boyle, *Introduction to Roman Tragedy* (London and New York: Routledge, 2006) has a markedly political focus. E. Lefèvre, "Die politische Bedeutung der römischen Tragödie und Senecas *Oedipus*," *Aufstieg und Niedergang der römischen Welt* II.32.2 (1985): 1242–62 covers all Roman tragedy. Compare the discussion of Greek tragedy and tyranny by Andújar in this volume.

2. Notable recent reassertions of tragedy as non-subversively pro-democratic are W. Allan and A. Kelly, "Listening to Many Voices: Athenian Tragedy as Popular Art," in *The Author's Voice in Classical and Late Antiquity*, ed. A. Marmodoro and J. Hill (Oxford: Oxford University Press, 2013); A. Kelly, "Aias in Athens: The Worlds of the Play and the Audience," *Quaderni Urbinati di Cultura Classica* 111 (2015): 61–92; S. Mills, "*Ektos sumphorās*: Tragic Athens," *Polis* 34 (2017): 208–25. Notable representatives of the questioning interpretation include S. Goldhill, "The Great Dionysia and Civic Ideology," in *Nothing to do with Dionysos? Athenian Drama in its Social Context*, ed. J.J. Winkler and F. I. Zeitlin (Princeton: Princeton University Press, 1990); N. Croally, *Euripidean Polemic* (Cambridge: Cambridge University Press, 1994); P. Cartledge, "'Deep Plays': Theatre as Process in Greek Civic Life," in *The Cambridge Companion to Greek Tragedy*, ed. P. Easterling (Cambridge: Cambridge University Press, 1997); P. Pucci, *Euripides' Revolution under Cover: An Essay* (Ithaca: Cornell University Press, 2016).

3. The seminal work is P.J. Rhodes, "Nothing to do with democracy: Athenian drama and the polis," *Journal of Hellemic Studies* 123 (2003): 104–19, whose ideas are variously developed and challenged by chapters and responses in D.M. Carter, ed. *Why Athens?: a reappraisal of tragic politics* (Oxford: Oxford University Press, 2011).

4. J. Griffin, "The social function of Greek tragedy," *Classical Quarterly* 48 (1998): 39–61, with the response of R. Seaford, "The social function of Attic tragedy: a response to Jasper Griffin," *Classical Quarterly*, 50 (2000): 30–44. On individual plays, P.J. Finglass, "Is there a *polis* in Sophocles' *Electra*?" *Phoenix* 59 (2005): 199–209 and "Sophocles' *Ajax* and the Polis," *Polis* 34 (2017): 306–17.

5. Cf. "the most profound questioning of democracy . . . is not to be found by searching through the tragic texts for any direct engagement with specific political policies or concrete issues of foreign or domestic strategy. Tragedy's politics is to be found rather in the searing exploration of the basic elements of democratic principle: responsibility, duty, masculinity, decision-making, self-control, and so on." S. Goldhill, "Undoing in Sophoclean Drama: *Lusis* and the Analysis of Irony," *Transactions of the American Philological Association* 139 (2009): 48.

6. For form and politics in tragedy, see esp. P. Burian, "Athenian tragedy as democratic discourse," in Carter, *Why Athens?*; and V. Wohl, *Euripides and the Politics of Form* (Princeton: Princeton University Press, 2015).

7. On this passage and its relationship with Sophocles' Ajax: T.K. Hubbard, "Pindar and Sophocles: Ajax as Epinician Hero," *Echos du Monde Classique* 19, no. 3 (2000): 315–32; D. Cairns, "Virtue and Vicissitude: the Paradoxes of the *Ajax*," in *Dionysalexandros: Essays on Aeschylus and his fellow tragedians in honour of Alexander F. Garvie*, ed. D. Cairns and V. Liapis (Swansea: The Classical Press of Wales, 2006).

8. On the many voices in the play, see P. Burian, "Polyphonic *Ajax*," in *A Companion to Sophocles*, ed. K. Ormand (Malden: Wiley-Blackwell, 2012).

9. On rhetoric in tragedy: V. Bers, "Tragedy and rhetoric," in *Persuasion: Greek rhetoric in action*, ed. I. Worthington (London: Routledge, 1994); S. Halliwell, "Between Public and Private: Tragedy and Athenian Experience of Rhetoric," in *Greek Tragedy and the Historian*, ed. C. Pelling (Oxford: Clarendon Press, 1997).

10. Eur. *Her.* 140–69. On this agon, see esp. R. Hamilton, "Slings and Arrows: The Debate with Lycus in the *Heracles,*" *Transactions of the American Philological Association* 115 (1985): 19–25.
11. On stichomythia: R.B. Rutherford, *Greek Tragic Style: Form, Language, and Interpretation* (Cambridge: Cambridge University Press, 2012), 164–79.
12. On the agon: M. Lloyd, *The Agon in Euripides* (Oxford: Clarendon Press, 1992); Rutherford, *Greek Tragic Style,* 190–200.
13. D. Sansone, *Greek Drama and the Invention of Rhetoric* (Malden MA: Wiley-Blackwell, 2012).
14. S. Goldhill, *Reading Greek Tragedy* (Cambridge: Cambridge University Press, 1986), 107–37; J. Gregory, *Euripides and the Instruction of the Athenians* (Ann Arbor: University of Michigan Press, 1991), 51–84.
15. See P. Wilson, *The Athenian Institution of the Khoregia: The Chorus, the City and the Stage* (Cambridge: Cambridge University Press, 2000).
16. The classic study is Goldhill, "The Great Dionysia and Civic Ideology." For more on performance contexts, see Andújar, Weiss, and Visvardi in this volume.
17. See Andújar and Visvardi in this volume.
18. R. Parker, "Gods Cruel and Kind: Tragic and Civic Theology," in Pelling, *Greek Tragedy and the Historian.*
19. For the issue in Aeschylus' *Oresteia,* see M. Griffith, "Brilliant Dynasts: Power and Politics in the *Oresteia,*" *Classical Antiquity* 14 (1995): 62–129; and in Euripides' *Medea,* S. Perris, "Is There a *Polis* in Euripides' *Medea*?", *Polis* 34 (2017): 318–35.
20. On hero-cult in tragedy, see esp. A. Henrichs, "The tomb of Aias and the prospect of hero cult in Sophokles," *Classical Antiquity* 12 (1993): 165–80; B. Kowalzig, "The Aetiology of Empire? Hero-Cult and Athenian Tragedy," in *Greek Drama III: Essays in Honour of Kevin Lee,* ed. J. Davidson, F. Muecke, and P. Wilson (London: Institute of Classical Studies, 2006).
21. J. Wilkins, "The State and the Individual: Euripides' Plays of Voluntary Self-Sacrifice," in *Euripides, Women and Sexuality,* ed. A. Powell (London and New York: Routledge, 1990).
22. On the negative or positive depiction of Athenian practice in the mirror of Ajax, contrast S. Goldhill, "The Great Dionysia and Civic Ideology" and Kelly, "Aias in Athens."
23. On tragic audiences, see M. Revermann, "The Competence of Theatre Audiences in Fifth- and Fourth-Century Athens," *Journal of Hellenic Studies* 126 (2006): 99–124; D.K. Roselli, *Theater of the people: spectators and society in ancient Athens* (Austin: University of Texas Press, 2011).
24. For a thought-experiment along these lines involving Euripides' *Medea,* see C. Pelling, *Literary Texts and the Greek Historian* (London and New York: Routledge, 2000), 196–208.
25. For further discussion of tragedy under tyranny, see Andújar in this volume. On the implications of reperforming Euripides' *Children of Heracles* in Heracleia, see W. Allan, "Euripides in Megale Hellas: Some Aspects of the Early Reception of Tragedy," *Greece and Rome* 48 (2001): 67–86. On *Archelaus,* see also M. Revermann, "Euripides, Tragedy and Macedon: Some Conditions of Reception," in *Euripides and Tragic Theatre in the Late Fifth Century, ICS* 24–5, ed. M. Cropp, K. Lee, and D. Sansone (Champaign, IL: Stipes Publishing, 1999–2000); L. Di Giuseppe, "Euripide e la grecità dei Macedoni: Archelao presso Cisseo," *Prometheus* 30 (2004): 125–8; A.G. Katsouris, "Euripides' *Archelaos*: a reconsideration," in *Euripide e i papyri, atti del Convegno internazionale di studi, Firenze, 10-11 giugno 2004,* Studi e testi di papirologia, n.7, ed. G. Bastianini and A. Casanova (Firenze: Istituto papirologico G. Vitelli, 2005); on the *Women of Aetna*: C. Dougherty, "Linguistic Colonialism in Aeschylus' *Aetnaeae,*" *Greek, Roman, and Byzantine Studies* 32, no.2 (1991): 119–32;

L. Poli-Palladini, "Some Reflections on Aeschylus' *Aetnae(ae),*" *Rheinisches Museum für Philologie, Neue Folge* 144, no. 3–4 (2001): 287–325; A. Duncan, "Nothing to do with Athens? Tragedians at the Courts of Tyrants," in Carter, *Why Athens?*; A.M. Seminara, "Eschilo tra democrazia e tirannide: dai *Persiani* alle *Etnee,*" *Sileno* 35 (2009): 69–86.

26. On the remoteness of tragedy's settings: Allan and Kelly, "Listening to Many Voices"; Kelly, "Aias in Athens."
27. On anachronism in Attic tragedy: P.E. Easterling, "Anachronism in Greek Tragedy," *Journal of Hellenic Studies* 105 (1985): 1–10.
28. Kelly, "Aias in Athens."
29. On the demos in Attic tragedy, see D.M. Carter, "The demos in Greek tragedy," *Cambridge Classical Journal* 56 (2010): 47–94; on assemblies: D.M. Carter, "Reported assembly scenes in Greek tragedy," *Institute of Classical Studies* 38 (2013): 23–63.
30. Esp. F.I. Zeitlin, "Thebes: Theater of Self and Society in Athenian Drama," in Winkler and Zeitlin, *Nothing to do with Dionysus?*
31. On tyranny in tragedy; R. Seaford, *Reciprocity and Ritual: Homer and Tragedy in the Developing City-state* (Oxford: Clarendon Press, 1994), 231–4; L. Edmunds, "Oedipus as tyrant in Sophocles' *Oedipus Tyrannus,*" *Syllecta Classica* 13 (2002): 63–103; D.K. Picariello and A.W. Saxonhouse, "Aeschylus and the binding of the tyrant," *Polis* 32 (2015): 271–96.
32. See Sophie Mills, *Theseus, Tragedy and the Athenian Empire* (Oxford: Oxford University Press, 1997).
33. For a good recent overview of the play with up-to-date bibliography, see D. Cairns, *Sophocles: Antigone* (London and New York: Bloomsbury, 2016).
34. On the tragic royal household, see esp. Seaford, *Reciprocity and Ritual*, esp. 344–62.
35. On the Persians in historical context, see esp. T. Harrison, *The emptiness of Asia: Aeschylus' Persians and the history of the fifth century* (London: Duckworth, 2000).
36. On this incident: D. Rosenbloom, "Shouting 'fire' in a crowded theater: Phrynichos's *Capture of Miletos* and the politics of fear in early Attic tragedy," *Philologus* 137 (1993): 159–96; E. Badian, "Phrynichus and Athens' οἰκήϊα κακά," *Scripta Classica Israelica* 15 (1996): 55–60.
37. On tragedies set in Athens, see esp. Mills, "*Ektos sumphorās*" with further bibliography.
38. Notably A. Harder, "Praxithea: A Perfect Mother?" in *Land of Dreams: Greek and Latin Studies in Honour of A.H.M. Kessels*, ed. A. Lardinois, M. van der Poel, and V. Hunink (Leiden: Brill, 2006).
39. D. Feeney, "The Beginnings of a Literature in Latin," *Journal of Roman Studies* 95 (2005): 226–40; *Beyond Greek: The Beginnings of Latin Literature* (Cambridge MA: Harvard University Press, 2016), esp. 122–51; R. Cowan, "A Stranger in a Strange Land. Medea in Roman Republican Tragedy," in *Unbinding Medea. Interdisciplinary Approaches to a Classical Myth*, ed. H. Bartel and A. Simon (Abingdon: Modern Humanities Research Association and Routledge, 2010); "240 BCE and All That: the Romanness of Republican Tragedy," in *Brill's Companion to Roman Tragedy*, ed. G.W.M. Harrison (Leiden: Brill, 2015).
40. E. Lefèvre, "Die politisch-aitiologische Ideologie der Tragödien des Livius Andronicus," *Quaderni di Cultura e di Tradizione classica* 8 (1990): 9–19, and, more cautiously, E. Weber, "Die altere Tragödie in Rom und die Legende von der trojanischen Abstammung," in *Identität und Alterität in der frühromischen Tragödie*, ed. G. Manuwald (Würzburg: Ergon Verlag, 2000).
41. P. Schierl, "Roman Tragedy—Ciceronian Tragedy? Cicero's influence on our perception of Republican Tragedy," in Harrison, *Companion to Roman Tragedy*; and cf. J. Zetzel, "The Influence of Cicero on Ennius," in *Ennius Perennis: The Annals and Beyond*, ed. W. Fitzgerald and E. Gowers (Cambridge: Cambridge University Press, 2000).

42. On the administration and staging of Republican drama, see G. Manuwald, *Roman Republican Theatre* (Cambridge: Cambridge University Press, 2011), 41–125.
43. E.S. Gruen, *Culture and National Identity in Republican Rome* (Ithaca: Cornell University Press, 1992), 183–222; Manuwald, *Roman Republican Theatre*, 49–54.
44. C. Campbell, "The Uncompleted Theatres of Rome," *Theatre Journal* 55 (2003): 67–79; J. Tan, "The Ambitions of Scipio Nasica and the Destruction of the Stone Theatre," *Antichthon* 50 (2016): 70–9. See Visvardi, in this volume.
45. On the politics of Republican tragedy, see Boyle, *Roman Tragedy*, 25–142; Gildenhard, "Buskins and SPQR."
46. On praetextae: G. Manuwald, *Fabulae praetextae: Spuren einer literarischen Gattung der Römer Zetemata* 108 (München: Beck, 2001); H. Flower, "*Fabulae Praetextae* in context: when were plays on contemporary subjects performed in Republican Rome?" *Classical Quarterly* 45 (2005): 170–90.
47. B. Biliński, *Accio ed i Gracchi. Contributo alla storia della plebe e della tragedia romana* (Rome: Signorelli, 1958).
48. R. Beacham, *The Roman Theatre and its Audience* (London: Routledge, 1991), 156–63; E. Champlin, "*Agamemnon* at Rome: Roman Dynasts and Greek Heroes," in *Myth, History and Culture in Republican Rome. Studies in honour of T.P. Wiseman*, ed. D. Braund and C. Gill (Exeter: University of Exeter Press, 2003), 295–305; M. Erasmo, *Roman Tragedy: Theatre to Theatricality* (Austin: University of Texas Press, 2004) 81–101; Boyle, *Roman Tragedy*, 143–59.
49. Att. 2.19.3
50. Cic. *Sest.* 120–4.
51. See esp. Champlin, "*Agamemnon* at Rome."
52. Fam. 7.1.2.
53. On the politics of Senecan tragedy, see esp. Boyle, *Roman Tragedy*, 85–111; S. Grewe, *Die politische Bedeutung der Senecatragödien und Senecas politisches Denken zur Zeit der Abfassung der Medea* (Wurzburg: Ergon Verlag, 2001); G. Manuwald, "The Concepts of Tyranny in Seneca's *Thyestes* and in *Octavia*," *Prudentia* 35 (2003): 37–59; O. Schwazer, "Senecas *Thyestes* und der 'Fürstenspiegel' für Nero," *Mnemosyne* 69 (2016): 1008–28, though many other studies at least touch on political issues.
54. The standard study of Seneca's life and work is M.T. Griffin, *Seneca: A Philosopher in Politics* (Oxford: Clarendon Press, 1976). See also E. Wilson, *The Greatest Empire: A life of Seneca* (Oxford University Press 2014).
55. The issues are summarized and debated in G.W.M. Harrison, ed., *Seneca in Performance* (London: Duckworth with the Classical Press of Wales, 2000), to which T. Kohn, *The Dramaturgy of Senecan Tragedy* (Ann Arbor: University of Michigan Press, 2013) is the most significant addition.
56. Pantomime: B. Zimmermann, "Seneca and Pantomime," in *New Directions in Ancient Pantomime*, ed. E. Hall and R.Wyles Oxford: Oxford University Press, 2008); A. Zanobi, *Seneca's tragedies and the aesthetics of pantomime* (London: Bloomsbury, 2014); gladiators: G.W. Most, "*Disiecti membra poetae*: The Rhetoric of Dismemberment in Neronian Poetry," in *Innovations of Antiquity*, ed. R. Hexter and D. Selden (London/New York: Routledge, 1992).
57. Most notably J.D. Bishop, *Seneca's daggered stylus: political code in the tragedies* (Königstein: Anton Hain, 1985).
58. Suet. *Tib.* 61.3.
59. Tyrants in Roman political invective: R. Dunkle, "The Greek Tyrant and Roman Political Invective of the Late Republic," *Transactions of the American Philological Association* 98

(1967): 151–7; in declamation: M. Beard, "Looking (harder) for Roman myth: Dumézil, declamation and the problems of definition" in *Mythos in mythenloser Gesellschaft: das Paradigma Roms*, ed. F. Graf (Stuttgart: Teubner, 1993).

60. On Atreus, see esp. C. Littlewood, "Seneca's *Thyestes*: the tragedy with no women?" *Materiali e Discussioni* 38 (1997): 57–86; A. Schiesaro, *The Passions in Play: Thyestes and the Dynamics of Senecan Drama* (Cambridge: Cambridge University Press, 2003).

61. In this respect, I disagree with the conclusions of the excellent discussion by C. Star, "Commanding *Constantia* in Senecan Tragedy," *Transactions of the American Philological Association* 136 (2006): 207–44.

Chapter Seven

1. A fixed date for the *Poetics* cannot be established, see S. Halliwell, *Aristotle's Poetics* (London: Duckworth, 1986; reprint Chicago: University of Chicago Press, 1998), appendix I. I would like to thank Richard Seaford, Emily Wilson, and Dallin Lewis for comments on this chapter as it was developing; errors are my own.

2. *Poetics* 1453a16–22. For more on these families, see below. Cf. also the comments of E. Belfiore, *Murder Among Friends: Violations of Philia in Greek Tragedy* (Oxford: Oxford University Press, 2000), xv: "harm to *philoi* is in several respects characteristic of Greek tragedy as a genre . . . [it is] a central element in nearly all the extant tragedies." Cf. *Poetics* 1453b18–21.

3. Aeschylus could describe his own work as "slices from Homer's banquet" (Athenaeus 8.39.17).

4. R. Seaford has developed this view over a long series of books and articles; I will be referencing in particular the overarching view proposed in his *Reciprocity and Ritual: Homer and Tragedy in the Developing City-State* (Oxford: Clarendon Press, 1994).

5. Seaford, *Reciprocity and Ritual*, xvi, "Both genres are a product of the *polis* but at different stages of its development," and ibid. 233, "The mythological themes of epic and tragedy originate in pre-*polis* society . . . the Homeric epics are . . . a product of the *polis* . . . Tragedy, a product of the *polis* in a later stage of its development." On the importance of the family in Greek tragedy, e.g., the remarks of Belfiore, *Murder Among Friends*, xvi.

6. Seaford, *Reciprocity and Ritual*, 12 remarks upon the "Homeric tendency to downplay intrafamilial killing."

7. W. Lacey, *The Family in Classical Greece* (Ithaca: Cornell University Press, 1968), 33, "In the society of the Homeric poems the ambition, hopes, desires and fears of the heroes are centered in their families."

8. S. Pomeroy, *Families in Classical and Hellenistic Greece: Representations and Realities* (Oxford: Clarendon Press, 1997), 33, "The archaic period is marked by the exogamy of aristocrats and are of tyrants who used international marriages to secure political alliances."

9. Seaford, *Reciprocity and Ritual*, 200.

10. Seaford, *Reciprocity and Ritual*, 98, cf. 103. Cf. Belfiore, *Murder Among Friends*, 10; B. Strauss, *Fathers and Sons in Athens: Ideology and Society in the Era of the Peloponnesian War* (London: Routledge, 1993), 44.

11. On Solon's funerary legislation, see S. Humphreys, *The Family Women and Death: Comparative Studies* (1983; Reprint, Ann Arbor: University of Michigan Press, 1993), 85–8 and Pomeroy, *Families*; cf. J. Oakley, "Death and the Child," in *Coming of Age in Ancient Greece: Images of Childhood from the Classical Past*, ed. J. Neils and J. Oakley (New Haven: Yale University Press, 2003), 166.

12. Seaford, *Reciprocity and Ritual*, 181, "there is a contradiction between the PanHellenic nature of Homeric epic and the traditionally local nature of hero-cult."
13. Seaford, *Reciprocity and Ritual*, 111 speaks of the "power of hero-cult . . . to unite a group not united by kinship." Cf. also ibid. 116, "Participation by non-kin is a criterion for distinguishing hero-cult from ancestor worship."
14. Pomeroy, *Families*, 18.
15. Lacey, *The Family*, 156. Cf. Seaford, *Reciprocity and Ritual*, 208; Pomeroy, *Families*, 126. The expectation was even more pronounced for male citizens: B. Knox, "Sophocles and the Polis," in *Sophocle: sept exposés suivis de discussions (Entretiens sur L'Antiquité classique 29)*, ed. J. de Romilly (Genève: Fondation Hardt, 1983) 1; cf. Pomeroy, *Families*, 141.
16. For the two disputed plays, *Prometheus Bound* and *Rhesus*, see M. Griffith, *The Authenticity of the Prometheus Bound* (Cambridge: Cambridge University Press, 1977) and V. Liapis, *A Commentary on the Rhesus Attributed to Euripides* (Oxford: Oxford University Press, 2012) respectively. In neither play do family relations loom especially large: the trials and travails of the family seem to have become less of a concern for tragedy, though New Comedy would take up its own interest in the household.
17. Indeed, tragedy is the one genre often left out of scholarly accounts of the family of this period, see e.g., the comment of Lacey, *The Family*, 10. Comedy, however, Lacey insists is "always potentially useful" (ibid. 10), a predilection for which Pomeroy, *Families*, 2 faults his study of the classical family. See Strauss, *Fathers and Sons in Athens*, 18–20 for further discussion on what type of evidence (i.e., genres) should or should not be taken into account by way of reconstructing the historical family of the fifth century. Such difficulties and considerations of what is in the last analysis only indirect evidence lead some to question whether we can really know that much at all (L. Nevett, *House and Society in the Ancient Greek World* (Cambridge: Cambridge University Press, 1999), 6–7).
18. R. Seaford, "The Structural Problems of Marriage in Euripides," in *Euripides, Women and Sexuality*, ed. A. Powell (New York: Routledge, 1990), 151–2, "Almost every marriage is therefore a conjunction of two households, and as such contains the possibility of competing claims." While this is more or less the situation assumed in the genre of tragedy, it seems that the historical record of aristocratic families features a high proportion of marriages between first cousins and thus minimized the distance broached by the marriage; see the conclusions of W. Thompson, "The Marriage of First Cousins in Athenian Society," *Phoenix* 21 (1967): 279.
19. For a working definition of the *oikos*, see, e.g., the comments of M. Arthur, "'Liberated' Women: The Classical Era," in *Becoming Visible: Women in European History*, ed. R. Bridenthal and C. Koonz (Boston: Houghton-Mifflin, 1977), 67, "a small holding corporation composed of its male head, his wife, their children, and the slaves who served it and worked the land that was its economic base." For a more archaeological approach to the family in the fifth to the third centuries BCE, see Nevett, *House and Society*.
20. See further discussion by Ormand in this volume.
21. Pomeroy, *Families*, 123, "The nearest male relative of their father is obliged to marry the *epikleroi*. If either spouse is already married, he or she must divorce his or her current mate." For qualification of this last statement, see Lacey, *The Family*, 140, "The next of kin was not absolutely obliged to marry her," and the discussion which follows.
22. S. Hübner and D. Ratzen, "Fatherless Antiquity? Perspectives on 'Fatherlessness' in the Ancient Mediterranean," in *Growing up Fatherless in Antiquity*, ed. S. Hübner and D. Ratzen (Cambridge: Cambridge University Press, 2009), 9.
23. Seaford, "The Structural Problems of Marriage," 151.

24. Belfiore, *Murder Among Friends*, 7, "the bride retains important ties to her family of birth and is 'foreign' to her husband's family." Cf. Pomeroy, *Families*, 8, "A woman's natal family retained ultimate control over her dowry and reproductive potential," and, ibid. 20, "the position of women in this legal definition of the family is ambiguous and cannot be clarified simply by referring to the categories of marriage or blood relationship." Pomeroy later speaks of brides adding a "second family" to their identity (ibid. 67). Cf. also the discussion of J. Maitland, "Dynasty and Family in the Athenian City: A View from Attic Tragedy," *Classical Quarterly* 42 (1992): 33–4 on Demosthenes 41, wherein it appears that one Polydeuctus marries a daughter to his adopted brother Leocrates only later to quarrel with him and summarily dissolve the marriage he had contracted between his daughter and "brother." In this way the natal family, through the offices of the *kyrios* ("male legally recognized as the family's head"), realizes its latent right to "reappropriate" its women.
25. The father's word alone guaranteed the status of his daughter's citizenship status, see Pomeroy, *Families*, 79.
26. Lacey, *The Family*, 103 concludes that "the desire to ensure that all girls were found husbands was most important"; Pomeroy, *Families*, 33–4 observes that "Pericles' citizenship law ... was anticipated by actual practice"; Seaford, *Reciprocity and Ritual*, 214, "The *polis* endogamy produced by Pericles' law represents the culmination of a progressive definition of the category of citizenship."
27. Pomeroy, *Families*, 33, "The archaic period is marked by the exogamy of aristocrats and of tyrants who used international marriages to secure political alliances."
28. J.P. Vernant, *Myth and Society in Ancient Greece*, trans. J. Lloyd (The Harvester Press Limited 1980; Third Printing, New York: Zone Books, 1996), 60. Strauss, *Fathers and Sons in Athens*, 6–7.
29. Again see Ormand in this volume.
30. Iambl. *Vit. Pyth.* 84. Cf. Belfiore, *Murder Among Friends*, 7, "the bride retains important ties to her family of birth and is 'foreign' (*othneia*) to her husband's family." But cf. C. Cox, *Household Interests: Property, Marriage Strategies, and Family Dynamics in Ancient Athens* (Princeton: Princeton University Press, 1998), 72, "There may be some distrust of the wife at first, but when she begins to bear children for the *oikos* a deep respect and trust develops." Both the evidence for and general validity of such statements, *pace* Cox, are difficult to establish given the nature of our access to the family. Contrary examples are not difficult to find: e.g., the situation between Xanthippe and her husband, Socrates, who seems less than respectful toward one who has borne his children, cf. *Phaedo* 60a and 116b.
31. Pomeroy, *Families*, 82, "Indeed, it is precisely the lack of explicit identity in her natal family that permits a bride to leave it and join another." But cf. Lacey, *The Family*, 44, "Daughters, however, did not wholly lose contact with their own families at marriage." Occasions for renewed contact could include childbirth and festival attendance. Indeed in Euripides' *Electra* the eponymous heroine tricks her mother Clytemnestra into entering her house to perform rites for her newborn child.
32. Lacey, *The Family*, 138–9.
33. D. MacDowell, *The Law in Classical Athens* (Ithaca: Cornell University Press, 1978), 84.
34. Cox, *Household Interests*, 92, "The primary dyad is that of father and son ... the father-daughter dyad is ignored."
35. Cf. Strauss, *Fathers and Sons in Athens*, 7. Funerary imagery also seems often to convey "an intimacy between fathers and infant sons" (Oakley, *Death and the Child*, 170).
36. Griffith, "The King and Eye: The Rule of the Father in Greek Tragedy," *Proceedings of the Cambridge Philological Society* 44 (1998): 31; Strauss, *Fathers and Sons in Athens*, 8;

M. Golden, "Childhood in Ancient Greece," in Neils and Oakley, eds. *Coming of Age*, 24–5.
37. Strauss, *Fathers and Sons*, 17.
38. Indeed such was the scarcity of legitimate children after 415 that men were permitted to introduce as legitimate those children they bred outside of marriage proper; see the discussion of Lacey, *The Family*, 112.
39. Other plays having to do with father-conflict include *Ajax*, *Oedipus Rex*, *Alcestis*, *Hippolytus*, *Heracles Furens*, *Phoenissae*, *Trachiniae*, and, of course, *Antigone*.
40. Cf. the comments of Griffith, "The King and Eye," 62.
41. On the destruction of the ruling family as ideological, see Seaford, *Reciprocity and Ritual*, 342. Cf. the comments of Griffith, "The King and Eye," 78.
42. Strauss, *Fathers and Sons in Athens*, passim.
43. Cf. P.J. Finglass, ed. *Sophocles' Ajax*, Cambridge Classical Texts and Commentaries 48 (Cambridge: Cambridge University Press, 2011): "brutality is to be the hallmark of Eurysaces' education ... Ajax wants his offspring to be inculcated into his violent ways immediately."
44. For a father exiling a son on false charges, cf. *Hippolytus* no discussion in what follows.
45. Ajax seems to be affected by her arguments during the "deception speech" (646–92), where he claims to have been "made soft" (651) by Tecmessa's words. Yet he never veers from the course of action first imagined as he contemplates his father's reaction to his dishonor. On the Deception Speech see, *inter alios*, J. Gibert, *Change of Mind in Greek Tragedy*, Hypomnemata Heft 108 (Göttingen: Vandenhoeck and Ruprecht, 1995), chapter 3 and A. Lardinois, "The Polysemy of Gnomic Expressions and Ajax' Deception Speech," in *Sophocles and the Greek Language: Aspects of Diction, Syntax and Pragmatics*, ed. A. Rijksbaron and I. de Jong (Leiden: Brill, 2006).
46. The very rarity of the word, a *hapax legomenon* in the feminine, may reveal its "elevated form"; see Finglass, *Sopocles' Ajax*.
47. The literature on the *Trügrede* is voluminous; see R.C. Jebb, *Sophocles: Plays, Ajax*, ed. P.E. Easterling, with an introduction by P. Wilson (London: Bristol Classical Press, 2004), xxxii–xxxviii.
48. On the expectation that children take care of their parents until death, see, e.g., the comments of D. Mastronarde, ed. *Euripides' Medea* (Cambridge: Cambridge University Press, 2002) on *Medea* 1033–4. Cf. Cox, *Household Interests*, 81.
49. Cf. the comments of P.W. Rose, "Historicizing Sophocles' *Ajax*," in Goff, ed., *History, Tragedy, Theory*, 71–2. For a corrective, see J. Griffin, "Sophocles and the Democratic City," in *Sophocles Revisited: Essays Presented to Sir Hugh Lloyd-Jones*, ed. J. Griffin (Oxford: Oxford University Press, 1999), 83–4. To his arguments against Rose, I would add that Ajax is consistently presented not so much a *strategos* as a redoubtable warrior and that the aspect of Menelaus as the "Spartan menace" adduced by Rose is far less developed than it would be in the plays of Euripides.
50. See, e.g., P. Burian, "Supplication and Hero Cult in Sophocles' Ajax," *Greek, Roman and Byzantine Studies* 13 (1972): 151–6. That Tecmessa forms part of the familial tableau at the tomb, however, need not indicate her incorporation into a close-knit tie with Ajax and his family, inasmuch as one of the distinguishing features of hero-cult was to offer a public, open forum for lament in place of the more *oikos*-restricted practice of the past, cf. note 13 above.
51. In favor of the connection, see R. Scodel, "Aetiology, Autochthony, and Athenian Identity in *Ajax* and *Oedipus Coloneus*," *Bulletin of the Institute of Classical Studies*, Supplement 87

(2006): 68, "This aspect of the quarrel is surely related to the Periclean citizenship law of 451"; *contra*, Finglass, *Sophocles' Ajax*, on *Aj.* 1262–3, "Even if the play was first performed after that date (which is uncertain), and even if we allow that tragedy made such political allusions, the reference would be irrelevant: the issue at stake is Hellenicity, not membership of an individual *polis*."

52. Cf. E. Rawson, "Family and Fatherland in Euripides' *Phoenissae*," *Greek, Roman, and Byzantine Studies* 11, no. 2 (1970): 114, "it is not merely the House of Labdacus (and, we should add, Creon and his family, who are not Labdacids, and even Adrastus, connected only by marriage) that we are to consider; it is family life as such, in a period of strife and war . . . [there is a] perpetual stress on family relationships, family duties, family feelings."

53. Rawson, "Family and Fatherland," 117, "Teiresias, in this play, is a man whose dependence on his family is complete; for Euripides has replaced the usual anonymous attendant with the seer's own daughter."

54. The end of the play may have been interpolated. D. Mastronarde, ed., *Euripides'* Phoenissae, *Cambridge Classical Texts and Commentaries* 29 (Cambridge: Cambridge University Press, 1994), 591–3 largely defends the text as authentic except where there is "accidental" corruption.

55. Griffith, "The King and Eye."

56. Jocasta was probably fifteen (the traditional age of the bride in the fifth century) when she married Laius and may have had Oedipus at sixteen or so at the earliest. If we assume Oedipus was between eighteen and twenty-one when he arrived in Thebes to solve the riddle of the Sphinx and marry Jocasta, this would have meant she was in her mid-thirties when she had her children, thus making her around fifty in the action of *Phoenissae*.

57. The use of such terms as "sympathetic" and its converse, while less clear-cut than other conceptual categories, continues to be a part of the modern critical vocabulary, see, *inter alios*, H. Bloom, *Shakespeare: The Invention of the Human* (New York: Riverhead Books, 1998) 106, 237, and 370.

58. The play ends with Creon facing a dilemma over what to do with the bodies of Eteocles and Polynices respectively (cf. Sophocles' *Antigone*): once again a ruler of Thebes chooses the purely political over any familial concerns.

59. Hermione blames this state of affairs upon Andromache and then launches into a diatribe about barbarians' (foreigners) propensity for incest (173–6)!

60. Set against the *topos* of the doubled-family, the two parts of the play may be seen to be more closely related than scholars have realized; cf. the comments of D. Kovaks, ed. and trans., *Euripides: Children of Heracles, Hippolytus, Andromache, Hecuba* (Cambridge, MA: Harvard University Press, 1995), 267, "[I]t (*Andromache*) combines two stories that have no necessary connection with one another."

61. For the ritualized relationship between these deaths, see M. Widzisz, *Chronos on the Threshold: Time, Ritual, and Agency in the* Oresteia (Lanham: Lexington Books, 2012), 26–36.

62. In Sophocles' *Electra*, Clytemnestra is given the chance to explain the motivation(s) behind her decision to kill Agamemnon, among which his deference to Menelaus is central (cf. *El.* 537–45).

63. Cf. the comments of Widzisz, *Chronos on the Threshold*, 31, "The second sacrifice, once completed, is deemed effective . . . and nothing detains the army any longer."

64. R. Meridor, "Aeschylus' *Agamemnon* 944–57: Why does Agamemnon give in?" *Classical Philology* 88 (1987): 38–43 and V. Wohl, *Intimate Commerce: Exchange, Gender, and Subjectivity in Greek Tragedy* (Austin: University of Texas Press, 1998), 111, "Cassandra . . . is Agamemnon's 'bride.'"

65. She later speaks of Aegisthus as tending to their household fire inside, demonstrating that she considers him to be her husband, see 1434–6.
66. Aegisthus' own desire for revenge figures into his part of the plan, see *Ag.* 1604.
67. Orestes' punishment, should he fail to avenge his father, is couched in extreme terms, see *Cho.* 291–6.
68. See Widzisz, *Chronos on the Threshold*, 205n86.
69. The argument, however, fails to win the day on its own: over half of the Athenian jurors vote against Orestes' acquittal. See M. Gagarin, *Aeschylean Drama* (Berkley: University of California, 1976), 121–7 and R. Seaford, "Historicizing tragic ambivalence: the vote of Athena," in B. Goff, ed. *History, Tragedy, Theory*.
70. Seaford, "The Structural Problems of Marriage," 153–5 discusses three strategies a family can use to produce a legitimate male heir: have a son by another woman, find a man separated from his native family, or resort to endogamy.
71. These infamous lines have been the subject of much scholarly discussion, for a more recent treatment see S. West, "The *Antigone* and Herodotus Book 3," in Griffin, ed. *Sophocles Revisited*.
72. See L.P.E. Parker, ed. *Euripides' Alcestis* (Oxford: Clarendon Press, 2007), xx–xxiv.
73. On Alcmaeon, see *OCD* s.v. Alcmaeon.
74. We do know, however, that Sophocles wrote a trilogy on the subject of Telephus and that Aeschylus wrote an eponymous play on the hero in addition to a play entitled *Mysians* in which he also treated the Telephus myth. Euripides' version was parodied by Aristophanes in *Thesmophoriazusae*.
75. Recounted in Sophocles' *Aleadae*.
76. Some of Shakespeare's plays have elements of this same dynamic: in *Romeo and Juliet*, the lovers cannot openly declare their bond as husband and wife because of their obligations as son and daughter; in *Lear*, the king's demand for an absolute declaration of love from his daughters amounts to suborning the affection due to a husband.
77. Cf. S. Murnaghan, *Disguise and Recognition in the* Odyssey (Princeton: Princeton University Press, 1987) 38, "While a marriage begins without any kinship between husband and wife, it creates kinship between them through their children." This, of course, leaves out the possibility that the couple was indeed kin before their marriage; see note 18 above.
78. In Aeschylus' *Agamemnon*, Clytemnestra will register publicly her awareness of his perfidy, calling her husband the "darling of [all] the Chryseïdes at Troy" (*Ag.* 1439).
79. Cf. Murnaghan, *Disguise and Recognition*, 138, "the poem [the *Odyssey*] shows us that Penelope's behavior is imposed on her by her impossible role as faithful wife of a man who is absent."

Chapter Eight

1. It is necessary to state here that the vast majority of our sources from Classical Greece are written by, and presumably for, elite men. What elite women (to say nothing of non-elite women), lower-class members of society, and slaves of either sex thought about the proscriptions of gender roles is something that can only be inferred from elite male sources, and by reading against the grain.
2. Aristotle's *Problems* 4.26 investigates the possible physiological causes of this "unnatural" desire, concluding that desiring to be penetrated can become "a second nature" if such behavior is habitual. See the discussion of J.J. Winkler, *The Constraints of Desire: The Anthropology of Sex and Gender in Ancient Greece* (New York: Routledge, 1990), 67–9.
3. Winkler, *Constraints of Desire*, 50.

4. See B. Holmes, *Gender: Antiquity and its Legacy* (Oxford: Oxford University Press, 2012), 14–46, for a useful discussion of the "one-sex" model of gender and its limitations.
5. I summarize here my own views about a topic with a vast bibliography. See Winkler, *The Constraints of Desire*; D. Halperin, *One Hundred Years of Homosexuality and Other Essays on Greek Love* (New York: Routledge, 1990); a recent counter-argument is presented by J. Davidson, *The Greeks and Greek Love: A Bold New Exploration of the Ancient World* (New York: Random House, 2007).
6. See K. Dover, "Two Women from Samos," in *The Sleep of Reason: Erotic Experience and Sexual Ethics in Ancient Greece and Rome*, ed. M.C. Nussbaum and J. Sihvola (Chicago: University of Chicago Press, 2002).
7. Plato's *Symposium* 180a suggests that Aeschylus depicted Achilles and Patroklos as lovers in his play *The Myrmidons* (which is lost).
8. F. Zeitlin, *Playing the Other: Gender and Society in Classical Greek Literature* (Chicago: University of Chicago Press, 1995), ch. 8 argues that the theater itself, with an emphasis on plotting and mimesis, carries explicitly feminine connotations. See also Holmes, *Gender: Antiquity and its Legacy*, 126–35, 150–68 for a brilliant discussion of gender in Sophocles' *Antigone*.
9. The heroic epics of the archaic period present a nostalgic, fantastic view of an idealized past, in which mortals had frequent and direct contact with the gods, and (at least in certain books of the *Odyssey*) fantastic creatures and semi-divine beings. In so far as these texts can provide us with information about women's lives, it is worth noting that mortal women—even those of the elite classes—such as Penelope, though socially powerful, do seem to lead relatively sequestered lives in the household. More active, powerful female characters, such as Circe, Calypso, and even Helen, are either divine or half-divine. We do have significant poetry written by Sappho (a woman), and this provides a fascinating, but unique, window into female life, erotics, and poetics. But we know little about Sappho's historical existence. What was once supposed to be historical data is now considered nothing more than extrapolations from her poetry, and the scholarly reconstruction of her conditions of existence and production of poetry resembles modern fan fiction more than history. See H. Parker, "Sappho Schoolmistress," *Transactions of the American Philological Association* 123 (1993): 309–51; M. Lefkowitz, *The Lives of the Greek Poets*, 2nd edn. (Baltimore: Johns Hopkins University Press, 2012).
10. An excellent discussion is D. Schaps, "What was Free about a Free Athenian Woman?," *Transactions of the American Philological Association* 128 (1998): 161–88. See also H. Foley, "The Concept of Women in Athenian Drama," in *Reflections of Women in Antiquity*, ed. H. Foley (New York: Gordon & Break, 1981), 129–32.
11. See, among others Foley, "The Concept of Women," 133–5; E. Hall, "The Sociology of Athenian Tragedy," in *The Cambridge Companion to Greek Tragedy*, ed. P.E. Easterling (Cambridge: Cambridge University Press, 1997), 93.
12. The scholarship on this issue is vast. Among the most important works of the last thirty years are: Zeitlin, *Playing the Other*; H. Foley, *Female Acts in Greek Tragedy* (Princeton: Princeton University Press, 2001); N. Rabinowitz, *Anxiety Veiled: Euripides and the Traffic in Women* (Ithaca: Cornell University Press, 1993); V. Wohl, *Intimate Commerce: Exchange, Gender, and Subjectivity in Greek Tragedy* (Austin: University of Texas Press, 1998); D. McCoskey and E. Zakin, eds., *Bound by the City: Greek Tragedy, Sexual Difference, and the Formation of the Polis* (Albany: SUNY Press, 2009); B. Goff, ed., *History, Tragedy, Theory: Dialogues on Athenian Drama* (Austin: University of Texas Press, 1995). In addition there have been numerous studies on individual plays, and essays on the role of women in Greek tragedy. The

role of women and female desire in Roman tragedy has, so far, elicited considerably less interest.
13. See J.P. Gould, "Law, Custom, and Myth: Aspects of the Social Position of Women in Classical Athens," *Journal of Hellenic Studies* 100 (1980): 38.
14. Zeitlin, *Playing the Other*, 347.
15. M. Katz, "The Character of Tragedy: Women and the Greek Imagination," *Arethusa* 17 (1994): 108. See also the foundational article by Foley, "The Concept of Women."
16. C. Patterson, "Marriage in Sophocles: A Problem for Social History," in *A Companion to Sophocles*, ed. K. Ormand (Malden: Wiley-Blackwell, 2012), 382. See a similar approach in Hall, "Sociology of Athenian Tragedy," 93–4.
17. On this point, see, e.g., C. Patterson, "*Hai Attikai*: The Other Athenians," *Helios* 13 (1986): 49–67. Foley, "The Concept of Women," 150.
18. Presumably before this time, the offspring of a citizen man and a well-born woman from another city-state would have been a citizen; for an excellent discussion, seen C. Patterson, "Those Athenian Bastards," *Classical Antiquity* 9 (1990): 40–73. See Foley, *Female Acts*, 75–6 for a brief discussion. For wealthy Athenian men, this created a complex set of conflicting interests. See A. Duplouy, *Le Prestige des Élites: Recherches sur les modes de reconnaissance sociale en Grèce entre les xe et ve siècles avant J.-C.* (Paris: Les Belles Lettres, 2006), 94–108 for a discussion of the Athenian statesman Cimon, who first married a non-citizen woman, Kleitora, with whom he had three children. He later married a citizen, Isodike, whose children (with Cimon) were Athenian citizens and his heirs.
19. See Gould, "Law, Custom, and Myth," 50. B. Goff, *Citizen Bacchae: Women's Ritual Practice in Ancient Greece* (Berkeley: University of California Press, 2004) provides a comprehensive discussion of women's importance to the ritual life of the city. Chapter five discusses the representation of women's ritual in Greek drama; Goff sees a general progression through the fifth century, from a representation of women's ritual at odds with political values, to a gradual alignment of ritual practice and civic identity. For an ancient example, see [Demosthenes] 59.63; discussed by K. Ormand, "Electra in Exile," in McCoskey and Zakin, eds., *Bound by the City*, 255–7.
20. Foley, *Female Acts*, chap. 6 argues cogently that Antigone's defiance of Creon in the *Antigone* is consistent with social expectations for female family members in fifth-century Athens.
21. Probably a development of the fourth century; the legal case *Against Neiara* (dated to the 340s) assumes the existence of such a law.
22. This and all translations are by the author.
23. Compare *Iliad* 14.346–51, in which Zeus and Hera have sex, producing a "glimmering dew," and the earth beneath them spontaneously brings forth grass, clover, crocus, and hyacinths.
24. Noted by A.W. Gomme, "The Position of Women in the Fifth and Fourth Centuries," *Classical Philology* 20, no. 1 (1925): 5. In the *Odyssey*, Agamemnon's ghost repeatedly blames Clytemnestra: 11.405–34; 24.199–202; Athena seems to blame Clytemnestra first, though Aegisthus is mentioned as well: *Od.* 3.234–5. Zeus and Nestor blame Aegisthus for the actual killing, but also criticize Clytemnestra for her collusion with him: *Od.* 1.32–43 (Zeus); *Od.* 3.260–75, 3.301–10 (Nestor). None of these versions have Clytemnestra acting alone, and rejoicing in the spatter of her husband's blood.
25. In one of the many versions of this death in the *Odyssey*, Menelaos (recalling Proteus' narrative) tells Telemachos that Aigisthos killed Agamemnon "as one kills an ox in the manger" (*Od.* 4.535).
26. See R. Seaford, "Wedding Ritual and Textual Criticism in Sophocles' *Women of Trachis*," *Hermes* 114 (1986): 58–9; Wohl, *Intimate Commerce*, 17–37.

27. We also know that this play (Eu. *Hipp.*) is Euripides' second play on the same topic, and there is scholarly speculation—not entirely ironclad—that in the earlier version Phaedra was considerably more forward in her pursuit of Hippolytus, and that it is this aggressive display of female desire that made the play less successful and resulted in the comments about Phaedra as a morally corrupt woman in the comedies of Aristophanes. See W.S. Barrett, ed., *Euripides' Hippolytus* (Oxford: Oxford University Press, 1964): 10–45 for a careful, balanced treatment of the standard view. See also S. Goldhill, *Reading Greek Tragedy* (Cambridge: Cambridge University Press, 1986), 131. J. Gibert, "Euripides' *Hippolytus* Plays: Which Came First?" *Classical Quarterly* 47 (1997): 85–97, analyzes all the available evidence, and argues that we do not know why Euripides wrote two versions; we do not know which version came first; and we do not even know for certain what the audience response was to the first version, beyond knowing that it did not win the tragic competition that year.
28. Hall, "The Sociology of Athenian Tragedy," 122.
29. See the excellent discussion of V. Wohl, *Law's Cosmos: Juridical Discourse in Athenian Forensic Oratory* (Cambridge: Cambridge University Press, 2010), 82–97.
30. M. Alexiou, *The Ritual Lament in Greek Tradition* (Cambridge: Cambridge University Press, 1974), 14–23; Foley, *Female Acts*, 145–71.
31. Alexiou, *Ritual Lament*, 21.
32. See the excellent discussion by Foley, *Female Acts*, 145–71.
33. Foley, *Female Acts*, 150.
34. Foley, *Female Acts*, 151. Electra engages in a similar strategy in Euripides' *Electra* as well; see the useful discussion of F. Zeitlin, "The Argive Festival of Hera and Euripides' *Electra*," *Transactions of the American Philological Association* 101 (1970): 648–50.
35. See K. Ormand, *Exchange and the Maiden: Marriage in Sophoclean Tragedy* (Austin: University of Texas Press, 1999), 17–18; H.J. Wolff, "Marriage Law and Family Organization in Ancient Athens: A Study of the Interrelation of Public and Private Law in the Greek City," *Traditio* 2 (1944): 48–53.
36. See C. Cox, *Household Interests: Property, Marriage Strategies, and Family Dynamics in Ancient Athens* (Princeton: Princeton University Press, 1988), 94–9. Isaeus 3.64 is the passage most often cited to support the idea that a woman might have to divorce her husband to marry as an *epikleros*.
37. See especially R. Seaford, "The Tragic Wedding," *Journal of Hellenic Studies* 107 (1987): 106–30. Seaford argues that weddings in tragedy tend to represent the ritual as unfulfilled, and the bride's transition as incomplete, leading to a general failure of the household and, frequently, of the society at large. Hall, "The Sociology of Athenian Tragedy," 106 states that "Every single transgressive woman in tragedy is temporarily or permanently husbandless." This is not quite true of Medea, unless you consider the present Jason to be no longer her husband, having publicly announced his desertion of her.
38. See the useful discussion of H. Foley, "Tragedy and Democratic Ideology," in Goff, ed., *Tragedy, History, Theory*, 138–9; Foley, *Female Acts*, 32–3.
39. Gould, "Law, Custom, and Myth," 55. See also Foley, *Female Acts*, 71: "In comparison with the Homeric bride, the Attic wife remained to some extent a marginal and even suspect outsider in her marital family."
40. See Patterson, *Hai Attikai*, 56.
41. See F. Zeitlin, "The Politics of Eros in the Danaid Trilogy of Aeschylus," in *Innovations of Antiquity*, ed. R. Hexter and D. Selden (New York: Routledge, 1992). Zeitlin explores the connection, posited by Herodotus, between the Danaids and the establishment of the

Thesmophoria at Athens, and argues that "If this hypothesis is correct, the aim of the trilogy will be to teach the Danaids to accept the feminine role that subordinates them to men in the institution of marriage but that also acknowledges the significance of their maternal functions . . ." (235–6). Recently G. Bakewell, *Aeschylus' Suppliant Women: the Tragedy of Immigration* (Madison: University of Wisconsin Press, 2013) has analyzed the *Suppliants* as reflecting on an influx of resident aliens in Athens in the late sixth and early fifth centuries. In his elegant reading, the suppliant women are overdetermined as both foreign and female, in both senses "outsiders" to the political state.

42. Ormand, *Exchange and the Maiden*, 14–18, 72–5.
43. We must also note that the dowry is not, strictly speaking, a commercial transaction; a woman's dowry remained in some sense her own property, and had to be returned to her natal family in the case of divorce. See Ormand, *Exchange and the Maiden*, 17.
44. See Zeitlin, *Playing the Other*, 358: "Although deceit and intrigue are condemned in woman, they are also seen as natural to her sphere of operations and the dictates of her nature."
45. A concise discussion of this principle is M. Foucault, *The History of Sexuality, vol. 2: The Use of Pleasure*, trans. R. Hurley (New York: Vintage Books, 1985), 63–77.
46. Zeitlin, "Playing the Other," 350.
47. For a fuller discussion, see Wohl, *Intimate Commerce*, 9–10; Ormand, *Exchange and the Maiden*, 55–7.
48. Zeitlin, *Playing the Other*, 361.
49. K. Ormand, "Oedipus the Queen: Cross-dressing without Drag," *Theatre Journal* 55 (2003): 13.
50. See, for example, Plutarch's *Roman Questions* 274d-e.
51. See especially J. Walters, "Invading the Roman Body: Manliness and Impenetrability in Roman Thought," in *Roman Sexualities*, ed. J.P. Hallett and M. Skinner (Princeton: Princeton University Press, 1997), 30–2.
52. See, for example, Tacitus *Annals* 13.5.
53. See, for example, Seneca's *On the Happy Life*, 8. On Stoicism and its relationship to Senecan tragedy, also see the discussion by Busch in this volume.
54. Source texts are too many to enumerate; Seneca's *Letter 16 (to Lucilius)* gives a clear, concise overview. The Stoic development of "care of the self" as a form of pleasure is brilliantly discussed by Michel Foucault, *The History of Sexuality vol. 3: The Care of the Self*, trans. R. Hurley (New York: Random House, 1986), 39–68.
55. Foucault, *The History of Sexuality*, vol. 3, 66.
56. See, e.g., Seneca's *Consolatio ad Marciam*.
57. R. Meyer, *Seneca: Phaedra* (London: Duckworth, 2002), 43.
58. As Meyer, *Senaca: Phaedra*, 38 points out, "Her case cannot be faulted, either in Stoic or 'Hippolytean' terms (though of course her real purpose is perverted)."
59. A. Schiesaro, *The Passions in Play: Thyestes and the Dynamics of Senecan Drama* (Cambridge: Cambridge University Press, 2003), 20–1.

BIBLIOGRAPHY

Adam, J. ed. *The Republic of Plato, Edited Text with Critical Notes, Commentary and Appendices*. With an introduction by D.A. Rees. 2nd edn. 2 vols. Cambridge: Cambridge University Press, 1969.
Alexiou, M. *The Ritual Lament in Greek Tradition*. Cambridge: Cambridge University Press, 1974.
Allan, W. *The* Andromache *and Euripidean Tragedy*. Oxford: Oxford University Press, 2000.
Allan, W. "Euripides in Megale Hellas: Some Aspects of the Early Reception of Tragedy." *Greece and Rome* 48 (2001): 67–86.
Allan, W. ed. *Euripides: Helen*. Cambridge: Cambridge University Press, 2008.
Allan, W. and Kelly, A. "Listening to Many Voices: Athenian Tragedy as Popular Art." In *The Author's Voice in Classical and Late Antiquity*, edited by A. Marmodoro and J. Hill, 77–122. Oxford: Oxford University Press, 2015.
Allen, D.S. *The World of Prometheus: The Politics of Punishing in Democratic Athens*. Princeton: Princeton University Press, 2000.
Arthur, M. "'Liberated' Women: The Classical Era." In *Becoming Visible: Women in European History*, edited by R. Bridenthal and C. Koonz, 60–91. Boston: Houghton Mifflin, 1977.
Asmis, E. "Seneca on Fortune and the Kingdom of God." In Bartsch and Wray, *Seneca and the Self*, 115–38.
Badian, E. "Greeks and Macedonians." In *Macedonia and Greece in Late Classical and Early Hellenistic Times, Studies in History of Art 10*, edited by B. Barr-Sharrar and E. N. Borza, 33–51. Washington: National Gallery of Art, 1982.
Badian, E. "Phrynichus and Athens' οἰκήια κακά." *Scripta Classica Israelica* 15 (1996): 55–60.
Baertschi, A. "Drama and epic narrative: the test case of messenger speech in Seneca's *Agamemnon*." In Gildenhard and Revermann, *Beyond the Fifth Century*, 249–68.
Bakewell, G. *Aeschylus' Suppliant Women: the Tragedy of Immigration*. Madison: University of Wisconsin Press, 2013.
Bakhtin, M. *The Dialogic Imagination: Four Essays*, trans. C. Emerson and M. Holquist. Austin: University of Texas Press, 1981.
Barker, E.T.E. *Entering the Agon: Dissent and Authority in Homer, Historiography, and Tragedy*. Oxford: Oxford University Press, 2009.
Barrett, W.S. ed. *Euripides' Hippolytus*. Oxford: Oxford University Press, 1964.
Bartsch, S. *Decoding the Ancient Novel: The Reader and the Role of Description in Heliodorus and Achilles Tatius*. Princeton: Princeton University Press, 1989.
Bartsch, S. *Actors in the Audience*. Cambridge, MA: Harvard University Press, 1994.
Bartsch, S. and Wray, D. eds. *Seneca and the Self*. Cambridge: Cambridge University Press, 2009.
Bartsch, S. and Schiesaro, A. eds. *The Cambridge Companion to Seneca*. Cambridge: Cambridge University Press, 2015.
Battezzato, L. "Dithyramb and Greek Tragedy." In *Dithyramb in Context*, edited by B. Kowalzig and P. Wilson, 93–110. Oxford: Oxford University Press, 2013.

Beacham, R.C. *The Roman Theatre and its Audience*. London: Routledge, 1991.

Beard, M. "Looking (harder) for Roman myth: Dumézil, declamation and the problems of Definition." In *Mythos in mythenloser Gesellschaft: das Paradigma Roms*, edited by F. Graf, 44–64. Stuttgart: Teubner, 1993.

Beard, M., North, J., and Price, S. *Religions of Rome, Volume 1: A History*. Cambridge: Cambridge University Press, 1998.

Behler, E. "A.W. Schlegel and the nineteenth-century *damnatio* of Euripides." *Greek, Roman, and Byzantine Studies* 27 (1986): 335–67.

Belfiore, E. "Plato's Greatest Accusation against Poetry." *Canadian Journal of Philosophy*, Suppl. Vol. 9 (1983): 39–62.

Belfiore, E. *Murder Among Friends: Violations of Philia in Greek Tragedy*. Oxford: Oxford University Press, 2000.

Bergmann, B. and Kondoleon, C. eds. *The Art of Ancient Spectacle*. New Haven and London: NGA and Yale University Press, 2000.

Bers, V. "Tragedy and rhetoric." In *Persuasion: Greek rhetoric in action*, edited by I. Worthington, 176–95. London: Routledge, 1994.

Berthold, R.M. *Rhodes in the Hellenistic Age*. Ithaca: Cornell University Press, 1984.

Biliński, B. *Accio ed i Gracchi. Contributo alla storia della plebe e della tragedia romana*. Rome: Signorelli, 1958.

Bishop, J.D. *Seneca's daggered stylus: political code in the tragedies*. Königstein: Anton Hain, 1985.

Blondell, R. *Helen of Troy: Beauty, Myth, Devastation*. Oxford: Oxford University Press, 2013.

Bloom, H. *Shakespeare: The Invention of the Human*. New York: Riverhead Books, 1998.

Bobzien, S. *Determinism and Freedom in Stoic Philosophy*. Oxford: Oxford University Press, 1998.

Bosher, K. ed. *Theater Outside Athens: Drama in Greek Sicily and South Italy*. Cambridge: Cambridge University Press, 2012.

Bosher, K. "Hieron's Aeschylus." In Bosher, *Theater outside Athens*, 97–111.

Bosworth, A.B. *Alexander and the East. The Tragedy of Triumph*. Oxford: Clarendon Press, 1996.

Bosworth, A.B. "Alexander, Euripides, and Dionysos: The Motivation for Apotheosis." In *Transitions to Empire: Essays in Greco-Roman History, 360–146 BC in honor of E. Badian*, edited by R.W. Wallace and E.M. Harris, 140–66. Norman, OK and London: University of Oklahoma Press, 1996.

Boyle, A.J. *Tragic Seneca: An Essay in the Theatrical Tradition*. London: Routledge, 1997.

Boyle, A.J. *Introduction to Roman Tragedy*. London and New York: Routledge, 2006.

Boyle, A.J. ed. and trans. *Seneca: Medea*. Oxford: Oxford University Press, 2014.

Braden, G. *Renaissance Tragedy and the Senecan Tradition: Anger's Privilege*. New Haven: Yale University Press, 1985.

Braund, D. and Hall, E. "Theatre in the fourth-century Black Sea region." In Csapo et al. *Greek Theatre in the Fourth Century BC*, 371–90.

Braund, S.M. and Gill, C. eds. *The Passions in Roman Thought and Literature*. Cambridge: Cambridge University Press, 1997.

Bridenthal, R. and Koonz, C. eds. *Becoming Visible: Women in European History*. Boston: Houghton Mifflin, 1977.

Broggiato, M. "Aristophanes and Aeschylos' *Persians*: Hellenistic Discussions on Ar. *Ran.* 1028f." *Rheinisches Museum für Philologie, Neue Folge* 157, no. 1 (2014): 1–15.

Budelmann, F. *The language of Sophocles: communality, communication and involvement*. Cambridge: Cambridge University Press, 2000.

Budelmann F. "The Reception of Sophocles' Representation of Physical Pain." *American Journal of Philology* 128, no. 4 (2007): 443–67.
Buraselis, K. "Appended Festivals: The Coordination and Combination of Traditional Civic and Ruler Cult Festivals in the Hellenistic and Roman East." In *Greek and Roman Festivals: Content, Meaning and Practice*, edited by J. Rasmus Brandt and J.W. Iddeng, 247–66. Oxford: Oxford University Press, 2012.
Burian, P. "Supplication and Hero Cult in Sophocles' Ajax." *Greek, Roman and Byzantine Studies* 13 (1972): 151–6.
Burian, P. "Athenian tragedy as democratic discourse." In Carter, *Why Athens?*, 95–118.
Burian, P. "Polyphonic *Ajax*." In Ormand, *A Companion to Sophocles*, 69–83.
Burkert, W. "Greek Tragedy and Sacrificial Ritual." *Greek, Roman, and Byzantine Studies* 7, no. 2 (1966): 87–121.
Burnett, A.P. *Catastrophe Survived: Euripides' Plays of Mixed Reversal*. Oxford: Oxford University Press, 1971.
Busch, A. "*Versane Natura Est*? Natural and Linguistic Instability in the *Extispicium* and Self-Blinding of Seneca's *Oedipus*." *The Classical Journal* 102, no. 3 (2007): 225–67.
Busch, A. "Dissolution of the Self in the Senecan Corpus." In Bartsch and Wray, *Seneca and the Self*, 255–82.
Bushnell, R. ed. *A Companion to Tragedy*. Malden, MA: Blackwell Publishing, 2005.
Cairns, D. "Virtue and Vicissitude: the Paradoxes of the *Ajax*." In Cairns and Liapis, *Dionysalexandros*, 99–132.
Cairns, D. and Liapis, V. eds. *Dionysalexandros: Essays on Aeschylus and his fellow tragedians in honour of Alexander F. Garvie*. Swansea: The Classical Press of Wales, 2006.
Cairns, D. *Sophocles: Antigone*. London and New York: Bloomsbury, 2016.
Campbell, C. "The Uncompleted Theatres of Rome." *Theatre Journal* 55 (2003): 67–79.
Carter, D.M. *The Politics of Greek Tragedy*. Liverpool: Liverpool University Press, 2007.
Carter, D.M. "The demos in Greek tragedy." *Cambridge Classical Journal* 56 (2010): 47–94.
Carter, D.M. ed. *Why Athens?: a reappraisal of tragic politics*. Oxford: Oxford University Press, 2011.
Carter, D.M. "Reported assembly scenes in Greek tragedy." *Institute of Classical Studies* 38 (2013): 23–63.
Cartledge, P. "'Deep plays': Theatre as process in Greek civic life." In Easterling, *Cambridge Companion to Greek Tragedy*, 3–35.
Ceccarelli, P. "Le Dithyrambe et la Pyrrhique: à propos de la nouvelle liste de vainqueurs aux Dionysies de Cos (Segre, *ED* 234)." *Zeitschrift für Papyrologie und Epigraphik* 108 (1995): 287–305.
Ceccarelli, P. "Tragedy in the Civic and Cultural Life of Hellenistic City-States." In Gildenhard and Reverman, *Beyond the Fifth Century*, 99–150.
Champlin, E. "*Agamemnon* at Rome Roman Dynasts and Greek Heroes." In *Myth, History and Culture in Republican Rome. Studies in honour of T.P. Wiseman*, edited by D. Braund and C. Gill, 295–319. Exeter: University of Exeter Press, 2003.
Chaniotis, A. "Theatricality Beyond the Theater. Staging Public Life in the Hellenistic World." In B. Le Guin *De la scène aux gradins. Théâtre et représentations dramatiques après Alexandre le Grand* (= *Pallas* 47), edited by B. Le Guen, 219–59. Toulouse: Presses Universitaires du Mirail, 1997.
Chappell, T. *Reading Plato's Theaetetus*. Indianapolis: Hackett, 2005.
Coleman, K.M. "Fatal Charades: Roman Executions Staged as Mythological Enactments." *Journal of Roman Studies* 80 (1990): 44–73.

Conacher, D. *Euripides and the Sophists: Some Dramatic Treatments of Philosophical Ideas.* London: Duckworth, 1998.

Cowan, R. "A Stranger in a Strange Land. Medea in Roman Republican Tragedy." In *Unbinding Medea. Interdisciplinary Approaches to a Classical Myth*, edited by H. Bartel and A. Simon, 39–52. Abingdon: Modern Humanities Research Association and Routledge, 2010.

Cowan, R. "240 BCE and All That: The Romanness of Republican Tragedy." In Harrison, *Companion to Roman Tragedy*, 63–89.

Coward, T. "Poetry and Performance on Hellenistic Rhodes." In *Hellenistic Poetry beyond Callimachean Aesthetics*, edited by M. Leventhal and T. Nelson, forthcoming.

Cox, C. *Household Interests: Property, Marriage Strategies, and Family Dynamics in Ancient Athens*. Princeton: Princeton University Press, 1998.

Croally, N. *Euripidean Polemic*. Cambridge: Cambridge University Press, 1994.

Csapo, E. "Later Euripidean Music." *Illinois Classical Studies* 24–5 (1999–2000): 399–426.

Csapo, E. "Some social and economic conditions behind the rise of the acting profession in the fifth and fourth centuries BC." In *Le statut de l'acteur dans l'Antiquité grecque et romaine: Actes du colloque qui s'est tenu à Tours les 3 et 4 mai 2002 organisé par l'UMR 5189 "Histoire et sources des mondes anciens"*, edited by C. Hugoniot, F. Hurlet, and S. Milanezi, 53–76, Tours: Presse Universitaire François Rabelais, 2004.

Csapo, E. "The Men Who Built Theatres: *Theatropolai, Theatronai*, and *Arkhitektones*." In Wilson, *Theatre and Festivals*, 87–115.

Csapo, E. *Actors and Icons of the Ancient Theater*. Chichester: Wiley Blackwell, 2010.

Csapo, E. and Slater, W.J. *The Context of Ancient Drama*. Ann Arbor: University of Michigan Press, 1995.

Csapo, E., Goette, H.R., Green, J.R., and Wilson, P. eds. *Greek Theatre in the Fourth Century BC*. Berlin: De Gruyter, 2014.

Csapo, E. and Wilson, P. "The Finance and Organization of the Athenian Theater in the Time of Eubulus and Lycurgus." In Csapo et al., *Greek Theatre in the Fourth Century BC*, 393–424.

Csapo, E. and Wilson, P. "Drama Outside Athens in the Fifth and Fourth Centuries BC." In Lamari, *Reperformances*, 316–95.

Curley, D. *Tragedy in Ovid: Theater, Metatheater, and the Transformation of a Genre*. Cambridge: Cambridge University Press, 2013.

D'Angour, A. "The New Music: So What's New?" In *Rethinking Revolutions through Ancient Greece*, edited by R. Osborne, 276–83. Cambridge: Cambridge University Press, 2006.

Davidson, J. *The Greeks and Greek Love: A Bold New Exploration of the Ancient World*. New York: Random House, 2007.

Davie, J. trans. *Seneca: Dialogues and Essays*. With an introduction and notes by T. Reinhardt. Oxford: Oxford University Press, 2007.

Dawson, S. "The Theatrical Audience in Fifth-Century Athens: Numbers and Status." *Prudentia* 19 (1997): 1–14.

Dearden, C.W. "Fourth-Century Drama in Sicily." In *Greek Colonists and Native Populations: Proceedings of the First Australian Congress of Classical Archaeology held in honour of Emeritus Professor A. D. Trendall*, edited by J.-P. Descoeudres, 231–42. Oxford: Clarendon Press, 1990.

De Unamuno, M. *The Tragic Sense of Life*, translated by J.E. Crawford Flitch. 1921; reprint New York: Cosimo Classics, 2005.

Di Giuseppe, L. "Euripide e la grecità dei Macedoni: Archelao presso Cisseo." *Prometheus* 30 (2004): 125–8.

Dillon, J. "Euripides and the Philosophy of His Time." *Classics Ireland* 11 (2004): 47–73.

Dillon, J. and Gergel, T. trans. *The Greek Sophists*. London: Penguin, 2003.
Donovan, B. R. "The Project of Protagoras." *Rhetoric Society Quarterly* 23, no. 1 (1993): 35–47.
Dougherty, C. "Linguistic colonialism in Aeschylus' *Aetnaeae*." *Greek, Roman, and Byzantine Studies* 32, no. 2 (1991): 119–32.
Douglas, A.E. ed. and trans. *Tusculan disputations 2 & 5, Cicero*. Warminster: Aris & Phillips, 1990.
Dover, K. "Two Women from Samos." In *The Sleep of Reason: Erotic Experience and Sexual Ethics in Ancient Greece and Rome*, edited by M.C. Nussbaum and J. Sihvola, 222–9. Chicago: University of Chicago Press, 2002.
Dunbabin, K.M.D. "Convivial Spaces: Dining and Entertainment in the Roman Villa." *Journal of Roman Archaeology* 9 (1996): 66–80.
Dunbabin, K.M.D. *The Roman Banquet: Images of Conviviality*. Cambridge: Cambridge University Press, 2003.
Duncan, A. "Nothing to do with Athens? Tragedians at the Courts of Tyrants." In Carter, *Why Athens?*, 69–84.
Duncan A. "Political Re-Performances of Tragedy in the Fifth and Fourth Centuries BC." In Lamari, *Reperformances*, 297–315.
Dunkle, R. "The Greek Tyrant and Roman Political Invective of the Late Republic." *Transactions of the American Philological Association* 98 (1967): 151–7.
Dunn, F. *Tragedy's End: Closure and Innovation in Euripidean Drama*. Oxford and New York: Oxford University Press, 1996.
Duplouy, A. *Le Prestige des Élites: Recherches sur les modes de reconnaissance sociale en Grèce entre les xe et ve siècles avant J.-C.* Paris: Les Belles Lettres, 2006.
Easterling, P.E. "Anachronism in Greek Tragedy." *Journal of Hellenic Studies* 105 (1985): 1–10.
Easterling, P.E. "The end of an era? Tragedy in the early fourth century." In *Tragedy, Comedy and the Polis*, edited by A. Sommerstein, S. Halliwell, J. Henderson, and B. Zimmermann, 559–70. Bari: Levante editori, 1993.
Easterling, P.E. "Euripides Outside Athens: A Speculative Note." *Illinois Classical Studies* 19 (1994): 73–80.
Easterling, P.E. ed. *The Cambridge Companion to Greek Tragedy*. Cambridge: Cambridge University Press, 1997.
Easterling, P.E. "From Repertoire to Canon." In Easterling, *Cambridge Companion to Greek Tragedy*, 211–27.
Easterling, P.E. "A Show for Dionysus." In Easterling, *Cambridge Companion to Greek Tragedy*, 36–53.
Easterling, P.E. "Actor as Icon." In Easterling and Hall, *Greek and Roman Actors*, 327–41.
Easterling, P.E. and Hall, E. eds. *Greek and Roman Actors: Aspects of an Ancient Profession*. Cambridge: Cambridge University Press, 2002.
Edmunds, L. "Oedipus as tyrant in Sophocles' *Oedipus Tyrannus*." *Syllecta Classica* 13 (2002): 63–103.
Erasmo, M. *Roman Tragedy: Theatre to Theatricality*. Austin: University of Texas Press, 2004.
Fantham, E. ed. and trans. *Seneca's Troades*. Princeton: Princeton University Press, 1982.
Fantham, E. "Orator and/et actor." In Easterling and Hall, *Greek and Roman Actors*, 362–76.
Fantham, E. *The Roman World of Cicero's De Oratore*. Oxford: Oxford University Press, 2004.
Feeney, D. "The Beginnings of a Literature in Latin." *Journal of Roman Studies* 95 (2005): 226–40.
Feeney, D. *Beyond Greek: The Beginnings of Latin Literature*. Cambridge, MA: Harvard University Press, 2016.

Ferrari, G.R.F. "Plato and Poetry." In *The Cambridge History of Literary Criticism, Vol. 1: Classical Criticism*, edited by G.A. Kennedy, 92–148. Cambridge: Cambridge University Press, 1993.

Finglass, P.J. "Is there a *polis* in Sophocles' *Electra*?" *Phoenix* 59 (2005): 199–209.

Finglass, P.J. ed. *Sophocles' Ajax, Cambridge Classical Texts and Commentaries 48*. Cambridge: Cambridge University Press, 2011.

Finglass, P.J. "Sophocles' *Ajax* and the Polis." *Polis* 34 (2017): 306–17.

Fitch, J.G. ed. *Seneca's Hercules Furens: A Critical Text with Introduction and Commentary*. Ithaca: Cornell University Press, 1987.

Fitch, J.G. "Playing Seneca?" In Harrison, *Seneca in Performance*, 1–12.

Fitch, J.G. ed. and trans. *Seneca VIII: Tragedies I: Hercules, Trojan Women, Phoenician Women, Medea, Phaedra*. Cambridge, MA: Harvard University Press, 2002.

Fitch, J.G. ed. and trans. *Seneca IX: Tragedies II: Oedipus; Agamemnon; Thyestes; Hercules on Oeta; Octavia*. Cambridge: Harvard University Press, 2004.

Fletcher, J. *Performing Oaths in Classical Greek Drama*. Cambridge: Cambridge University Press, 2012.

Fletcher, R. and Hanink, J. eds. *Creative Lives in Antiquity*. Cambridge: Cambridge University Press, 2016.

Flower, H. "*Fabulae Praetextae* in context: when were plays on contemporary subjects performed in Republican Rome?" *Classical Quarterly* 45 (2005): 170–90.

Folch, M. *The City and the Stage: Performance, Genre, and Gender in Plato's Laws*. Oxford: Oxford University Press, 2015.

Foley, H. "The Concept of Women in Athenian Drama." In *Reflections of Women in Antiquity*, edited by H. Foley, 127–68. New York: Gordon & Break, 1981.

Foley, H. *Ritual Irony: Poetry and Sacrifice in Euripides*. Ithaca: Cornell University Press, 1985.

Foley, H. "Tragedy and Democratic Ideology." In Goff, *History, Tragedy, Theory*, 131–50.

Foley, H. *Female Acts in Greek Tragedy*. Princeton: Princeton University Press, 2001.

Fontaine, M. and Scafuro, A. eds. *The Oxford Handbook of Greek and Roman Comedy*. Oxford: Oxford University Press, 2014.

Foucault, M. *The History of Sexuality*, vol. 2: *The Use of Pleasure*. Translated by R. Hurley. New York: Vintage Books, 1985.

Foucault, M. *The History of Sexuality*, vol. 3: *The Care of the Self*. Translated by R. Hurley. New York: Vintage Books, 1986.

Fountoulakis, A. "When Dionysus Goes to the East: On the Dissemination of Greek Drama Beyond Athens." In Fountoulakis, Markantonatos, and Vasilaros, *Theater World*, 75–117.

Fountoulakis, A., Markantonatos, A. and Vasilaros, G. eds., *Theater World: Critical Perspectives on Greek Tragedy and Comedy. Studies in Honor of Georgia Xanthakis- Karamanos*. Trends in Classics 45. Berlin: De Gruyter, 2017.

Frangoulidis, S., Harrison, S.J., and Manuwald, G. eds. *Roman Drama and its Contexts*, Trends in Classics, Supplementary volume 34. Berlin: De Gruyter, 2016.

Gabrielsen, V. *The Naval Aristocracy of Hellenistic Rhodes*. Aarhus/Oxford: Aarhus University Press, 1997.

Gadamer, H.G. *Dialogue and Dialectic: Eight Hermeneutical Studies on Plato*. Translated by P.C. Smith. New Haven: Yale University Press, 1980.

Gagarin, M. *Aeschylean Drama*. Berkeley: University of California, 1976.

Gentili, B. *Theatrical Performances in the Ancient World: Hellenistic and early Roman Theatre*. Amsterdam: Gieben, 1979.

Gibert, J. *Change of Mind in Greek Tragedy, Hypomnemata Heft 108*. Göttingen: Vandenhoeck and Ruprecht, 1995.
Gibert, J. "Euripides' *Hippolytus* Plays: Which Came First?" *Classical Quarterly* 47 (1997): 85–97.
Gildenhard, I. "Reckoning with Tyranny: Greek Thoughts on Caesar in Cicero's Letters to Atticus in early 49." In *Ancient Tyranny*, edited by S. Lewis, 197–209. Edinburgh: Edinburgh University Press, 2006.
Gildenhard, I. *Paideia Romana: Cicero's Tusculan Disputations*. Cambridge: Cambridge Philological Society, 2007.
Gildenhard, I. "Buskins & SPQR: Roman Receptions of Greek Tragedy." In Gildenhard and Revermann, *Beyond the Fifth Century*, 153–85.
Gildenhard, I. and Revermann, M. eds. *Beyond the Fifth Century: Interactions with Greek Tragedy from the Fourth Century BCE to the Middle Ages*. Berlin: De Gruyter, 2010.
Ginsberg, L.D. "Tragic Rome? Roman Historical Drama and the Genre of Tragedy." In Harrison, *Companion to Roman Tragedy*, 216–37.
Ginsberg, L.D. "History as Intertext and Intertext as History in the *Octavia*." In Frangoulidis, Harrison, and Manuwald, *Roman Drama and its Contexts*, 417–32.
Goette, H. "An Archaeological Appendix." In Wilson, *Theatre and Festivals*, 116–21.
Goff, B. *Citizen Bacchae: Women's Ritual Practice in Ancient Greece*. Berkeley: University of California Press, 2004.
Goff, B. ed. *History, Tragedy, Theory: Dialogues on Athenian Drama*. Austin: University of Texas Press, 1995.
Goldberg, S. "The Fall and Rise of Roman Tragedy." *Transactions of the American Philological Association* 126 (1996): 265–86
Goldberg, S. "Cicero and the Work of Tragedy." In *Identität und Alterität in der frühömischen Tragödie*, edited by G. Manuwald, 49–60. Würzburg: Ergon Verlag, 2000.
Golden, M. "Childhood in Ancient Greece." In Niels and Oakley, *Coming of Age*, 13–30.
Goldhill, S. *Reading Greek Tragedy*. Cambridge: Cambridge University Press, 1986.
Goldhill, S. "The Great Dionysia and Civic Ideology." In Winkler and Zeitlin, *Nothing to do with Dionysus?*, 97–129.
Goldhill, S. "The audience of Athenian tragedy." In Easterling, *Cambridge Companion to Greek Tragedy*, 54–68.
Goldhill, S. "Undoing in Sophoclean Drama: *Lusis* and the Analysis of Irony." *Transactions of the American Philological Association* 139 (2009): 21–52.
Goldhill, S. *Sophocles and the Language of Tragedy*. Oxford: Oxford University Press, 2012.
Goldhill, S. and Osborne, R. eds. *Performance Culture and Athenian Democracy*. Cambridge: Cambridge University Press, 1999.
Gomme, A.W. "The Position of Women in the Fifth and Fourth Centuries." *Classical Philology* 20, no. 1 (1925): 1–25.
Gould, J.P. "Law, Custom, and Myth: Aspects of the Social Position of Women in Classical Athens." *Journal of Hellenic Studies* 100 (1980): 38–59.
Gould, T. *The Ancient Quarrel between Poetry and Philosophy*. Princeton: Princeton University Press, 1990.
Graver, M. *Stoicism and Emotion*. Chicago: University of Chicago Press, 2007.
Graver, M. and Long, A.A. trans. *Letters on Ethics*. Chicago: University of Chicago Press, 2015.
Green, J.R. "On Seeing and Depicting the Theatre in Classical Athens." *Greek, Roman, and Byzantine Studies* 32 (1991): 15–50.
Green, J.R. *Theatre in Ancient Greek Society*. London: Routledge, 1994.

Green, J.R. "Theatre Production: 1996–2006." *Lustrum* 50 (2008): 7–302.
Gregory, J. *Euripides and the Instruction of the Athenians*. Ann Arbor: University of Michigan Press, 1991.
Gregory, J. "Sophocles and Education." In Markantonatos, *Companion to Sophocles*, 513–35.
Grewe, S. *Die politische Bedeutung der Senecatragödien und Senecas politisches Denken zur Zeit der Abfassung der Medea*. Wurzburg: Ergon Verlag, 2001.
Griffin, J. "The social function of Greek tragedy." *Classical Quarterly* 48 (1998): 39–61.
Griffin, J. "Sophocles and the Democratic City." In Griffin, *Sophocles Revisited*, 73–94.
Griffin, J. ed. *Sophocles Revisited: Essays Presented to Sir Hugh Lloyd-Jones*. Oxford: Clarendon Press, 1999.
Griffin, M.T. *Seneca: A Philosopher in Politics*. Oxford: Clarendon Press, 1976.
Griffith, M. *The Authenticity of the Prometheus Bound*. Cambridge: Cambridge University Press, 1977.
Griffith, M. "Aeschylus, Sicily and Prometheus." In *Dionysiaca: Nine Studies in Greek Poetry By Former Pupils Presented to Sir Denys Page on his Seventieth Birthday*, edited by R.D. Dawe, J. Diggle, and P.E. Easterling, 105–39. Cambridge: Cambridge University Press, 1978.
Griffith, M. "Brilliant Dynasts: Power and Politics in the *Oresteia*." *Classical Antiquity* 14 (1995): 62–129.
Griffith, M. "The King and Eye: The Rule of the Father in Greek Tragedy." *Proceedings of the Cambridge Philological Society* 44 (1998): 20–84.
Griffith, M. *Greek Satyr Play: Five Studies*. Berkeley: University of California Press, 2013a.
Griffith, M. *Aristophanes' Frogs*. Cambridge: Cambridge University Press, 2013b.
Gruen, E.S. *Culture and National Identity in Republican Rome*. Ithaca: Cornell University Press, 1992.
Habicht, C. *Gottmenschentum und griechische Städte*. München: Beck, 1956.
Hall, E. *Inventing the Barbarian*. Oxford: Oxford University Press, 1989.
Hall, E. "Is There a Polis in Aristotle's *Poetics*?" In Silk, *Tragedy and the Tragic*, 295–309.
Hall, E. "The Sociology of Athenian Tragedy." In Easterling, *Cambridge Companion to Greek Tragedy*, 93–126.
Hall, E. "Actor's Song in Tragedy." In Goldhill and Osborne, *Performance Culture*, 96–124.
Hall, E. "The Singing Actors of Antiquity." In Easterling and Hall, *Greek and Roman Actors*, 3–38.
Hall, E. *Greek Tragedy: Suffering under the sun*. Oxford: Oxford University Press, 2010.
Hall, E. *Adventures with Iphigenia in Tauris: A Cultural History of Euripides' Black Sea Tragedy*. Oxford: Oxford University Press, 2013.
Hall, E. and Wyles, R. eds. *New Directions in Ancient Pantomime*. Oxford: Oxford University Press, 2008.
Halliwell, S. "Between Public and Private: Tragedy and Athenian Experience of Rhetoric." In Pelling, *Greek Tragedy and the Historian*, 121–41.
Halliwell, S. *Aristotle's Poetics*. London: Duckworth, 1986; reprint Chicago: University of Chicago Press, 1998.
Halliwell, S. *The Aesthetics of Mimesis: Ancient Texts and Modern Problems*. Princeton NJ: Princeton University Press, 2002.
Halliwell, S. *Between Ecstasy and Truth: Interpretations of Greek Poetics from Homer to Longinus*. Oxford: Oxford University Press, 2011.
Halperin, D. *One Hundred Years of Sexuality and Other Essays on Greek Love*. New York: Routledge, 1990.
Hamilton, R. "Slings and Arrows: The Debate with Lycus in the *Heracles*." *Transactions of the American Philological Association* 115 (1985): 19–25.

Hammond, N.G.L. and Griffith, G.T. *A History of Macedonia, vol. 2 550–336 B.C.* Oxford: Clarendon Press, 1979.
Hanink, J. "The Classical Tragedians, from Athenian Idols to Wandering Poets." In Gildenhard and Revermann, *Beyond the Fifth Century*, 39–67.
Hanink, J. *Lycurgan Athens and the Making of Classical Tragedy*. Cambridge: Cambridge University Press, 2014.
Hanink, J. "Literary Evidence for New Tragic Production: The View from the Fourth Century." In Csapo et al., *Greek Theatre in the Fourth Century BC*, 189–206.
Hanink, J. and Uhlig, A.S. "Aeschylus and his Afterlife in the Classical Period: 'My Poetry Did Not Die with Me.'" In *The Reception of Aeschylus' Plays through Shifting Models and Frontiers*, Metaforms 7, edited by S. E. Constantinidis, 51–79. Leiden: Brill, 2016.
Hanson, J.A. ed. and trans. *Apuleius*. Metamorphoses *Books 7–11*. Cambridge, MA: Harvard University Press, 1989.
Harder, A. ed. *Euripides' Kresphontes and Archelaos*. Leiden: Brill, 1985.
Harder, A. "Praxithea: A Perfect Mother?" In *Land of Dreams: Greek and Latin Studies in Honour of A.H.M. Kessels*, edited by A. Lardinois, M. van der Poel, and V. Hunink, 146–59. Leiden: Brill, 2006.
Harrison, G.W.M. ed. *Seneca in Performance*. London: Duckworth with the Classical Press of Wales, 2000.
Harrison, G.W.M. ed. *Brill's Companion to Roman Tragedy*. Leiden: Brill, 2015.
Harrison, S.J. *Framing the Ass: Literary Texture in Apuleius' Metamorphoses*. Oxford: Oxford University Press, 2013.
Harrison, T. *The emptiness of Asia: Aeschylus' Persians and the history of the fifth century*. London: Duckworth, 2000.
Harvey, D. "Phrynichos and his Muses." In *The Rivals of Aristophanes: Studies in Athenian Old Comedy*, edited by D. Harvey and J. Wilkins, 91–134. London: Duckworth, 2000.
Heath, M. "Should There Have Been a *Polis* in the *Poetics*?" *The Classical Quarterly* 59 (2009): 389–402.
Henrichs, A. "The Last of the Detractors: Friedrich Nietzsche's Condemnation of Euripides." *Greek, Roman, and Byzantine Studies* 27 (1986): 369–97.
Henrichs, A. "The tomb of Aias and the prospect of hero cult in Sophokles." *Classical Antiquity* 12 (1993): 165–80.
Henrichs, A. "Anonymity and Polarity: Unknown Gods and Nameless Altars at the Areopagus." *Illinois Classical Studies* 19 (1994): 27–58.
Henrichs, A. "'Why Should I Dance?': Choral Self-Referentiality in Greek Tragedy." *Arion* 3, no. 1 (1994–5): 56–111.
Herrington, C.J. "Aeschylus in Sicily." *Journal of Hellenic Studies* 87 (1967): 74–85.
Hill, T. *Ambitiosa Mors: Suicide and Self in Roman Thought and Culture*. London: Routledge, 2004.
Hine, H.M. ed. *L. Annaei Senecae Naturalium Quaestionum Libros*. Stuttgart: Teubner, 1996.
Hine, H.M. trans. *Natural Questions*. Chicago: University of Chicago Press, 2010.
Holford-Strevens, L. "Sophocles at Rome." In Griffin, *Sophocles revisited*, 219–59.
Holmes, B. *Gender: Antiquity and its Legacy*. Oxford: Oxford University Press, 2012.
Holst-Warhaft, G. *Dangerous Voices: Women's Laments and Greek Literature*. London and New York: Routledge, 1992.
Hubbard, T.K. "Pindar and Sophocles: Ajax as Epinician Hero." *Echos du Monde Classique* 19, no. 3 (2000): 315–32.

Hübner, S. and Ratzen, D. "Fatherless Antiquity? Perspectives on 'Fatherlessness' in the Ancient Mediterranean." In *Growing up Fatherless in Antiquity*, edited by S. Hübner and D. Ratzen, 3-26. Cambridge: Cambridge University Press, 2009.

Hübner, S. and Ratzen, D. eds. *Growing Up Fatherless in Antiquity*. Cambridge: Cambridge University Press, 1986.

Humphreys, S. *The Family, Women and Death: Comparative Studies*. 1983. Reprint, Ann Arbor: University of Michigan Press, 1993.

Hutchinson, G.O. *Greek to Latin: Frameworks and contexts for intertextuality*. Oxford: Oxford University Press, 2013.

Inwood, B. *Reading Seneca: Stoic Philosophy at Rome*. Oxford: Oxford University Press, 2005.

Irwin, E. *Solon and Early Greek Poetry: The Politics of Exhortation*. Cambridge: Cambridge University Press, 2005.

James, P. "Apuleius' Metamorphoses: A Hybrid Text?" In *A Companion to the Ancient Novel*, edited by E.P. Cueva and S.N. Byrne, 317–29. Chichester: Blackwell, 2014.

Jebb, R.C. *Sophocles: Plays, Ajax*. Edited by P.E. Easterling, with an introduction by P. Wilson. London: Bristol Classical Press, 2004.

Jocelyn, H.D. "Greek poetry in Cicero's prose writings." *Yale Classical Studies* 23 (1973): 61–111.

Jones, C.P. "Dinner Theater." In *Dining in a Classical Context*, edited by W.J. Slater, 185–98. Ann Arbor: University of Michigan Press, 1991.

Jones, C.P. "Greek Drama in the Roman Empire." In *Theater and Society in the Classical World*, edited by R. Scodel, 39–52. Ann Arbor: University of Michigan Press, 1993.

Jones, E. *The Origins of Shakespeare*. Oxford: Oxford University Press, 1977.

Kassel, R. and Austin, C. eds. *Poetae Comici Graeci Vol. 2*. Berlin: De Gruyter, 1991.

Kaster, R.A. "Controlling Reason: Declamation in Rhetorical Educations at Rome." In *Education in Greek and Roman Antiquity*, edited by Y. Lee Too, 317–37. Leiden: Brill, 2001.

Kaster, R.A. and Nussbaum, M.C. trans. *Anger, Mercy, Revenge*. Chicago: University of Chicago Press, 2010.

Katsouris, A.G. "Euripides' *Archelaos*: a reconsideration." In *Euripide e i papyri, atti del Convegno internazionale di studi, Firenze, 10–11 giugno 2004. Studi e testi di papirologia, n.7*, edited by G. Bastianini and A. Casanova, 205–26. Firenze: Istituto papirologico G. Vitelli, 2005.

Katz, M. "The Character of Tragedy: Women and the Greek Imagination." *Arethusa* 17 (1994): 81–109.

Keith, A.M. *Engendering Rome: Women in Latin Epic*. Cambridge: Cambridge University Press, 2000.

Kelly, A. "Aias in Athens: The Worlds of the Play and the Audience." *Quaderni Urbinati di Cultura Classica* 111 (2015): 61–92.

Klotz, A. ed. Scaenicorum Romanorum Fragmenta: I. Tragicroum Fragmenta. Adiuvantibus *Ottone Seel et Ludovico Voit*, Munich: R. Oldenbourg, 1953.

Knox, B. "Sophocles and the *Polis*." In *Sophocle: sept exposés suivis de discussions (Entretiens sur L'Antiquité classique 29)*, edited by J. de Romilly, 1–37. Genève: Fondation Hardt, 1983.

Kohn, T. *The Dramaturgy of Senecan Tragedy*. Ann Arbor: University of Michigan Press, 2013.

Kotlińska-Toma, A. *Hellenistic Tragedy: Texts, Translations and a Critical Survey*. London: Bloomsbury, 2015.

Kovaks, D. ed. and trans. *Euripides: Children of Heracles, Hippolytus, Andromache, Hecuba*. Cambridge, MA: Harvard University Press, 1995.

Kowalzig, B. "Changing Choral Worlds: Song-Dance and Society in Athens and Beyond." In *Music and the Muses: The Culture of "Mousikē" in the Classical Athenian City*, edited by Penelope Murray and Peter Wilson, 39–65. Oxford: Oxford University Press, 2004.

Kowalzig, B. "The Aetiology of Empire? Hero-Cult and Athenian Tragedy." In *Greek Drama III: Essays in Honour of Kevin Lee*, edited by J. Davidson, F. Muecke, and P. Wilson, 79–98. London: Institute of Classical Studies, 2006.

Lacey, W. *The Family in Classical Greece*. Ithaca: Cornell University Press, 1968.

Lada-Richards, I. *Silent Eloquence: Lucian and Pantomime Dancing*. London: Duckworth, 2007.

Laidlaw, W.A. "Cicero and the Stage." *Hermathena* 94 (1960): 56–66.

Lamari, A. ed. *Reperformances of Drama in the Fifth and Fourth Centuries BC: Authors and Contexts, Trends in Classics* 7.2. Berlin: De Gruyter, 2015.

Lamari, A. *Reperforming Greek Tragedy. Theater, Politics, and Cultural Mobility in the Fifth and Fourth Centuries BC, Trends in Classics* 52. Berlin: De Gruyter, 2017.

Lardinois, A. "The Polysemy of Gnomic Expressions and Ajax' Deception Speech." In *Sophocles and the Greek Language: Aspects of Diction, Syntax and Pragmatics*, edited by A. Rijksbaron and I. de Jong, 213–23. Leiden: Brill, 2006.

Lefèvre, E. "Die politische Bedeutung der römischen Tragödie und Senecas *Oedipus*." *Aufstieg und Niedergang der römischen Welt* II.32.2 (1985): 1242–62.

Lefèvre, E. "Die politisch-aitiologische Ideologie der Tragödien des Livius Andronicus." *Quaderni di Cultura e di Tradizione classica* 8 (1990): 9–19.

Lefkowitz, M. "Impiety and Atheism in Euripides' Dramas." *Classical Quarterly* 39 (1989): 70–82.

Lefkowitz, M. *The Lives of the Greek Poets*, 2nd edn. Baltimore: Johns Hopkins University Press, 2012.

Lefkowitz, M. *Euripides and the Gods*. Oxford: Oxford University Press, 2015.

Lefteratou, A. "Iphigenia Revisited: Heliodorus' *Aethiopica* and der Tod und das Madchen pattern." In *Intende, Lector – Echoes of Myth, Religion and ritual in the Ancient Novel*, edited by M.P. Futre Pinheiro, A. Bierl, and R. Beck, 200–22. Berlin: De Gruyter, 2013.

Le Guen, B. "Théâtre et cités à l'époque hellénistique." *Revue des Études Greques* 108, no. 1 (1995): 59–90.

Le Guen, B. ed. *De la scène aux gradins. Théâtre et représentations dramatiques après Alexandre le Grand (= Pallas 47)*. Toulouse: Presses Universitaires du Mirail, 1997.

Le Guen, B. *Les associations de Technites dionysiaques à l'époque hellénistique*. Nancy: Association pour la diffusion de la recherche sur l'antiquité, 2001.

Le Guen, B. "L'activité dramatique dans les îles grecques à l'époque hellénistique." In *Les îles de l'Égée dans l'Antiquité, Actes du colloque international (Bordeaux, 12/13 novembre 1999)*, edited by P. Brun, 261–98. Pessac: Revue des Études anciennes, 2001.

Le Guen, B. "Theatre, Religion and Politics at Alexander's Travelling Royal Court." In Csapo et al. *Greek Theatre in the Fourth Century BC*, 249–74.

Leo, F. *De Senecae Tragoediis observationes criticae*. Berlin: Weidmann, 1878.

Lesky, A. *Greek Tragic Poetry*, trans. M. Dillon. New Haven: Yale University Press, 1983.

Liapis, V. *A Commentary on the* Rhesus *Attributed to Euripides*. Oxford: Oxford University Press, 2012.

Lightfoot, J.L. "Nothing to do with the technītai of Dionysus?" In Easterling and Hall, *Greek and Roman Actors*, 209–24.

Littlewood, C. "Seneca's *Thyestes*: the tragedy with no women?" *Materiali e Discussioni* 38 (1997): 57–86.

Littlewood, C. *Self-Presentation and Illusion in Senecan Tragedy*. Oxford: Oxford University Press, 2004.

Littlewood, C. "Theater and Theatricality in Seneca's World." In Bartsch and Schiesaro, *The Cambridge Companion to Seneca*, 161–73.

Lloyd, M. *The Agon in Euripides*. Oxford: Clarendon Press, 1992.

Long, A. *Language and Thought in Sophocles: A Study of Abstract Nouns and Poetic Technique*. London: Athlone Press, 1968.

Loraux, N. *The Invention of Athens: The Funeral Oration and the Classical City*. Cambridge, MA: The MIT Press, 1986.

Loraux, N. *Mothers in Mourning*. Ithaca, NY: Cornell University Press, 1998.

Loraux, N. *The Mourning Voice: An Essay on Greek Tragedy*. Ithaca: Cornell University Press, 2002.

Lowe, N.J. *Comedy, Greece and Rome, New Surveys in the Classics* 37. Cambridge: Cambridge University Press, 2008.

Lundström, S. *Ein textkritisches Problem in den Tusculanen*. Uppsala: Almqvist & Wiksell International, 1982.

Luraghi, N. *Tirannidi arcaiche in Sicilia e Magna Grecia: da Panezio di Leontini alla caduta dei Dinomenidi*. Firenze: Olschki, 1994.

MacDowell, D. *The Law in Classical Athens*. Ithaca: Cornell University Press, 1978.

Macleod, C. "Thucydides and Tragedy." In *The Collected Essays of Colin Macleod*, edited by O. Taplin, 140–58. Oxford: Clarendon Press, 1997.

Maitland, J. "Dynasty and Family in the Athenian City: A View from Attic Tragedy." *Classical Quarterly* 42 (1992): 26–40.

Manuwald, G. ed. *Identität und Alterität in der frühömischen Tragödie*. Würzburg: Ergon Verlag, 2000.

Manuwald, G. *Fabulae praetextae: Spuren einer literarischen Gattung der Romer, Zetemata* 108. München: Beck, 2001.

Manuwald, G. "The Concepts of Tyranny in Seneca's *Thyestes* and in *Octavia*." *Prudentia* 35 (2003): 37–59

Manuwald, G. *Roman Republican Theatre*. Cambridge: Cambridge University Press, 2011.

Manuwald, G. and Frangoulidis, S. "Introduction: Roman Drama and its Contexts." In Fragoulidis, Harrison, and Manuwald, *Roman Drama and its Contexts*, 1–12.

Markantonatos, A. ed. *Brill's Companion to Sophocles*. Leiden: Brill, 2015.

Marshall, C.W. "Alcestis and the Problem of Prosatyric Drama." *The Classical Journal* 95 (2000): 229–38.

Marshall, C.W. *The Structure and Performance of Euripides' Helen*. Cambridge: Cambridge University Press, 2014.

Mason, H.J. "*Fabula Graecanica*: Apuleius and his Greek Sources." In *Aspects of Apuleius' Golden ass: a collection of original papers*, edited by B.L. Hijmans Jr. and R. Th. van der Paardt, 1–15. Groningen: Bouma's Boekhuis, 1978.

Mason, H.J. "The *Metamorphoses* of Apuleius and its Greek sources." In *Latin Fiction: the Latin Novel in Context*, edited by H. Hofmann, 103–12. London: Routledge, 1999.

Mastronarde, D. "The Optimistic Rationalist in Euripides: Theseus, Jocasta, Teiresias." In *Greek Tragedy and its Legacy: Essays Presented to D. J. Conacher*, edited by M. Cropp, E. Fantham, and S.E. Scully, 201–11. Calgary: The University of Calgary Press, 1986.

Mastronarde, D. ed. *Euripides'* Medea. Cambridge: Cambridge University Press, 2002.

Mastronarde, D. ed. *Euripides'* Phoenissae, *Cambridge Classical Texts and Commentaries 29*. Cambridge: Cambridge University Press, 1994.

Mastronarde, D. *The Art of Euripides: Dramatic Technique and Social Context*. Cambridge: Cambridge University Press, 2010.

May, R. *Apuleius and Drama: the Ass on Stage*. Oxford: Oxford University Press, 2006.

McClure, L. "Maternal Authority and Heroic Disgrace in Aeschylus's *Persae*." *Transactions of the American Philological Society* 136, no. 1 (2006): 71–97.

McCoskey, D. and Zakin, E. eds. *Bound by the City: Greek Tragedy, Sexual Difference, and the Formation of the Polis*. Albany: SUNY Press, 2009.

Meridor, R. "Aeschylus' *Agamemnon* 944–57: Why does Agamemnon give in?" *Classical Philology* 88 (1987):38–43.

Meyer, R. *Seneca: Phaedra*. London: Duckworth, 2002.

Michelakis, P. *Euripides: Iphigenia at Aulis*. London: Duckworth, 2006.

Mikalson, J. "Gods and heroes in Sophocles." In Markantonatos, *Companion to Sophocles*, 429–46.

Mills, S. "*Ektos sumphorās*: Tragic Athens." *Polis* 34 (2017): 208–25.

Mills, S. *Theseus, Tragedy and the Athenian Empire*. Oxford: Oxford University Press, 1997.

Moloney, E. "*Philippus in acie tutior quam in theatro fuit*... (Curtius 9.6.25): The Macedonian Kings and Greek Theatre." In Csapo et al., *Greek Theatre in the Fourth Century BC*, 231–482.

Moore. T. "Music in Roman Tragedy." In Frangoulidis, Harrison, and Manuwald, *Roman Drama and its Contexts*, 345–62.

Moretti, J-C. "The Evolution of Theatre Architecture Outside Athens in the Fourth Century." In Csapo et al., *Greek Theatre in the Fourth Century BC*, 107–37.

Morgan, J.R. "The story of Knemon in Aethiopica." *Journal of Hellenic Studies* 109 (1989): 99–113.

Morgan, J.R. and Harrison, S. "Intertextuality." In *The Cambridge Companion to Greek and Roman Novel*, edited by T. Whitmarsh, 218–36. Cambridge: Cambridge University Press, 2008.

Morgan, K. "A prolegomenon to performance in the West." In Bosher, *Theater outside Athens*, 35–55.

Morgan, K. *Pindar and the construction of Syracusan monarchy in the fifth century B.C.* Oxford: Oxford University Press, 2015.

Morgan, T. *Literate Education in the Hellenistic and Roman Worlds*. Cambridge: Cambridge University Press, 1998.

Morrison, A.D. *Performance and Audiences in Pindar's Sicilian Victory Odes*, BICS Supplement 95. London: Institute of Classical Studies, School of Advanced Study, University of London, 2007.

Moss, J. "What is Imitative Poetry and Why is it Bad?" In *The Cambridge Companion to Plato's Republic*, edited by G.R.F. Ferrari, 415–44. Cambridge: Cambridge University Press, 2007.

Mossman, J. "Tragedy and Epic in Plutarch's *Alexander*." *Journal of Hellenic Studies* 108 (1988): 83–93.

Mossman, J. "Tragedy and the Hero." In *A Companion to Plutarch*, edited by M. Beck, 437–48. Chichester: Wiley-Blackwell, 2014.

Most, G.W. "*Disiecti membra poetae*: The Rhetoric of Dismemberment in Neronian Poetry." In *Innovations of Antiquity*, edited by R. Hexter and D. Selden, 391–419. London/New York: Routledge, 1992.

Murnaghan, S. *Disguise and Recognition in the* Odyssey. Princeton: Princeton University Press, 1987.

Naiden, F. *Ancient Supplication*. Oxford: Oxford University Press, 2006.

Nehamas, A. *Virtues of Authenticity: Essays on Plato and Socrates*. Princeton: Princeton University Press, 1999.

Neils, J. and Oakley, J. eds. *Coming of Age in Ancient Greece: Images of Childhood from the Classical Past*. New Haven: Yale University Press, 2003.

Nervegna, S. "Performing Classics: The Tragic Canon in the Fourth Century and Beyond." In Csapo et al., *Greek Theatre in the Fourth Century BC*, 157–88.

Nevett, L. *House and Society in the Ancient Greek World*. Cambridge: Cambridge University Press, 1999.

Nicolet, C. *The World of the Citizen in Republican Rome*. Translated by P.S. Falla. Berkeley and Los Angeles: University of California Press, 1980.

Nightingale, A.W. *Genres in Dialogue: Plato and the Construct of Philosophy*. Cambridge: Cambridge University Press, 1995.

Nussbaum, M.C. *The Therapy of Desire: Theory and Practice in Hellenistic Ethics*. Martin Classical Lectures, new series, v. 2. Princeton: Princeton University Press, 1994.

Nussbaum, M. *The Fragility of Goodness: Luck and ethics in Greek tragedy and philosophy*. Cambridge: Cambridge University Press, 1986; reprint 2001.

Oakley, J. "Death and the Child." In Niels and Oakley, *Coming of Age*, 163–94.

Ober, J. and Strauss, B. "Drama, Political Rhetoric, and the Discourse of Athenian Democracy." In Winkler and Zeitlin, *Nothing to do with Dionysus?*, 237–70.

O'Connell, P.E. *The Rhetoric of Seeing in Attic Forensic Oratory*. Ashley and Peter Larkin Series in Greek and Roman Culture. Austin: University of Texas Press, 2017.

O'Kell, E. "*Hercules Furens* and Nero: The Didactic Purpose of Senecan Tragedy." In *Herakles and Hercules: Exploring a Graeco-Roman Divinity*, edited by H. Bowden and L. Rawlings, 185–204. Swansea: The Classical Press of Wales, 2005.

Ormand, K. *Exchange and the Maiden: Marriage in Sophoclean Tragedy*. Austin: University of Texas Press, 1999.

Ormand, K. "Oedipus the Queen: Cross-dressing without Drag." *Theatre Journal* 55 (2003): 1–28.

Ormand, K. "Electra in Exile." In *Bound by the City: Greek Tragedy, Sexual Difference, and the Formation of the Polis*, edited by D. McCoslkey and E. Zakin, 247–73. Albany: SUNY Press, 2009.

Ormand, K. ed. *A Companion to Sophocles*. Malden: Wiley-Blackwell, 2012.

Panayotakis, C. ed. *Decimus Laberius. The Fragments*. Cambridge: Cambridge University Press, 2010.

Papaioannou, S., Serafim, A., and da Vela, B. eds. *The Theatre of Justice, Aspects of Performance in Greco-Roman Oratory and Rhetoric*. Mnemosyne Supplements 403. Leiden: Brill, 2017.

Papastamati-von Moock, C. "The Theater of Dionysus Eleuthereus in Athens: New Data and Observations on its 'Lycurgan' Phase." In Csapo et al., *Greek Theatre in the Fourth Century BC*, 15–76.

Parker, H. "Sappho Schoolmistress." *Transactions of the American Philological Association* 123 (1993): 309–51.

Parker, H. "The Observed of All Observers: Spectacle, Applause, and Cultural Poetics in the Roman Theater Audience." In *The Art of Ancient Spectacle. Studies in the History of Art* 56, edited by B. Bergmann and C. Kondoleon, 163–79. New Haven and London: NGA and Yale University Press, 2000.

Parker, L.P.E. ed. *Euripides'* Alcestis. Oxford: Clarendon Press, 2007.

Parker, R. "Gods Cruel and Kind: Tragic and Civic Theology." In Pelling, *Greek Tragedy and the Historian*, 143–60.

Paton, W.R. ed. and trans. *The Greek Anthology, Books VII–VIII*. Cambridge, MA: Harvard University Press, 1917.
Patterson, C. "*Hai Attikai*: The Other Athenians." *Helios* 13 (1986): 49–67.
Patterson, C. "Those Athenian Bastards." *Classical Antiquity* 9 (1990): 40–73.
Patterson, C. *The Family in Greek History*. Cambridge, MA: Harvard University Press, 1998.
Patterson, C. "Marriage in Sophocles: A Problem for Social History." In Ormand, *A Companion to Sophocles*, 381–94.
Pelling, C. ed. *Greek Tragedy and the Historian*. Oxford: Clarendon Press, 1997.
Pelling, C. "Dionysiac Diagnostics: Some Hints of Dionysus in Plutarch's *Lives*." In *Plutarco, Dioniso y el vino*, edited by J.G. Montes, M. Sánchez, and R. J. Gallé, 359–68. Madrid: Ediciones Clásicas, 1999.
Pelling, C. *Literary Texts and the Greek Historian*. London and New York: Routledge, 2000.
Peponi, A.E. ed. *Performance and Culture in Plato's Laws*. Cambridge: Cambridge University Press, 2013.
Perris, S. "Is There a *Polis* in Euripides' *Medea*?" *Polis* 34 (2017): 318–35.
Picariello, D.K. and Saxonhouse, A.W. "Aeschylus and the binding of the tyrant." *Polis* 32 (2015): 271–96.
Pickard-Cambridge, A.W. *Dithyramb, Tragedy, and Comedy*, 2nd edn, rev. T.B.L. Webster. Oxford: Clarendon Press, 1962
Pickard-Cambridge, A.W. *The dramatic festivals of Athens*, 2nd edn. rev. J. Gould and D.M. Lewis. Oxford: Clarendon Press, 1988.
Pletcher, J. "Euripides in Heliodorus' *Aethiopiaka* 7–8." *Gronigen Colloquia on the Greek and Roman Novel* 9 (1998): 17–27.
Poe, J.P. "The Sinful Nature of the Protagonist of Seneca's *Oedipus*." In *Seneca Tragicus: Ramus Essays on Senecan Drama*, edited by A.J. Boyle, 140–48. Berwick: Aureal Publications, 1983.
Pöhlmann, E. and West, M.L. *Documents of Ancient Greek Music*. Oxford: Clarendon Press, 2001.
Poli-Palladini, L. "Some Reflections on Aeschylus' *Aetnae(ae)*." *Rheinisches Museum für Philologie, Neue Folge* 144, no. 3–4 (2001): 287–325.
Poli-Palladini, L. *Aeschylus at Gela: An Integrated Approach*. Alessandria: Edizioni dell'Orso, 2013.
Pollard, T. *Greek Tragic Women on Shakespearean Stages*. Oxford: Oxford University Press, 2017.
Pomeroy, S. *Families in Classical and Hellenistic Greece: Representations and Realities*. Oxford: Clarendon Press, 1997.
Powell, A. ed. *Euripides, Women, and Sexuality*. London and New York: Routledge, 1990.
Power, T. "Sophocles and Music." In Markantonatos, *Companion to Sophocles*, 283–304.
Prauscello, L. *Performing Citizenship in Plato's Laws*. Cambridge: Cambridge University Press, 2014.
Pucci, P. *Euripides' Revolution under Cover: An Essay*. Ithaca: Cornell University Press, 2016.
Rabinowitz, N.S. *Anxiety Veiled: Euripides and the Traffic in Women*. Ithaca: Cornell University Press, 1993.
Rackham, H. *Cicero, On Ends*. Cambridge, MA: Harvard University Press, 1914.
Rawson, E. "Family and Fatherland in Euripides' *Phoenissae*." *Greek, Roman, and Byzantine Studies* 11, no. 2 (1970): 109–27.
Rawson, E. "Theatrical Life in Republican Rome and Italy." *Papers of the British School at Rome* 53 (1985): 97–113.

Redford, J. *Nature and Culture in the Iliad: The tragedy of Hector*. Durham: Duke University Press, 1994.

Rehm, R. "Aeschylus in Syracuse: The Commerce of Tragedy and Politics." In *Syracuse, The fairest Greek city: Ancient art from the Museo Archeologico Regionale "Paolo Orsi"*, edited by B. Daix Wescoat, 31–4. Rome: De Luca, 1989.

Rehm, R. *Greek Tragic Theatre*. London and New York: Routledge, 1992.

Rehm, R. *Marriage to Death: The Conflation of Wedding and Funeral Rituals in Greek Tragedy*. Princeton: Princeton University Press, 1994.

Revermann, M. "Euripides, Tragedy and Macedon: Some Conditions of Reception." In *Euripides and Tragic Theatre in the Late Fifth Century, ICS 24-5*, edited by M. Cropp, K. Lee, and D. Sansone, 451–67. Champaign, IL: Stipes Publishing, 1999–2000.

Revermann, M. "The Competence of Theatre Audiences in Fifth- and Fourth-Century Athens." *Journal of Hellenic Studies* 126 (2006): 99–124.

Revermann, M. "Situating the gaze of the recipient(s): theatre-related vase paintings and their contexts of reception." In Gildenhard and Revermann, *Beyond the Fifth Century*, 69–97.

Revermann, M. ed. *The Cambridge Companion to Greek Comedy*. Cambridge: Cambridge University Press, 2014.

Reynolds, L.D. ed. *L. Annaei Senecae Ad Lucilium Epistulae Morales*, 2 vols. Oxford: Clarendon Press, 1966.

Reynolds, L.D. ed. *L. Annaei Senecae Dialogorum Libri Duodecim*. Oxford: Clarendon Press, 1977.

Rhodes, P.J. "Nothing to do with democracy: Athenian drama and the polis." *Journal of Hellenic Studies* 123 (2003) 104–19.

Rose, P.W. "Historicizing Sophocles' *Ajax*." In Goff, *History, Tragedy, Theory*, 59–90.

Roselli, D.K. *Theater of the people: spectators and society in ancient Athens*. Austin: University of Texas Press, 2011.

Rosenbloom, D. "Shouting 'fire' in a crowded theater: Phrynichos's *Capture of Miletos* and the politics of fear in early Attic tragedy." *Philologus* 137 (1993): 159–96.

Rozik, E. *The Roots of Theatre: Rethinking Ritual and Other Theories of Origin*. Iowa City: Iowa University Press, 2002.

Rutherford, R.B. *Greek Tragic Style: Form, Language, and Interpretation*. Cambridge: Cambridge University Press, 2012.

Sansone, D. *Greek Drama and the Invention of Rhetoric*. Malden MA: Wiley-Blackwell, 2012.

Schaps, D. *Economic Rights of Women in Ancient Greece*. Edinburgh: Edinburgh University Press, 1979.

Schaps, D. "What was Free about a Free Athenian Woman." *Transactions of the American Philological Association* 128 (1998): 161–88.

Schierl, P. "Roman Tragedy – Ciceronian Tragedy? Cicero's Influence on Our Perception of Republican Tragedy." In Harrison, *Companion to Roman Tragedy*, 45–62.

Schiesaro, A. "La tragedia di Psiche: note ad Apuleio, *Met.* IV 28–35." *Maia* 40 (1988): 141–50.

Schiesaro, A. "Seneca's *Thyestes* and the Morality of Tragic *Furor*." In *Reflections of Nero: Culture, History & Representation*, edited by J. Elsner and J. Masters, 196–210. London: Duckworth, 1994.

Schiesaro, A. "Passion, Reason and Knowledge in Seneca's Tragedies." In *The Passions in Roman Thought and Literature*, edited by S.M. Braund and C. Gill, 89–111. Cambridge: Cambridge University Press, 1997.

Schiesaro, A. *The Passions in Play: Thyestes and the Dynamics of Senecan Drama*. Cambridge: Cambridge University Press, 2003.

Schiesaro, A. "Roman Tragedy." In *A Companion to Tragedy*, edited by R. Bushnell, 269–286. Malden, MA: Blackwell Publishing, 2005.

Schmidt, M. "Dionysien." *Antike Kunst* 10 (1967): 70–81.

Schwazer, O. "Senecas *Thyestes* und der 'Fürstenspiegel' für Nero." *Mnemosyne* 69 (2016): 1008–28.

Scodel, R. "The Poet's Career, the Rise of Tragedy, and Athenian Cultural Hegemony." In *Gab es das Griechische Wunder?: Griechenland zwischen dem Ende des 6. und der Mitte des 5. Jahrhunderts v. Chr. ; Tagungsbeiträge des 16. Fachsymposiums der Alexander von Humboldt-Stiftung, veranstaltet vom 5. bis 9. April 1999 in Freiburg im Breisgau*, edited by D. Papenfuss and V.M. Strocka, 215–228. Mainz: P. von Zabern, 2001.

Scodel, R. "Aetiology, Autochthony, and Athenian Identity in *Ajax* and *Oedipus Coloneus*." *Bulletin of the Institute of Classical Studies*, Supplement 87 (2006): 65–78.

Scodel, R. "Lycurgus and the State Text of Tragedy." In *Politics of Orality (Orality and Literacy in Ancient Greece 6)*, Mnemosyne Supplements 280, edited by C. Cooper, 129–52. Leiden: Brill, 2006.

Scullion, S. "Tradition and Invention in Euripidean Aitiology." *Illinois Classical Studies* 24–5 (1999–2000): 217–33.

Scullion, S. "'Nothing to do with Dionysos': Tragedy Misconceived as Ritual." *Classical Quarterly* 52, no. 1 (2002): 102–37.

Scullion, S. "Tragedy and Religion: The Problem of Origins." In *A Companion to Greek Tragedy*, edited by J. Gregory, 21–37. Malden, MA/Oxford: Blackwell Publishing, 2005.

Seaford, R. "Wedding Ritual and Textual Criticism in Sophocles' *Women of Trachis*." *Hermes* 114 (1986): 58–9.

Seaford, R. "The Tragic Wedding." *Journal of Hellenic Studies* 107 (1987): 106–30.

Seaford, R. "The Structural Problems of Marriage in Euripides." In Powell, *Euripides, Women and Sexuality*, 151–76.

Seaford, R. *Reciprocity and Ritual: Homer and Tragedy in the Developing City-State*. Oxford: Clarendon Press, 1994.

Seaford, R. "Historicizing tragic ambivalence: the vote of Athena." In Goff, *History, Tragedy, Theory*, 202–22.

Seaford, R. "The social function of Attic tragedy: a response to Jasper Griffin." *Classical Quarterly*, 50 (2000): 30–44.

Seaford, R. "Aitiologies of Cult in Euripides: A Response to Scott Scullion." In *The Play of Texts and Fragments: Essays in Honour of Martin Cropp*, edited by J.R. Cousland and J.R. Hume, 221–34. Leiden: Brill, 2009.

Segal, C. *Sophocles' Tragic World: Divinity, Nature, Society*. Cambridge, MA: Harvard University Press, 1995.

Segal, E. "'The Comic Catastrophe': An Essay on Euripidean Comedy." *Bulletin of the Institute of Classical Studies*, Supplement 66 (1995): 46–55.

Segre, M. ed. *Iscrizioni di Cos*, 2 vols. Roma: L'Erma di Bretschneider, 1993.

Seminara, A.M. "Eschilo tra democrazia e tirannide: dai *Persiani* alle *Etnee*." *Sileno* 35 (2009): 69–86.

Sewell-Rutter, N. *Guilt by Descent: Moral Inheritance and Decision Making in Greek Tragedy*. Oxford: Oxford University Press, 2007.

Shaw, C.A. *Satyric Play: The Evolution of Greek Comedy and Satyr Drama*. Oxford: Oxford University Press, 2014.

Shelton, J-A. "The Spectacle of Death in Seneca's *Troades*." In Harrison, *Seneca in Performance*, 87–118.

Sherwin-White, S.M. *Ancient Cos: An historical study from the Dorian settlement to the Imperial Period*. Göttingen: Vandenhoeck & Ruprecht, 1978.
Sifakis, G.M. *Studies in the History of Hellenistic Drama*. London: The Athlone Press, 1967.
Sifakis, G.M. "The Misunderstanding of Opsis in Aristotle's Poetics." In *Performance in Greek and Roman Theatre*. Mnemosyne Supplements 353, edited by G. Harrison and V. Liapis, 45–61. Leiden: Brill, 2013.
Silk, M. ed. *Tragedy and the Tragic: Greek Theatre and Beyond*. Oxford: Oxford University Press, 1996.
Silk, M. *Aristophanes and the Definition of Comedy*. Oxford: Oxford University Press, 2002.
Silk, M. and Stern, J.P. *Nietzsche on Tragedy*. Cambridge: Cambridge University Press, 1981.
Slater, N.W. "Nothing to Do with Satyrs? *Alcestis* and the Concept of Prosatyric Drama." In *Satyr Drama: Tragedy at Play*, edited by G.W.M. Harrison, 83–101. Swansea: The Classical Press of Wales, 2005.
Slater, W.J. "The Theatricality of Justice." *Classical Bulletin* 71 (1995): 143–57.
Smith, D.G. "Sicily and the identities of Xuthus: Stesichorus, Aeschylus' Aetnaeae, and Euripides' Ion." In Bosher, *Theater outside Athens*, 112–36.
Solmsen, F. "Onoma and ΠΠΑΛΜΑ in Euripides' *Helen*." *The Classical Review* 48, no. 4 (1934): 119–21.
Sommerstein, A. "Orestes' Trial and Athenian Homicide Procedure." In *Law and Drama in Ancient Greece*, edited by E. Harris and D. Leão, 25–38. London: Duckworth, 2010.
Sourvinou-Inwood, C. *Tragedy and Athenian Religion*. Lanham: Lexington Books, 2003.
Spahlinger, L. *Tulliana simplicitas: zu Form und Funktion des Zitats in den philosophischen Dialogen Ciceros*. Göttingen: Vandenhoeck & Ruprecht, 2005.
Star, C. "Commanding *Constantia* in Senecan Tragedy." *Transactions of the American Philological Association* 136 (2006): 207–44.
Star, C. "Roman Tragedy and Philosophy." In Harrison, *Companion to Roman Tragedy*, edited 238–59.
Staley, G.A. *Seneca and the Idea of Tragedy*. New York: Oxford University Press, 2010.
Stehle, E. "Prayer and Curse in Aeschylus' *Seven Against Thebes*." *Classical Philology* 100, no. 2 (2005): 101–22.
Stewart, E. *Greek Tragedy on the Move: The Birth of a Panhellenic Art Form c. 500–300 B.C.* Oxford: Oxford University Press, 2017.
Stinton, T.W. "'Si Credere Dignum Est': Some Expressions of Disbelief in Euripides and Others." *Proceedings of the Cambridge Philological Society* 22 (1976): 60–89.
Strauss, B. *Fathers and Sons in Athens: Ideology and Society in the Era of the Peloponnesian War*. London: Routledge, 1993.
Sutton, D.F. *Seneca on Stage*. Leiden: Brill, 1986.
Swift, L. *The Hidden Chorus: Echoes of Genre in Tragic Lyric*. Oxford: Oxford University Press, 2010.
Tan, J. "The Ambitions of Scipio Nasica and the Destruction of the Stone Theatre." *Antichthon* 50 (2016): 70–9.
Taplin, O. *The Stagecraft of Aeschylus: the dramatic use of exits and entrances in Greek tragedy*, Oxford: Clarendon Press, 1977.
Taplin, O. "Fifth-century Tragedy and Comedy: A *synkrisis*." *Journal of Hellenic Studies* 106 (1986): 163–74.
Taplin, O. *Comic Angels: and other approaches to Greek drama through vase-paintings*. Oxford: Clarendon Press, 1993.

Taplin, O. "Spreading the word through performance." In Goldhill and Osborne, *Performance Culture*, 33–57.
Taplin, O. "Aeschylus' *Persai*—The Entry of Tragedy into the Celebration Culture of the 470s?" in Cairns and Liapis, *Dionysalexandros*, 1–10.
Taplin, O. *Pots and Plays: Interactions between Tragedy and Greek Vase-Painting of the Fourth Century B.C.* Los Angeles: Getty Publications, 2007.
Taplin, O. "How was Athenian tragedy played in the Greek West?" In Bosher, *Theater outside Athens*, 226–46.
Taplin, O. "How Pots and Papyri Might Prompt a Re-Evaluation of Fourth-Century Tragedy." In Csapo et al. *Greek Theatre in the Fourth Century BC*, 141–55.
Tarrant, R.J. ed. *Seneca's Thyestes (American Philological Association Textbook Series)*. Atlanta: Scholar's Press, 1985
Tatum, J. "The Tales in Apuleius' *Metamorphoses*." In *Oxford Readings in The Roman Novel*, edited by S.J. Harrison, 157–94. Oxford: Oxford University Press, 1999.
Taylor, C.C.W. and Lee, M. "The Sophists." In *The Stanford Encyclopedia of Philosophy*, edited by E.N. Zalta, 2016. Available online: https://plato.stanford.edu/archives/win2016/entries/sophists/
Thompson, W. "The Marriage of First Cousins in Athenian Society." *Phoenix* 21 (1967): 273–282.
Torrance, I. "Euripides' *IT* 72–5 and a *Skene* of Slaughter." *Hermes* 137 (2009): 23–7.
Torrance, I. *Metapoetry in Euripides*. Oxford: Oxford University Press, 2013.
Torrance, I. "The 'Sophoclean' Oath." In Torrance and Sommerstein, *Oaths and Swearing*, 86–111.
Torrance, I. "The tongue and the mind: responses to Euripides, *Hippolytus* 612." In Torrance and Sommerstein, *Oaths and Swearing*, 289–94.
Torrance, I. "Distorted Oaths in Aeschylus." *Illinois Classical Studies* 40, no. 2 (2015): 281–95.
Torrance, I. *Euripides*, London: I.B. Tauris, 2018.
Torrance, I. and Sommerstein, A. eds. *Oaths and Swearing in Ancient Greece*. Berlin: De Gruyter, 2014.
Trinacty, C. "Senecan Tragedy." In Bartsch and Schiesaro, *The Cambridge Companion to Seneca*, 29–40.
Vahtikari, V. *Tragedy Performances Outside Athens in the Late Fifth and the Fourth Centuries BC, Papers and Monographs of the Finnish Institute at Athens 20*. Helsinki: Suomen Ateenan-Instituutin säätiö (Foundation of the Finnish Institute at Athens), 2014.
Vernant, J.P. "The Historical Moment of Tragedy in Greece: Some of the Social and Psychological Conditions." In *Myth and Tragedy in Ancient Greece*, trans. J. Lloyd, edited by J.P. Vernant and P. Vidal-Naquet, 23–8. New York: Zone, 1988.
Vernant, J.P. *Myth and Society in Ancient Greece*, trans. J. Lloyd. The Harvester Press Limited, 1980; Third Printing, New York: Zone Books, 1996.
Verrall, A. *Euripides the Rationalist: A Study in the History of Art and Religion*. Cambridge: Cambridge University Press, 1895.
Versenyi, L. "Protagoras' Man-Measure Fragment." *The American Journal of Philology* 83, no. 2 (1962): 178–84.
Vickers, M. *Sophocles and Alcibiades*. Ithaca: Cornell University Press, 2008.
Villacèque, N. *Spectateurs de paroles! Délibération démocratique et théâtre à Athènes à l'époque classique*. Rennes: Presses Universitaires de Rennes, 2013.
Visvardi, E. *Emotion in Action: Thucydides and the Tragic Chorus*. Mnemosyne Supplements 377. Leiden: Brill, 2015.

Volonaki, E. "Euripides' *Erectheus* in Lycurgus' *Against Leocrates*." In Fountoulakis, Markantonatos, and Vasilaros, *Theater World*, 251–68.

Wallace, R.W. and Harris, E.M. eds. *Transitions to Empire: Essays in Greco-Roman History, 360–146 BC in honor of E. Badian*. Norman, OK: University of Oklahoma Press, 1996.

Walters, J. "Invading the Roman Body: Manliness and Impenetrability in Roman Thought." In *Roman Sexualities*, edited by J.P. Hallett and M. Skinner, 29–44. Princeton: Princeton University Press, 1997.

Webb, R. *Demons and Dancers: Performance in Late Antiquity*. Cambridge, MA: Harvard University Press, 2008.

Weber, E. "Die altere Tragödie in Rom und die Legende von der trojanischen Abstammung." In Manuwald, *Identität und Alterität*, 135–41.

Weiss, N. "Noise, Music, Speech: The Representation of Lament in Greek Tragedy." *American Journal of Philology* 138 (2017): 243–66.

Weiss, N. *The Music of Tragedy: Performance and Imagination in Euripidean Theater*. Berkeley: University of California Press, 2018.

Weiss, N. "Generic Hybridity in Athenian Tragedy." In *The Genres of Archaic and Classical Greek Poetry*, edited by M. Foster, L. Kurke, and N. Weiss. Leiden: Brill, forthcoming.

Wellenbach, M.C. "The Iconography of Dionysiac Choroi: Dithyramb, Tragedy, and the Basel Krater." *Greek, Roman, and Byzantine Studies* 55 (2015): 72–103.

Wenkebach, E. ed. *In Hippocratis Epidemiarum librum III commentaria III: (Corpus Medicorum Graecroum 10.2.1)*. Leipzig: Teubner, 1936.

West, M.L. "The Early Chronology of Attic Tragedy." *The Classical Quarterly* 39, no. 1 (1989): 251–4.

West, M.L. *Studies in Aeschylus*. Stuttgart: Teubner, 1990.

West, S. "The *Antigone* and Herodotus Book 3." In Griffin, *Sophocles Revisited*, 109–36.

Widzisz, M. *Chronos on the Threshold: Time, Ritual, and Agency in the* Oresteia. Lanham: Lexington Books, 2012.

Wiedemann, T. *Emperors and Gladiators*. London and New York: Routledge, 1992.

Wiles, D. *Tragedy in Athens: performance space and theatrical meaning*. Cambridge: Cambridge University Press, 1997.

Wilkins, J. "The State and the Individual: Euripides' Plays of Voluntary Self-Sacrifice." In Powell, *Euripides, Women, Sexuality*, 177–94.

Williams, C.A. *Roman Homosexuality*, 2nd edn. Oxford: Oxford University Press, 2010.

Willis, C. "Conceptions of Language and Reality in Euripides' *Helen*." *Eras Journal* 5 (2003). Available online: http://artsonline.monash.edu.au/eras/1129-2/

Wilson, E. *Mocked with Death: Tragic overliving from Sophocles to Milton*. Baltimore: Johns Hopkins University Press, 2004.

Wilson, E. trans. *Seneca: Six Tragedies*. Oxford: Oxford University Press, 2010.

Wilson, E. "Sophocles and Philosophy." In Markantonatos, *Companion to Sophocles*, 537–62.

Wilson, E., *The Greatest Empire: A life of Seneca*. Oxford University Press 2014.

Wilson, P. "The *Aulos* in Athens." In Goldhill and Osborne, *Performance Culture*, 58–95.

Wilson, P. *The Athenian Institution of the Khoregia: The Chorus, the City and the Stage*. Cambridge: Cambridge University Press, 2000.

Wilson, P. "The Musicians Among the Actors." In Easterling and Hall, *Greek and Roman Actors*, 39–68.

Wilson, P. "Sicilian Choruses." In Wilson, *Theatre and Festivals*, 351–77.

Wilson, P. ed. *The Greek Theatre and Festivals, Documentary Studies*. Oxford: Oxford University Press, 2007.

Wilson, P. "Thamyris the Thracian: The Archetypal Wandering Poet?" In *Wandering Poets in Ancient Greek Culture*, edited by R. Hunter and I. Rutherford, 46–79. Cambridge: Cambridge University Press, 2009.

Winkler, J.J. *The Constraints of Desire: The Anthropology of Sex and Gender in Ancient Greece*. New York: Routledge, 1990.

Winkler, J.J. and Zeitlin, F.I. eds. *Nothing to Do with Dionysus? Athenian Drama in its Social Context*. Princeton: Princeton University Press, 1990.

Wohl, V. *Intimate Commerce: Exchange, Gender, and Subjectivity in Greek Tragedy*. Austin: University of Texas Press, 1998.

Wohl, V. *Law's Cosmos: Juridical Discourse in Athenian Forensic Oratory*. Cambridge: Cambridge University Press, 2010.

Wohl, V. *Euripides and the Politics of Form*. Princeton: Princeton University Press, 2015.

Wolff, H.J. "Marriage Law and Family Organization in Ancient Athens: A Study of the Interrelation of Public and Private Law in the Greek City." *Traditio* 2 (1944): 48–53.

Woodruff, P. "Didymus on Protagoras and the Protagoreans." *Journal of the History of Philosophy* 23, no.4 (1985): 483–97.

Wray, D. "Seneca and Tragedy's Reason." In Bartsch and Wray, *Seneca and the Self*, 236–54.

Wright, F.W. *Cicero and the Theater*. Northampton, MA: Smith College Classical Studies 11, 1931.

Wright, M. *Euripides' Escape-Tragedies: A Study of Helen, Andromeda, and Iphigenia among the Taurians*. Oxford: Oxford University Press, 2005.

Wright, M. *The Lost Plays of Greek Tragedy, vol. 1: Neglected Authors*. London: Bloomsbury, 2016.

Xanthakis-Karamanos, G. *Studies in Fourth-century Tragedy*. Athens: Ακαδημία Αθηνών, 1980.

Zanobi, A. "The Influence of Pantomime on Seneca's Tragedies." In Hall and Wyles, *New Directions in Ancient Pantomime*, 227–57.

Zanobi, A. *Seneca's Tragedies and the Aesthetics of Pantomime*. London: Bloomsbury, 2014.

Zeitlin, F.I. "The Motif of Corrupted Sacrifice in Aeschylus' *Oresteia*." *Transactions of the American Philological Association* 96 (1965): 463–508.

Zeitlin, F.I. "Postscript to Sacrificial Imagery in the *Oresteia* (*Ag.* 1235–37)." *Transactions of the American Philological Association* 97 (1966): 645–53.

Zeitlin, F.I. "The Argive Festival of Hera and Euripides' *Electra*." *Transactions of the American Philological Association* 101 (1970): 648–50.

Zeitlin, F.I. "Thebes: Theater of Self and Society in Athenian Drama." In Winkler and Zeitlin, *Nothing to do with Dionysus?*, 130–67.

Zeitlin, F.I. "The Politics of Eros in the Danaid Trilogy of Aeschylus." In *Innovations of Antiquity*, edited by R. Hexter and D. Selden, 203–40. New York: Routledge, 1992.

Zeitlin, F.I. "Playing the Other: Theater, Theatricality, and the Feminine in Greek Drama." In Winkler and Zeitlin, *Nothing to do with Dionysos?*, 63–96.

Zeitlin, F.I. *Playing the Other: Gender and Society in Classical Greek Literature*. Chicago: Chicago University Press, 1995.

Zetzel, J. "The Influence of Cicero on Ennius." In *Ennius Perennis: The Annals and Beyond*, edited by W. Fitzgerald and E. Gowers, 1–16. Cambridge: Cambridge University Press, 2000.

Zimmermann, B. "Seneca and Pantomime." In Hall and Wyles, *New Directions in Ancient Pantomime*, 218–27.

Zimmermann, M. ed. *Apuleius Madaurensis*, Metamorphoses: *Book X*. Groningen: Egbert Forsten, 2000.

Zwierlein, O. ed. *L. Annaei Senecae Tragoediae; Incertorum Auctorum Hercules (Oetaeus), Octavia*. Oxford: Clarendon Press, 1986.

Zwierlein, O. *Senecas* Phaedra *und ihre Vorbilder*. Stuttgart: Franz Steiner Verlag, 1987.

INDEX

Page numbers in **bold** refer to figures.

Accius, 111–12
Achilles, 3, **105**
actors, 18, 55–6, **56**, 60, 103, 110,
    164–5 n.5
Aeschines, 54
Aeschylus, 14, 18, 24, 35–6, 54, 90
    choruses, 10
    extant plays, 2, 17, 149 n.2
    language, 10
    number of plays, 151 n.1
    in Sicily, 36–7
    see also individual works
Aesopus, 60
Aethiopica (Heliodorus), 47–8
aetiology, 89
Aetnaeans, The (Aeschylus), 29
Against Leocrates (Lycurgus), 54
Against Timarchos (Aeschylus), 145
Agamemnon, 7, 10, 11, 27, 51, 85, 88, 92,
    112, 114, 117, 122, 126, 130,
    135–6
Agamemnon (Aeschylus), 12, 86, 102, 135–6
Agamemnon (Seneca), 96, 97–9
Agathon, 2, 7
Agen (Python of Catana), 30
agnothesia, 41
agônothetês, 58
Ai Khanoum, 39
Ajax, **105**, **122**, 183 n.45
Ajax (Sophocles), 11, 23, 83, 89, 104, 120–2
Alcestis (Euripides), 26, 86, 120, 128
Alcibiades, 24
Alcmaeon, 129
Alcmene, **88**
Alexander the Great, 39
    successors, 40
    theatrical activities, 39–40, 57
Alexiou, M., 139
anachronism, politics of, 104–9
Anaximander of Miletus, 7
Andromache (Euripides), 87, 125–6

Andújar, R., 29
anger, 50–1, 68
Anthesteria festival, 84
Antigone (Sophocles), 6, 86, 91, 106, **107**
Antigonous, 43
Antiphon, 43
Antiphon 1, 138
Apollo, 90, 127
appropriation, politics of, 109–11
Apuleius, *Metamorphoses*, 47–8
Archelaus, 37–8, 56
Archelaus (Euripides), 38–9
aristocrats, curtailment of, 117–18
Aristophanes, 6
    Birds, 27
    Clouds, 17
    Frogs, 17, 27, 28, 51, 103
Aristotle, 13, 33, 37, 65
    on Euripides, 1–2, 19, 20, 95
    limitations, 9, 19–20
    Nichomachean Ethics, 9
    on sexual desire, 185 n.2
    on tragedy, 8–10, 18–19, 26–7, 54–5, 117,
        129
    see also Poetics (Aristotle)
Arrian, 39
Artavasdes II of Armenia, 29
Artemis, 27
Athenaeus, 65
Athenocentrism, 29
Athenodorus, 57
Athens, 2, 11, 17, 23–6, 41, 103–4
    community life, 52–3
    cultural industry, 53–4
    democracy, 49–51
    fourth century, 52–6
    kings, 106–7
    Lycurgan era, 53–4
Atreus, 114–16
audience, 49–50, 58–9
    responses, 1–2, 104

audience experience, 20
augury, 83
Augustus, 169 n.105
autarkeia, 13
authoritative voice, 101
autocracies, fifth-century, 35–40
autonomy, 78, 80

Bacchae (Euripides), 12, 22, 83, 89–90, 91, 128, 144–5, 158 n.34
Bacchus, 95
Baertschi, Annette, 46
Bakhtin, M., 47
bigamy, 124–5
Birds (Aristophanes), 27
body, the, 13
Braden, G., 80
burial, 13
Busch, A., 13

Caligula, 62, 98, 113, 114
canon, 2
Cassandra, 27
catharsis, 8, 19
Cato, 74
character, 9
characters, 4, 6, 13, 19, 102
    female, 28, 50, 70, 135
Children of Heracles (Euripides), 86, 87, 89, 104, 106, 108–9
choral passages, 2
choral performance, 25
chorality, 49
chorēgia, 25, 41, 43, 49, 53
choreography, 23
choruses, 6, 18, 20, **25**, 30, 85
    Aeschylus, 10
    Aristotle on, 19, 55
    language, 10
    professionalization, 58
Cicero, 44, 46, 59, 61, 110, 111–12
    exile, 60
    philosophic dialogues, 46–7
    The Tusculan Disputations, 46
citizenship, 16, 118, 134
City Dionysia, 2, 24, 26, 49, 49–50, 52, 85, 103–4
civic role, 23–6, 35, 49–63
Clastidium (Naevius), 31
Claudius, 114, 146
Cleon, 51, 63
Clouds (Aristophanes), 17

Clytemnestra, 85, 87, 126, **127**, 129, 130, 135–6, 141, 143
Clytemnestra (Accius), 112
coins, **38**
collective memory, 53
comedy, 5, 6, 24, 27, 30, 105
Commodus, **97**
community building, 62–3
community life, impact on, 52–3
community relations, 55–6
competitions, 23–4, 41, 58, 85, 159 n.58
composition, 2
Consolation to Marcia (Seneca), 72, 76, 81
content, 1
context, 10–16
    politics of, 103–4
corporeal penetration, 70–1, 74–6, 131–2, 145–6
Cos, 41–3
costumes, 11, 20
Cowan, R., 14
Creon, 106, 107, 114–15
Critias, 91
cross-fertilization, with comedy, 27
cultural appropriation, 33
cultural differences, 66
cultural impact, 16
cultural industry, Athens, 53–4
curses, 92, 94
Cyclic poems, 3
cyclical family murder, 7
Cyclops (Euripides), 5, 26, 85

dance, 20, 21–2
De Beneficiis (Seneca), 96
dead, the, 98
death, 13–14
    representation of, 52
    self-willed, 74–6
debate, 102–3
Deianeira, 136, **137**
democracy, associations with, 24, 25, 40–3, 49–51, 53, 101, 103–4
developments, 28–33
dialogue, 2, 3, 18
diction, 9, 19
Dictyulci (Aeschylus), 5
Didymus the Blind, 65–6
Diodorus, 36
Diogenes Laertius, 65, 66
Diogenes of Apollonia, 94
Diomedes Grammaticus, 37

INDEX

Dionysius I of Syracuse, 37
Dionysos, festival of, 12, 14
Dionysus, 12, 20, 25–6, 26, 40, 84–5, **84**, 89–90, 144–5
Dioscorides, 23
dithyramb, 3, 24, 26, 84, 85
divine, 83
dowry, 119, 140, 182 n.24, 189 n.43

Ecbatana, 40
Edonoi (Aeschylus), **15**
education, 25, 46–7
 women, 133
Egypt, 43
Electra (Euripides), 2, 7, 12, 19, 86–7
Electra (Sophocles), 7, 27, 87, 92, 140, 141
elements, 3
emergence, 11
emotions, 1–2, 8
empathy, 52
endings, 2
engagement, 55
 modes of, 60, 61–3, **61**
Ennius, 44, 110
epic, 3, 101–3
epiklerate, 130
epikleros, 118, 140
epiphanies, 89–90
Epistle 66 (Seneca), 67–8, 69–70
Epistle 76 (Seneca), 69
Epistle 85 (Seneca), 68
Epistle 116 (Seneca), 76, 80–1
Erechtheus (Euripides), 86, 104, 106
Eros, **84**
ethical self, 67–81
 Medea, 71–3
 Thyestes, 73–4
Euctemon, 138
Eumenides (Aeschylus), 83
 and anger, 50–1, **50**
 Binding Song, 23, 28
 cycle of blood-feud, 109
 epiphanies, 90
 oaths, 92–3, 94
 representations of gods, 89
 statue of Athena, 87
Euripides, 4, 29, 54
 Aristotle on, 1–2, 19, 20, 95
 cross-fertilization with comedy, 27
 endings, 2
 epiphanies, 89
 extant plays, 2, 17

language, 10
in Macedon, 37–9
number of plays, 151 n.1
and philosophy, 65–7
representations of gods, 90–1
sacrificial practice, 86
see also individual works
extant plays, 2, 17, 33, 59, 65–7, 149 n.2
Ezekiel, 29

fabula Atellana, 31
fabula praetexta, 6, 31, 59–60, 83, 110, 167 n.81, 168 n.85
fabulae crepidatae, 3, 6
family and family structures, 15–16, 117, 130
 relationship between males within, 119–20, 120–2
 relationships within, 123–4, 124–9, **125**, **127**, 182 n.24
 tragic, 124–9, **125**, **127**
 women and, 118–19
fantasy, 105
female characters, 28, 50, 70, 135
femininity, 131
filial loyalty, 119–20
flexibility, 33
Foley, H., 139
form, politics of, 101–3
fortune, reversal of, 8
Foucault, M., 131
freedom, 70
Frogs (Aristophanes), 17, 27, 28, 51, 103
funding, 103
Furies, 92–3, 93–4

gender, 70, 131–5, 148
genres, 26–8
Gnaeus Naevius, 6
gods, the, 83, 89–92, 186n
Goldberg, S., 46
Golden Age, 53
Great Asclepieia, 42
Great Dionysia *see* City Dionysia

Halperin, D., 131
Harder, A., 38
Hecuba (Euripides), 12, 50, 51, 86
Helen (Euripides), 2, 27, 65–7, 87–8
Heliodorus, *Aethiopica*, 47–8
Hellenistic period, 29–30, 58–9
Hellenization, 29
Heracles (Euripides), 94, 102

Heracles/Hercules, 38, 39, 47, 97–8, **97**, 136, **137**, 144
Hercules Oetaeus (Seneca), 47, 97–8
Herodotus, 6, 36–7, 108, 149 n.2
hexameter poetry, 3
Hieron, 36, 43
Hippolytoi (Euripides), 48
Hippolytus (Euripides), 12, 38, 88, 90, 94–5, 103, 136–7, 146, 148, 188 n.27
historiography, 7
Homer, 3, 10, 106, 132
    Iliad, 2, 3, 117, 130
    Odyssey, 3, 117, 130
homoerotic desire, 132
homosexuality, 131
Horace, 29, 109
humor, 19
hypertextuality, 48

iambic trimeter, 2, 18
Ichneutae (Sophocles), 5
ideas, tragedy and, 7–10
Iliad (Homer), 2, 3, 117, 130
infanticide, 71–3
inserted tales, 48
interiority, politics of, 113–16
Inwood, B., 70
Io, 26
Ion (Euripides), 2, 89
Iphigenia, 85, **86**, 92
Iphigenia (Euripides), 48
Iphigenia among the Taurians (Euripides), 2, 19, 86, 87, 88, 90, 94
Iphigenia at Aulis (Euripides), 85, 92, 158 n.34
Isaeus, 138
isegoria, 102

Jason, 71–3
Jocasta, 13, 78, 95, 123–4, 128, 184 n.56

language, 10, 62, 143
Laws (Plato), 25, 52–3
Lefteratou, A., 48
Lenaia, 52
Lesbos, 43
Letters to Lucilius (Seneca), 113–14
Libation Bearers (Aeschylus), 19, 28, 88, 141
linguistic diversity, 10
Livius Andronicus, 5–6, 30, 31, 44, 59, 109–10, 110
Livy, 83

Lucretius, 74–6
Lycurgan era, 53–4
Lycurgus, **15**, 25, 53–4, 90
    Against Leocrates, 54
lyric poetry, 3, 19, 101–3, 132

Macedonia, 37–39, **38**, 56–7, 166 n.53
Macrobius, 36
maiden songs, 27
Marcus Marius, 112
marriage, 118–19, **119**, 130, **133**, 134, 140, 143, 181 n.18, 185 n.77
    to death, 85–6
masculinity, 4, 70, 131–2, 144–5, 145–6
masks, 11, **31**, **32**, **42**, **45**, **56**
mass entertainment, 58
May, R., 47
Medea, 12, 71–3, **71**, 141–3, **142**
Medea (Euripides), 38, 106, 124, **125**, 141–3
Medea (Seneca), 71–3, 81, 96, 96–7, 114–15
Meleager, 129
melody, 21
men, sexuality, 131–2, 144–5, 148, 150–1 n.31
messenger scenes, 46
messenger speeches, 18
Metamorphoses (Apuleius), 47–8
Metamorphoses (Ovid), 33
metaphor, 10
meter, 2, 3, 10, 18
military context, 14
Miller, Arthur, 2
mime, 5
Moloney, E., 38
mourning, 139–40, **139**
music, 19, 21–3, **32**
musical theater, tragedy as, 19–23, **21**, **22**
musical traditions, 27
Mytilene, 43

Naevius, 44, 95
    Clastidium, 31
narrative structures, 1
narrators, 101
natural law, 69, 70
Natural Questions (Seneca), 77–8, 79, 80, 81
nature, 69, 84, 96
negative dogmatism, 65–6
Neophron, 2
Neoptolemus, 57
Nero, 62, 114, 146
Nietzsche, F., 90–1

nondramatic lyric, 27
Nussbaum, M.C., 72

oaths, 92–4, 97
Octavia, 60, 98
Odysseus, 3, 5
Odyssey (Homer), 3, 117, 130
Oedipus, 79, 91, 127–8, 129, 184 n.56
Oedipus (Seneca), 76, 95
Oedipus at Colonus (Sophocles), 88, 89, 93–4, 120
Oedipus Rex (Sophocles), 127–8
Oedipus Tyrannos (Sophocles), 10, 12, 13, 83, 91, 150 n.17
On Anger (Seneca), 68, 75, 81, 114
On Clemency (De Clementia) (Seneca), 114
On the Happy Life (Seneca), 147
oracles, 91–2
oratory, 7
orchēstra, 22
Oresteia (Aeschylus), 7, 10, 85, 87, 92, 92–3, 126–7
Orestes, 50, 86–7, 117, 126–7, **127**, 129
Orestes (Euripides), 101, 105–6, 128–9
Orestes papyrus, 21
origins, 23–4, 26–7, 35, 84, 102
    Roman tragedy, 109–11
Ormand, K., 11–12, 16
Ovid, 47
    Metamorphoses, 33

Pacuvius, *Teucer*, 30
Panathenaic Festival, 3
participatory dynamics, 49
passion, 68
pathos, 13
patronage, 35
Peisistratus, 24
Peloponnesian War, 14, 120
Pentheus, 12, 13
performance conditions, 10–11
performance context, 2, 114
performance traditions, Rome, 44
Pericles, 118, 134, 150 n.17
perjurers, 94–5
Persian Wars, 14, 36, 37, 107–8, **108**
Persians (Aeschylus), 20, 27, 36–7, 83, 88, 107–8, 120, 132
Phaedra, 48, 136–7, 146–8, **147**
Phaedra (Seneca), 12, 48, 95, 98, 99, 146–8
Phaedra (Sophocles), 48
Phileonus, 138

Philip II, of Macedon, 39, 57
Philoctetes (Sophocles), 83, 93, 135
philosophical dialogue, tragedy as, 80–1
philosophy, 65–81
    definition, 65
    and Euripides, 65–7
    Greek, 65–81
    Medea, 71–3, 81
    negative dogmatism, 65–6
    and Senecan tragedy, 65, 67–81
    sophistic, 65–7
    stoicism, 67–81, 83–4, 96, 113, 146–8
    Thyestes, 73–4
    tragedy as dialogue, 80–1
    Troades, 74–6
Phoenician Women (Euripides), 46–7, 86, 91, 92, 104, 123–4
Phrynichus the tragedian, 2, 37, 149 n.2
physical body, representation of, 4
piety, 6
Pindar, 101–2, 106, 156 n.12
Pisistratos, 3
Plato, 7, 63, 65
    Laws, 25, 52
    Republic, 7–8, 39, 52
    Theaetetus, 65, 66
    on tragedy, 7–8, 52–3, 54
pledges, 72–3
Pleiad, 29
plot devices, 19
plot elements, 4
plot structures, 2
plots, 1, 30
Plutarch, 24, 37, 39, 40
    Life of Nicias, 37
Poe, J. P., 79
poetic traditions, 3
Poetics (Aristotle), 1–2, 4, 17, 23, 29, 30, 54–5, 84
    and epiphanies, 90–1
    on Euripides, 1–2
    limitations, 19–20
    on tragedy, 8–10, 18–19, 26–7, 117, 129
polis, 54–5, 117–18
political allusions, 59–60
political rhetoric, 54
political valences, 11
politics, 101–16
    of anachronism, 104–9
    of appropriation, 109–11
    of context, 103–4
    democratic, 102

of form, 101–3
of interiority, 113–16
and religion, 104
Politics (Aristotle), 20
Pollux, 27
Polynices, 120
Polyphemus, 5
Polyphrasmon, 90
Polyxena, 74–6, 86
Pompeii, 59, **71**, **84**
    House of the Tragic Poet, **61**
Pompey the Great, 111–12
porn songs, 28
portents, 77–8
post-classical tragedies, 1
power, abuse of, 51
prayer, 94–5, 97, 99
pre-play rituals, 104
private theater, 56–7, 166 n.53
producers, 55
professionalization, 58
Prometheus Luomenos (Prometheus Unbound)
    (Aeschylus), 47, 89, 90
Pronomos Vase, 20–1, **22**, 26
prophecy, 89, 91–2
prose elements, 2
Protagoras, 65–7
Ptolemy III Euergetes, **41**, 43
public life, 54
Pythagoras, 119
Python of Catana, 30

Ransom of Hector (Euripides), 37
reason, 9, 67–8
Rehm, R., 36–7
religion, 10
    and Athenian tragedy, 83, 84–95
    critiques of, 91
    and politics, 104
    and Roman tragedy, 83–4, 95–9
religious settings, 87–8
Republic (Plato), 7–8, 39, 52
Revermann, M., 40
rhetoric, 103
    Senecan, 62
rhetorical tragedies, 32
Rhodes, 41–3
riddling, 10, 93
ritual context, 83
Roman tragedy, 11, **32**, 44, 46
    actors, 110
    comparison with Athenian, 3–4

composers, 110
cultural context, 5–6
developments, 30–3
modes of engagement, 60, 61–3, **61**
origins, 30, 109–11
performance context, 110–11
philosophical engagement, 67, 67–81
polyglossic, 47–8
under the principate, 113–16
and religion, 83–4, 95–9
Republican, 109–12
role of, 59–61
subject-matter, 31
romanization, 109–11
Rome, 2–3, 16, 43–8
    education, 46–7
    emperors, 61–2
    Greek tragedy in, 44, **45**, 46
    imperial period, 47–8
    performance traditions, 44
    the principate, 113–16
    sexuality and sexual desire, 145–8, **148**
    theatres, 59
    tragedy comes to, 109–11
Rural Dionysia, 24, 52

sacrificial practice, 83, 92, 95–6, 98
    abnormal, 85–7, **86**
Salamis, Battle of, 107–8
Sappho, 186 n. 9
satirical blame poetry, 3
satyr plays, 2, 4–5, 26, 85
satyrs, 4, **5**, **42**
self, boundaries of, 13
self-control, 131, 144–5
Seneca and Senecan tragedy, 4, 7, 12, 13, 26,
    32–3, 46, 83–4
    on community building, 62–3
    and corporeal penetration, 70–1, 74–6
    extant plays, 59
    performance context, 114
    and philosophy, 65, 67–81
    under the principate, 113–16
    and religion, 95–9
    representation of the divine, 97–9
    rhetoric, 62
    stoicism, 96, 113, 146–8, **148**
    see also individual works
Seven against Thebes (Aeschylus), 88, 91, 92,
    102
sexuality and sexual desire, 4, 131–2, 135–8,
    145–8, 150–1 n.31

INDEX

Shakespeare, William, 2, 185 n.76
Sicily, 11, 156 n.18
    Aeschylus in, 36–7
Silenus, 4
single-mindedness, 13
slaves, agency, 12
social conflict, 12
social reintegration, costs of, 3–4
social status, 6
social worlds, 4
Socrates, 65
songs, 9, 18, 20
sophistic philosophy, 65–7
Sophocles, 14, 18, 29, 54, 102
    characters, 13
    extant plays, 2, 17
    and Herodotus, 6
    musical themes, 22–3
    number of plays, 151 n.1
    representations of gods, 91
    see also individual works
sparagmos, 12
Sparta, 11, 109
spectacle, 9, 55, 63
stage properties, religious, 87–8
Stesichorus, 66
stichomythia, 102–3
stoicism, 67–81, 83–4, 96, 113
    Medea, 71–3, 81
    and nature, 69, 84
    Oedipus, 76
    and sexuality, 146–8, 148
    and suicide, 74–6
    Troades, 75
subject-matter, 30
    Roman tragedy, 31
Suda, 24, 151 n.2
suffering, 8
suicide, 74–6, 121–2, **122**
Suppliant Women (Aeschylus), 21–2, 26, 87, 88, 102, 140–1
Suppliant Women (Euripides), 86, 87, 101, 106, 108–9
supplication, 87

Taplin, O., 36
technitai, 58
Technitai of Dionysus, 29
Telephus, 129
Teucer (Pacuvius), 30
Thamyras (Sophocles), 23
Theaetetus (Plato), 65, 66

Theater of Dionysus, 17, 24, 35, 53
theatrical experience, 10
Thebes, 107, 120
Theoric Fund, 53, 103
Thucydides, 2, 63
Thyestes, 4, 129
Thyestes (Seneca), 73–4, 80, 96, 97, 98, 99, 114–16
Tiberius, 114
Torrance, I., 16
Trachinian Women (Sophocles), 124–5, 136, 144
tradition, 1
tragedy, 17–33
    Aristotle on, 8–10, 18–19, 26–7, 54–5, 117, 129
    components of, 9, 18–19
    definition, 1
    formal aspects, 18–19
    generalizations, 3
    and ideas, 7–10
    meaning of name, 23
    Plato on, 7–8, 52, 54
tragic poetry, 55
Troades (Seneca), 74–6, 81
Trojan Women (Euripides), 12, 27–8, 94, 101
Trojan Women (Seneca), 96, 98
Tusculan Disputations, The (Cicero), 46
Tympanistae (Sophocles), 22–3
tyranny, associations with, 24, 35–40, 101, 106, 114–15

Vahtikari, V., 39
vases, 5, 15, 20–1, **21**, **22**, 25, 26, 50, 84, 86, 87, **105**, **107**, **108**, **119**, **137**
verse drama, 2
violence, 6
virtue, 67–9, 70, 146, 148
Visvardi, E., 14

Weiss, N., 14
Widzisz, M., 11–12, 16
Willis, C., 66
wives, place of, 11–12
women
    as citizens, 132–3, 134
    control over, 11–12
    education, 133
    exclusion from political life, 134
    and the family, 118–19
    gender roles, 131–5
    impenetrable, 70

non-citizen, 135
portrayal of, 134
responsibilities, 139–43, **139**, **142**
sexuality and sexual desire, 131, 135–8, 146–8, **147**
status, 132–5, 140, 182 n.24, 182 n.30, 182 n.31
Women of Aetna (Aeschylus), 36

Women of Trachis (Sophocles), 93
Wray, David, 80

Xenophon, 106, 133
Xerxes, 13, 120

Zeitlin, F., 134, 141, 144
Zeus, 26, **88**, 94